Second Edition

Straight Talk about
COMMUNICATION
RESEARCH METHODS

Christine S. Davis
University of North Carolina, Charlotte

Heather Powell
State Farm Insurance Company

Kenneth A. Lachlan
University of Massachusetts, Boston

Kendall Hunt
publishing company

Book Team

Chairman and Chief Executive Officer *Mark C. Falb*
President and Chief Operating Officer *Chad M. Chandlee*
Vice President, Higher Education *David L. Tart*
Director of Publishing Partnerships *Paul B. Carty*
Senior Editor *Angela Willenbring*
Vice President, Operations *Timothy J. Beitzel*
Assistant Vice President, Production Services *Christine E. O'Brien*
Senior Production Editor *Mary Melloy*
Senior Permissions Coordinator *Renae Horstman*
Cover Designer *Heather Richman*

Cover image © 2013, Shutterstock, Inc.

Kendall Hunt
publishing company

www.kendallhunt.com
Send all inquiries to:
4050 Westmark Drive
Dubuque, IA 52004-1840

BRIEF CONTENTS

CONTENTS

Chapter 4: Writing a Literature Review   73

Chapter 5: Understanding Research Ethics   99

PART 3: RESEARCH UNDER THE QUANTITATIVE PARADIGM   197

Chapter 10: Survey Research   199

Chapter 11: Quantitative Analysis of Text and Words: Content and Interaction Analysis   233

Chapter 12: Experiments 251

Chapter 15: Collecting Qualitative Data   345

Chapter 16: Writing, Analyzing, and Critiquing Qualitative Research   375

PREFACE

Welcome to *Communication Research Methods*! Through this textbook we hope you will catch our excitement with research. Your three authors are researchers who—amazingly enough— love doing research. We may be crazy, and we may be academic nerds, but that's not why we love research. We think research is FUN! We feel investigating, following leads, and solving puzzles is exciting.

According to Albert Einstein (as cited in Eves, 1987, p. 31), "It is, in fact, nothing short of a miracle that the modern methods of instruction have not entirely strangled the holy curiosity of inquiry." It is our hope that in this book we give you enough information about the foundations of research methods, the choices we as scholars make, and the methodological decisions driving communication scholarship; balancing your desire to know and inquire into interesting communication questions while instilling an enthusiasm about the process!

We think conducting research is like being a detective. Both are trying to find something out. Both are asking and answering questions. Both are trying to put together a puzzle to come up with a solution. In both, answering questions leads to more questions. And, in both, seeing patterns is crucial to solving the puzzle.

There is much about the social world that most of us think we know already; yet, there is also much left to learn. This book will ask you to question what you know, why you know what you know, and where that belief came from. While much of the material here is sometimes difficult to understand, we tell our students that their struggle with this material will allow them a place to store the other knowledge about communication and society. We also suggest that when your head begins to hurt, you have really begun the work of thinking about this material. Research Methods may not be an easy "A" class, but it's worth it! You'll learn a lot in this class—perhaps more information you'll use the rest of your career than many other classes. Our students will tell you that we also encourage them to talk with each other about this material. As communication scholars, we often overlook the powerful learning tool of discussing informally what we learn in the classroom. As you learn to talk about these conceptual ideas, you will begin to crystallize your understanding of both communication research methods and theory.

We hope that through this course you'll discover your own joy in conducting research. Some communication students are intimidated when they first encounter research methods, and we'd like to lessen the intimidation factor for you. To do this, we want to introduce to you a model of the stages of learning (Dubin, 1962; Howell & Fleishman, 1982; Kirkpatrick, 1971).

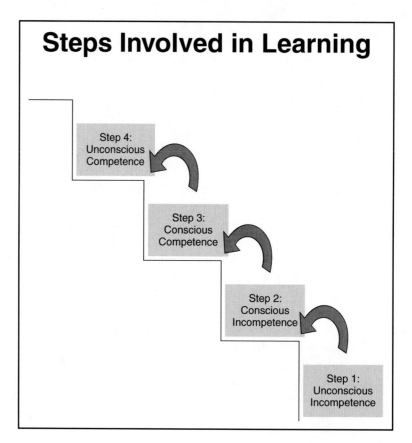

Steps Involved in Learning

Step 4:
Unconscious
Competence

Step 3:
Conscious
Competence

Step 2:
Conscious
Incompetence

Step 1:
Unconscious
Incompetence

You're in Step 1 right now: Unconscious Incompetence. That means you know so little, you don't even know what you don't know! This is a pretty blissful place to be, but we're about to move you out of your comfort zone. We're about to move you to Step 2. We're about to tell you what you don't know. We're going to teach you how to do things and you will spend much of the semester moving between Steps 2 and 3. We'll teach you something, and you'll be very conscious of the fact that you're learning something new. These stages are always uncomfortable because new learning feels awkward. Remember when you were first learning how to drive a car? There was a time when you had to remind yourself to push in the clutch, and check your rear view mirror, and for awhile that felt very uncomfortable. Luckily for you (and your parents), that stage didn't last long, and soon you were in the stage of Unconscious Competence in your driving—you could get in the car and drive without even thinking about it! We promise that by the end of the semester, you will be in this final stage for research. You will be able to do things that, right now, you don't even know exist! And, you'll enjoy it!

We've based the structure of this textbook on adult learning theory. Adult learning scholars suggest that learning for adults must be experiential—taking into account the learners' experiences, and integrating the materials into their own lives, combining active experimentation with theory and practical life skills as participants learn both formally and informally through application of course materials to experiences (Dinmore, 1997; Knowles, 1984; O'Dell, 1997; Tice, 1997). Research has also shown that adult learners best remember concepts given to them as spaced repetition—repeated in intervals over time (Spieler & Balota, 1996; Wulf & Schmidt, 1997). In this textbook, we give you information in small chunks that build upon each other, repeating then expanding knowledge. We'll give you multiple passes over concepts—introducing you to concepts in early chapters; then telling you more about those concepts in subsequent chapters. That's why it's going to be important for you to keep up with the material throughout the semester—you don't want to miss any of the early passes over the information.

When you graduate with a degree in Communication Studies, we as a department are certifying that you are properly socialized into our field. We are indoctrinating you into our community of knowledge—and, like every community of knowledge, we have ways of knowing, ways of seeing the world, ways of thinking, and ways of deciding. We require that you take classes in Communication Theory so you will learn how we in our community think about things. We require that you take classes in Research Methods so you will learn how we know things, describe things, and decide if something is true or not. You're probably a junior or senior undergraduate when you take this course, and by now you've probably had at least ten courses in our field. You've been told a lot of things about the world, given a lot of facts, and memorized a lot of theories. Have you ever wondered where all these things, facts, and theories came from? Did someone just make them up so you could have something to be tested on? We know sometimes it feels that way, but this semester you'll learn how to do the same type of research that communication scholars before you have done. You'll see firsthand how theories (and other research questions) begin as a curiosity—an "I wonder if . . ."—and how these musings and wonderings turn into full-blown research, then into facts, knowledge, and theories. Who knows? You might discover that you're the next George Herbert Mead, Barnett Pearce, Kenneth Burke, Elisabeth Noelle-Neumann, or Marshall McLuhan!

You'll also learn how people in our community prove a point. You'll learn that not everything you read or hear is true, and, as we said, you'll learn how to question what you hear and believe, and how to determine if you want to continue believing it. You'll learn how to make credible claims and how to back them up with evidence so other people will believe what you have to say.

By the way, throughout this textbook we are using the term Communication Studies to refer to our field of study. The field of Communication or Communication Studies is incredibly diverse. In most universities, our community of scholars can include people in fields as varied as health communication, interpersonal communication, organizational communication, rhetoric, mass media, public relations, broadcasting, and film studies, to name only some. At some universities, study of Communication is under an umbrella of Communication Studies; and at other universities, study in a field called Communication Studies is under an umbrella called

Communication. When we use either term—Communication or Communication Studies—we are using the term to be inclusive of all scholarship in all forms of human communication—mediated or interpersonal, organizational or rhetorical.

Confused—or curious? For now, don't worry about what you don't yet know. Just sit back, relax, and enjoy the ride!

▼ Student-Oriented Pedagogy

Because we recognize the importance of assessing student learning, we have included features in each chapter that facilitate student learning and help instructors measure learning outcomes.

- Chapter Outlines serve as a map to guide you through the content of the text and focus on key points.
- Key Terms list shows important terms to focus on as you read the chapter.
- Chapter Objectives help you focus on the overall concepts, theories, and skills discussed in the chapter.
- Running Glossary provides the definition of a key term in the margin for quick clarification when reading the material.
- Chapter Summary reviews the key points explored in the text.
- Chapter Glossary serves as a helpful reference tool at the end of each chapter.
- References list documents the research cited within the chapter.

▼ Instructional Online Enhancements

Both students and instructors have access to online content that is integrated chapter by chapter with the text to enrich student learning. The Web access code is included on the inside front cover of the textbook.

Look for the Web icon in the text margins to direct you to various interactive tools.

▼ References

Dinmore, I. (1997). Interdisciplinary and integrative learning: An imperative for adult education. *Education*, 117(3), 452–468.

Dubin, P. (1962). *Human relations in administration.* Englewood Cliffs, NJ: Prentice-Hall.

Eves, H. W. (1987). *Return to mathematical circles: A fifth collection of mathematical stories and anecdotes.* Prindle, Weber, and Schmidt.

Howell, W. C., & Fleishman, E. A. (Eds.). (1982). *Human performance and productivity: Information processing and decision making.* Hillsdale, NJ: Erlbaum.

Kirkpatrick, D. L. (1971). *A practical guide for supervisory training and development.* Reading, MA: Addison-Wesley.

ACKNOWLEDGMENTS

The authors wish to gratefully acknowledge the support and encouragement by Kendall Hunt for this book, especially Paul Carty and Angela Willenbring. We would also like to thank and acknowledge the hard work and help of graduate assistants Jennifer Medieros, Jeff Brucato, Julia Nelson, and Kaitlin Rogers, and the extensive feedback and supportive comments from the reviewers.

Christine Davis dedicates this book to the memory of Horace Kelly, my early research and career mentor. Horace is responsible for (almost) everything I know about market research, quantitative methods, and focus group research. I would also like to acknowledge the help and encouragement given to me by my husband, Jerry, without whose support this research would never have been achieved; Carolyn Ellis, Art Bochner, Buddy Goodall, and Stacy Holman-Jones, who taught me everything I know about qualitative writing and research; and my family, friends, and colleagues, Barbara Eudy, Deborah Breede, Robin Davis Kumako, Kathleen Salkin, and Colleen Salkin, who have loved and encouraged me despite many long absences on my part. I would also like to thank my colleagues and friends at the University of South Florida and the University of North Carolina at Charlotte for their incredible mentoring, encouragement, inspiration, and support. I also want to thank my colleagues Heather Powell and Ken Lachlan who have made working on this book a joy. Finally, I want to thank God, who makes all things possible.

Ken Lachlan would like to thank his graduate school mentors, Bradley S. Greenberg, Chuck Atkin, Stacy Smith, and in particular Ron Tamborini; the training and mentorship I have received and continue to receive from him has been immeasurably valuable to my career. In addition to being just about the best mentor one could ask for, in the years since, I have learned more from Ron about life, people, and relationships than he will likely ever realize, and I am forever grateful to be his advisee.

I would also like to thank Patric Spence for his friendship and collaboration. Patric's dedication to his craft, work ethic, and outlook on what our field can and should be continue to awe and inspire me, and I am very lucky to have him in my corner. Thanks also to our frequent collaborators Jennifer Burke, Christine Eith, Donyale Griffin, J. J. McIntyre, Lin Nelson, Matt Seeger, Tim Sellnow, Ashleigh Shelton, Paul Skalski, and David Westerman.

Finally I extend my deepest thanks to my wife, Heather Gallant-Lachlan. Words cannot adequately express my gratitude for her ongoing love, support, patience, and encouragement. I thank God every day that she randomly decided to give me—a total stranger—better directions on the subway one night, and that we haven't been able to stop talking since.

Heather Powell wishes to acknowledge the scholars who first shared the study of communication with me: Mark Nuss, Beverly Davenport-Sypher, and Tracy Russo. I still don't have the words to adequately express my gratitude to Chris Segrin for his professional and personal mentorship. He is my advisor for life.

Additional thanks to my colleagues along the way for believing in me, supporting me, and always being willing to talk theory and research methods with me: Bill Stuart, Kenci Lewis, Beth Bonham, Bell O'Neil, Barbara DeSanto, Holli Frazier, and Rich Furman. I am appreciative to my colleagues at UNC-Charlotte and State Farm for their encouragement as this process progressed. Many thanks to Cris and Ken for making this a fabulous experience.

I am forever grateful to my family for their unconditional love and support, my parents, Dennis and Cheryl Powell; my brother, T. J. Powell; and my daughter, Darbe Gallardo. She has been God's greatest blessing and has sacrificed more than anyone through this endeavor. Finally, this book is dedicated to each and every student who gave me a chance to teach them research methods.

We gratefully acknowledge the constructive comments of the colleagues who provided reviews for the text. The reviewers include:

Jonathan Amsbary
University of Alabama–Birmingham

Mia Consalvo
Ohio University

Sean Baker
Towson University

Linda Crumley
Southern Adventist University

Ralph Beliveau
University of Oklahoma

Christopher Darr
Indiana University–Kokomo

Kristen Berkos
Bryant University

Sara DeTurk
University of Texas–San Antonio

Brian Brantley
University of Texas of the Permian Basin

Cliff Fortenberry
Mississippi College

Sharee Broussard
Spring Hill College

Robert Gass
California State University–Fullerton

Richard Caplan
University of Akron

Jennifer Gregg
University of Louisville

Dawn Carusi
Marietta College

Laurel Hellerstein
Endicott College

Dane Claussen
Point Park University

Andrew Herman
SUNY Geneseo

Lawrence Hosman
University of Southern Mississippi

Steve Howard
Ohio University

Dorothy Imrich Mullin
University of California–Santa Barbara

Michelle Johnson
The College of Wooster

Bill Jong-Ebot
Florida Memorial University

John Jordan
University of Wisconsin-Milwaukee

Janis King
Missouri State University

David Kintsfather
Kutztown University of Pennsylvania

Young Lin
University of Akron

Hsin-I Liu
University of Incarnate Word

Faye Mangrum
Southeastern Oklahoma State University

Robert McPhee
Arizona State University

Jefrey McQuillen
University of Texas–Pan American

Mary Meares
Washington State University

Lisa Millhous
West Chester University

Gretchen Norling
University of West Florida

Mary Beth Oliver
Penn State University

Andy Opel
Florida State University

Bryant Paul
Indiana University

Andrew Rancer
University of Akron

Charles Robert
East Tennessee State University

William Robinson
Purdue University Calumet

Jimmy Roux
Lynchburg College

Carmen Russell
Fontbonne University

Susan Seymour
Webster University

Linda Sampson
Southern Connecticut State University

Claire Sullivan
University of Maine

Melissa Wall
California State University–Northridge

Alex Wang
University of Connecticut–Stamford

Kenneth Yang
University of Texas–El Paso

ABOUT THE AUTHORS

Christine Davis is Associate Professor at the University of North Carolina–Charlotte. Before coming to UNCC, she was a research faculty member at the Florida Mental Health Institute. Her area of academic expertise is in Communication Studies, specializing in the intersection of health, family, interpersonal, and group communication. Christine has been involved in research on children's mental health systems of care, hospice organizations, family communication and disability, and health literacy in the context of patient-provider communication. Her preferred methodologies are autoethnography, narrative, and critical ethnography. She is involved with NIH (National Institutes of Health)-funded research, and regularly partners with healthcare organizations on research projects. Christine has over 20 years of research and corporate consulting experience, including owner of a national marketing research firm and executive director of a nonprofit for-older adults. She obtained all three of her degrees in Communication Studies. Her BA is from Virginia Polytechnic Institute and State University (more commonly known as Virginia Tech), her M.A. is from the University of North Carolina–Greensboro, and her Ph.D. is from the University of South Florida. Christine has a husband, a daughter and a son-in-law, and a Sheltie named Maggie. In addition to conducting research and teaching, she loves to sail, hike, jog, and swim.

Heather Powell is an Agency Field Specialist for State Farm Insurance, in Hot Springs, Arkansas. Before making the transition to her current corporate position, Heather was Assistant Professor at the University of North Carolina–Charlotte. Before coming to UNCC, was Assistant Professor at Saginaw Valley State University in Saginaw, Michigan. Her area of academic expertise is in Communication Studies, specializing in interpersonal and family communication in the context of health. Much of her research has explored sexual risk taking and sexual communication within relationships, and how romantic relationships are negotiated and experienced when living with depression. Although trained as a quantitative scholar, Heather is a renaissance academic, preferring to answer interesting questions with the appropriate methodology. She has conducted research ranging from experimental design to autoethnography. Heather holds a B.G.S. and an M.A. from the University of Kansas, and a Ph.D. from the University of Arizona, all in Communication Studies. She is most proud of her autoethnographic narrative published in the *Journal of Divorce & Remarriage* with her daughter Darbe on how they have co-constructed their relationship. In addition to her work, Heather enjoys scrapbooking, screaming at the television during college football, basketball (Go Jayhawks!), and NASCAR (Go Bowyer!), throwing impromptu dinner parties, traveling, and spending time with her friends and family.

Ken Lachlan is Associate Professor and Founding Chair of the Communication Department at the University of Massachusetts–Boston. Prior to his academic career, he worked in public radio and television promotions for several years. His research interests include the psychological effects of mass media, health and risk communication, media violence, and new media technologies. Recent publications have appeared in the *Journal of Broadcasting and Electronic Media*, *Media Psychology*, and the *Journal of Applied Communication Research*, to name a few. Ken considers himself mostly a quantitative scholar, preferring experimental and survey methodologies in investigating his areas of interest. He has also served as a consultant statistician for various companies and government agencies. He holds a dual B.A. in Communication and Sociology from Wake Forest, an M.A. in Mass Communication from Bowling Green State University, and a Ph.D. in Communication from Michigan State. An avid jogger and diehard hockey fan, Ken lives in Boston with his wife and their cat.

INTRODUCTION TO COMMUNICATION RESEARCH

PART **1**

WHAT IS COMMUNICATION RESEARCH?

1

CHAPTER OUTLINE

KEY TERMS

A priori

Authority

Communication researchers

Epistemology

Experience

Health communication scholars

Hypotheses

Interpersonal communication

Media research

Organizational communication

Research

Scientific reasoning

Social research

Tenacity

Theory

CHAPTER OBJECTIVES

1. To introduce the concept of communication research
2. To explain the ways of thinking behind communication research
3. To explain what exactly it is that communication researchers do
4. To give examples of communication research

▼ # What Will You Do with the Information You Learn in this Course?

Imagine you're in your first job after college, a Research Assistant for an advertising and marketing research company. You've been working there for about six months, and one day you find yourself standing in front of a room of corporate executives. Your company has conducted advertising testing for its products, and the executives are waiting anxiously to hear you discuss the results. The information you're about to give them will help them make some major corporate decisions: Should they keep the same advertising agency or hire another? Should they change their marketing slogan or continue using the same one they've been using? Should they change the language or images in their ad? And, finally, they want an answer to their most important question: Does their advertising really make a difference in their product sales? This is the day you've been waiting for. You've been training for this presentation for years. You took Public Speaking as a college freshman, and you feel confident as you prepare to begin your presentation. You took Research Methods, and you know how to explain and justify the methods your company undertook to test the advertising. You also took Communication Theory, Persuasion, Mass Media, and Public Relations in college, and you understand the theories that explain why the consumers reacted the way they did to the advertising. You understand the importance of this presentation—the corporate executives will make million-dollar advertising decisions based on your presentation. This is not simply a made-up scenario—one of your books' authors (Christine Davis) actually faced this situation in her first job out of college.

communication researchers
Scholars and professionals who study communication.

> *I (Christine) had no idea when I graduated from college with an undergraduate degree in Communication Studies that I would end up taking a job as a* **communication researcher***. I just wanted a job that would let me use what I had learned in my major—communication—the conveyance of symbols and information from one party to another in order to elicit a particular response. When I took my Communication Research Methods course as an undergraduate, I didn't realize how much I would end up using what I'd learned in my career. Yet, my Communication Research Methods course got me my first job and my first career.*

It might get you your first job, too, or it might be responsible for your first promotion or a pat on the back by your boss. You might, for example, get a job with an Internet consulting company and be asked to study the ways people deceive others when using e-mail and Facebook. You might end up working for a political candidate, helping him or her understand the rhetorical strategies used by political pundits in advancing his or her agendas. You might work for a public relations company using information on the ways people may respond to accidents and public crises by turning to different news outlets under different conditions. You might be hired by a major television network and might use research about the declining ratings of reality programming and what this might mean for the television industry.

Some of your classmates might decide they want to use their knowledge of communication research methods to change the world for the better. They might join a social marketing firm and use research findings to develop campaigns to convince students to practice safe sex or make more healthful lifestyle choices. They might get a job for a health department in which they study or use different intervention strategies and effective ways of convincing people to get tested for HIV infection. They might work for a research think tank and focus on communication with, and understanding of, people from different cultures or with different needs than their own.

Communication, as a field, is exceptionally diverse. Those who dedicate their careers to either researching or using research on the conveyance of meaning do so in a number of ways. Some conduct surveys to measure opinions and behavior that may be related to these symbols. Some conduct experiments using human participants, examining people's attitudes and opinions before and after receiving messages. Others conduct long interviews and look for themes that may emerge from people's responses, or they may immerse themselves in certain social interactions as participant-observers.

Still others are more interested in what the information looks like, as opposed to how people will respond. They may try to systematically analyze the content of a particular program, genre, or network. They may try to identify certain rhetorical devices and argumentation strategies to figure out *how* influence may occur. They may even be more concerned with the underlying biases and issues of power that make information look a certain way.

There are literally dozens of approaches to the study of communication as a discipline. While communication researchers often engage in spirited academic debate about the pros and cons of looking at things in different ways, there is really no right or wrong approach. Rather, the prevailing wisdom in our field is that different approaches to communication research are appropriate for different research questions.

What Is Research? ▼

Research

Research is the activity of conducting intellectual investigations into the observable world. Researchers are generally concerned with discovering and investigating the means by which things work, in order to advance human knowledge with the goal of better understanding our world. Generally speaking,

research
The activity of conducting intellectual investigations into the observable world.

research involves the asking and answering of questions. These questions may be derived from observations of the world, a lack of understanding of observed phenomena, or the questioning of previously held assumptions about the ways in which something may work. Research is often driven by a desire to improve the human condition, as one of its fundamental motivations is the assumption that more and better knowledge can only serve to help humanity.

Very often, when we think of research, our minds first turn to research in the natural sciences. As a matter of fact, when we say research, your mind might go back to your eighth-grade Science Fair project. You can probably think of dozens of examples of research in physics, chemistry, biology, and engineering that have served to advance human knowledge. For example, in recent years, much attention (and controversy) has surrounded research concerning the viability of using human stem cells to cure a wide array of physical ailments. Advances in biomedical research have extended the life expectancies associated with certain types of cancers, while early twentieth century research in inoculations for childhood diseases has dramatically reduced infant mortality rates in the Western world. Research in engineering has helped make our automobiles, planes, and working environments far safer than they were fifty years ago. Computer science research has allowed us to carry cell phones that are more powerful than computers that took up entire buildings during the 1970s. The list goes on and on.

Communication as Social Research

social research
This research focuses less on the observable world in which human beings interact and more on the interactions themselves, how they come into existence, how they function, and how they affect the human experience. Research in communication, psychology, sociology, economics, political science, and anthropology are typically classified as social research.

Perhaps less well known is the process of **social research**. Social researchers are more concerned with human interactions and the ways in which human beings make sense of their world. This research focuses less on the observable world in which human beings interact, and more on the interactions themselves, how they come into existence, how they function, and how they affect the human experience. Research in psychology, sociology, economics, political science, and anthropology are typically classified as social research.

Communication research can also be classified as social research. Communication researchers study parts of the observable world as it interacts with us—symbol-producing and symbol-using humans. We study the ways in which human beings use information and symbols to create meaning among ourselves. This process will be discussed at great length throughout this text, but in basic terms, social science communication researchers often attempt to solve problems and answer questions associated with the exchange of information between human beings.

Communication as Humanities Research

Many communication researchers conduct research that could be classified as research in the humanities, rather than a social science. Rather than looking at how we exchange information per se, communication humanities scholars tend to look at how we co-construct meaning through communication. Performance studies scholars, for example, create and present performances that exemplify societal or interactional phenomena to help both themselves and their audiences understand the communication phenomena at a deep level. Other communication scholars use novelistic elements to write narratives that pull the reader into the story and evoke meaning and understanding. Others use poetry, art, or music to more deeply understand a communication act or culture.

Communication as Critical or Cultural Research

There are other scholars in the field of communication studies who look at the construction, use, and abuse of power and control in a culture, situation, organization, or community. They might look at how communication perpetuates or reifies power, or how communication is used by marginalized groups to resist power by dominant groups in a society. Other scholars might study how communication creates identity within a culture, or how cultures use communication to construct meaning.

How Is Research Knowledge Distributed? ▼

Academic Publishing

Of course, answering these questions is not a particularly useful endeavor if no one knows about it. In both the natural sciences and in social research, the most common way of distributing the answers to the questions asked by researchers is through academic publishing. As you will see in Chapter 3, there are a number of scholarly journals in the field of communication that provide an outlet for the distribution of these findings. Communication scholars often publish books and volumes of selected studies that report the findings to their questions. They are also known to publish their work in journals and volumes outside the field, or in collaboration with scholars from other disciplines. Communication scholars frequently publish alongside psychologists, sociologists, management scholars, and public health researchers, just to name a few.

One common misconception surrounding academic publishing is the notion of the ivory tower. People often think that social researchers, such as communication scholars, sit around mulling over grand ideas that have little bearing on the real world. Many people would also say no one outside of academia reads scholarly research, or places much value in its findings and conclusions.

Social Dialogue and Public Policy

Nothing could be further from the truth. Social researchers and communication scholars, in particular, have a long history of contributing to social dialogue on the relevant issues of the day. Government agencies, policymakers, and businesses frequently look to research published in academic journals to inform their decision making.

Take this example: A hotly contested social issue is the unrealistic portrayal of body image on television. Public health officials, psychologists, and communication researchers have become increasingly concerned with the abundance of dangerously thin people in mainstream media, and in particular what impact this may have on self-esteem and eating disorders among adolescents. Further, they have become concerned with the ways in which television may influence our perceptions of people of varying sizes and how this may contribute to various forms of stereotyping. In 1999, a team of communication researchers led by Bradley S. Greenberg decided to examine television characters in terms of both their body sizes and the ways in which they were portrayed. Generally speaking, they found that a little less than a third of the women on television can be classified as dangerously underweight, while larger characters on television are often ridiculed or presented in other unflattering ways.

The article was presented at an academic convention in Quebec and was eventually published in the *American Journal of Public Health* (Greenberg, Eastin, Hofshire, Lachlan, & Brownell, 2003). However, realizing that there may be a wider market that could use this information, Greenberg's research team created a press release and distributed it to varying media outlets.

This press release (shown on page 9) caught the attention of *USA Today*, who promptly ran a story on the findings (*USA Today*, October 8, 2001). Thus the findings of the study were made available not just to other scholars interested in the subject matter, but the general public, policymakers, parents, and activists.

There are numerous other examples of communication research being disseminated not only to those in academic circles, but also to the general public and to those in positions of authority. Communication researchers have even *testified before Congress* regarding the implications of their findings. Notably, a large number of communication researchers played a pivotal role in the 1972 Surgeon General's Commission Report on television violence and aggressive behavior. Communication researchers have presented testimonies on the influence and impact of alcohol advertising on young consumers, tobacco advertising, violence in video games, sexual television content, and numerous others.

Here's another, very different example. The May 26, 2009, edition of the *Charlotte Observer* reported on a play put on by a writing company, a university professor, and staff and residents of a residential maternity home. The play, performed for the public, depicts—through the use of drama and performance—stories and experiences of the home's clients—pregnant women, children in foster care, and at-risk adolescents. The purpose of the play is to inspire empathy (Toppman, 2009, p. 5D), and it's a great example of performance studies being used for social dialogue.

Communication in the Popular Press

Communication scholars often release the results of their academic work to the popular press in hopes that it will draw the attention of those in business and government. Our field even has an online publication—*Communication Currents*—that makes recent communication research accessible to the general public. A recent issue reported on teasing and bullying in school, communication about the economy, representation of gay families in the news, Twitter and its impact on American governance, communication about grief, and talking about sex with teens and adolescents.

Other communication scholars have published books based on their research that made their way to the popular press. H. L. Goodall, for example, conducted an autoethnographic exploration of his father's work for the CIA and published a novel titled *A Need to Know* (Goodall, 2006).

newsroom.msu.edu

TV PORTRAYALS OF OBESE CHARACTERS PERPETUATE NEGATIVE STEREOTYPES, MSU RESEARCHER FINDS

Contact: University Relations (517) 355-2281, or hodack@msu.edu

10/8/2001

EAST LANSING, Mich. - Overweight and obese television characters have fewer romantic interactions, fewer interactions with friends and fewer leadership characteristics, Michigan State University research shows. Larger characters also were less likely to date and have sex.

Bradley Greenberg, university distinguished professor of communication and telecommunication, will present these and other findings today at the annual scientific meeting of the North American Association for the Study of Obesity in Quebec City, Quebec. His talk: "How Commercial Television Treats Obesity and other Body Types." Co-researchers on the project are Linda Hofshire and Ken Lachlan, also at MSU, Matt Eastin of Ohio State University and Kelly Brownell of Yale University.

Greenberg's research examined portrayals of overweight characters in 275 episodes from 56 different series across six commercial broadcast networks. The study looked at the 10 primetime fictional series with the highest Nielsen ratings in the 1999-2000 television season on ABC, CBS, Fox, NBC, UPN and WB.

Findings compared the distribution of body types on primetime TV on a scale ranging from very underweight to very overweight, with the national distribution of body types using the official Body Mass Index of the National Institutes of Health.

"The female differences were staggering," Greenberg said. "Whereas one in four American women in reality is obese, the TV figure is three in 100. And whereas 5 percent of all women in reality are underweight, nearly one in three on television has that body type."

More generally, Greenberg added, half of all women in real life are average or underweight, yet on TV the number is almost nine out of every 10.

Males in real life are three times more likely to be obese than their television peers, and male TV characters are six times more likely to be underweight than their counterparts in real life, the study noted.

According to the Centers for Disease Control and Prevention, obesity increased 50 percent between 1991 and 1998 - from 12 percent to 18 percent of the American population. Further,

file:///C|/Documents%20and%20Settings/LACHLAN/Desktop/methods%20textbook/gberg%20press%20release.htm (1 of 2)6/2/2008 1:03:30 PM

How Do We Know What We Know?

Where Does Knowledge Come From?

Of course, in order to answer these and other questions, we are forced to confront difficult issues concerning knowledge itself. These aren't likely to be questions that you ask yourself every day. Most of us, communication researchers included, go through our everyday lives with a fairly comfortable understanding of what is and what is not. Our view of the world may come from a variety of sources, and we generally don't stop to think about what those sources may be. We certainly don't often stop to ask ourselves the question: Where does knowledge come from?

epistemology
The study of knowledge.

The study of knowledge itself is known as **epistemology** (Babbie, 1995). Before examining communication research, the questions it asks, and methods of exploring those questions, it may be helpful to think about different ways of understanding what it is that we know to be true. This serves to illustrate both how we make sense of our world, and how scholarly inquiry into communication and other social phenomena may deviate from these means of gathering knowledge. The philosopher Charles Peirce identified four methods of knowing: tenacity, authority, a priori, and science (Buchler, 1955). We'll discuss these plus a few others—personal experience; traditions, customs, and faith; magic, superstition, and/or mysticism; and intuition or hunches.

We should begin to learn about knowledge building by considering how it is we come to know something in our everyday life. Much communication research is dedicated to things that we see in our everyday lives, the functionality of everyday interactions, and ways in which we make sense of the world around us. In fact, if we think about it for a minute, there are countless examples of everyday behaviors that can be informed by communication research.

When you go home after class, there is a good chance you turn on the television. Why do you watch what you watch? There are entire programs of communication research dedicated to uncovering the motives for your media consumption. Maybe you have very general reasons for selecting certain programs, like desiring entertainment or needing a score in the big game. Maybe there are far more specific reasons, like needing to relax when you are stressed or excitement when you are bored. Communication research can answer this question.

Maybe you are walking across campus one day, and someone approaches you and asks if you would like to buy some raffle tickets for a local charity. While you don't mind helping a good cause, you realize that before you knew it your wallet was out and you were handing over cash. How was this person so convincing? Why were you so willing to comply?

You get into an argument with your significant other. You don't feel that he is spending enough time with you, while he thinks he is doing the right thing by not trying to smother you or monopolize your time. How did this disconnect take place? How can two people in a relationship see that relationship so differently?

Let's say you go to your doctor for your annual checkup. There is nothing to worry about, you are in perfect health, and everything is fine. But for some reason you walk away with a strange feeling. You have been going to this doctor for years, but you feel as though she was completely unsympathetic to your questions and barely knows who you are. Why do you not feel as though you and your doctor are on the same page?

Perhaps you are at work and your boss is being very demanding. Your boss constantly rides you about how you need to spend more hours at your job and how you don't seem particularly dedicated to it. You don't understand because you think you take your job seriously and do it well. Then you find out that your boss's supervisor has been criticizing him about his performance. Why is your boss taking it out on you? And why didn't you know that people further up the ladder had concerns about your boss's performance?

While communication research can help inform issues of policy, activism, and government, it is also very useful in understanding our everyday interactions and in helping us make sense of the world. These are only a few examples of real life questions that can be informed by communication research. Almost every interaction you can possibly have—be it with mediated information or in a face-to-face setting—can be informed by the study of the conveyance of meaning.

Experience.   One of our best teachers is often personal **experience**. Many of us learn much of understanding of the social world by experiencing. The easiest example of this type of knowledge conforms to the adage that sometimes we have to learn the hard way. Touching a hot stove with your hand is a pretty good teacher. Not many experiences with a hot stove are necessary before you have complete knowledge of what will happen if you touch another hot item. Our experience with people is no different. We may have had previous experiences with specific people, similar people, or situations that we can then use as a guide to anticipate and interpret a new experience and/or situation. This is known as generalizing and is an important aim for some scientific research. The value of this type of knowing is that it can be a fruitful beginning, upon which we build to gain knowledge.

> **experience**
> *A common way of understanding the social world.*

Tenacity.   Think of some things about the world that everybody knows. For example, "everybody knows" that if you toss a coin off the Empire State Building, it will kill whomever it lands upon. Likewise, "everybody knows" that a dog's mouth is actually cleaner than a human's; bad guys in the Old West always wore black hats; and when you cross the equator, toilets begin flushing in the opposite direction.

There is just one problem with all of these statements: None of them are true. A coin tossed off a skyscraper does not have enough mass, relative to resistance from the air below it, to accelerate to a speed that could kill someone. Think about how you bathe and how your dog bathes. Lawmen and outlaws in the Old West wore hats that came in a variety of colors. Toilets will flush in the direction that water enters them (usually counterclockwise), whether they are in New York or Melbourne. So how, then, do statements such as those above become accepted as "facts"?

Part of the reason may be our tendency to rely on **tenacity** as a method of knowing. Tenacity is simply the assumption that something is true because it always has been said to be true. Knowledge is passed from person to person and generation to generation through cultural norms and assumptions. You may believe that the sun rises in the morning because the sun god Ra wills it so; if you do, chances are it's because that's what your parents, grandparents, and great-grandparents believed. Furthermore, consensus plays a critical role in tenacity as a source of knowledge: the frequent repetition of these so-called facts

> **tenacity**
> *The assumption that something is true because it has always been said to be true.*

makes them seem more likely to be true (Kerlinger, 1992). Even in the face of conflicting information, people will hold onto their beliefs and rationalize away evidence that flies in the face of what they already hold to be true.

Of course, tenacity is not inherently bad as a means of knowing. It comes in handy in a variety of different scenarios, mostly because, as humans, we don't have the time or energy to consider all possible explanations for every observation we ever make. And very often, it provides us with knowledge that is useful and accurate. We don't really need to formally test the notion that stepping out in front of traffic is a bad idea, or that it is more likely to rain if it is cloudy outside, or that your lawn will grow if you water it. These are things that most of us have always accepted as being true, have heard repeated over and over, and for the most part are correct.

authority

The reliance upon someone in a position of power to determine what is factual. This power may be derived from a variety of places, such as expertise, political power, religious authority, or interpersonal trust.

Authority.   Another important instructor in everyday knowledge is **authority**. Authority is when we turn to experts to help us make sense out of a particular situation. Authority has less to do with the repetition of information and more to do with the perceived credibility of the source of that information. Very often, people realize they are not experts on a given subject, to the extent that they may not even be able to comprehend or make sense of their observations. In these instances, they often rely on someone in a position of power to tell them what is factual. This power may be derived from a variety of places, such as expertise, political power, religious authority, or interpersonal trust.

Consider this common example. Many people, including this author (Ken), have a geek. This is the person they go to for information about anything having to do with computers, software, or technology. This person may have been assembling and disassembling computers since he was a child, or he may be more of a programmer type who enjoys cracking the source code on various software applications. In any case, this person can probably tell you how to turn on the computer, as this will be child's play given their level of expertise. This person could tell you practically anything, and you would assume it to be true (at least until you try it out, and even then you might assume that you are not following his or her instructions correctly, since he, after all, is the expert).

Advertisements using celebrity spokespersons are good examples of how authority guides our knowledge building. If Michael Jordan tells us to purchase Hanes underwear, then we think we should since we have trust in him. After all, Michael wouldn't lie to us, would he? Authority only works as a source of knowledge if I have faith in the authority figure or she has some control over me. For example, one of your authors once served on a jury. One of the experts brought to testify in the case was a drug specialist for the state of North Carolina. Her job was to explain to us the laboratory tests conducted on the white substance found in the defendant's car and convince us that it was, in fact, crack cocaine. Due to her experience, her education, and the way in which she presented herself, the jury never debated over whether the substance was actually crack cocaine. Her authority created knowledge for us.

Consider another example: Most of us have experienced our parents' authority, and you can probably remember how smart your parents were when you were a small child and how stupid they became when you reached adolescence!

If they haven't already, they'll become much smarter in your eyes as you move through college and into adulthood. You probably have believed your parents' authority when they told you that vegetables were good for your health, and you might someday use your mom's advice for making stock market picks!

Authority has value, if we believe the authority to be reliable, because it saves us time from having to find out everything for ourselves. What's the downside of relying on information from an authority without checking it out for ourselves? Authorities are sometimes wrong, or they may have biased information or opinions. I (Christine) once worked as Executive Director for a nonprofit organization that served older adults. One of our older adult volunteers asked me how to do something, and I gave her instructions. Several hours later, it became apparent that my instructions were wrong, and she commented, "That didn't sound right when you told me!" I asked her, "Then why in the world didn't you question me?" and she replied, "You sounded so sure of yourself when you told me!" What she didn't understand was that I'm a communication expert and I'm trained to sound confident, even when I'm clearly wrong! Her mistake was relying on my perceived authority.

Traditions, Customs, and Faith.   Traditions, customs, and faith are also great teachers. **Health communication scholars** are experts at understanding the role traditions, customs, and faith play in communicating health information. A perfect example is the adage "an apple a day keeps the doctor away." An adage is a type of tradition, and while we all know eating one apple a day really will not ensure our not getting sick, we also know eating a healthy diet, including fruits, does increase the likelihood of living a healthy life.

Think about the things you've come to know by the traditions your family followed and the knowledge passed down from one generation to the next. Take the tradition of the Easter basket. In a recent conversation with another mother, who is a friend of one of your authors, we were discussing Easter baskets for our daughters. She detailed her search for just the right basket this year, as she couldn't reuse last year's basket, or her daughter might catch on. I (Heather) responded that at our house the Easter bunny uses the basket that we already have, which I place out in the house for decoration during the Easter season. What our daughters know about the Easter bunny is based upon the traditions each family follows. Her daughter is convinced the Easter bunny is wealthy, while my daughter knows that the Easter bunny is concerned with the environment! Another great example comes from the same friend. She grew up in the South during the 1960s and 1970s and loved Pepsi. It was a treat not often allowed in her youth. Because her family expected each child to drink a glass of milk with each meal, my friend Dianne would guzzle down her glass of milk, hoping for a chance to have her cherished beverage. However, Dianne's mother explained to her that drinking Pepsi after milk would upset her stomach and cause her to be sick. It was not until away at college that Dianne realized she had been duped. This demonstrates how we know or believe things to be true because we've been told or taught by others to believe them early on in life. While the latter examples may not ring true, many customs, such as eating an apple a day, are based upon solid evidence.

health communication scholars
Communication scholars who look at the interpersonal exchanges between doctors and patients, public health campaigns, the flow of information in public health organizations, and other aspects of health.

Magic, Superstition, and/or Mysticism.

Another way we believe we know is through magic, superstition, and/or mysticism. When you study for an exam, are you superstitious? Do you have a lucky item of clothing, a particular feeling about some numbers, a routine that if deviated from undermines your confidence? If so, then you already have a clear understanding of how we can come to know something through magic, superstition, and/or mysticism. Some of us have been known to change clothes during a Kansas basketball game, as it seems that some t-shirts are luckier than others, and we know that what we wear influences how our team performs! How many of you know your sign and read your horoscope, swearing it is accurate? No, we are not here to argue about its accuracy, rather to point out we like to believe we gain knowledge of the world around us through these particular mechanisms. We experience some things that are unexplainable; we often attribute these things to mystery. If we struggle to find a clear understanding, we often chalk it up to magic, mysticism, or superstition. The value of this method of knowledge is that, in fact, there are some things we cannot know scientifically.

Intuition or Hunches.

Most of us also have some form of knowledge we believe is based upon intuition. Intuition is that feeling we get that we often call our *gut feeling*. It is some internal-based instinct we have about a situation, issue, or experience. It is not unusual for us to accept certain things as true, just because it makes sense. Some people see intuition as a "leap of insight." Again, intuition can produce useful ideas, but since we are unable to explain why, it can be difficult to investigate.

A slightly more difficult concept to articulate is the method of knowing known as **a priori**. This method is one that has its roots in early philosophers contemplating epistemology, such as Plato and Aristotle. It is the first to consider the relationship between knowledge and one's own observations; that is to say that what we observe with our senses may be the most effective means of determining what is true (regardless of how things have always been or what someone in a position of authority has to say about it).

a priori
A form of reasoning based on hunches and observations that have been accumulated over time; it intuitively makes sense that something is true.

For lack of a better way of putting it, a priori reasoning is based on hunches. Based on what someone has seen before, it may just stand to reason that things are a certain way (Kerlinger, 1992). Based on observations that have been accumulated over time, it intuitively makes sense that something is true.

Let's say you are trying to move an enormous couch into your apartment. It weighs about 300 pounds, and you and your roommate have been trying to get it up a stairwell for half an hour. It isn't working. You decide that you need to ask a passerby for help, and you see two gentlemen walking in opposite directions. The first is six feet six inches tall, with approximately the same physique as a professional bodybuilder. The second is about five foot eleven, in pretty good shape, but not a large person by any stretch of the imagination. You need to determine a conditional truth: Who would be a better person to ask for help?

Of course you ask the big guy. It just stands to reason that a big, strong person will be more able to help than a person of average size. Clearly the bigger of the two men is the one you should ask for help. One could perhaps argue that more often than not you would be right. But what if, in this case, the bodybuilder has an elbow injury? Or that the smaller of the two men has a black belt in jiu-jitsu, thus making him not only deceptively strong for his size, but an expert in balance and leverage? Under either or both of these circumstances, the smaller man would be a better choice.

It is very unlikely that you will have to someday choose between an injured bodybuilder and a martial arts expert when seeking help with your couch. However, this example illustrates the major shortcoming of a priori reasoning: exceptions to one's hunches. While accumulated experience in related matters may lead to an assumption about a specific observation, there is always the possibility that this particular scenario deviates from past experiences. In this case, the truth that you determine may be called into question, as your past observations are not exactly the same as the present situation. Believing the past predicts the future results in illogical reasoning. Look up the "gambler's fallacy." A gambler keeps gambling because he or she believes that his or her "number is bound to come up eventually," despite the fact that every dice roll, roulette spin, or hand of cards is an independent statistical event. Regardless of how many hands you have lost in a row, the odds are still in favor of the "house."

● ●

What's Wrong with Everyday Ways of Knowing?   ▼

While the everyday ways of knowing we have detailed above do provide a starting point for building knowledge, there are numerous problems inherent in these ways of knowing. People tend to trust their beliefs from personal experience, more than evidence that may be contrary to their own experience. We must consider some of these problems with everyday ways of knowing.

Accuracy

First, all in all, the majority of us are not very accurate at making observations. We tend to be pretty casual observers. Think back for a minute to the last person you saw before reading this textbook. Who was that person? What was he or she wearing? What kind of shoes? Do you remember the details? Most of us do not.

Overgeneralization

Another problem with our everyday ways of knowing is overgeneralization. As individuals, we prefer our world to be orderly and, as such, we tend to generalize our knowledge to a broader reach. This can be problematic when we base this knowledge on just a few experiences or observations. For example, we might generalize that people with college degrees are less likely to get divorced. However, what if our experience is atypical? We need to be cautious when it comes to generalizing based on limited data in any form.

Cognitive Conservatism

Yet, another difficulty with everyday knowing is that once we believe something, we tend to pay special attention to experiences and situations that are consistent with our beliefs, and disregard those that are inconsistent with our beliefs. This is called cognitive conservatism, the idea that how we view the world is often based upon our prior beliefs. Allport and Postman (1945) conducted a series of studies that demonstrate how cognitive conservatism works. In this research, they played a game called "Rumor," where a message is given to the first person who then must whisper in his or her neighbor's ear, each in turn, until the message is shared aloud by the last participant. For their study on racial prejudice, they showed white subjects a picture of a fight between a white man and a black man on a train. The white man was holding a razor to the black man in the picture. What do you suppose participants experienced? Yes, that's right; the razor typically changed hands. Allport and Postman noted information that does not fit the predisposition of a perceiver is likely to be forgotten or changed in memory.

Contradictory Knowledge

Everyday ways of knowing can lead to contradictions in what we know. For example, if you've ever been in a long-distance relationship, you've likely heard the expression "absence makes the heart grow fonder," and that makes logical sense. However, you might have also experienced the effects of "if you can't be with the one you love, love the one you're with." So you know that both could be true. Your parents or other authorities (including your friends) might have given you advice on one side or the other about that reality, and they could probably cite everyday evidence to support each claim.

• •

▼ Scientific Reasoning

This leads us to the final way of knowing, identified by Buchler (1955): science. The scientific method attempts to address the problems with these everyday ways of knowing. **Scientific reasoning** begins with a priori assumptions, but goes a step further—it includes *self-correction* (Kerlinger, 1992). Under the method of science, one has a hunch about how things ought to be, then tests this hunch by making observations. As you will see in Chapter 6, these hunches are often called **hypotheses**, or educated guesses, about a social phenomenon based on prior observations. Scientists propose hypotheses and then make observations in order to test them.

One major misconception of science as a way of knowing is that science *proves* things. Scientific reasoning by its very nature is skeptical, and scientists are reluctant to make claims about the truth in black-and-white terms. Rather, scientists are more likely to talk about *probability* and confidence in their conclusions. They discuss their conclusions in terms of the likelihood of their explanations and observations being true. In fact, the process of scientific reasoning is largely concerned with the *disproving* of a priori statements, as opposed to looking for ways of finding out that they are correct (which we will discuss in further detail in Chapters 10 through 13). Scientists start from a

scientific reasoning
A way of knowing where one has a hunch about how things ought to be, then tests that hunch by making observations.

hypotheses
Educated guesses about a social phenomenon based on prior observations.

position of skepticism, assuming their hunches to be wrong, and evaluate their observations in terms of how they may refute or fail to refute their hypotheses. They then repeat their procedures in order to build more confidence in these conclusions. In order to do so, science must remain objective, without the biases, values, or attitudes of the scientist interfering with the interpretation of this data.

Take our furniture-moving example from above. If you really wanted to know whether the best choice to help with moving a couch is a big person or an average-sized person, as a scientist, you would form the same hypothesis as that in the example above: The bigger of the two men will be of more help. You may then test this hypothesis by asking both men to help to see who can lift the couch. You may then find ten other large muscular men, and ten other men of average size, and repeat this experiment over and over. Despite the presence of the injured bodybuilder and the small martial arts expert, you would likely find that nine times out of ten the bigger person is better at moving furniture. You could then offer support for your initial hypothesis: It is not the case that bigger men are *always* better at moving furniture, but by making repeated observations you can state that it is more often than not the case.

This example illustrates perhaps the most useful advantage to scientific thinking: the ability to *predict*. By establishing a certain amount of confidence in their findings, if faced with the same dilemma sometime in the future our struggling movers would have a theory to work with regarding who could help the most. They wouldn't be under the misconception that it always works that way, but would understand that it is *more likely* that in the future the larger person could help out.

Of course, this example also illustrates how cumbersome science can be as a way of understanding our everyday experiences. If you are lugging a couch up a stairwell, you don't have time to conduct a series of tests to determine the best course of action; you just need someone to lift the couch. If your hard drive crashes, you probably don't want to conduct a series of tests of different procedures that may fix the problem; you just want it fixed immediately! If a conclusion drawn from tenacity or authority accomplishes this task, then so be it.

Science is, however, very useful in the understanding of more complex social phenomena such as communication. The repeated testing of hypotheses in an academic or applied research environment or an in-depth exploration to understand a phenomenon on a detailed description of a communication act may lead to the basic goal of science: the development of **theory**. Accumulating these statements over time may lead to the formation of a theory, otherwise known as "a set of interrelated constructs, definitions, and propositions that present a systematic view of phenomena by specifying relations among variables, with the purpose of explaining and predicting the phenomena" (Kerlinger, 1992, p. 9). In plain terms, this is to say that systematically seeking to answer questions and understand phenomena can lead to useful heuristics and allow us to make informed predictions and understandings about social behavior under different circumstances. Theoretical work derived from academic research can then serve to inform everyday problems and issues.

theory
A set of interrelated constructs, definitions, and propositions that present a systematic view of phenomena by specifying relations among variables, with the purpose of explaining and predicting the phenomena.

▼ What Do Communication Researchers Do?

What Specific Areas Do Communication Researchers Study?

Now that we have established an epistemological framework for the systematic study of communication, let us turn our attention to some of the more specific subject areas that communication researchers study. The following pages will detail some of the phenomena that communication researchers address using assumptions and techniques derived from a scientific or humanistic approach to the study of human interactions.

As stated earlier, communication as a discipline deals fundamentally with the use of symbols and information to convey meaning to others. The conveyance of meaning can exist in several contexts. For example, communication researchers may be concerned with the impact of mediated information—transmitted through media channels such as film, television, and the Internet—on public opinion, attitudes, and behaviors. Others may be more concerned with communication in interpersonal contexts, such as face-to-face interactions, conversations between family members, or those in romantic relationships. Still others may study the ways in which information is transmitted through different levels of organizations and businesses.

Scholarly Research

Generally speaking, communication researchers draw a distinction between *scholarly research* and *applied research*. When we speak of scholarly research, this usually refers to primary research conducted by communication professors and academics and distributed through academic publications. As stated above, scholarly research is often driven by the desire to build or explain *theory*. Those conducting scholarly research are typically concerned with the theoretical implications of their findings and building or contributing to theories.

Let's take one well-known example of the development of a theory that is widely used in both communication and psychology research: the Theory of Reasoned Action (Ajzen & Fishbein, 1980). Frustrated with past research in persuasion, Ajzen and Fishbein began conducting a series of experiments during the 1970s and 1980s looking at other things they thought might be important in the process of compliance. Through numerous studies, they came to the conclusion that while there is a link between attitude change and actual behaviors, there are other things that are important as well. Most notably, they identified people's intentions as a critical factor that had been overlooked. The Theory of Reasoned Action argues (to put it in the simplest terms possible) that attitudes don't directly affect people's behavior; they affect people's intentions to behave in a certain way, which then may or may not result in a change of behavior.

For example, a commercial advocating that people stop smoking might be effective in changing a person's attitude toward smoking (e.g., "Okay, now we see that smoking is a bad idea"), but this does not necessarily mean she will quit. Instead, the Theory of Reasoned Action would argue that not only does she have to realize that it is a bad idea, but also actually *decide* that she is going to quit before doing so. Of course, there are a number of reasons why things might break down; the person in question may or may not actually decide to quit, and then may or may not actually do it.

Still, something was missing. Adding a person's intentions into the equation did a better job of explaining persuasion, but did not explain it completely. As Ajzen and Fishbein continued these experiments throughout the 1980s and 1990s, they came to the conclusion that an important consideration might be people's belief that they could actually get it done. They (and others) have called this "behavioral control." In fact, they found that attitudes were more likely to drive intentions, and intentions were more likely to drive behavior, if people actually believed that they could successfully perform the behavior in question. To tie it in to our smoking example above, a person may experience a shift in her attitude toward smoking; this attitude shift is much more likely to lead her to attempting to quit if she *believes* that she can quit. Likewise, if she tries to quit, she is more likely to actually do so if she believes she can. The committed smoker, who has been doing it for years and years and has given up on the idea of ever quitting, may form an increasingly negative view of the habit, but she will not likely try to quit, and if she does try, she will likely fail.

By adding in a person's behavioral control to the theory, Ajzen and Fishbein modified their original theory and gave it a new title: Theory of Planned Behavior (Ajzen, 1995). Through decades of fine tuning and adjustment, the results of their studies led to a well-informed and commonly applied theory that has been used to explain persuasion in a variety of contexts, including smoking, drinking, signing up for treatment programs, using contraceptives, dieting, wearing seatbelts or safety helmets, exercising regularly, voting, and breast-feeding (Fishbein, Middlestadt, & Hitchcock, 1994).

Applied Research

Fishbein and Ajzen's work has proved to be a major contribution to communication thinking. Developing their framework through scholarly research has helped inform not only theoretical development on the topic of persuasion, but also numerous studies evaluating the utility of the theory in real-world contexts.

Such research is often labeled *applied research*. Communication scholars, like other social, behavioral, and humanities researchers, will take the theoretical lessons learned in their academic studies and further apply them to varying real-life contexts. Applied research is typically concerned with investigating whether theoretical developments can be taken outside of the academic setting and used to solve more tangible, social problems. While applied research can often be found in the same journals and texts as theoretical research, the goal of applied research is quite different—to test theory in the field to see if it can be used to solve problems.

Often, applied research addresses very specific concerns. For example, Roberto, Krieger, Katz, Goei, and Jain (2011) tested the Theory of Planned Behavior, as described above, to see if it could be applied to pediatricians' likelihood to get their daughters tested for the HPV virus. After mailing out a survey measuring attitudes, norms, perceived control, intentions, and behaviors, the authors analyzed the links between these data points to see if TPB held in this context. They report that it did, and that positive attitudes toward the vaccine, subjective norms regarding its use, and perceptions of behavioral control all combined to predict the likelihood that the subjects would get their daughters the vaccine. Thus, the authors offered evidence that this theory was effective in explaining one highly specific, real life problem.

Nothing as Practical as a Good Theory

Let's think about this a little further. Communication scholars and other social researchers are quick to draw a line between scholarly and applied research. Yet at the same time, applied research is defined as that which takes theoretical work and tests it in the field. We do this so that we can have more confidence in our theories, and also so that we may witness the contributions of theory in solving real-life problems.

Might it be the case that this distinction is not as stark as we make it out to be? Certainly, the theoretical insights offered by academic research can be useful in applied contexts. By the same token, if we test our theories in the field, and they do not work so well, then we need to refine them just as we would with results from a laboratory. Further, we frequently build theories from applied research; in fact, in the example above, Ajzen, Fishbein, and colleagues conducted research that could be classified as both scholarly and applied, using these criteria.

It really depends on how we piece together our studies. Sometimes we start with theories and then go out and test them. Other times we build our theories from a number of observations, without preexisting ideas of what might happen. But that is a discussion for Chapter 2.

● ●

organizational communication ▼
This field of communication studies the ways in which people exchange information to accomplish goals. The exchange of information in organizational contexts can take on a variety of different forms, including relationships between managers and subordinates, relationships with constituents outside the organization, different ways that organizations deal with crises and emergencies, and so on.

What Are Some Examples of Communication Research?

Where Do Communication Researchers Study?

Now that we have talked a little bit about both theoretical and applied research, let's look at some examples of each across a wide range of communication subject areas. The examples below don't go into a great deal of detail, nor are they all-inclusive by any stretch, but a few examples of different research topics are presented to give you an idea of the range of subject matter in which communication researchers may be interested.

In Businesses and Organizations. **Organizational communication**, as a subfield, is dedicated to studying the ways in which people exchange information in order to accomplish group or individual goals (Miller, 2005). The exchange of information in organizational contexts can take on a variety of different forms, including relationships between managers and subordinates, relationships with constituents outside the organization, different ways that organizations deal with crises and emergencies, and so on.

Here are a few examples of studies that illustrate the diversity of communication research in organizations. Coombs and Holladay (2004) developed a means of measuring how tolerant employees are of aggressive behavior in their organizations, hoping that this tool could be used to improve relationships between employees and managers. Daft and Lengel (1986) looked at the role of media richness in computer-mediated work teams, and the impact it would have on productivity. Sellnow, Seeger, and Ulmer (2002) examined emergency messages surrounding the 1999 Red River floods, arguing that these messages hindered the goals of those organizations responding to the crisis. Ehrlich and Shami (2010) explored the use of microblogs such as Twitter inside and outside the workplace as a form of information gathering within the workplace. James and Minnis (2004) looked at the role of organizational storytelling in corporate leadership. Stohl and Stohl (2005) examined communication networks associated with the founding of the United Nations and the Universal Declaration of Human Rights. Real and Putnam (2005) examined organization-employee relationships by looking at the message strategies of a group of airline pilots who went on strike. Mignerey, Rubin, and Gordon (2005) examined the processes through which new employees reduce uncertainty upon arriving in organizations and their exposure to organizational assimilation processes. Davis (2008) used an ethnographic method to look at the role of leadership in interorganizational peer-led teams. Organizational communication may include the study of individuals, organizational entities, groups, or messages themselves and how they serve to meet certain goals.

In Media.   Some communication researchers explore research questions and hypotheses related to the mass media. Again, these research questions can take on a variety of different forms. Much attention in the media literature has been paid to the influence of media messages on attitudes and behaviors, such as persuasion, aggressive behavior, attitudes toward sexuality, and political opinion. Other research has focused more on what it is that people choose to watch, and their motivations for seeking out different types of information that meet different needs. Other studies are more concerned with the *content* of media, analyzing the messages themselves to look for different types of messages that might be important.

Media research relies heavily on several different methods that will be discussed in this volume. It uses surveys, laboratory experiments, and content analysis to answer questions about our uses of and responses to mediated information. Whether the information in question is used for entertainment purposes, acquiring information, or facilitating social interactions, examining mediated information can be useful in understanding how humans convey meaning.

Katz, Blumler, and Gurevitch (1973), for example, conducted a long program of research exploring the reasons why people choose to use different types of media, select different channels, and what they get out of the experience on the whole. McCombs and Shaw (1972) explored the role media

media research
This type of research uses surveys, laboratory experiments, and content analysis to answer questions about the uses of and responses to mediated information and can be useful in understanding how humans convey meaning.

coverage plays in highlighting specific political issues that people consider when voting. Gerbner, Gross, Morgan, and Signorielli (1986) studied the ways in which heavy television viewers tended to believe that the real world looks like that on television, and in particular whether the presence of violence and policing on television made people more fearful; similarly, Lowry, Nio, and Leitner (2003) compared the extent of network crime reporting to FBI crime statistics, revealing a disconnect between people's fears and their actual likelihood of becoming a victim. The National Television Violence Study (Wilson et al., 1998) quantified not only the amount of violence on mainstream television, but also how often violence was presented in a way known to lead to aggression, fear, and desensitization among viewers. Dixon and Linz (2000) explored the underrepresentation of Latinos and African Americans in mainstream television. Raney (2002) examined the relationship between moral judgment and enjoyment of crime dramas. Nabi, Moyer-Guse, and Byrne (2007) explored the relationship between televised political humor and attitude change. Both Ledbetter et al. (2011) and Greenhow and Robelia (2009) have examined the way in which Facebook affects our communication. Ledbetter et al. (2011) found support for the idea that our self-disclosure and social connections were directly related to both our Facebook communication and relational closeness.

In Health Care.   Communication researchers are increasingly turning their attention to the role of information exchange in the context of health care. This research also tackles a wide range of subject matters. Some health communication scholars look at the interpersonal exchanges between doctors and patients or how an illness or disability affects family communication. Others look at public health campaigns designed to encourage healthy behaviors or how our culture constructs ideas of health, wellness, and illness. Still, others look at the flow of information in public health organizations, just to name a few.

For example, a number of studies have looked at the ways in which people can be scared into engaging in healthy behaviors (like quitting smoking or practicing safe sex); these fear appeal studies, such as Dillard, Plotnick, Godbold, Freimuth, and Edgar (1996), have looked at the extent to which audiences can be scared into compliance and any unintended effects associated with this fear. Other campaign studies have looked at the effectiveness of health messages in very specific contexts, such as sun protection (Silk & Parrott, 2006), gun safety (Meyer, Roberto, & Atkin, 2003), or bicycle helmets (Witte, Stokols, Ituarte, & Schnieder, M., 1993). Still other studies have examined the role communication plays in the experience of social support for cancer survivors as they return to their workplace (Yarker, Munir, Bains, Kalawsky, & Haslam, 2010). Laura Ellingson (2005) used ethnography to examine *backstage* communication in a health-care setting. Carolyn Ellis used a technique called *autoethnography* to examine her relationship with her colleague and husband Gene Weinstein as he died from emphysema (1995). Christine Davis co-constructed a narrative with her sister Kathy Salkin (Davis & Salkin, 2005) to describe and explain the experience of being and having a sibling with a disability.

In Interpersonal Interactions.   Perhaps the most diverse subset of communication research is research in interpersonal exchanges. The exchange of information in face-to-face settings has fascinated communication scholars for nearly a century. Along the way, interpersonal scholars have developed areas of study too numerous to cover in their entirety. However, there are a few major areas of focus that should be mentioned.

A large body of **interpersonal communication** research has been devoted to the study of compliance gaining and social influence; persuading people to adopt certain attitudes or behaviors. Relational scholars have looked at the dynamic and exchange of information between those in romantic relationships or members of families; Burleson and McGeorge (2002), for example, explored the ways in which people in relationships effectively provide social support during difficult times. Segrin, Woszidlo, Givertz, Bauer, and Murphy (2012) examined the role "helicopter parenting" has on parent child communication and the relationship between overparenting and adaptability and entitlement attitudes in adult children. They found that lower quality parent-child communication is associated with overparenting and that this was a significant predictor of adult children's sense of entitlement. Powell (2011) explored the dissolution of her marriage through a retrospective analysis of letters she wrote to her husband.

Deception scholars have long studied the use of both verbal and nonverbal cues to indicate when someone is lying. In a study conducted by Dunleavy, Chory, and Goodboy (2010), they found that liars who withhold information rather than distort it are perceived as being more competent and of higher character within the workplace, while coworkers perceived as having the highest character and being most trustworthy are colleagues who told the truth rather than lied.

Nonverbal scholars study the use of gesture, inflection, and other forms of self-presentation in conveying meaning to others. Okora and Washington (2011) examined the connection between faculty attire and students' nonverbal behaviors and attitudes. They explored the idea that faculty attire functions as a form of nonverbal communication, impacting student perception of quality of instruction. Conversation analysts study the patterns of verbal exchanges between individuals. Others study conflict negotiation and resolution between individuals in both everyday and political contexts. The list goes on and on.

interpersonal communication
The study of compliance gaining and social influence; persuading people to adopt certain attitudes or behaviors; establishing identity, information gathering, building understanding with each other; and creating and maintaining relationships in a variety of contexts.

So What?

In summary, the field of communication is exceptionally diverse. Communication researchers are in the business of answering questions related to these and dozens of other matters. The prevailing theme throughout all aspects of communication research—to reiterate the opening of this chapter—is that communication researchers seek the answers to questions regarding the use of symbols and information to convey meaning. This volume will give a basic overview and explanation of the ways in which these questions are formulated, how they are explored, and how the answers to these questions are reported. It is a how-to guide on the practice of communication research.

Glossary

A priori
This form of reasoning is based on hunches and observations that have been accumulated over time; it intuitively makes sense that something is true.

Applied Research
Research that takes the theoretical lessons learned in academic studies and applies them to varying real life contexts.

Authority
The reliance upon someone in a position of power to determine what is factual. This power may be derived from a variety of places, such as expertise, political power, religious authority, or interpersonal trust.

Cognitive Conservatism
The idea that how someone views the world is often based upon his or her prior beliefs.

Communication Researchers
Scholars and professionals who study communication.

Critical or Cultural Research
Research that looks at the construction, use, and abuse of power and control in a culture, situation, organization, or community.

Epistemology
The study of knowledge.

Experience
A common way of understanding the social world.

Health Communication Scholars
Communication scholars who look at the interpersonal exchanges between doctors and patients, public health campaigns, the flow of information in public health organizations, and other health issues.

Humanities Research
Research that uses performative or artistic elements to look at how we co-construct meaning through communication.

Hypotheses
Educated guesses about a social phenomenon based on prior observations.

Interpersonal Communication
The study of compliance gaining and social influence; persuading people to adopt certain attitudes or behaviors; establishing identity, information gathering, building understanding with each other, and creating and maintaining relationships in a variety of contexts.

Intuition
An internal-based instinct that people have about a situation, issue, or experience.

Media Research
This type of research uses surveys, laboratory experiments, and content analysis to answer questions about the uses of and responses to mediated information. It can be useful in understanding how humans convey meaning.

Organizational Communication
This field of communication studies the ways in which people exchange information to accomplish goals. The exchange of information in organizational contexts can take on a variety of different forms, including relationships between managers and subordinates, relationships with constituents outside the organization, different ways that organizations deal with crises and emergencies, and so on.

Overgeneralization
A problematic way of knowing in which individuals base their knowledge on just a few experiences or observations.

Research
The activity of conducting intellectual investigations into the observable world.

Scientific Reasoning
A way of knowing where one has a hunch about how things ought to be, then tests that hunch by making observations.

Scholarly Research
Primary research conducted by academic researchers and distributed through academic publications with the desire to build theory.

Social Research
This research focuses less on the observable world in which human beings interact, and more on the interactions themselves, how they come into existence, how they function, and how they affect the human experience. Research in communication, psychology, sociology, economics, political science, and anthropology are typically classified as social research.

Tenacity
The assumption that something is true because it has always been said to be true.

Theory
A set of interrelated constructs, definitions, and propositions that present a systematic view of phenomena by specifying relations among variables, with the purpose of explaining and predicting the phenomena.

References

Ajzen, I. (1995). Attitudes and behavior. Beliefs. Theory of reasoned action. Theory of planned behavior. In A. S. R. Manstead & M. Hewstone (Eds.), *The Blackwell dictionary of social psychology.* Oxford, UK: Blackwell.

Ajzen, I., & Fishbein, M. (1980). *Understanding attitudes and predicting social behavior.* Englewood Cliffs, NJ: Prentice-Hall.

Allport, G. W., & Postman, L. J. (1945). The basic psychology of rumor. *Transactions of the New York Academy of Sciences, 8,* 61–81.

Babbie, E. (1995). *The practice of social research.* Belmont, CA: Wadsworth.

Buchler, J. (1955). *Philosophical writings of Peirce.* New York: Dover.

Burleson, B. R., & MacGeorge, E. L. (2002). Supportive communication. In M. L. Knapp & J. A. Daly (Eds.), *Handbook of interpersonal communication* (3rd ed., pp. 374–424). Thousand Oaks, CA: Sage.

Coombs, T., & Holladay, S. J. (2004). Understanding the aggressive workplace: Development of the workplace aggression tolerance questionnaire. *Communication Studies, 55*(3), 481–497.

Daft, R. L., & Lengel, R. H. (1986). Organizational information requirements, media richness, and structural design. *Management Science, 32,* 554–571.

Davis, C. S. (2008). Dueling narratives: How peer leaders use narrative to frame meaning in community mental health care teams. *Small Group Research, 39*(6), 706–727.

Davis, C. S., & Salkin, K. A. (2005). Sisters and friends: Dialogue and multivocality in a relational model of sibling disability. *Journal of Contemporary Ethnography, 34*(2), 206–234.

Dillard, J. P., Plotnick, C. A., Godbold, L. C., Freimuth, V. S., & Edgar, T. (1996). The multiple affective consequences of AIDS PSAs: Fear appeals do more than scare people. *Communication Research, 23,* 44–72.

Dixon, T. L., & Linz, D. (2000). Overrepresentation and underrepresentation of African Americans and Latinos as law-breakers on television news. *Journal of Communication, 50,* 131–154.

Dunleavy, K. N., Chory, R. M., & Goodboy, A. K. (2010). Responses to deception in the workplace: Perceptions of credibility, power, and trustworthiness. *Communication Studies, 61,* 239–255.

Ehrlich, N., & Shami, S. (2010). Microblogging inside and outside the workplace. USA Proceedings of the Fourth International AAAI Conference on Weblogs and Social Media. May 23–26, 2010. Washington DC. Association for the Advancement of Artificial Intelligence.

Ellingson, L. L. (2005). *Communicating in the clinic: Negotiating frontstage and backstage teamwork.* Cresskill, NJ: Hampton Press.

Ellis, C. (1995). *Final negotiations: A story of love, loss, and chronic illness.* Philadelphia: Temple University Press.

Fishbein, M., Middlestadt, S. E., & Hitchcock, P. J. (1994). Using information to change sexually transmitted disease-related behaviors. In R. J. DiClemente & J. L. Peterson (Eds.), *Preventing AIDS: Theories and methods of behavioral interventions.* New York: Plenum Press.

Gerbner, G., Gross, L., Morgan, M., & Signorielli, N. (1986). Living with television: The dynamics of the cultivation process. In J. Bryant & D. Zillman (Eds.), *Perspectives on media effects* (pp. 17–40). Hillsdale, NJ: Lawrence Erlbaum Associates.

Goodall, H. L. (2006). *A need to know: The clandestine history of a CIA family.* Walnut Creek, CA: Left Coast Press.

Greenberg, B. S., Eastin, M. S., Hofshire, L., Lachlan, K. A., & Brownell, K. (2003). Portrayals of overweight and obese individuals in commercial television. *American Journal of Public Health, 93*(8), 1342–1348.

Greenhow, C., & Robelia, E. (2009). Old communication, new literacies: Social network sites as social learning resources. *Journal of Computer-Mediated Communication, 14,* 1130–1161.

James, C.H., & Minnis, W.C. (2004). Organizational storytelling: It makes sense. *Business Horizons, 3,* 23–32

Katz, E., Blumler, J. G., & Gurevitch, M. (1973). Uses and gratifications research. *Public Opinion Quarterly, 37*(4), 509–523.

Kerlinger, F. (1992). *Foundations of behavioral research.* Fort Worth, TX: Harcourt Brace.

Ledbetter, A. M., Mazer, J. P., DeGroot, J. M., Meyer, K. R., Mao, Y., & Swafford, B. (2011). Attitudes toward online social connection and self-disclosure as predictors of Facebook communication and relational closeness. *Communication Research, 38,* 27–53.

Lowry, D. T., Nio, T. C., & Leitner, D.W. (2003). Setting the public fear agenda: A longitudinal analysis of network TV crime reporting, public perceptions of crime, and FBI crime statistics. *Journal of Communication, 53,* 61–73.

McCombs, M., & Shaw, D. (1972). The agenda-setting function of mass media. *Public Opinion Quarterly, 36*(2), 176–187.

Meyer, G., Roberto, A. J., & Atkin, C. K. (2003). A radio-based approach to promoting gun safety: Process and outcome evaluation implications and insights. *Health Communication, 15*(3), 299–318.

Mignerey, J.T., Rubin, R.B., & Gorden, W.I. (2005). Organizational entry: An investigation of newcomer communication behavior and uncertainty. *Communication Research, 22,* 54–85.

Miller, K. (2005). *Organizational communication: Approaches and processes.* Boston: Thomson Wadsworth.

Nabi, R. L., Moyer-Guse, E., & Byrne, S. (2007). All joking aside: A serious investigation into the persuasive effect of funny social issue messages. *Communication Monographs, 74*(1), 29–54.

Okoro, E., & Washington, M. (2011). Communicating in a multicultural classroom: A study of students' nonverbal behavior and attitudes toward faculty attire. *Journal of College Teaching and Learning, 8,* 27–38.

Powell, H. L. (2011). Letters to Louis: Marital dissolution through the social construction of lived experience. *Journal of Divorce & Remarriage, 52,* 19–32.

Raney, A. A. (2002). Punishing criminals and moral judgment: The impact on enjoyment. *Media Psychology, 7*(2), 145–163.

Real, K., & Putnam, L. L. (2005). Ironies in the discursive struggle of pilots defending the profession. *Management Communication Quarterly, 19*(1), 91–119.

Roberto, A. J., Krieger, J. L., Katz, M., Goei, R., & Jain, P. (2011). Predicting pediatricians communication with parents about the Human Papillomavirus (HPV) vaccine: An application of the Theory of Reasoned Action. *Health Communicaiton, 26*(4), 303–312.

Segrin, C., Woszidlo, A., Givertz, M., Bauer, A., & Murphy, M. T. (2012). The association between overparenting, parent-child communication, and entitlement and adaptive traits in adult children. *Family Relations, 61,* 237–352.

Sellnow, T. L., Seeger, M. W., & Ulmer, R. R. (2002). Chaos theory, informational needs, and natural disasters. *Journal of Applied Communication Research, 30*(4), 269–292.

Silk, K. J., & Parrott, R. L. (2006). All or nothing . . . or just a hat?: Farmers' sun protection behaviors. *Health Promotion Practice, 7*(2), 180–185.

Stohl, M., & Stohl, C. (2005). Human rights, nation states, and NGOs: Structural holes and the emergence of global regimes. *Communication Monographs, 72*(4), 442–467.

Toppman, L. (2009, May 26). Mothers' bare emotions burst out in "Miracle Kick." *Charlotte Observer,* pp. 1D, 5D.

U.S. Surgeon General's Scientific Advisory Committee on Television and Social Behavior. (1972). *Television and growing up: The impact of televised violence* (DHEW Publication No. HSM 72-9086). Washington, DC.

Wilson, B. J., Kunkel, D., Linz, D., Potter, W. J., Donnerstein, E., Smith, S. L., et al. (1998). *National television violence study: Vol. 1. Violence in television programming overall: University of California–Santa Barbara study.* Thousand Oaks, CA: Sage.

Witte, K., Stokols, D., Ituarte, P., & Schnieder, M. (1993). Testing the health belief model in a field study to promote bicycle safety helmets. *Communication Research, 20,* 564–586.

Yarker, J., Munir, F., Bains, M., Kalawsky, K., & Haslam, C. (2010). The role of communication and support in return to work following cancer-related absence. *Psycho-oncology, 19,* 1078–1085.

METATHEORETICAL CONSIDERATIONS, RESEARCH PERSPECTIVES, AND RESEARCH PARADIGMS

2

CHAPTER OUTLINE

KEY TERMS

Axiology

Critical perspective

Deductive model

Epistemology

Hermeneutics

Inductive model

Interpretivism

Metatheory

Nominalist

Objectivist

Ontology

Positivism

Proprietary research

Qualitative research

Quantitative research

Realist

Scholarly research

Social constructionist

Subjectivist

CHAPTER OBJECTIVES

1. To explain metatheory and its primary components
2. To understand the differences between the research perspectives and paradigms discussed in this chapter
3. To understand how our beliefs, values, and the ways we see the world influences our research choices
4. To become familiar with the different types of research

▼ ## What Are the Goals and Methods of Communication Scholars and Everyday Observers?

The primary goal of both social scientists and humanities scholars is to understand the world around us. Communication scholars are interested in questions and ideas relating to how we communicate. These goals have grown out of everyday concerns, a type of common sense allowing us to better understand the world we live in. From an early age, we observe things in our everyday life as they occur around and to us. Many of us try to understand why these things happen to or around us. We wonder about specific happenings, while also making general conclusions about why we behave as we do, as well as why others are the way they are.

Consider this example: We observe teenagers waiting in line at an amusement park speaking rudely to one another, yet they appear to be friends. We want to know why they speak to each other in this manner. What would you do? We could ask them; we could observe their behavior before and after the incident; we could ask an expert in teenage behavior. We may conclude that speaking rudely to one another in conversation is a way to demonstrate affiliation and to project identity. To reach some conclusion about the experience we have observed, we must formulate a research question and/or hypothesis, gather data, and draw conclusions until we are satisfied with the conclusion we've drawn.

▼ ## Metatheoretical Considerations

All forms of communication research are built upon researchers' own unique metatheoretical considerations, which are inherent in the research question(s) and/or hypotheses at study. **Metatheory** is theory about theory and allows us to understand the philosophy driving our decisions about research methods, design, and even analysis. Metatheory is a tool allowing us to recognize what aspects about the social world we think about and study. There are three primary components of metatheory: ontology, epistemology, and axiology. These three components are inherent within all of us—researchers and even students. It may be you have never identified or studied your beliefs about the world yet; we invite you to do so here.

metatheory
Theory about theory that allows people to understand the philosophy driving their decisions about research methods, design, and analysis.

Ontology

First, we need to consider the metatheoretical consideration, called ontology. **Ontology** is simply the study of the nature of reality. It answers the question: How do we know about the world around us? What do we believe exists in the world and how do we know it exists is the crux of our ontological perspective. As with all metatheoretical considerations, a continuum of knowing about the reality of the world exists. Some scholars take a **realist** stance; they believe the world exists out there and is tangible. This is an objective perspective, because they believe there is an objective reality independent of anything else. These scholars are at one end of the continuum of ontology. At the opposite end of the continuum we find scholars who take a subjective position. They believe that without individual cognition, the social world is arbitrary. Therefore, if we take this **nominalist** stance, we can never be certain about the reality of the world, outside of understanding an individual's unique cognitive experience of that thing. Between the realist and nominalist stance on the ontological continuum is an area of social reality that is neither objective nor subjective, but somewhere in between, that perhaps depends on the piece of social reality we desire to know.

Consider this example to help us sort out where you fall on the ontological continuum. Have you ever been asked, "If a tree falls in the forest, does it make a sound?" Most of us have a gut reaction response to this question. When we ask our classes this, we sort out the ontological foundations inherent in most people pretty quickly. For example, some students will immediately nod their heads with an emphatic yes, as though we have asked a rhetorical question. Their explanations often verge on the scientific explanations of physics about the fact that when the tree is falling and hits the ground, sound waves are created and must expand out into space. Thus, whether anyone is there to hear it, the sound exists because of what these students believe about physical space. These students are taking a realist stance; they believe without a shadow of a doubt that because the tree exists as a creation of certain types of cells, regardless of their knowledge of that specific tree, and because of their understanding of sound waves and basic physics, that indeed the tree that falls makes a noise.

However, almost as immediately upon hearing this question and response, many students start to disagree. They suggest almost the exact opposite. They propose that without actually being present at the moment in which the tree falls, they can in no way be certain the tree that fell made an actual noise. In other words, they must see it and hear it to know that the tree did, indeed, make a sound. The key here is individual cognition, and suggests this group of students is taking a nominalist stance to the question. As we discuss both the nominalist and realist perspective in relation to our tree question, another section of the classroom begins to look confused. These students are the students who like to answer the question with something along the lines of, "Well, it depends." These folks are likely our **social constructionist** perspective. They argue it is possible that the tree, which falls, makes a noise under certain conditions, but not others. We discuss all the possibilities that could and should be

ontology
The study of the nature of reality.

realist
The belief that the world exists and is tangible.

nominalist
The belief that without individual cognition, the social world is arbitrary.

social constructionist
The belief that our ideas about reality are constructed through societal and interpersonal communication.

factored in if we take this perspective. Usually, students suggest the tree could hit something besides just the ground; they consider weather conditions and all types of possibilities. The fact remains that they are undecided.

Often, students will want to know who is right. (Can you guess what ontological perspective these students usually have? Likely, they are realists—believing as they do that the world is absolute.) This is when we point out that all three ontological perspectives are right and valid. For many students, their ontological perspective is inherent and unwavering; still for other students, their ontological perspective will vary with different topics and as they learn and grow through life. What we do strive for with students is that they are able to articulate what they believe and can recognize the other perspectives in others and, more importantly, look for it as we read and study communication research. It is inherent within the research questions we ask and the hypotheses we seek to support.

Epistemology

epistemology
The study of the nature of knowledge.

Our second metatheoretical consideration, called **epistemology**, is simply the study of the nature of knowledge. It answers the questions: What can we know? Or, how do I approach studying the world as a scholar? As with all metatheoretical considerations, a continuum of belief about knowledge exists.

objectivist
The belief that it is possible to know and explain the world.

Some scholars take an **objectivist** position, which believes it is possible to know and explain the world. They search for regularities and patterns to communication behavior. They are most often interested in global understandings of life. Many individuals taking an objectivist epistemological perspective prefer a separation between the researcher and the subject, with the goal of not interfering with the outcome. People with this epistemology believe they know by discovery. They believe there is an objective reality outside of humans that can be observed by all. They believe they can study this objective reality in an unbiased, precise (accurate), systematic, and reliable manner through repetition, generalization, and discrimination.

subjectivist
The belief that knowledge is relative and can only be understood from the point of view of the individual involved.

On the other end of the continuum of epistemology is a **subjectivist** perspective. These scholars believe knowledge is relative and can only be understood from the point of view of the individual involved. They are most often interested in local understandings of life within a specific context. People with this epistemology believe they know by interpretation—that more than one reality can be known, so they use interpretation to guide their understanding of the different perspectives.

Axiology

axiology
The study of values.

The third metatheoretical consideration, called **axiology**, is the study of values. While scholars once believed it was possible to separate our value system from influencing scientific exploration, most scholars have come to realize that, in fact, it is a matter of how values influence our science. Some researchers believe, for example, that it is important for a researcher to be objective and that the researcher is the expert authority on his or her research. Others believe it is important to make sure multiple perspectives of participants are heard and that authority comes from all research participants, including the people in the group or culture being researched. What we value in research determines what research questions we ask, what types of studies we conduct, how we design those studies, and how we analyze the data. Essentially, it is impossible to eliminate the influence of values from scholarship. More importantly, many argue we should not separate values from scholarship and that good scholarship is based upon our values and ethics, which will be discussed in Chapter 5. As research is bounded in context, it is unlikely and unwise to ignore the values embedded within that context. However, as we have suggested about both our ontological and epistemological perspectives, a continuum of axiological perspective still exists. This reflects how strongly a researcher feels these values should be considered as part of the research.

Research Perspectives and Paradigms   ▼

From our metatheoretical considerations, we can build a composite picture of several different perspectives and paradigms we might take in conducting research. Our metatheoretical considerations are the foundation on which we build research, while research perspectives and paradigms are the overarching principles we use to conduct research. They are a way of experiencing and acting upon reality, to study communication. Like other areas of research, communication studies utilize a paradigm to determine the rules of gathering data and evidence and how such data should be interpreted. These might also be considered common boundaries established for what constitutes legitimate research practices. Research paradigms are shared by scholars across academic fields and agreed upon as a shared language within each paradigm. As they are understood across a community, they are jointly constructed by the intellectual community. Some scholars have suggested that paradigms enforce a particular view of the world. We prefer to think of paradigms of different views of the world that inform our research.

While our metatheoretical considerations tend to be intuitive and learned through everyday ways of knowing, early in our lives, research paradigms are more often taught. We learn research paradigms through our formal education. The academic community, through trial and error, has found research paradigms to be more useful than the everyday ways of knowing we discussed earlier. As research paradigms have been created through an intellectual community based on education, it is possible that research paradigms can be revised and changed through new discoveries and knowledge. Each research paradigm commits itself to its own standards and rules, including what problems can and cannot be addressed and studied. While a research paradigm is an important concept for understanding research methods, the idea is not free from disadvantages. Communication does not come neatly in one research paradigm or another. It is inherently messy and difficult to carve up. Some scholars become so entrenched in their own research paradigm, that they may not see what does not fit into their own paradigm. We will talk about three research perspectives and paradigms: positivist, interpretivist, and critical.

Positivism

Positivism is most often thought of as the most traditional research perspective. Individuals who identify themselves as preferring this perspective believe scientific evidence is superior to other types of knowing. They tend to prefer empirical data and formal theoretical perspectives as the way to gain knowledge about the physical and social world. In terms of their metatheoretical considerations, they are usually realists in their ontology, yet many recognize the possibility that multiple realities may exist. Objectivists in their epistemology believe social regularities exist. The social world, such as communication, occurs in patterns and can and should be studied using the tenants of social scientific methods. While original positivists would have argued for the exclusion of values in research, meaning that the researcher's values had no place contaminating data collection, most modern postpositivists recognize that our values, if in no other way, impact our research by the choices we make in what to study. If it had no value, why would we study it (Miller, 1986)?

Positivism as a research perspective began with scholars in the social sciences during the 1920s and 1930s (Miller, 1986). These researchers were interested in verifying social science through analysis and often experiments. Eventually, researchers using the verification approach recognized the difficulty of proving any particular fact and switched gears. They decided instead that what they should be doing is ruling out alternatives; in other words, attempting to prove that something is not true, rather than true. This is known as falsification and differentiates classic positivism from postpositivism, which most scholars taking this approach use today. This is also where we get the notion of the null hypothesis, which will be addressed later. It is also the reason most communication research methods instructors we know cringe when a student uses the word *prove*, because what we are really doing is ruling out alternatives.

A postpositivist approach to research often attempts to explore research questions concerned with explanation, prediction, and/or control of communication phenomenon. We can answer questions about why something will happen (explanation), forecast what will happen under similar circumstances (prediction), and attempt to create particular outcomes (control). For example, if a positivist or postpositivist scholar wanted to study relationship development, they might develop a hypothesis (see Chapter 6) predicting that the longer the relationship, the more time couples spend together. They might design a study considering people in three groups: those in relationships fewer than six months, those in relationships between six months and five years, and those in relationships over five years. The researcher might ask the study participants to keep a journal of their time spent together, then might conduct a statistical analysis to determine if there is a causal relationship between time in relationship and time spent together.

Positivists know by discovery. These scholars believe they must come to understand the world and the communication within it from an objective stance of observation. They feel strongly about precision and conduct research with an eye toward the systematic procedures of data collection and analysis and the ability to replicate their findings. These scholars tend to use experimental design and survey research to study communication.

Interpretivism

Interpretivism as a research perspective began with scholars such as Immanuel Kant and Max Weber. Both were pioneers contributing to a new understanding of the social world. Kant argued our understanding of the social world begins with intuition and a subjective spirit; a sense, essentially, that we are interpreting the world through our own perspective. Weber similarly advocated for moving to a more interpretive social science, which allowed room for studying the subjective reality of all individuals involved in interaction, rather than just knowing an objective reality. A term often connected with interpretive approaches to research is *phenomenology*. Phenomenology is most often considered an ontological consideration concerned with the essence of what we experience from an individual's firstperson perspective. It is an intentional analysis of lived experience. Again, the reason for this viewpoint is the emphasis on the importance of understanding from each person's perspective. This perspective provides primacy to an individual's own perceptions and interpretations of their experience. If we take this perspective to research, individual consciousness is the source of knowledge. Here we experience ourselves and others through the act of communication or dialogue.

In understanding what it means to take an interpretivist lens to research practice, we must also understand the metatheoretical commitments inherent within this choice. The epistemological position associated with interpretivism is that of a subjective stance, emphasizing that we can only understand reality from the person living it. In order to access this type of data, scholars taking this perspective are comfortable with minimal distance between themselves and their research participants. Interpretivism is based upon the epistemological consideration that knowledge is created in individual consciousness. Therefore, meaning will depend upon our own perceptions, backgrounds, and life experience. For example, consider your own perception when we ask you to consider a cat. How many of you picture a soft, cuddly kitty cat that you would love to pet and hold? How many of you think of a cat as a mean, independent, and smelly creature that you wish would stay away from you? Do any of you experience swelling throat, burning eyes, a tight chest, and trouble breathing when you are around cats? When we say "cat," do any of you think about the cats we might encounter at a zoo or circus? Our knowledge of cats is influenced by whether we like animals, whether we had a bad experience with a particular cat, whether we are allergic to cats, or whether we grew up with a cat we loved. Scholars who take this approach to research are truly interested in the individual perspective and meaning embedded within that experience. Based on what you know so far, what do you think an interpretive scholar's ontological tendencies are? Are they a realist, a social constructionist, a nominalist? Most likely they have nominalist leanings. A nominalist stance on ontology preferences individual cognition. Interpretive scholars utilize this axiological approach in their work, while acknowledging that they see the world through their own biases and perspective. As such, they encourage their values to be part of the discussion and the analysis, rather than striving toward an artificial attempt to eliminate their own value system.

interpretivism
A research perspective in which understanding and interpretation of the social world is derived from one's personal intuition and perspective.

Scholars who follow interpretive perspectives believe that more than one reality can be known and that interpretation is their guide to understanding. These scholars tend to use qualitative research techniques such as ethnography (described fully in Chapter 14). An interpretive scholar might study relational development by looking at his own relationship and, perhaps, write a narrative about the history of that relationship. He might also want to include the perspective of his partner and coconstruct a narrative written by both of them. Interpretive scholars might also include the perspectives of other significant people in their lives—perhaps other family members and close friends might contribute to the narrative as well.

Critical Perspective

critical perspective
This perspective uses research methods as a tool to challenge unjust discourse and communication practices, with the goal of using knowledge as a tool to create social change.

The third perspective, known as the **critical perspective**, essentially questions the primary goals associated with positivist and interpretivist perspectives. Remember that positivists' primary goal in research is explanation, while interpretivists are interested in understanding. Critical scholars think both of these representations are lacking. According to critical tradition, they see research methods as a tool to challenge unjust discourse and communication practices. There are several foundations of this perspective. One comes from the German Frankfurt School, which embraced Karl Marx's tradition of critiquing society. Another comes from French philosopher Foucault, whose work was especially important in understanding power and deviance as it is experienced and conveyed in everyday practices, discourses, and discursive rules, and in understanding how discourses and associated practices come to be accepted as true or legitimate (Deveaux, 1994; Foucault, 1965, 1972, 1973, 1995).

As they are critical of contemporary society and the practices found within our social structure, critical theorists typically challenge three components of contemporary society that are particularly useful to communication students. First, the structure and control of language perpetuates power imbalances in our society. Second, individuals become less sensitized to repression through the role of the mass media. Third, they suggest we have relied too heavily on the scientific method and accept all empirical findings, without adequate critique. The goal of most critical scholars is to use knowledge as a tool to create social change. Most of them are crusaders and/or activists of sorts working actively in reforming and changing the world with their research. Critique was originally suggested as a way to focus on the ways in which we alienate people.

What are the metatheoretical considerations of the critical perspective? Hopefully, by now, you are starting to see how the metatheoretical considerations of epistemology, ontology, and axiology begin to guide our choices of perspective. What might be most interesting about critical scholars is that they have some unique characteristics in terms of their metatheoretical considerations. They range from one side of the epistemological perspective to the other; being both positivistic in ways, while also exhibiting social constructionist tendencies, and even sometimes nominalist beliefs. Let me explain. Habermas

(1968) suggested that critical theory is a form of **hermeneutics**. Hermeneutics is essentially a way to study textual data through interpretation to create meaning. In other words, hermeneutics is a way to gain knowledge via interpretation. As the focus in these instances is upon explanation and interpretation, it could be considered as having a realist or social constructionist epistemological stance. However, other scholars taking the critical approach call into question the values and norms of a society, exploring how society adopts and reinforces dominant power structures. These scholars see realization of these dominant power structures and subsequent change as the goal of research. They clearly take a more nominalist stance, believing that knowledge comes from the cognitive process of recognizing the flaws of the society we live within. Similarly, in terms of their ontology, scholars taking the critical perspective can range from an objectivist stance to a more subjectivist stance. However, it is most common for contemporary communication scholars who take the critical perspective to reside more on the subjective side. As the goal for all critical theorists is identifying the power structures that bind our communication, they would argue that values not only are part of scholarship, but that they should drive scholarship. Critical theorists would suggest that values are the motivation behind their research, since they use research to be agents of societal change.

Many critical scholars are interested in work related to cultural studies. This work explores the idea of culture as a viable framework for understanding how one's values and beliefs are woven together and guide their experience of the world. Still, other critical scholars ground their work in feminist theory, which recognizes gender as among the most important defining features of social life. It is their belief that women throughout social life have been silenced or muted. This type of scholarship highlights the oppression women face in our society.

Scholars following the critical perspective believe that everything about how we communicate is shaped by values. The world is socially constructed and critical theorists study it through understanding knowledge for the purpose of bringing about social change. These scholars use different types of research, such as rhetorical criticism and critical ethnography, to understand the communication of our world.

Critical scholars might study relational development by asking a question such as: How do traditional relationships marginalize women or constrain the empowerment of women? They might use mixed methods such as observation, indepth interviews, and perhaps focus groups to gather information that will help them understand how social relationships construct power among people of different genders.

The following chart summarizes the different research perspectives and paradigms. In summary, postpositivists typically conduct research using strict scientific methods with bias-free inquiry as the goal, using objective methods. Their analysis is conducted at the conclusion of data collection as a separate step of the research process. Interpretivists, on the other hand, prefer to conduct research driven by empirical observation—in other words, grounded in the theory, with their primary goal to understand, rather than measure or explain. Unlike postpositivists, their data analysis occurs throughout the data collection

hermeneutics
A way to study textual data through interpretation to create meaning; knowledge gained via interpretation.

process. They are guided by the question: Does this research provide in-depth understanding? Critical scholars conduct research using a variety of methods, as you will see throughout this book. However, most important is the idea that they are warriors on an ethical agenda of identifying with human suffering and working toward changing the human condition.

		Ontological Assumptions (What do we believe about reality?)	Epistemological Assumptions (What can we know and study?)	Axiological Assumptions (What do we value in research and knowledge?)
Realist ↕ **Nominalist/Social Constructionist**	Positivism/ Postpositivism	Reality is orderly, fixed, and measurable.	We can know and study objective reality.	We value research that is objective and researchers who are expert authority.
	Critical/Cultural	May believe reality is orderly, measurable, objective. May believe reality is subjective.	We can know and study reality that is either objective or subjective. We can know and study reality that is interpreted or observed as is.	We value research that includes marginalized voices. We value research in which the researcher shares power with participants.
	Interpretivism	Reality is both orderly and chaotic. Reality is subjective.	We can know and study subjective reality as it is constructed, mediated, and biased.	We value research in which all participants are equal authorities and in which all perspectives are represented.

▼ **Types of Research**

As we have considered the metatheoretical foundations, research perspectives, and possible paradigms guiding scholarly research, we have yet to consider the characteristics of research. In other words, how do we conduct research? Research involves disciplined inquiry; we study communication in a systematic or planned approach. We take a scientific approach to research, no matter our metatheoretical considerations, our paradigm, or our method. We work to avoid the problems we encounter in our everyday ways of acquiring knowledge. There are two types of research: proprietary and scholarly. Most of you at one point or another will be responsible for or involved in both types of research.

Proprietary Research

Proprietary research is research conducted for a specific audience, which is not shared beyond the intended audience. Many corporations and businesses conduct research to examine anything from their business practices, to satisfaction with employee benefits programs, to marketing new products and services within potential clients or consumers. When one of your authors (Christine Davis) (see Chapter 1) worked for a market research consulting firm, she conducted proprietary research for clients. Many of you may end up doing this type of research for your career.

proprietary research
Research that is conducted for a specific audience, which is not shared beyond the intended audience.

Scholarly Research

Scholarly research is research conducted for the goal of contributing to knowledge for public consumption. While most research methods courses focus on scholarly research, it is important to realize that the steps, methods, and/or approaches for how to conduct research don't change, regardless of what type of research you are conducting.

scholarly research
Research conducted to contribute to generalizable knowledge for public consumption.

Characteristics of Scholarly Research.   Research is question-oriented. Academic scholarship is always interested in answering interesting questions. For communication scholars, the crux of our questions must involve questions related to communication. These questions are remaining questions about communication that, to date, remain unanswered. Questions come in all forms, from a variety of places. Sometimes we come up with questions through our experience and other everyday ways of knowing, recognizing the limitations of this type of knowledge. This is often a good way to come up with questions, but is only a starting point. Other questions come about from reading scholarly work and recognizing questions left unanswered from previous research.

Research is methodological. As we suggested earlier, without fail research involves planning and following a systematic approach for data collection and analysis. Regardless of the research questions or the area of communication studies we study, research follows rules. These rules may differ depending upon the research methodology we choose; yet, there are rules nonetheless.

Research is creative. This is often a characteristic of research that many students fail to recognize about research. We are in the process of creating new knowledge or adding to existing knowledge, and there are a variety of ways we can do this. Selecting (or inventing!) the best ways to know is a delightfully creative process.

Research is self-critical. As researchers, we are obligated to examine our own work from a critical vantage point. We should always be the first critic of our own work, fairly assessing the strengths and weaknesses of our scholarship. It is imperative that we remember there is no *perfect* research study; there is always more to learn. Good scholarship acknowledges the limitations of the work as a method of advancing our understanding. This self-critical view also suggests areas of future research.

Research is public. As we discussed earlier, academic research is conducted for public consumption. Researchers typically view scholarship as a mechanism for serving useful social purposes. If you ask most scholars what they most love about conducting research, it is the idea that they can work toward scholarship that may be useful to someone.

Research is both cumulative and self-correcting. All research is built upon previous scholarship. Good scholarship begins with the ability to gather scholarly research and critically assess the results of the work. This provides researchers the opportunity to correct mistakes made in other work. While we often think of correcting others' research, scholars often have the opportunity to improve upon their own previous research.

Research is cyclical. All research occurs in stages. The stages are determined first and foremost by the type of research question(s) we ask. The research question(s) determine the methodological design of the research project and the way we analyze the data we gather. Ultimately, while research answers questions, it also generates new questions that need to be answered.

••

▼ Two Logical Systems

The purpose of social science, including communication research, is to build knowledge that contributes to our understanding of communication behaviors. In some cases, we hope to be able to predict communication behaviors and even control these behaviors. However, in order to explain, predict, and/or control communication behaviors, we collect data and gather evidence to evaluate our understanding of these behaviors. There are two logical systems that allow social scientists to do just that. It is important to remember that the type of question determines which logical system we use. Neither is better than the other; in fact, they are merely different entry points into the same system.

Inductive Model

inductive model
This approach to research is often referred to as grounded theory. Communication scholars begin the research process by gathering data, observing patterns and idiosyncrasies within the data, and developing theory based upon that data. Most scholars who prefer this method of inquiry use qualitative research methods.

One system is the **inductive model**. This approach to research is often referred to as grounded theory, and it is often appropriate when we know little about a topic. Inductive methods can help create theory that can be tested with deduction (our second system). With inductive methods, instead of starting out with a theory and testing the theory, communication scholars begin the research process by gathering data, observing patterns and idiosyncrasies within the data, and developing theory based upon that data. Most scholars who prefer this method of inquiry use qualitative research methods. It is said that inductive reasoning moves us from the specific (the research study) to the general (the theory), while deductive reasoning moves us from the general (the theory) to the specific (the research study).

One interesting example of induction comes from a study on physicians' disclosure of confidential patient information. Maria Brann (2006) wondered how physicians balanced families' caregiving needs for information with patients' confidentiality rights. Using grounded theory, she interviewed physicians and used a detailed thematic coding process. Her findings theorized that the nature and severity of the patient's impairment influenced physician disclosures. She determined that federal privacy laws (HIPAA regulations) did not seem to discourage physicians from disclosing information, primarily because they were motivated by concern for the patient and belief in their own judgment. In other words, she developed a theoretical conclusion based on her research findings, which is an inductive approach.

Deductive Model

The other system is the **deductive model**. This model is typically referred to as theory driven. Communication scholars preferring a deductive approach begin with a theory and gather evidence to evaluate that theory. Most scholars who prefer this method of inquiry use quantitative research methods.

> **deductive model**
> *This model is typically referred to as theory driven. Communication scholars preferring a deductive approach begin with a theory and gather evidence to evaluate that theory. Most scholars who prefer this method of inquiry use quantitative research methods.*

One example of a deductive approach is Geddes' 2001 study on the impact of speech style such as gender/power on the perception of employee satisfaction and speaker effectiveness. She created both male- and female-delivered messages with one of three speech styles: powerless, powerful, and a mix of powerless and powerful. Union members were asked to evaluate one of these speech styles reporting on the effectiveness of the manager's speech style, as well as the employee satisfaction they experienced viewing the message. Geddes (2001) found that both male and female managers using the mixed speech style were rated both most effective and elicited the most satisfaction. This study demonstrates a deductive approach.

Another example of a deductive approach is Mark Morman's 2000 study on the use of fear appeals to motivate men to practice testicular self-exam (TSE) to detect cancer. Building on Witte's Extended Parallel Process Model (EPPM), Morman designed and tested alternative messages to motivate men to perform TSE. His findings supported the EPPM, which suggests that messages that create fear by communicating perceived severity of the threat and perceived susceptibility to the threat (the reaction will be bad and I could get it) and that communicate perceived efficacy (I can do something effective about it) are the most effective to motivate action. Morman started with an existing EPPM, developed a study to test it in a specific context, then evaluated the model in that new context. This is also a deductive approach.

An interesting example of a deductive approach using qualitative methods is Alexander Lyon's research (2007) on Merck's marketing of the pain medication Vioxx. Building on Deetz's theory about systematically distorted communication, Lyon used a multiple case study approach to analyze Merck's corporate communication. He determined that Merck used neutralization, topic avoidance, and disqualification to reduce the amount of open information patients and physicians received about the drug, and to thus stifle their decision-making ability. Lyon used a deductive approach—starting with Deetz's theory, developing a study to apply that theory, then evaluating the theory in the context of Merck's communication.

Model of Deduction/Induction

Although we have discussed these two types of systems as separate and different, in reality, they are really two parts of the same process. Another way to think about them is that they both begin at different points in the process. All social scientific research proceeds in a circular fashion. You can see how this would work because if we looked back to the EPPM study, someone might pick up after this experiment and start researching this from a deductive stance. For example, we might say, "Well, if the EPPM is true, then women who believe they could get breast cancer and who think they can prevent it through breast selfexam (BSE) should be more likely to practice BSE." So, we conduct a survey and if it is true, then the EPPM receives further support.

We can also start with inductive reasoning and ask, "Why do some women practice BSE and some don't?" We might conduct interviews or focus groups with women to examine their beliefs and practices, and might use grounded theory to come up with a model or theory (perhaps much like the EPPM) to determine what might make women more likely to practice BSE.

▼ # Qualitative and Quantitative Research

Finally, to conclude our discussion of research perspectives and paradigms, we must consider the overarching concepts of qualitative and quantitative research. It is paramount that you understand what the differences are, as well as understand that the research question we ask must always drive our methodological decision making. Therefore, if we ask a question best suited to qualitative methods, even though we prefer quantitative methods, we have to consider whether we are both able and willing to step outside our comfort zone to answer the question appropriately. We suggest to our students that a good scholar will, despite her own individual preferences, come to appreciate and understand the utility of both qualitative and quantitative methods. Neither method is a better method; they just address different questions using different methods, all contributing to our understanding of the world around us.

One way to distinguish between qualitative and quantitative research is to think: Is the research what you might call *art-based* or is it *science-based*? Qualitative research is sometimes thought of more like art, while quantitative research is more like science.

Qualitative Research

qualitative research
Research, usually studying words or texts, that uses methods that embrace a naturalistic, interpretive paradigm typically from an inductive discovery based point of view.

Qualitative research methods embrace a naturalistic, interpretive paradigm typically conducting research from an inductive discovery based point of view. Here they often seek to answer research questions that consider how our reality is constructed in interaction. They are less concerned with generalizing to a wider population or other cases; rather they tend to focus on studying the way in which their research participants understand, describe, and see the world.

Qualitative research methods are best used when there is not much previously known about the topic, when the topic is personal, and when you want to know more in great detail about a small unit or event. Some of the research tools that qualitative researchers make use of include: observation, participation, interviews, focus groups, reviewing documents, gathering life histories, exploring one's own life, field notes, transcripts, and narrative forms of coding data. Qualitative research strives toward the goals of preserving human behavior, analyzing its qualities, and representing different worldviews and experiences. Qualitative researchers see themselves as part of the process of creating knowledge and meaning through understanding what's going on. Another important point about qualitative research is that what differentiates scholars using these approaches from those taking a quantitative approach is that qualitative scholars not only see themselves as observing the meaning behind communication, but also see themselves as actually being part of the process of meaning making (Krauss, 2005).

Quantitative Research

Quantitative research methods embrace a postpositivist paradigm typically conducting research from a deductive explanatory based point of view. Here they often seek to answer research questions based on the premise that reality is knowable and measurable. Scholars taking the quantitative approach are most interested in generalizing to a wider audience, and they believe that knowledge is something objective that is found and measured. Quantitative methods are best used when you seek to learn something about a lot of people and/or when you are interested in generalizing from your sample to a larger group of people; or when you seek to generalize to a similar situation. Some of the research tools that qualitative researchers make use of include experiments, questionnaires, surveys, interviews, statistical methods, theory testing, secondary data analysis, and numerical coding. The primary goals of quantitative research include representing and explaining objective reality with the overarching goal of simplifying, organizing, predicting, and controlling human behavior.

quantitative research
Research, usually studying numerical data (or reducing words to numerical data), that uses methods that embrace a postpositivist paradigm typically from a deductive explanatory based point of view.

Here is a summary of the basic differences between qualitative and quantitative research:

Qualitative	Quantitative
Impressionist	Realist
Inductive	Deductive
Goal is to discover, preserve form and content of human behavior, represent different world views, create knowledge and meaning, understand what's going on.	Goal is to explain, subject the world to statistical transformations, predict and control, represent and explain objective reality.
Assumption is that reality is construction in interaction.	Assumption that reality is objective and measureable.

Qualitative	Quantitative
Believes that knowledge is created.	Believes that knowledge is found and received.
Generalizes research findings to other cases or similar phenomena.	Generalizes research findings as widely as possible.
The purpose is to understand, describe, get close to those studied, to understand how participants see the world.	The purpose is to measure relationships among variables, test hypotheses, predict, and control.
Is appropriate when you want to know a lot about a small unit, where not much is known about the topic, when the topic is something you can be immersed in, when you have a desire to make the strange familiar or the familiar strange.	Is appropriate when you want to know something about a lot of people, when you want to generalize from your sample to a large group.

Using our previous language on ontology, epistemology, and axiology, quantitative researchers tend toward the realist end of the spectrum, while qualitative researchers tend toward the nominalist or social constructionist end of the spectrum.

		Ontological Assumptions (What do we believe about reality?)	Epistemological Assumptions (What can we know and study?)	Axiological Assumptions (What do we value in research and knowledge?)
Realist QUANTITATIVE ↕ **Nominalist/Social Constructionist QUALITATIVE**	Positivism/ Postpositivism	Reality is orderly, fixed, and measurable.	We can know and study objective reality.	We value research that is objective and researchers who are expert authority.
	Critical/Cultural	May believe reality is orderly, measurable, objective. May believe reality is subjective.	We can know and study reality that is either objective or subjective. We can know and study reality that is interpreted or observed as is.	We value research that includes marginalized voices. We value research in which the researcher shares power with participants.
	Interpretivism	Reality is both orderly and chaotic. Reality is subjective.	We can know and study subjective reality as it is constructed, mediated, and biased.	We value research in which all participants are equal authorities and in which all perspectives are represented.

As we've said several times in this chapter and book, the method you choose depends entirely on your research question—different methods are most appropriate for answering different research questions. However, as you've seen, because qualitative and quantitative research methods represent different ontologies, epistemologies, and axiologies, researchers tend toward one or the other. In other words, since how you see the world determines the type of research questions you ask, this influences the type of research methods you tend to use. So, for fun, let's see where you fall on the spectrum of beliefs and methods.

You might be a qualitative researcher if you:

> Like ambiguity and complexity.
>
> Like to ask questions.
>
> Like to interact/be with people.
>
> Like to analyze immediate experience.
>
> Fantasize about what goes on behind people's windows/phone calls.
>
> Concentrate on episodic, emotional aspects of social life.
>
> Question authority.

You might be a quantitative researcher if you:

> Like to simplify, organize, manage the world, categorize the world.
>
> Like math and formulas.
>
> Usually think there's a separate, objective reality to be captured.
>
> Concentrate on rational, patterned order of social life.
>
> Write in authoritative, declarative sentences.

So What?

As you can see, both quantitative and qualitative research methods answer interesting questions and help us come closer to understanding both the world around us and the people within it. And while some researchers claim that one method is better than another, there are benefits to both methods. It is our goal to objectively consider the strengths and limitations with all types of research practices. Remember that the research question and/or hypotheses drive our decision about how to pursue our research and the research methods we follow.

Glossary

Axiology
The study of values.

Critical perspective
This perspective uses research methods as a tool to challenge unjust discourse and communication practices, with the goal of using knowledge as a tool to create social change.

Deductive model
This model is typically referred to as theory driven. Communication scholars preferring a deductive approach begin with a theory and gather evidence to evaluate that theory. Most scholars who prefer this method of inquiry use quantitative research methods.

Epistemology
The study of the nature of knowledge.

Hermeneutics

A way to study textual data through interpretation to create meaning; knowledge gained via interpretation.

Inductive model

This approach to research is often referred to as grounded theory. Communication scholars begin the research process by gathering data, observing patterns and idiosyncrasies within the data, and developing theory based upon that data. Most scholars who prefer this method of inquiry use qualitative research methods.

Interpretivism

A research perspective in which understanding and interpretation of the social world is derived from one's personal intuition and perspective.

Metatheory

Theory about theory that allows people to understand the philosophy driving their decisions about research methods, design, and analysis.

Nominalist

The belief that without individual cognition, the social world is arbitrary.

Objectivist

The belief that it is possible to know and explain the world.

Ontology

The study of the nature of reality.

Positivism

The most traditional research perspective with the belief that scientific evidence is superior to other types of knowing.

Proprietary research

Research that is conducted for a specific audience, which is not shared beyond the intended audience.

Qualitative research

Research, usually studying words or texts, that uses methods which embrace a naturalistic, interpretive paradigm typically from an inductive discovery based point of view.

Quantitative research

Research, usually studying numerical data (or reducing words to numerical data), that uses methods which embrace a postpositivist paradigm typically from a deductive explanatory based point of view.

Realist

The belief that the world exists and is tangible.

Scholarly research

Research conducted to contribute to generalizable knowledge for public consumption.

Social constructionist

The belief that our ideas about reality are constructed through societal and interpersonal communication.

Subjectivist

The belief that knowledge is relative and can only be understood from the point of view of the individual involved.

References

Brann, M. (2006). The influence of illness factors on physicians' likelihood of disclosing confidential health information to relatives of patients. *Communication Studies, 57*(3), 259–276.

Deveaux, M. (1994). Feminism and empowerment: A critical reading of Foucault. *Feminist Studies, 20,* 223–248.

Foucault, M. (1965). *Madness and civilization: A history of insanity in the age of reason.* New York: Random House.

Foucault, M. (1972). *The archaeology of knowledge and the discourse on language.* New York: Pantheon Books.

Foucault, M. (1973). *The birth of the clinic: An archaeology of medical perception* (A. M. S. Smith, Trans.). New York: Pantheon Books.

Foucault, M. (1995). *Discipline and punish: The birth of the prison* (A. Sheridan, Trans.). New York: Random House.

Geddes, D. (2001). Sex roles in management: The impact of varying power of speech style on union members' perception of satisfaction and effectiveness. *The Journal of Psychology, 126,* 589-607.

Habermas, J. (1968). The idea of the Theory of Knowledge as Social Theory. In J. Habermas, *Knowledge & Human Interest.* Cambridge, UK: Polity Press.

Krauss, S. E. (2005). Research paradigms and meaning making: A primer. *The Qualitative Report, 10,* 758–770.

Lyon, A. (2007). "Putting patients first": Systematically distorted communication and Merck's marketing of Vioxx. *Journal of Applied Communication Research, 35*(4), 376–398.

Miller, T. G. (1986). Goffman, positivism, and the self. *Philosophy of the Social Sciences, 16,* 177–195.

Morman, M. T. (2000). The influence of fear appeals, message design, and masculinity on men's motivation to perform the testicular selfexam. *Journal of Applied Communication Research, 28*(2), 91–116.

DISCOVERING WHAT'S ALREADY KNOWN: LIBRARY RESEARCH

CHAPTER OUTLINE

1. What Are the Purposes of Library Research?
2. Types of Research
   a. Primary Research
   b. Secondary Research
3. Phases of Research
4. Using Library Research to Come Up with Your Research Question
5. Research Sources
   a. Scholarly Journals
      i. How Do You Access Scholarly Journals?
   b. Finding Research Sources Using Search Strategies
   c. Evaluating Research Sources
6. How to Read a Journal Article
7. Taking Notes on Research
8. So What?

KEY TERMS

Academic journals

Applied research

Basic research

Body of knowledge

Boolean search

Databases

Peer review

Primary research

Secondary research

Study objectives

CHAPTER OBJECTIVES

1. To explain reasons to conduct library research
2. To explain how to evaluate data sources
3. To explain how to use library research in your own research

▼ # What Are the Purposes of Library Research?

Throughout your scholarly career (from elementary school through college), you've likely had to write a lot of research papers and conduct a lot of library research to do so. In this chapter, we'll help you understand how library research is part of the bigger process of scholarly research. We'll teach you to move from your academic research to library research and back again. We'll explain how to find and evaluate sources, and perhaps most importantly, how to actually read, understand, and use a journal article. One main purpose of this research you've been doing since possibly elementary school was to learn more about the subject you were studying. That's still one main purpose of the library research you're going to conduct in your Communication Research Methods course, and it's still one main reason that all scholars conduct library research. However, it's not the only purpose.

There are five main purposes of library research:

1. To determine what's already known about the topic and related topics.
2. To define the problem and formulate possible solutions. The assembling and analyzing of available secondary data will almost always provide a better understanding of the problem and its context, will frequently suggest solutions not considered previously, and will identify gaps in the body of knowledge for which research is needed. In addition, you don't want to directly duplicate what's already been done (Hart, 2001).
3. To plan the collection of primary data. You can examine the methods and techniques used by previous research efforts in similar studies, which will be useful in planning your present study. Also, this may be of value in establishing classifications that are more compatible with past studies, so that you can more readily analyze trends.
4. To define the population and select the sample in your primary information collection. This may be valuable in helping you choose areas for most productively interviewing participants.
5. To supply background information that will fill out what you find in your primary research. You may also find information against which you can compare your own findings and experience.

body of knowledge
Research that has already been conducted.

One basic premise of academic research is that it creates, and builds upon, a **body of knowledge**. There is very little (if anything) that has not been studied in some way, by some person. Your job as a scholar is to build on the research that has already been done by contributing to it, updating it, replicating it, and/or extending it (Booth, Colomb, & Williams, 1995; Rossman, 1995). In order to find out what's already been done, you conduct library research.

Types of Research   ▼

As we explained in Chapter 1, research is the way we find answers to questions. One good way to discover what you're interested in is to listen to the voice in your head that says, "I wonder. . . ." What types of things do you find yourself wondering about? You might be sitting around your apartment talking to friends and wonder, "Why don't guys call when they say they're going to?" or "How many people my age have issues with their parents telling them what to do?" Or, perhaps, you're reading a newspaper and ask, "Why do women in abusive relationships refuse to leave the relationships?" or "What causes people to become homeless?" or "How do movies depict smoking behaviors?" Regardless of how you attempt to find the answer, your method of answering your question is research. As Booth and colleagues said, "Research is simply gathering the information you need to answer a question and thereby help you solve a problem"(Booth et al., 1995, p. 6). Your research may be systematic and valid, or it may not be, but it's still research. If you ask a few friends if they have the same issues with their parents, you're conducting research. If you do a Google search on the Internet to identify the causes of homelessness, you're conducting research. The purpose of this book is to teach you how to conduct research that is considered, in our field (and related fields), to be valid (defensible). Defensible research is planned and conducted in an organized, orderly, methodical manner (Alberts, Hecht, Buley, & Petronio, 1993).

When you ask your friends questions, you're actually conducting what's called primary research; you are generating your own data. If you look up information on the Internet, you're conducting what's called secondary research; you're looking at other people's data.

Primary Research

If you were answering a question with **primary research**, you would be conducting a study to specifically answer that question. Primary research is research that is conducted to answer a specific problem or question. A primary source is the original, or first, published account of research findings (Galvan, 2006). Most research papers you read in journals are examples of primary research (unless it is a synthesis of the literature), so, don't get confused. When you are writing a literature review, you will be reading published articles reporting on primary research. Those articles include a literature review section, which is secondary research (because it summarizes and reports on other people's research). Consequently, your literature review is secondary research, because it summarizes and reports on other people's research.

primary research
Research that is conducted to answer a specific problem or question and produces original data.

Secondary Research

Secondary data is information that has been collected or conducted previously. If you were answering a question with **secondary research**, you would be looking for the answer in papers or books that summarize other studies, or you

secondary research
Research that has been previously collected or conducted.

would be looking at the other studies yourself. Textbooks are classic examples of secondary research. This textbook gives you lots of information, and all of it is taken from other sources, from research previously conducted (and published) by other people. Other examples of secondary research are literature reviews. When you write the results of your library research into a paper, you're writing a literature review. By the way, if you're writing a review of the literature for a class project, you're actually conducting secondary research. When a stand-alone literature review is published in a journal, it's often called a *synthesis of the literature*, and that's another example of a secondary research report. An additional example is the literature review *sections* of research reports.

No research project should ever be conducted without first searching secondary information sources. Why? Because all scholarly research builds upon the scholarly community's body of knowledge, and you have to conduct secondary research to find out what that body of knowledge is. Think of research like a conversation. When you are conducting research, you are entering into a scholarly conversation. You'd never walk up to a conversation and just start talking without finding out the other people are talking about, right? In the same way, to enter a scholarly conversation, you need to find out what the conversation is about.

▼ Phases of Research

This chapter assumes that you have (or want to have) a research question for which you want to find the answer. Let's say your instructor has given you a research assignment for a class, or you want to do an independent study research project on a topic that's intrigued you. When you decide you want to conduct a research project (or when your instructor gives you a research assignment for a class), the first thing you need to do is come up with a topic. Sometimes you have a specific topic in mind, sometimes you have a vague idea of what your topic might be, and other times you have no idea of where to even begin when choosing a topic!

Since this is a book on Communication Research Methods, the first thing to do is to make sure your topic is *communication* related. That's not necessarily as easy as it sounds. Remember, from Communication Theory or other communication classes you've taken, the scholarly definition of communication: "Communication is a transactional process involving a cognitive sorting, selecting, and sending of symbols in such a way as to help a listener elicit from his or her own mind a meaning or response similar to that intended by the communicator" (Ross, 1977, p. 11). What does that mean exactly? It's a process that is ongoing, circular, and continual, and it consists of give-and-take messages and feedback, feedback and messages. Since it's a process, it has no definite beginning or end point, so it's a complicated process. It's also about using symbols to create meaning. Words are symbols; gestures are symbols; language, pitch, or tones are symbols. Because messages are transmitted through nonverbal means, and because communication is an on going process, you cannot not communicate; all behavior is potentially communication, because there is the potential for transmission of meaning, regardless of intent. This meaning or interpretation is based on each of our filters—our individual ways of seeing the world, based on our experiences, culture, history, and so on—and noise—those voices in our head that distract us, or beliefs we have that convince us we're wrong, and so forth. Why are we reminding you of all this? Because pretty much any element in the communication process is subject to communication research. You can create a communication-related research question about the message sender or receiver, the message, feedback to the message, meaning, channel (medium) of the message, noise, context, culture, and so on.

Therefore, you can pretty much study any behavior, but you have to study it in the context of transmitting meaning. For example, you may be interested in exercise behavior. Studying how jogging leads to weight loss has nothing to do with communication. However, studying what jogging (as the *message*) communicates to others does. Or, studying how you can use communication to persuade people to jog is, obviously, about communication. Communication research answers questions about the sender, receiver, message, meaning, or channel that describe, explain, and/or predict communication related behavior (Alberts et al., 1993).

We'll come back to your research question in a minute. First, let's talk about the phases of research. The first phase is called *conceptualization*—forming an idea. Ideas are built on the body of knowledge that's already been created. Your idea builds on the research that's already been done on your topic or related topics.

Once you've formed an idea for your research project, you've got to plan it. You've got to determine exactly what you're looking at and decide how you're going to define your terms. This is called *operationalization*—defining your terms as you're using them in your research project. You often operationalize your data based on how other people have operationalized the same variables—you find this out based on your library research. You've got to decide how to study it and what research methodology to use to collect your data. You've got to know how you're going to analyze your data. One step in planning your research and methodology is to look at what other people have done with the same or similar projects—what worked for them, what didn't work, and what they recommended to do differently.

Then, when you're done planning, you've got to carry out the research. When you write up your research, you do what's called *reconceptualization*—you reconnect it back to the larger body of knowledge.

So, before conducting any type of research, there are two things you must do: determine exactly what information is already known about your topic and determine exactly what you want to know. You have to have a starting point. You have to start with knowing the assumptions the community of knowledge already has and build your information on that. You don't want to spend time, money, and energy gathering information that's already been gathered. Funding agencies won't fund research that's "so what" research, and publications won't publish it. One of the characteristics of academic research is that it builds on a *body of knowledge*—other research that has already been done on your topic or on related topics. So, the first use of library research is to determine what background information already exists about your topic.

▼ # Using Library Research to Come Up with Your Research Question

By the time you're ready to plan your library research, you'll need to be able to articulate a statement of the problem ("The topic of this study is____"), the objective of the study ("This research will determine_____"), and the questions to be answered (Rossman, 1995).

How do you find possible research topics when your mind is blank? Here's where library research can help you. We recommend you start by browsing through your textbooks. Did you especially like Interpersonal Communication? Or Mass Media? Or Public Relations? Pull out your old text book and look at what topics interest you. Delve a little deeper in the topic by searching the Internet (Booth et al., 1995). Or browse newspapers or magazines to see if there's a topic or story that interests you. Once you have a general topic, you can conduct a library search (we'll explain how to do this later in this chapter) on that topic to see what research other people have done on the topic to help you refine your objective and decide your ultimate research question.

Next, you need to determine your **study objectives**—what do you want to answer with this research? This is probably the most important step of any research study. All other steps stem from the objective. Good researchers refer back to the objectives every step of the way, and ensure that everything they are doing answers these objectives. Usually, there is one main objective and several related secondary objectives. Your objectives should be precise and specific.

Finally, a well defined objective might take the form, "I am studying X because I want to find out [who/what/when/where/whether/why/how]. . ." (Booth et al., 1995, p. 43). Your research question maybe what's called *pure* research, in that you just want to know something that is not already known. Or it may be what's called **applied research**, in that what you find out will result in some sort of specific action (Booth et al., 1995). So, you might want to formulate a pure research question about domestic violence, "I wonder if family communication patterns affect levels of domestic violence?" Or you might want to formulate an applied research question about domestic violence, "I wonder how we can persuade women to leave violent relationships?"

By the time you've finished your library research and are ready to begin collecting your own data, you'll need to be able to articulate the theoretical or conceptual frame work for the research (how this issue relates to other issues or other research, or how it explains or adds to existing theories), the questions to be answered (they will be more developed or refined at this point and will usually be either in the form of a research question or a hypothesis), and the significance of the study (Why is my research important to society? How does my research idea fit into the body of knowledge that already exists?) (Rossman, 1995).

Once you have a good problem statement and objective, you're ready to conduct library research. You're done with your library research when you have a theoretical or conceptual framework, a well-defined research question or hypothesis, and when you fully understand the significance of your study.

study objectives
What it is that researchers hope to answer through their research. Good researchers refer back to the objectives every step of the way and ensure that everything they are doing answers these objectives. Usually, there is one main objective, and several related secondary objectives.

applied research
Research that tests theory in real life contexts to see if it can be used to solve problems.

Research Sources ▼

Let's say you have a vague idea of a general topic area, but aren't sure how to narrow your idea from there. The first thing you might want to do is browse journals and books in your topic area to get ideas from what other people have studied. There are many sources of literature for your library research; some are more suited to academic purposes than others:

- Books—often give the original (or primary) information on a topic or theory, but typically are more out-of-date since there is a much longer lag time from writing to publication.
- Articles—in scholarly journals, tend to be up-to-date and therefore often cutting-edge; in peer-reviewed journals, have met academic standards.
- Governmental statistical data—often available online, usually up-to-date and available (Hart, 2001).
- Other sources, such as magazines, newspapers, and websites— typically not appropriate for a scholarly review of the literature.

There are several good sources of secondary research in Communication Studies: handbooks, textbooks, edited books, and journals. Scholarly type books consist of monographs (often published by communication associations or key publishers in our field), anthologies or edited books, textbooks, and reference books (Hart, 2001). Books are more difficult than journals to identify as scholarly versus nonscholarly, but one good rule to evaluate books is to look at their references—if the book itself cites scholarly references, then it is likely a scholarly book.

Scholarly Journals

The key journals in the field of Communication Studies are published by communication associations:

→**The International Communication Association (ICA) publishes five journals:**

- *Journal of Communication*—publishes primary research reports on all aspects of communication.
- *Human Communication Research*—publishes primary research reports on human communication with a social science focus.
- *Communication Theory*—publishes articles and essays introducing, suggesting, critiquing, or extending communication theory; publishes articles based on both primary and secondary sources.
- *Journal of Computer-Mediated Communication*—publishes primary research reports related to communication via the Web.
- *Communication, Culture, and Critique*—publishes primary research reports that are related to media and cultural studies topics.

→**The National Communication Association (NCA) publishes ten journals:**

- *Communication and Critical/Cultural Studies*—publishes both primary and secondary research-based articles related to criticisms of cultural power and issues of class, race, ethnicity, marginalization, and so on.
- *Communication Education*—publishes primary research related to communication instruction.
- *Communication Monographs*—publishes primary research articles on interpersonal, group, organizational, cultural, and media communication.
- *Communication Teacher*—publishes teaching and classroom suggestions for Communication courses.
- *Critical Studies in Media Communication*—publishes primary research in mass media topics.
- *Journal of Applied Communication Research*—publishes primary research on applied communication topics, often related to organizational, group, and health communication.
- *Journal of International and Intercultural Communication*—publishes primary research related to cultural and international contexts.
- *Quarterly Journal of Speech*—publishes primary research that specifically uses different forms of rhetorical analysis as the methodology.
- *Review of Communication*—an online journal that publishes reviews of other communication-related publications.
- *Text and Performance Quarterly*—publishes primary research that is related to communication performance, communication-as-performance, and "Performance Studies."

There are several regional communication associations, each of which also publishes journals:

- The Southern States Communication Association (SSCA) publishes a journal called *Southern Communication Journal*, which includes articles on primary research from a wide variety of communication contexts and topics.
- The Central States Communication Association publishes *Communication Studies*, which also includes primary research from a variety of communication areas.
- The Western States Communication Association publishes two general communication journals, *Western Journal of Communication* and *Communication Reports*.
- The Eastern Communication Association (ECA) publishes two general communication journals, *Communication Quarterly* and *Communication Research Reports*, and one journal that focuses on qualitative research, *Qualitative Research Reports in Communication*.

In addition, most states have communication associations that publish journals or yearbooks. Carolina's Communication Association, for example, publishes *The Carolina Communication Annual*.

→**The Association for Education in Journalism and Mass Communication (AEJMC) publishes three journals:**

- *Journalism and Mass Communication Quarterly*—publishes primary research on journalism and mass communication.
- *Journalism and Mass Communication Educator*—publishes teaching and classroom suggestions for journalism and mass communication courses.
- *Journalism and Communication Monographs*—publishes primary research on journalism and mass communication and theory-related topics.

The Public Relations Society of America (PRSA) publishes the *Public Relations Journal* which includes primary research on public relations related topics.

→**The American Marketing Association publishes four journals in the field of advertising and marketing:**

- *Journal of Marketing*
- *Journal of Marketing Research*
- *Journal of International Marketing*
- *Journal of Public Policy and Marketing*

The Advertising Educational Foundation publishes an online journal called *Advertising and Society Review*, and the Advertising Research Foundation publishes the *Journal of Advertising Research*.

There are also many specialized and interdisciplinary journals that may be of interest to students in our field:

- The Organization for Research on Women and Communication publishes *Women's Studies in Communication*, which includes primary research on gender and feminist issues.
- Students interested in health communication (and related areas) may want to look at *Journal of Health Communication: International Perspectives, Health Communication, Journal of Loss and Trauma, Journal of Qualitative Health Research*, and *Disability Studies Quarterly*.
- Students interested in looking at qualitative research could browse *Qualitative Inquiry; Qualitative Research; Journal of Contemporary Ethnography; International Review of Qualitative Research; Storytelling, Self, and Society;* and *Qualitative Communication Research*.

A journal introduced in 2012, *Journal of Qualitative Communication Research*, is published by Left Coast Press and also publishes qualitative research in our field.

- Students interested in interpersonal and family communication could look at *Symbolic Interaction, Journal of Family Communication, Journal of Loss and Trauma, Journal of Social and Personal Relationships*, and *Journal of Divorce and Remarriage*.
- Students interested in cultural studies should check out the journals *Cultural Studies and Cultural Studies-Critical Methodologies*.
- Students interested in public relations should also investigate *Public Relations Quarterly, Public Relations Review*, and *Journal of Public Relations Research*.

- Students interested in rhetoric and advocacy could look at *Rhetoric and Public Affairs* and *Rhetoric Society Quarterly*.
- Students interested in mass communication should look at *Critical Studies in Media Communication*.
- *Howard Journal of Communication* publishes research related to culture and ethnicity.
- Students interested in organizational communication might want to look at management journals such as *MIT Sloan Management Review*, *Management Communication Quarterly*, *Journal of Business Communication*, *Small Group Research*, and *Journal of Organizational Behavior*.

How Do You Access Scholarly Journals?   Now you've got lots of names of journals, but how do you access the journals? If you Google the journal name, you will likely be able to access a table of contents and maybe a list of abstracts. Perhaps this is all you need to begin forming ideas. For example, let's say you think you might be interested in family communication. Google the *Journal of Family Communication*. The first listing gives you the Web page for the journal. On the right side of the page there is a link to "online contents."

When you click on that link, it takes you straight to the listing for the current issue of that journal. Notice that this listing gives "volumes" and "issues." The volume represents a year for the journal; for example, in the *Journal of Family Communication*, 2012 journals are all Volume 12. With in a year, each journal is represented by an issue. The *Journal of Family Communication* publishes four issues per year. In the example below, two of the four issues are listed (the other two weren't published yet when this book went to press).

Take a look at the page for the current issue: Volume 12, Issue 2.

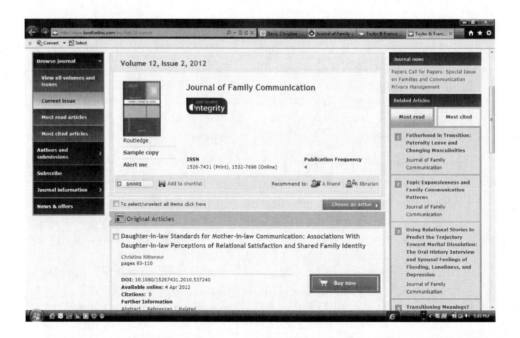

You get a list of the five articles in that issue. The first one sounds interesting. Let's see if you can get more information about it. Click the link for the abstract.

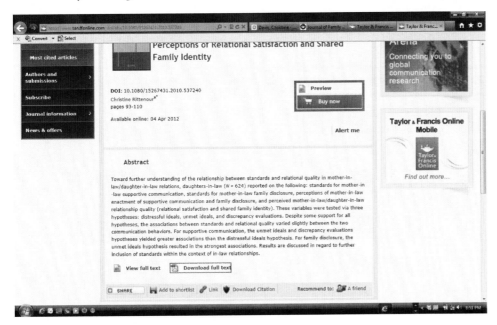

The abstract is a short description (usually 100–300 words) of the article. If you're only looking for general ideas, the abstract may be all you need for right now. But let's say you're intrigued and want to read the actual article. This is as far as you're allowed to go on the Internet without subscribing to the journal. However, you haven't really hit a dead end.

Your university library subscribes to many of these journals. Let's see if your library subscribes to this one. Go to the Web page for your university library. Below is the Web page for University of North Carolina–Charlotte:

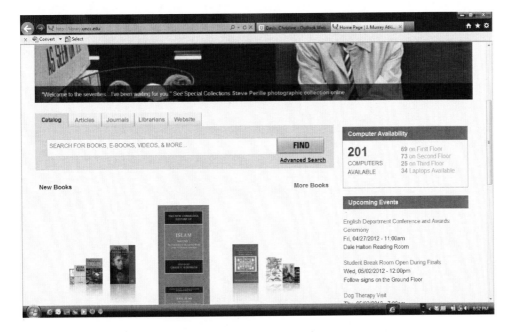

Yours is probably similar. The opening screen has a place to search the library catalog for books, then a tab for articles, and a tab for journals. Since you're looking for a journal, click this last link.

Let's see what happens when you type in the journal title, *Journal of Family Communication*.

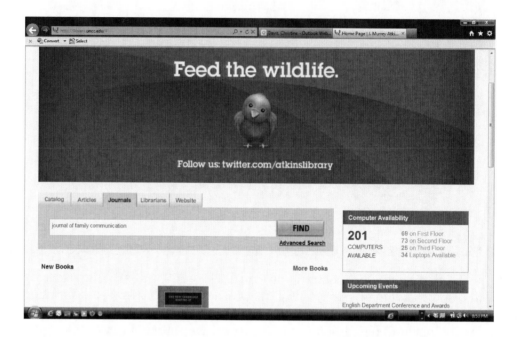

You're in luck. The library subscribes to it and it's available online through the Communication and Mass Media Database. Click that link.

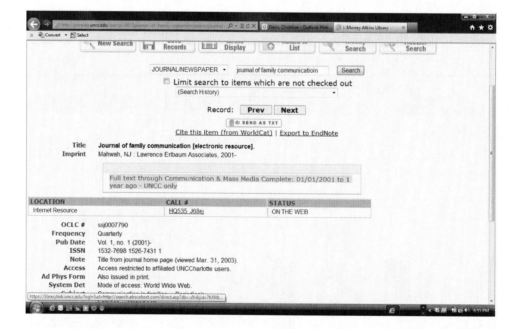

If your library doesn't subscribe to the journal, you can ask the reference librarian to order it via Interlibrary Loan. Interlibrary Loan (sometimes called ILL) usually takes a few days to a few weeks, so you'd have to allow time for that.

You're back to a listing of volumes for this journal. Remember that you were looking for an article in Volume 12, Issue 2. And remember that Volume 12 was 2012, so look at 2012, then select Issue 2. This time, when you click on the article from the list, it will open the article. For right now, you can either print it or read it online.

Finding Research Sources Using Search Strategies

Now let's say through browsing journals and the Internet, talking to friends, and reading the newspaper, you've decided on your communication-related topic: "What communication is like in long-distance relationships." Your study objective is: "This research will determine how couples in long-distance relationships communicate." Your next step is to find out what other research has been done on this and related topics. Let's identify the key concepts in this objective: "relational communication" and "long-distance relationships." Before you start searching, think of alternative or related concepts you can use if you need them. For example, for the first concept—relational communication: "couples communication," "communication," and "relationships." For the second concept—long-distance relationships: "distance" and perhaps "virtual."

Let's use your library Web page to search for journal articles on the topic. You conduct this search through **databases**—sources that search through many journals at a time. There are untold databases you can use, and there are a

databases
Sources that search through many journals at a time.

Boolean search
A search function that is used to connect two or more concepts in a search engine. Common Boolean search operators are "and" and "or."

academic journals
Collections of published, peer-reviewed scholarly research that are often consulted by academic scholars, government agencies, policy makers, and businesses to inform their decision making.

few that tend to work best for the field of communication studies. Some of our favorites are "Academic Search Premier," "Web of Science," "WorldCat," and "Communication and Mass Media Complete." While Google is an inappropriate search engine to use for academic research, Google Scholar might yield useful information because it includes peer-reviewed papers and articles (Munger & Campbell, 2007). Google Scholar also might include some sites that aren't appropriate for academic research, so you'll need to be a bit more discerning if you search through that source.

Again, your library website will look a little differently from ours, but in the UNCC website, you can search by specific database:

Let's start by using your first two concepts to search: "relational communication" AND "long-distance relationships." The word "AND" is in all caps because it is a **Boolean search** term, and you are using it to connect the two concepts. You are telling the search engine that you want only articles that have both of your terms in the keywords. It's really important to make sure you also check the box for "scholarly (peer-reviewed) journals" because you are only interested in scholarly or **academic journals** for this research project.

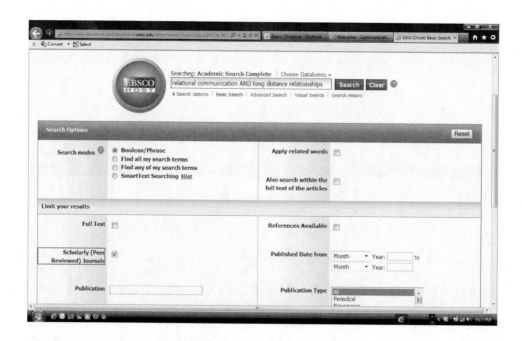

This search gives you two choices, and the first one looks interesting. Take a look at the full text of the article "When Distance is Problematic."

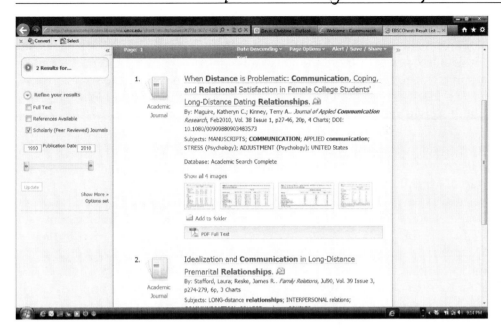

Clicking the "PDF full text" link pulls up the full text of the article.

Evaluating Research Sources

Not all sources are created equal. As Booth and colleagues (1995) said, "One good source is worth more than a score of mediocre ones, and one accurate summary of a good source is sometimes worth more than the source itself" (p. 71). The first step in evaluating your source is to read it—all of it. And read it slowly and carefully (Booth et al., 1995).

First of all, make sure it really is an article in a scholarly journal. You selected that check box, but databases sometimes make errors, so you need to make sure it's really a scholarly journal you're looking at. If you recognize the journal name from the list earlier in the chapter, you're in luck. All of the names we gave you are scholarly journals. The reason that this is an important distinction is because scholarly research falls under the practice of **peer review**—a "self regulatory practice designed to protect against the publication of flawed research or unsound scholarship, and to recognize and promote innovative and cutting-edge studies," says Art Bochner, NCA President (Bochner, 2008, p. 3). In other words, peer review is the way a scholarly field determines which research is acceptable, sound, and valid, and which is not. Make sure you understand the requirements of your assignment, but for most literature reviews or library research assignments for college classes, your professor will either prefer or require that you use scholarly sources. If you don't recognize the name of the journal, how else can you tell? Simply put, many journals have the word "journal" in their name. Many will state that they are published by a scholarly association. It's sad to say, but you can also use this general rule: If it looks as if it's fun to read, it might not be a scholarly journal. If it looks like a magazine article with lots of pictures and white space, it's probably a magazine article, and not a journal. If it is more dense, with more complex language, usually with footnotes, endnotes, references, and citations, it's more likely to be a scholarly journal. Watch out here, though. Some people publish what look like scholarly articles on websites that are not peer reviewed and are not in scholarly journals. Don't be fooled. You want to use articles that are in recognized peer-reviewed journals, unless otherwise instructed by your professor.

In some cases, you might need additional information that is not available from academic sources. For example, suppose you are doing library research on domestic violence and you want to provide statistics on the number of people who were killed by spouses last year. An academic journal would not likely have up-to-date information on that subject, but the Internet very likely might (Munger & Campbell, 2007). You have to be careful with Internet sources, however. Anyone can create a website or post to a blog, and the Internet has no standards under which posted messages must fall. Look at who the sponsor of the site is and try to determine where the information came from (Munger & Campbell, 2007).

Just like not all sources are equal, not all journals are equal either. As a general rule, international journals are rated more highly than national journals, which are rated more highly than regional journals, and so on.

There are several other criteria to evaluate sources. The most straightforward is the year of publication. How current is the research? In most cases, the

peer review
The way in which a scholarly field determines which research is acceptable, sound, and valid, and which is not.

more recent, the better. For some reason, certain topics have peaks and valleys; some years there is a lot published on a topic, and in other years, not so much (Rossman, 1995). You may find this to be the case. Notice how the research has evolved in each peak—the topic likely has a slightly (or largely) different focus from one peak to another. Make sure you know which focus you're interested in. Knowing when the study was done will help determine if replicability is needed or warranted. Maybe the research you're looking at is old—does it need to be updated? If you're suggesting updating outdated research, then you should go a head and cite the research you're updating. Generally, though, this textbook was published in 2012, and we probably wouldn't cite any sources older than 2007. The exception would be if you are citing a source that is considered a *classic* in the field of communication studies. For example, if you're talking about the concept of symbolic interactionism, you'd need to cite Blumer, who wrote the original book on the topic, *Symbolic Interactionism: Perspective and Method*, in 1969.

Another consideration is the reputation of the author. How well known is this person? How much has this person published? How prestigious are the journals or publishers of this person's work? How often have the author and this article been cited? You may not have been in this field long enough to know the answers to all of these questions, but if you have a few communication classes under your belt, you may have heard some names related to some of the key theories or concepts in our field. If they're in your textbook, and if you're studying them in a general survey class of communication theory, they're important names. So, for example, if you're citing symbolic interactionism, you might want to cite what someone currently said about it, but you'd definitely want to cite what Blumer (1969) said.

Other evaluation variables concern how the research was conducted. Is it relevant to you? How does this relate to your topic? How was the population sampled? How does this population relate to your objectives? Is the perspective of the article local, regional, national, or international? Why was the study conducted? What problem was the researcher looking at?

Finally, is this a primary or secondary source? For most of the literature reviews you are writing, you will be synthesizing primary sources, that is, you will be reporting on primary research reports that describe actual research studies. Occasionally, however, you might, in the course of your library research, find that someone has published a synthesis of the literature on your topic. Feel free to use this, but use it properly. If such synthesis says anything new, such as commenting on, critiquing, or extending the literature they're reviewing, cite that source. Otherwise, to cite the sources they are citing, you must go to the primary source. In other words, if someone named Smith cites Blumer, you must go directly to Blumer to cite Blumer. You cannot count on Smith properly explaining and summarizing Blumer. It is very bad form and lazy research to stop at the secondary source. Booth and colleagues (1995) suggest that you cite both the primary and secondary sources and reiterate that you must go to the primary source and read it before you use it. Booth and colleagues (1995) also say, "You will soon discover that you cannot trust researchers to quote reliably. It is intellectually lazy not to look up an important quotation in its original context if that source is easily available" (p. 75). Instead of relying only on the secondary source, use it to point you in the right direction. Feel free to look up references, and once you've read them yourself, then you can use them.

● ●

▼ How to Read a Journal Article

We've said that you need to read the journal article thoroughly. But how do you read a journal article? If you start reading at the beginning and move through it, for most articles, you'll get bogged down in the "Findings" section before figuring out what you're reading.

Papers differ slightly in their headings and organization, but most articles have the following sections in roughly this order: Abstract, Introduction, Literature Review, Findings, Discussion, Limitations, and Conclusion. We suggest you read them out of order. We know this may feel odd, but we have a good reason to suggest this. We generally read research articles in this order:

1. Abstract
2. Introduction
3. Conclusion
4. Literature Review
5. Method
6. Discussion
7. Findings
8. Limitations
9. References

Read to gather the following information, in this order:

a. What is the *research topic*?
b. What are the *main points* and *findings*?
c. What *claim* is this article making?
d. What is the *evidence* for that claim?
e. Is this *basic* or *applied* research?
f. Does this have a *research question* or a *hypothesis*? What is it?
g. How highly regarded is the journal?
h. How recent is the research?
i. What is the *methodology*? Is it clearly detailed?
j. How in-depth was the research?
k. How recent are the sources?
l. What *relevant quotes* might you use from this in your literature review?

If, at any point answering these questions, you find that the article is not appropriate for your library research, move on to another article; don't waste any more time on one that's not relevant to your needs.

Let's consider the article we found above in the *Journal of Applied Communication Research* by Katheryn C. Maguire and Terry A. Kinney (2010) called "When Distance is Problematic: Communication, Coping, and Relational Satisfaction in Female College Students' Long-Distance Dating Relationships." The keywords under the abstract tell you that the article is about long-distance dating relationships; stress; coping; relationship maintenance; and relational satisfaction. Sounds interesting so far.

The abstract is always found directly after the title, before the body of the paper begins. It is often in italics, centered, or otherwise set apart from the rest of the text. What do you know from the abstract? You know the topic of the research concerns the distress of long distance relationships. You know that the author's findings relate to the themes of helpfulness and coping strategies. From the abstract, this appears to be **basic research**, although you don't yet know the research question or hypothesis. You also know that this is a highly regarded journal (if nothing else, you know we gave you the name of the journal in the list earlier in the chapter of scholarly journals in our field), and that it is a recent article.

basic research
Research that is carried out to advance knowledge, address curiosities of researchers, or develop theory regardless of its immediate usefulness or practicality.

From "When Distance is Problematic" by Katheryn Maguire & Terry Kinney, *Journal of Applied Communication Research*, Vol. 38, No. 1. Copyright © 2010. Reprinted by permission of Taylor & Francis Ltd, www.informaworld.com.

To find out more, you'll have to read further. Jump to the Introduction. Right up front, you know that this is a significant problem for society because long-distance relationships are so common.

There is not a "Conclusion" section in this paper; however, you'll notice that the section called "Discussion" really serves to tie together what's been reported, so go to that section (another way to know to go to that section is to notice that it is the final section in the paper, so it must be a concluding section). Since the paper does not have separate "Conclusion" and "Discussion" sections, you'll look at the "Discussion" section now.

As you can see, this section summarizes the results of the study: "that communicative coping strategies were differentially helpful for various stressors depending on whether the participants were in a low or high distress LDDR [long distance dating relationship]" (p. 38). As you read throughout this section, it summarizes and explains the results and also discusses the significance of the results to the larger body of knowledge on long distance relationships, distress, and coping.

Now that you know what Maguire and Kinney found in their research, you might decide that this paper is relevant to your own research. Take a step back and look at their "Literature Review" to get a sense about what's known thus far (before Maguire and Kinney's research) on these topics:

The Literature Review also provides the different concepts and definitions Maguire and Kinney are using to design this study: physical distance, amount of time apart, sources of external and internal stress, primary and secondary appraisals

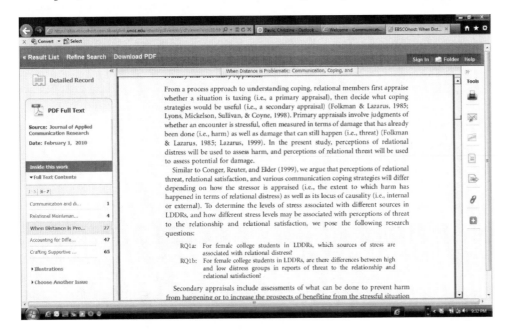

of the situation, and method of coping. You'll note that Maguire and Kinney use the literature to inform their Research Questions (see p. 30, for example).

Next, take a look at the methodology section and see how Maguire and Kinney did what they did. "Participants" tells who they interviewed, where and how they found the people to interview, and describes the participants.

As Maguire and Kinney move through this section, they describe the survey in great detail and list and describe the questions they asked the study participants.

Finally, in the Results section, Maguire and Kinney tell how they came up with their findings—how they statistically analyzed their data. While you may not yet be familiar with the terminology or statistics they use in this paper, you can still begin to form opinions as to whether their methods seem appropriate, or if they make sense to you.

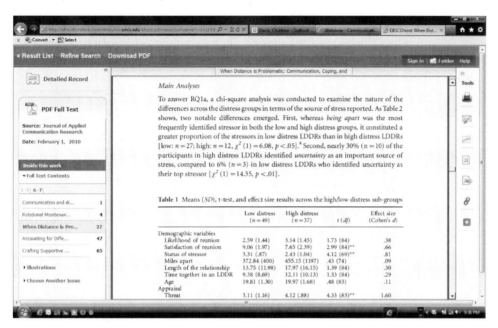

Most published research articles have a "Limitations" section, so let's take a look at theirs. Their limitations section also suggests future directions to take this research, and you can use this section as suggested topics or variations for your own research.

The last thing to look at is their references. You are looking for two things in her "Reference" section. First, how old are their sources? They range from 1978 to 2007, but most are from the 2000s. Some of the oldest ones are classics. Perhaps you've heard of Lazarus and Folkman in a health or psychology class when you were talking about stress and coping, or Leslie Baxter or Daniel Canary in your interpersonal communication class. So, while some of their references may be a little dated, they do include classic sources, and they does tell you that they are extending these concepts theories in to a more up-to-date manner. You have to evaluate the age of their sources with the rest of their research—was it conceptually, methodologically, and analytically sound? Perhaps you could discuss your opinions of that in class. You'll learn more specifics about how to critique research throughout this textbook.

▼ **Taking Notes on Research**

You've read an article and have begun to critique it. You've gotten to the point where you think this article will be a great one to include in your library research and literature review. Now you have to take notes on it. You're taking notes for two purposes: to make sure you have the information you need to use this in your paper (to make sure you have it down thoroughly and accurately) and to make sure you have the information you need to properly cite your source.

In order to make sure your notes give you enough information to really understand and remember what you've read, Booth and colleagues (1995) suggest that you write down not only the single idea you want to use, but also the paragraph or several paragraphs around it so you can fully understand the concept or argument the author is making.

Many students find it helpful to use "old-fashioned" bibliography notes written on index cards. Other students type out the information on their word processor. There is also software available to categorize information, such as Endnotes, and Munger and Campbell (2007) suggest creating a personal blog (blogger.com or livejournal.com) to capture your information. However you capture the information, it's a good idea to put the information for each citation on separate pages or index cards so you can sort and resort through them later as you're organizing your synthesis. At a minimum, you want to put down your citation information, the abstract, a summary of the findings, and the key points from the discussion. To avoid unintentional plagiarism (we'll discuss plagiarism in Chapter 4), make sure you are clear about summarizing, paraphrasing, or quoting (Booth et al., 1995). If you're using quotes, make sure you put down the page number for the quote, and make sure you put the quote in quotation marks so you remember it's a direct quote. We'll talk about citations in Chapter 4, but at this point, you need to know that you must cite your sources accurately to avoid charges of plagiarism. Plagiarism can ruin careers, derail graduations, and cause students to fail courses.

Take a look at the APA, MLA, or Chicago Manual of Style citation requirements to make sure you're getting all the information you need for your citation. There's nothing worse than wanting to use a source, but not being able to because you left off an important piece of citation information and can no longer find the article or book to get it again. When you put down the citation information for a book, for example, you'll need first and last names of all the authors (in the same order listed on the book cover), year of publication, exact name, publication location, and publishing company. When you put down the citation information for a journal article, you'll need the first and last names of all the authors (in order), year of publication, name of journal, volume number, issue number, and page numbers of the article. If you've accessed the article via the Web, it would also be helpful to put the URL so you can find it again, if necessary (Munger & Campbell, 2007).

When you're taking notes on the findings or main points, make sure you get the exact quotes and page numbers for direct quotations. Make sure you correctly read the article so that you understand it and are getting the context and claim right. If you used a source to go to one of their sources, make sure you are properly differentiating between primary and secondary sources.

When taking notes, you might find it helpful to follow this format, answering each question:

- What is the correct citation for the article?
- What is the purpose statement?
- What is the research question or hypothesis?
- What are the key concepts or variables under study?
- What is the method of data collection?
- What are the key findings or conclusions?
- What are other key pieces of information you found in the article that might be relevant to your research?

So What?

In this chapter, we've shown you how to conduct library research and how to choose and use databases, journals, and scholarly articles from our field of Communication Studies. We've shown you how to evaluate and read scholarly research. In short, we've shown you how communication scholars begin their scholarship. Communication scholars use systematic, scholarly, scientific methods to conduct research from the minute they get a research idea to the publication of that research idea. In Chapter 4, we'll show you the next step in the scholarship process—what to do with your library research.

Glossary

Academic journals
Collections of published, peer-reviewed scholarly research that are often consulted by academic scholars, government agencies, policy makers, and businesses to inform their decision making.

Applied research
Research that tests theory in real life contexts to see if it can be used to solve problems.

Basic research
Research that is carried out to advance knowledge, address curiosities of researchers, or develop theory regardless of its immediate usefulness or practicality.

Body of knowledge
Research that has already been conducted.

Boolean search
A search function that is used to connect two or more concepts in a search engine. Common Boolean search operators are "and" and "or."

Databases
Sources that search through many journals at a time.

Peer review
The way in which a scholarly field determines which research is acceptable, sound, and valid, and which is not.

Primary research
Research that is conducted to answer a specific problem or question and produces original data.

Secondary research
Research that has been previously collected or conducted.

Study objectives
What it is that researchers hope to answer through their research. Good researchers refer back to the objectives every step of the way, and insure that everything they are doing answers these objectives. Usually, there are one main objective and several related secondary objectives.

References

Alberts, J., Hecht, M., Buley, J., & Petronio, S. (1993). Methods for studying interpersonal communication research. In S. Petronio, J. Alberts, M. Hecht, & J. Buley (Eds.), *Contemporary perspectives on interpersonal communication* (pp. 18–24). Dubuque, IA: Wm. C. Brown.

Bochner, A. (2008, May). The case against the anonymous culture of peer review. *Spectra, 44*(5), 3.

Booth, W. C., Colomb, G. G., & Williams, J. M. (1995). *The craft of research.* Chicago: University of Chicago Press.

Galvan, J. L. (2006). *Writing literature reviews: A guide for students of the social and behavioral sciences.* Glendale, CA: Pyrczak.

Hart, C. (2001). *Doing a literature search: A comprehensive guide for the social sciences.* London: Sage.

Maguire, K. C., & Kinney, T. A. (2010). When distance is problematic: Communication, coping, and relational satisfaction in female college students' long-distance dating relationships. *Journal of Applied Communication Research, 38*(1), 27–46. doi:10.1080/00909880903483573

Munger, D., & Campbell, S. (2007). *What every student should know about . . . researching online.* New York: Pearson Longman.

Ross, R. S. (1977). *Speech communication: Fundamentals and practice.* Englewood Cliffs, NJ: PrenticeHall.

Rossman, M. H. (1995). *Negotiating graduate school: A guide for graduate students.* Thousand Oaks, CA: Sage.

WRITING A LITERATURE REVIEW

4

CHAPTER OUTLINE

1. What's the Purpose of a Literature Review?
2. What Is a Literature Review?
3. Annotated Bibliography versus Synthesis of the Literature
4. Organizing the Literature Review
5. Citations
6. Avoiding Plagiarism
7. Writing Styles
   a. American Psychological Association (APA) Style
      i. Body of the Paper
      ii. Reference List
      iii. In-Text Citations
   b. Modern Language Association (MLA) Style
   c. Chicago Style
8. Common Grammatical Errors
9. So What?

KEY TERMS

American Psychological Association (APA) style

Annotated bibliography

Chicago style

Modern Language Association (MLA) style

Plagarism

CHAPTER OBJECTIVES

1. To understand the purpose and use of a literature review
2. To understand how to synthesize literature
3. To understand how to write a literature review, using appropriate grammar, style, and organization
4. To understand how to properly use citations in a literature review

▼ # What's the Purpose of a Literature Review?

This chapter assumes you are writing a stand-alone literature review that serves the express purpose of synthesizing the existing literature on the topic. In Chapter 3, we taught you how to find good-quality research. In this chapter, we'll teach you how to use it—we'll discuss the definition and purposes of a literature review. Then we'll teach you how to synthesize the literature and how to write up the literature review: how to organize it, use proper citation to avoid plagiarism, and use appropriate writing and citation styles.

You may later write a literature review that becomes part of another project, such as a research proposal or a research paper, but we're assuming for now that your literature review will specifically be a summary and critique of the previous (usually academic) literature on a given topic, organized thematically or topically (Rossman, 1995). Its purpose is to give the reader a clear overview of what is known about the topic, point out common themes in existing research, and draw conclusions about what knowledge there is in the topic area. Literature reviews such as these are often called a *synthesis of the literature* because they combine and blend what's already been researched on a topic.

There are other purposes for conducting a literature review that you should be aware of, however. You might also write a literature review as part of a research proposal. This type of literature review not only summarizes existing literature but also builds your argument on why your study is necessary to be done, in the way you are proposing to do it. You might also write a literature review as part of a research paper reporting on your research findings. This type of literature review also summarizes existing literature, explains why you did the research the way you did it, and also shows the theories and concepts on which you built your study (remember the deductive paradigm) and the prior research that influenced the ways you operationalized (defined) and measured your variables. Often, with a literature review, you are building your case for your research study, so your literature review will provide evidence of what important questions remain to be explored and why your study can address those questions. This is why all research reports and proposals begin with a literature review, because a literature review shows your expertise and knowledge about your topic area, and shows you are up-to-date on the literature (Rossman, 1995).

In this chapter, we will discuss the elements of a good literature review; how a literature review is differentiated from another similar assignment that students frequently confuse it with—annotated bibliographies; specific skills related to writing a literature review such as synthesizing the literature and organizing the paper; and other writing elements related to writing literature reviews, such as proper citation, avoiding plagiarism, and avoiding common grammatical mistakes. In short, in Chapter 3 we told you how to find your literature. In this chapter, we will tell you everything you need to know to write up your findings.

What Is a Literature Review?

▼

A literature review is not a list of separate summaries of your various sources; that would be a form of an **annotated bibliography**. Instead, a literature review is a single summary, of several things: research conclusions previously made on your topic, the various methods that have been used to investigate your topic, and what areas still remain to be investigated on your topic. Your literature review places your research in the context of current and past studies. It compares your proposed research with what others have done—what they've studied and what they haven't, and what problems and successes they had in their design and methodology (and how they addressed any problems they had). Your literature review will help you decide what design and methodology you should use based on what has worked and has not worked for other people.

annotated bibliography
A list of separate summaries of various sources.

Your literature review gives you the ammunition to argue for your research: how is your study different from and/or better than other research that's already been done? It lets you justify the importance of your topic area. Finally, your literature review will help you decide on the theoretical or conceptual framework you will be basing your research on (Rossman, 1995).

Annotated Bibliography versus Synthesis of the Literature

▼

The number one problem students have in writing literature reviews is synthesizing the literature. Many first-time literature reviews read like annotated bibliographies—a listing of summaries of research studies, one at a time, with no link or connection between them. Here's an annotated bibliography that was published in a journal, *Technical Communication Quarterly*, to describe specific research published about organizational culture. Notice how, even though the research studies are compared to each other, the bibliography summarizes the research one study at a time, keeping each of the summaries separate from each other.

Paige, Michael. *Education for the Intercultural Experience.* Yarmouth, ME: Intercultural P, 1994.
    In this edited collection, Paige compiles articles and essays from the field of intercultural communication. These articles address the ways in which individuals are affected by and react to the different cultural dimensions encountered in international and intercultural immersion experiences. They discuss in more

Continued

From "Organizational & Intercultural Communication: An Annotated Bibliography" by H. Constantinides, K. St., Amant & C. Kampf, *Technical Communication Quarterly,* *10(1),* 2001; reprinted by permission of the publisher, Taylor & Francis Group, www.informaworld.com.

Continued

depth many of the issues raised by Adler with respect to cross-cultural managers, such as culture shock, intercultural adjustment, and reentry. However, the articles also address other topics such as Milton Bennett's model of intercultural sensitivity, the effects of intercultural experience on the individual, methods for preparing individuals to live in another culture, and ways to recognize and deal with the stress inherent in intercultural communication.

In contrast to Adler, the articles in this book focus exclusively on the personal aspects of and preparation for intercultural experiences. As such, they are useful for helping individuals develop empathy for people from other cultures, people whom they may encounter as co-workers, audiences, and clients in international business contexts. These essays also can help global employees prepare for assignments that immerse them in different cultures.

Storti, Craig. *Cross-Cultural Dialogues: 74 Brief Encounters with Cultural Differences.* Yarmouth, ME: Intercultural P, 1994.
Storti gives examples of intercultural miscommunication for the reader to

In contrast, look at the literature review section of the article "Cultural Identity Tensions in a Post-Acquisition Organization" by Pepper and Larson, 2006, in the *Journal of Applied Communication Research*.

From "Cultural Identity Tensions in a Post-Acquisition Organization: by G. L. Pepper & G. S. Larson, *Journal of Applied Communication Research,* Vol. 34, No. 1, January 2, 2006, reprinted by permission of Taylor & Francis Group, www.informaworld.com.

Identification and Disidentification with Cultural Premises

When people experience identity tensions, what they are wrestling with are cultural premises. Organizational culture refers to "patterns of human action and its recursive behaviors (including talk and its symbolic residues) and meanings" (Eisenberg & Riley, 2001, p. 294). Thus, organizational culture includes practices, as well as organizationally embedded values, assumptions, and expectations (Pacanowsky & O'Donnell-Trujillo, 1982, 1983; Schrodt, 2002).

Organizations are multi-cultural (Nicotera, Clinkscales, & Walker, 2003), and these multiple cultures are held together by what Parker (2000) refers to as "stabilizations of meaning" (p. 81). Culture and organization construct each other, resulting in both fragmentation and unity (Alvesson & Berg, 1992; Koene, Boone, & Soeters, 1997; J. Martin, 2002). Thus, "organizations are collective but also divided – not either one or the other" (Parker, 2000, p. 223). Organizational culture is a composite reflection of stakeholder stories (Mills, Boylstein, & Lorean, 2001) that represent the sensemaking (Weick, 1995) of groups as diverse as managers, founders, salespeople, and customers. And, as shown at the opening of this paper and elsewhere (Dukerich, Golden, & Shortell, 2002; Lampe, 2002), culture can have both a positive and negative impact on both employees and organizational performance.

Because of the large potential impact of organizational culture, managers and organizational leaders will try to create and manipulate culture in ways consistent with corporate profit and success. These efforts at creating uniform values, beliefs, and behaviors are often futile because culture, especially in complex organizations, is difficult to manage from the top (J. Martin, 2002; Parker, 2000; Turner, 1999).

The relationship between identification and organizational culture is crucial to understand when trying to discern acquisition success and failure. Strong cultures often produce highly identified employees, which may then lead to highly committed workers and concertive control (Barker, 1999; Tompkins & Cheney, 1983). Strong

Notice how different this synthesis is from the annotated bibliography. Especially notice how the different references have been merged together, discussed under a common topic or finding. For example, in the second paragraph, notice the line that says: "Culture and organization construct each other, resulting in both fragmentation and unity (Alvesson & Berg, 1992; Koene, Boone, & Soeters, 1997; J. Martin, 2002)." This sentence references three different studies, all of which talk about how culture and organizations both fragment and unify each other. They have been merged, or synthesized, into this one idea.

The next sentence merges in a related thought from another research study, and uses a direct quote from that study to make their point: "Thus, 'organizations are collective but also divided—not either one or the other' (Parker, 2000, p. 223)."

This next sentence continues to talk about what organizational culture is, pulling together two more related-yet-different thoughts from two other references:

Organizational culture is a composite reflection of stakeholder stories (Mills, Boylstein, & Lorean, 2001) that represent the sensemaking (Weick, 1995) of groups as diverse as managers, founders, salespeople, and customers.

Here's another example of synthesis of sources. Here are three sources discussing communication competence (Cegala, Socha McGee, & McNeilis, 1996; McNeilis, 2001; Query & James, 1989):

From "The Relationship Between Interpersonal Communication Competence and Social Support Groups in Retirement Communities" by Jim L. Query and Anita C. James, *Health Communication, Vol, 1, No. 3*, January 7, 1989; reprinted by permission of the publisher, Taylor & Francis Group, www.informaworld.com.

human communication to create, maintain, and terminate relationships. The task portion of the continuum refers to how the interactants communicate job-related information to one another.

The preceding examination of communication competence has two implications for the present study. First, communication competence is a multidimensional concept. Second, communication competence is contextually bound. For the present study, *communication competence* is defined as the perceived ability to communicate one's view as well as to understand another's perspective across a variety of situations. Similar to the view of social skills previously advanced by Heller (1979) and by B. R. Sarason et al. (1985), this definition encompasses social support reception and provision. Addressing social support reception, individuals have to be able to symbolically influence interaction in order to mobilize their support group or social network. Concerning social support provision, social actors must be able to interpret another person's situation to render satisfactory social support.

guage-in-use), and it all but ignores the role of context. As an alternative, we propose an approach to research on competence that is grounded in communicative behavior and, as such, is inherently context-bound (see Cegala & Waldron, 1992). Our approach is by no means adverse to striving toward a general theory of communication, but it assumes that such a theory is likely to evolve from deep understanding of what competence is within several different contexts.

From "Components of Patients' and Doctors' Perceptions of Communication Competence During a Primary Care Medical Interview" by Donald J. Cegala; Deborah Socha McGee; Kelly S. McNeilis, *Health Communication, Vol. 8, No. 1*, January 1, 1996; reprinted by permission of the publisher, Taylor & Francis Group, www .informaworld.com.

promise of the CACS is its ability to provide assessments of linguistic communication competence at the dyadic level. On the basis of the results of the coding system applied to these data, some conclusions about communication competence in the medical consultation are made here.

Competence Assessments

Results of this coding scheme provide some insights into health communication processes between physicians and patients regarding their use of specific linguistic strategies for accomplishing various goals. In particular, the use of continuers and other similar strategies by physicians (and patients) were observed as a recurring pattern within information exchange portions of the consultation. This pattern in-

Now, here's a paragraph synthesizing those three sources:

From "Analyzing Communication Competence in Medical Consultations" by Kelly McNeilis, *Health Communication, Vol. 13, No. 1*, January 1, 2001; reprinted by permission of the publisher, Taylor & Francis Group, www. informaworld.com.

The concept of communication competence has been defined as "the perceived ability to communicate one's view as well as to understand another's perspective across a variety of situations" (Query & James, 1989, p. 171), and, as Cegala, Socha McGee, and McNeilis (1996), McNeilis (2001), and Query and James (1989) point out, communication competence is bound by context, situation, and goals.

Notice how important it is when you are synthesizing your literature, to take the time to thoroughly read and understand what the research claims and does. It would be impossible to merge and synthesize research articles without a thorough knowledge of what each article claims.

• •

▼ Organizing the Literature Review

Synthesizing your literature is easier if you organize your paper according to your synthesis. In your literature review, you are making an argument, a claim (Booth, Colomb, & Williams, 1995). Your claim answers your research question (RQ), which for your literature review might be along the lines of: "What have other researchers found out about _____ ?" (Your claim for that RQ would state: "Other researchers have discovered these three things: _____.") If you synthesize the literature within each element of the claim, both your synthesis and organization will flow naturally.

Here's how you do that. Since you are making a claim, you should start your paper with that claim. You will be building your argument on this claim, and you will offer evidence from your literature review to support your claim. In other words, you will claim that "these things are known," and then provide the literature that supports that claim (Booth et al., 1995).

Typically, you will follow this organizational pattern:

1. Introduction: Introduce the topic and provide a preview of what is to follow
   a. Claim: Briefly describe what this research will show
2. Literature Review: Organize around your claim
3. Conclusion: Restate your claim and summarize your main points

You will likely organize your literature review topically: "These three things are known." You might also organize it chronologically: "We used to think this, but now we think this," or comparatively: "It's done this way in Europe, but this way in the United States." Let your data tell you how to best organize it. As you read through your sources, ask yourself how they are best grouped—what are the areas in which they are similar or different? Where do topics overlap and what are the most important findings to come out of all the research you have read? What are the trends, themes, or key ideas the literature points to?

Know your organization scheme (and claim) before you begin writing, and as you are writing your literature review, make sure your organization follows your claim. For example, if your claim states that "three things are known," your literature review should have three distinct sections—one for each of the three themes. Make sure you use clean, smooth transitions between each of the themes. This can be as easy as saying: "Unlike this first theme, this next theme does_____," or "The next main area of research is_____."

You'll state your claim in the introduction, and you'll develop it in the literature review section, talking about each separate theme one at a time, making (in a sense) mini-claims for each theme. You'll cite the studies you read as illustrations or examples for each claim, and you'll use this literature to develop each point of your claim. You'll show how the studies are connected and how they relate to the themes. You can also critique the validity of the research, if possible, so if you read a study that didn't make sense to you or didn't seem to be conducted in a valid manner, you can say that in your literature review.

• •

Citations   ▼

As you are synthesizing your literature and writing up your findings, you need to remember to properly cite your sources. We'll talk about citation styles in a minute, but let's go back to the Pepper and Larson example and take a look at how they cited their sources. Note that they've listed all the authors (we'll discuss exceptions to that in a minute) in all the papers they are citing. Look at this example:

Culture and organization construct each other, resulting in both fragmentation and unity (Alvesson & Berg, 1992; Koene, Boone, & Soeters, 1997; J. Martin, 2002).

They are citing three different studies. The first was a 1992 study written by two authors, one with the last name of Alvesson and one with the last name of Berg. They are listed in that order (Alvesson first, and Berg second) because that's the order they were in the paper they cited. This is very important! Authorial order is important, and it's political and negotiated. At some universities, for example, first author position counts more toward tenure for a faculty member than second or subsequent position. First author position implies that the first person listed is the one who spearheaded the research and took charge of writing and revising it. The order of subsequent positions is negotiated between the authors based, at various times, on amount of effort, work performed, and seniority on the project and in the organization. Teams of researchers who do many studies together may decide to rotate order of authorship. The point you should understand is that the authors did not take this order lightly and neither should you. Always list authors in the order they have listed them.

The second study was one published in 1997 and written by three authors: the first, a person with the last name of Koene, the second, with the last name of Boone, and the third, with the last name of Soeters. The third study was one published in 2002 and was written by J. Martin. The first initial is listed here to differentiate the author by another author with the same last name.

Do you see what order the three studies are listed? No, not chronological (although that would also be true for this example). They are ordered alphabetically—Alvesson comes before Koene, and Koene comes before Martin.

How do we know they're citing three different studies and not one study with six authors? There are two clues. First, there are three years, which indicate three different publishing dates. And, second, while commas separate the names of authors in a single article, semicolons separate the articles.

▼ Avoiding Plagiarism

plagiarism
The failure to properly cite sources, which results in taking credit for someone else's words or ideas.

Why are we telling you how to cite your sources? Failure to cite your sources properly is called **plagiarism**. It is illegal because it is a violation of copyright laws. It is a form of cheating and stealing because you are taking credit for someone else's ideas and words. It is serious. It can get you kicked out of school, or can cause you to flunk a class or get a zero on an assignment. It can prevent you from graduating or from getting a job or a promotion. It can ruin your career and cause you to incur fines or even face legal charges. Now that so many sources are available on the Internet, it's very easy to plagiarize. However, you should know that it's also very easy to get caught. There are as many ways on the Internet to catch plagiarism as there are to plagiarize. We've already said that it's a mark of a good scholar to build on the ideas of other people, so we're not suggesting that you *not use* sources, we're just insisting that when you do, you give them proper credit. Look at it this way, after you're done conducting your research study and writing up the findings, would you want other people to take your work and claim it as theirs?

Booth and colleagues (1995) say it well:

Intentional plagiarism is theft, but of more than words. By not acknowledging a source, the plagiarist steals some of the little reward that an academic community has to offer, the enhanced respect that a researcher spends a lifetime trying to earn. The plagiarism steals from his (or her) community of classmates by making the quality of their work seem worse by comparison and then perhaps steals again by taking one of the few good grades reserved to reward those who do good work. By choosing not to learn the skills that research can teach [him or] her, the plagiarist not only compromises [his or] her own education but steals from the larger society that devotes its resources to training students to do reliable work later. Most important, plagiarism, like theft among friends, shreds the fabric of community (p. 257).

Plagiarism is still plagiarism, even if you didn't mean to do it (Booth et al., 1995). Many plagiarism cases happen when students get in a hurry taking notes from their sources, then when writing up the paper, they can't read their notes or find they don't contain all the needed information (Davis, 2007). What, exactly, do you need to make sure you *avoid plagiarism*? According to Booth and colleagues (1995), it's plagiarism when you use someone else's *words*, but fail to credit him or her; use someone else's *ideas*, but fail to credit him or her; or use someone's *exact words*, but fail to put the quote in quotation marks or block indentation, and/or fail to put page number references for the quote. So what's the bottom line? Give proper credit to your sources!

Usually, you'll be paraphrasing someone's words. It's a poorly written literature review that consists of one quote after another. A good general rule is that you paraphrase unless you are so enamored with the words the person used that you just have to use them. Be careful when paraphrasing, though. Make sure you rewrite the information sufficiently so that you're not plagiarizing. Remember that simply changing one or two words is not sufficient. To paraphrase, you must understand the entire idea and then restate it in your own words. Write it as if you're explaining it to a friend when the original source is not in front of you (Booth et al., 1995).

Here, for example, is a proper paraphrase of a research article:

The role of the empowered consumer implies that patients take on a problem-solving, collaborative role in their own care. Reports of medical miscommunication resulting from patients' misunderstanding of medical terminology; different perceptions and understandings of their health problems and goals; and obstacles between patient and provider, support the importance of a communication competence view of health literacy (Young & Flower, 2001).

Here's one of the pages from the original article that yielded some of the information for the paraphrase:

A major frustration among health care providers is the lack of patient compliance. Yet, patients usually have logical reasons for their behavior—perhaps a specific treatment

Continued

From "Patients as Partners, Patients as Problem-Solvers" by Amanda Young & Linda Flower, *Health Communication, Vol. 14, No. 1,* January 1, 2002; reprinted by permission of the publisher, Taylor & Francis Group, www.informaworld.com.

Continued

is too embarrassing, too painful, too costly, or too time-consuming. Perhaps the patient does not understand the providers' instructions. Perhaps the patient does not have the necessary coping strategies to endure a specific treatment. Patients with cystic fibrosis, for example, have often complained that doctors and therapists do not understand how sore they get from continual chest percussion or how much the treatment interferes with the whole family's schedule (A. Young,

The same article states, later on the same page:

Creating a Partnership Between Providers and Patients

An optimal medical encounter is an experience that validates the expertise of both patient and provider and that dignifies the patient's needs throughout the entire sequence of treatment. In a problem-solving relationship, patients and providers concentrate on negotiation and shared agency, rather than on compliance. Instead of a patient being given a choice to simply comply or not, patients and providers can jointly develop a plan of care that recognizes the social, psychological, and financial constraints of the patient. This partnership is dependent, however, on a reciprocal relationship that incorporates the strategies of CI.

The *SAFE Program*[7] is a clear illustration of how to create a patient–provider partnership (see Figure 2). Young women at Children's Hospital of Pittsburgh are

[7]SAFE is part of a 5-year longitudinal study directed by Melanie Gold, DO, at Children's Hospital of Pittsburgh. Young and Gold developed the computer program using the concepts of CI. The follow-up counseling is based on Miller's (1983) model of motivational interviewing.

You can see how this information (plus other information from the overall article) is properly paraphrased into the paragraph above. The general understanding and ideas came from this Young and Flower (2001) article, but it is rewritten in the author's own words.

· ·

▼ Writing Styles

When you cite your sources and write your paper, you'll be following one of a few accepted *styles*. If you are writing a paper for a class, your instructor will let you know which style he or she wants you to use. In the field of Communication Studies, you will likely be using one of three styles: **American Psychological Association (APA) style**, **Modern Language Association (MLA) style**, or

Chicago style. Each of the different styles came out of different academic traditions, and each is best for different types of papers. Most social science and communication scholars use APA, so this is the style we will talk about most in this chapter. A few communication-related or interdisciplinary journals use MLA or Chicago, so we will talk briefly about these two styles, as well.

The style manuals instruct you how to format your paper, how to cite your sources in the text (in the body of your paper), and how to list your references and cite your sources in a list at the end of your paper. Each style manual differs on how you list the author's name, where you place the publication date, where and how you use marks such as underlines, quotations, or capitalization, and where and how you list the publisher's name, among many other things (Weidenborner, Caruso, & Parks, 2005). You should refer to the original manuals for specific, detailed information about each of the styles, but following is some general information about them. We recommend that you use this chapter to help remind you what details you should attend to for each style. Please remember, however, that this chapter is not intended to replace the use of the original style manuals.

Regardless of the style, you must develop an eye for detail to adhere to the proper style. In your citations, the number of spaces between words and punctuation marks is important. When to italicize and when not to italicize is important. How to list an author's name, when to underline, and when to capitalize is important. In writing your paper, you need to know exactly how wide your margins should be, what font should be used, as well as what font size should be used. In addition, you need to know the difference in citation style between a journal article, a book, and a chapter in an edited book.

Here are some tips for each of the styles used in our field:

American Psychological Association (APA) Style (6ᵗʰ edition)

Many of the NCA journals (*Communication Education, Communication Monographs, Communication Teacher, Critical Studies in Media Communication, Journal of International and Intercultural Communication, Journal of Applied Communication Research,* and *Review of Communication*) use APA style.

Body of the Paper. First of all, for you journalism majors, APA is not the same as AP. They are extremely different styles. Written in APA style, your paper will have 1" margins top, bottom, right, and left. Your right margin will be nonjustified. You will use 12-point type, in Times New Roman font. You will have a title page, an abstract page (in most cases), the body of your paper, and a reference section.

Your title page will include a header line, which includes the "running head," flush left, then on the same line, the page number, flush right. The running head includes the words "Running head," then a colon, then (in all caps) a short version of your title. The title page is numbered page one. About one-half to one-third of the way down the page, you will have the long version of your title on one or two lines, your name on the next line, your university affiliation on the next line, and, depending on the needs of your paper, separate lines for your course name, instructor name, and contact information. All of

American Psychological Association (APA) style
The editorial style most commonly used by social science and communication scholars, this style features a list of references and specifies the names and order of headings, among other elements. (Please refer to the Publication Manual of the American Psychological Association *for the most up-to-date style rules and guidelines.).*

Modern Language Association (MLA) style
An editorial style sometimes used by communication scholars that features an alphabetical list of works cited and brief parenthetical citations in the text, among other elements. (Please refer to the MLA Handbook for Writers of Research Papers *and the* MLA Style Manual and Guide to Scholarly Publishing *for the most up-to-date style rules and guidelines.).*

Chicago style
An editorial style sometimes used by communication scholars that is useful for providing detailed information about sources, and features footnotes and endnotes, among other elements. (Please refer to the Chicago Manual of Style *for the most up-to-date style rules and guidelines.).*

these lines will be centered, and double-spaced. Here's a sample title page in APA style:

Running head: DUELING NARRATIVES   1

Dueling Narratives: How Peer Leaders Use Narrative

to Frame Meaning in Community Mental Health Care Teams

Christine S. Davis, Ph.D.

Assistant Professor

University of North Carolina at Charlotte

Department of Communication Studies

9201 University City Blvd., Colvard 5004

Charlotte, North Carolina 28223

704-687-6638

Fax: 704-687-6900

csdavis2@email.uncc.edu

From page two on, your header will consist of your running head (WITH-OUT the words "running head") flush left, and the page number flush right. Your header is in all caps. Note that your header MUST be on the same line as your page number. You accomplish this in the "Insert Header" function in Word. Tip: In Word, within "Insert Header" go to "Edit Header," and check "different first page" to let you change the header from page one to two.

Page two includes your abstract. The abstract is (usually) a 100- to 250-word brief summary of your paper (Booth et al., 1995). It provides the RQ, key themes, and the main point of the research. It begins with a line centered that says, "Abstract." The abstract begins on the very next line, with *no* first line indent. If you have keywords, they go on the next line, right after the abstract, flush left, with the word "keywords" in italics. From here, throughout the rest of the paper, you will double-space. Here's a sample abstract page:

DUELING NARRATIVES   2

Abstract

Successfully leading an interorganizational peer-led team, a team of people from different backgrounds and organizations that are at comparable hierarchical levels with the leader, is a challenge, as is leading such a group to a new model in which the traditionally dominant frame is no longer valid. This research, reporting on observations of 118 child and family team meetings in a community children's mental health system of care, looks at peer leaders' narrative discourse to reframe meaning and assume leadership of the team. Leaders' use of strong narratives to frame consistent, clear, and congruent messages leads to both narrative power and their own desired outcomes.

Keywords: Narrative power, Narrative discourse, Team leadership, Peer-led teams

The body of your paper begins on page three. The first line is the long title, centered. The second line begins your paper. In the prior version of APA (the 5th edition), you used to include a header called "Introduction," but in the newest 6th edition, you no longer have that initial header. In APA, there are no extra lines between headers or between headers and the body of your paper, anywhere in the paper. Here's a sample of the first page of a paper:

DUELING NARRATIVES   3

Dueling Narratives: How Peer Leaders Use Narrative

to Frame Meaning in Community Mental Health Care Teams

In this research, I examine peer leadership within children's community mental health

system of care child and family team meetings and specifically look at the acquisition of power

and leadership through team leaders' and members' use of narrative to frame and reframe

meaning.

This research contributes to current knowledge by studying an interorganizational peer-

led team—a team of individuals from different organizations, all of whom are at comparable

status levels to each other and to the official team leader. I specifically address the paradox of

power from a seemingly power-less leader, by describing and giving examples of narrative

Your *first* level of section heading is reserved for the main sections of your paper, usually "Literature Review," "Study Objectives," "Discussion," and "Conclusion," for example. This level of heading is on its own line, centered, and boldface, with the first letter of each word capitalized. Your *second* level of section heading is for your subheadings. For example, if you are making three main points within your "Literature Review" section, you would have three sub-heads—one for each point. As in the example below, this level of subhead is on its own line, boldface, and flush left. The first letter of each word is capitalized.

If you have a *third* level of header, it is on the first line of the paragraph, tabbed (1/2-inch tab), and boldface, with only the first letter of the first word capitalized, and a period at the end of the header. Your paragraph would continue on the same line.

DUELING NARRATIVES   8

through sensemaking--communicating, managing, constructing, and creating a shared

understanding of experience (Drath & Palus, 1994; Lennie, 1999; Witherspoon, 1997).

This paper will show the child and family team leader, with no other formal source of

power, must coordinate and direct team participants in a way that creates a new meaning that

follows a system of care orientation. It will specifically discuss the team leaders' and members'

use of narrative to frame and reframe meaning and acquire power and leadership of the team.

Literature Review

Narrative as a Framing Device

Definition of narrative. Narratives can be defined as "the discursive way in which we

organize, account for, give meaning to, and understand, that is, give structure and coherence to,

the circumstances and the events in our lives . . . for and with ourselves and others" (Anderson,

1997, p. 212). People use narratives or stories to organize, make sense of, interpret, direct, and

create meaning from their experiences. Leaders use storytelling to enact meaning-making (Drath

& Palus, 1994). Our narratives evolve through interaction, language, and conversation; come

from our individual perspectives; and influence the way people behave and interact in society

(Anderson, 1997; Freeman & Lobovits, 1993; Herman, 2001; Parry & Doan, 1994).

Understanding the discourse in these child and family team meetings as narratives, as stories

with a beginning, middle, and end, and with characters, history, action, and a plot, lets us

examine the conversational way in which the team leaders—and members—attempt to frame the

meaning in the meetings.

Stories as source of conflict. In fact, in these meetings, it is the stories—or the meanings

stories assign to actions and discourse—which are the source of team conflict. It is most likely

Reference List. In APA, your citations differ greatly depending on what type of citation you're using. Let's start with the citations at the end of your paper. This is called the "Reference" page, and this page begins a new page after the last page of the body of your paper. Your reference list is in alphabetical order. Any reference in this list *must* be used and cited in the body of the paper, and any reference used and cited in the body of the paper *must* be in this reference list. Your reference list has a *hanging indent*, which you access in Word through the "indent" dialogue box, using a 1/2-inch hanging indent.

DUELING NARRATIVES   32

References

Anderson, H. (1997). *Conversation, language, and possibilities: A postmodern approach to therapy.* NY: Basic.

Avery, C. M. (1999). All power to you: Collaborative leadership works. *The Journal for Quality and Participation, 22*(2), 36-40. Retrieved from: http://www.asq.org/

Barton, L. (1996). Sociology and disability: Some emerging issues. In L. Barton (Ed.), *Disability and society: Emerging issues and insights* (pp. 3-17). NY: Longman.

Bastien, D. T. & Hostager, T. J. (1992). Cooperation as communicative accomplishment: A symbolic interaction analysis of an improvised jazz concert. *Communication Studies, 43,* 92-104. Retrieved from: http://associationdatabase.com/aws/CSCA/pt/sp/journal

Bateson, G. (1972). *Steps to an ecology of the mind.* Chicago: University of Chicago Press.

On your "Reference" page, for a citation from a book, you would put the author's last name, then a comma, then the author's initial(s) (use whatever initials the author gave in the article itself and separate initials with a space), followed by a period, then the publication year in parenthesis, followed by a period. Next is the title of the book in italics. The only letters you capitalize are the first letter of the first word of the title, the first letter of the first word that follows a colon or period, or a proper noun. The title ends with a period, followed by the city/state or city/country of publication (the state/country can be left off if the city is well known), a colon, the publisher name, and a period. A citation for a single-authored book looks like this:

> Anderson, H. (1997). *Conversation, language, and possibilities: A postmodern approach to therapy.* New York: Basic Books.

If you have more than one author, you would put the author names in the order they have them in the article. You would have a comma between them, and a comma followed by an ampersand (&) before the last name:

> Drath, W. H., & Palus, C. J. (1994). *Making common sense:*
> *Leadership as meaning-making in a community of practice.*
> Greensboro, NC: Center for Creative Leadership.

The citation style for an article in a journal is very different. Notice that you start the same way, listing the authors' names using first initials, a comma between names, an ampersand before the last name, and the year in parenthesis followed by a period. The title of the article is *not* in italics. The only letters you capitalize in the article title are the first letter of the first word of the title, the first letter of the first word that follows a colon or period, or a proper noun. The title ends with a period. This is followed by the journal title in italics with the first letter of each word capitalized (*except* prepositions, conjunctions, and the words *the*, *a*, and *an*, unless it is the first word of the title). The journal title closes with a comma, followed by the journal volume number, followed by an issue number in parentheses (optional), followed by a comma, then the inclusive (all) page numbers of the article, followed by a period. Note that the volume number is also in italics, but the issue number and page numbers are *not* in italics:

> Bastien, D. T., & Hostager, T. J. (1992). Cooperation as commu-
> nicative accomplishment: A symbolic interaction analysis of an
> improvised jazz concert. *Communication Studies, 43,* 92–104.

Here's a citation of a journal article that includes an issue number also:

> Guerrero, L. K., & Andersen, P. A. (1991). The waxing and waning
> of relational intimacy: Touch as a function of relational stage,
> gender and touch avoidance. *Journal of Social and Personal*
> *Relationships, 8*(2), 147–165.

If the journal is available as a published (hard copy) journal but you accessed it online, you would add the DOI number to the end of the citation. DOI stands for Digital Object Identifier, and this is a new style guideline as of the new 6th edition of the APA Style Manual. This is a code consisting of numbers and/or letters, and it's easiest if you just cut and paste it from the article to your citation. The DOI number can be found either in the article itself or in the database record. If there isn't one, then instead add to the end of your citation: "Retrieved from [the home page URL of the journal]." Note that the term "doi" is all in lower case letters, and there is no period after a doi number.

An, S. (2008). Antidepressant direct-to-consumer advertising and social perception of the prevalence of depression: Application of the availability heuristic. *Health Communication, 23*(6), 499-505. doi: 10.1080/10410230802342127

An, S. (2008). Antidepressant direct-to-consumer advertising and social perception of the prevalence of depression: Application of the availability heuristic. *Health Communication, 23*(6), 499-505. Retrieved from http://www.erlbaum.com/Journals/journals/HC/hc.htm

If it's an online journal (a journal published *only* online), the citation is:

Bounds, P. (2008, May). Beyond *Ways of Seeing:* The media criticism of John Berger. Retrieved from http://www.fifth-estate-online .co.uk/criticsm/P.Bounds.html

There is no period after a URL.

You also might cite a chapter in an edited book. Again, you start with the author's last name and first initial, but this time you start with the author of the *chapter* you are citing. This is followed by the publication year in parenthesis. The title of the chapter is next, *not* in italics, with the only letters you capitalize being the first letter of the first word of the title, the first letter of the first word that follows a colon or period, or a proper noun. This is followed by the citation information for the book from which you took the chapter. The chapter title ends in a period, then you type "In [*book* editor's name]." Note that the book editors' names here are reversed—first initials followed by last name. Note that if there is more than one editor, you put an ampersand before the last one, but not a comma. Notice that after the last name there is no comma, and this is followed by the word "Ed." (one editor) or "Eds." (two or more editors). This is in parenthesis, followed by a comma, followed by the title of the edited book (in italics). The only letters you capitalize in the book title are the first letter of the first word of the title, the first letter of the first word that follows a colon or period, or a proper noun. The title does *not* end with a period, but is followed by the inclusive page numbers of the chapter you are citing in parenthesis. Note that the page numbers are preceded by the letters "pp" and a period. A period is also placed after the parenthesis and the citation ends with the city of publication, a colon, the name of the publisher, and a period:

Charmaz, K. (2000). Grounded theory: Objectivist and constructivist methods. In N. K. Denzin & Y. S. Lincoln (Eds.), *The handbook of qualitative research* (pp. 509–535). Thousand Oaks, CA: Sage.

In the end-of-text references, always include all authors' names regardless of how many there are. Remember, put them in the same order as they were in the original paper or book that was cited from.

Increasingly important is the proper citing of electronic sources such as websites and Web pages. When citing a Web page, your reference will begin with the author of the page in the same format you would use for a journal article or book. If no author is provided, the title of the page will be the first entry, followed by a period. The only letters you capitalize in the title are the first letter of the first word of the title, the first letter of the first word that follows a colon or period, or a proper noun. The year of publication, in parenthesis, follows. If no date is available, use "n.d." inside the parenthesis. A period is used on the outside of these parentheses, followed by a space. Complete the citation with "Retrieved from [insert URL]" (remember, there is no period after a URL).

> What's new in the sixth edition of the publication manual? (n.d.).
>
> Retrieved from http://www.apastyle.org/manual/whats-new.aspx

If you are citing an entire website, you need only to give the address in your in-text citation. No end-of-text reference is necessary.

> The APA style website is a great source for information on structuring your paper, grammar, and citation examples (http://www.apastyle.org).

In-Text Citations.   In addition to putting your citations in the reference list at the end of the paper, you also must cite within the text, at the point in which you are referring to the cite. This is called an in-text citation, and there are some different ways to do this. You might want to write your sentence, making your claim without using the name of the author specifically. If you do this, you would put the citation in parenthesis at the end of the sentence, such as in this example:

> Organizational theorists generally agree regardless of its source, leadership requires power or the ability to influence behavior (Stupak & Leitner, 2001).

Note that in-text you only list the author's last name. Notice that you have an ampersand, but no comma between the two names. You do, however, have a comma between the last name and the year. And your period to end the sentence is outside the parenthesis, *not* within it.

Perhaps you want to use the source's name in your sentence. To do this, you put the publication year in parenthesis after the name, as shown here:

> Anderson (1997) points out. . . .

If you're citing two authors' names in your sentence, always use *and* rather than an ampersand:

> Smircich and Morgan (1982) suggest that framing the meaning of a team requires the acquiescence to power among other team members.

If you're citing something in-text that has one or two authors, you must cite the author's or both authors' names every time. If there are three to five authors, you list all the names the first time you cite it, then omit every name after the first in subsequent times and replace them with "et al.":

> (Anderson et al., 2003).

In text, you can use the less awkward sounding:

> Anderson and colleagues (2003) said. . . .

If your text has six or more authors, you *always* (even the first time) only list the first name, then "et al." It is "et al." in the reference section also.

When citing websites or Web pages, there is often no author or editor listed. In these cases, you would begin the citation in parentheses at the end of the sentence with the title or abbreviated title of the Web page or article. This title should be surrounded by double quotation marks, with each word capitalized. A comma inside the quotation marks will separate the title from the year. Again, if no date is available, use "n.d." It is often helpful to include a paragraph number following the date. The date and paragraph number are also separated by a comma.

> ("What's New in the Sixth Edition," n.d., para 3).

There are many more details and other types of citations you may need; you should refer to the most recent edition of the *Publication Manual of the American Psychological Association* (American Psychological Association, 2009) for more information.

Modern Language Association (MLA) Style (7th edition)

One of the NCA journals (*Text and Performance Quarterly*) uses MLA style.

MLA differs from APA in many significant ways. For example, the references page is titled "Works Cited." It, too, is formatted with a hanging indent, with the works organized alphabetically, and the book or journal titles are also italicized. A journal article is placed in quotation marks. Instead of using the author's first initial, you spell out the first name. The first author is listed as "last name, first name, middle initial." Subsequent authors are listed as "first name, middle initial, last name."The publication year is placed at the end of the cite (in parentheses). The first letter of each word in titles is capitalized (*except* for articles such as *and*, *a*, and *the*, in the middle of the sentence). At the end of each listing, you add the medium of the source (Print, Web, DVD, CD-ROM, PDF, etc.). In addition to the volume number, you also include the issue number. This is written as "volume(period)issue". The three references we gave you earlier would look like this in MLA:

Anderson, Harlene. *Conversation, Language, and Possibilities: A Postmodern Approach to Therapy*. New York: Basic Books, 1997. Print.

Bastien, David T., and Todd J. Hostager "Cooperation as Communicative Accomplishment: A Symbolic Interaction Analysis of an Improvised Jazz Concert." *Communication Studies* 43.2 (1992): 92–104. Web.

Charmaz, Kathy. "Grounded Theory: Objectivist and Constructivist Methods." *The Handbook of Qualitative Research*. Ed. Norman K. Denzin and Yvonna S. Lincoln. Thousand Oaks, CA: Sage, 2000. 509–35. Print.

In text, each of these citations would be referred to parenthetically (in parenthesis) by name and page number (*not* by year), as follows:

Organizational theorists generally agree regardless of its source, leadership requires power or the ability to influence behavior (Stupak and Leitner 784–801).

Anderson (629) points out. . . .

Smircich and Morgan (543) suggest that framing the meaning of a team requires the acquiescence to power among other team members.

Chicago Style (16ᵗʰ edition)

Two of the NCA journals (*Communication and Critical/Cultural Studies* and *Quarterly Journal of Speech*) use Chicago style.

Instead of using the parenthetical, in-text style used by APA and MLA, the Chicago style uses an endnote or footnote system. In text, each citation is given a footnote or endnote notation and a note that refers to the numbered endnotes at the end of the manuscript or footnotes at the bottom of each page.

The three references we gave you earlier would be listed both in endnotes or footnotes, and also in a separate Bibliography at the end of the paper. Following is the format for the endnotes or footnotes. Note that the Bibliography style is slightly different, as well:

1. Harlene Anderson, *Conversation, Language, and Possibilities: A Postmodern Approach to Therapy* (New York: Basic Books, 1997), 483.

2. David T. Bastien and Todd J. Hostager, "Cooperation as Communicative Accomplishment: A Symbolic Interaction Analysis of an Improvised Jazz Concert," *Communication Studies* 43, no. 5 (May 1992): 92–104.

3. Kathy Charmaz, "Grounded Theory: Objectivist and Constructivist Methods," in *The Handbook of Qualitative Research*, ed. Norman K. Denzin and Yvonna S. Lincoln, (Thousand Oaks, CA: Sage, 2000), 509.

In the Bibliography, the citations would be in alphabetical order, would have a hanging indent, and would look like this:

Anderson, Harlene, *Conversation, Language, and Possibilities: A Postmodern Approach to Therapy.* New York: Basic Books, 1997.

Bastien, David T., and Hostager, Todd J. "Cooperation as Communicative Accomplishment: A Symbolic Interaction Analysis of an Improvised Jazz Concert." *Communication Studies* 43, no. 5 (1992).

Charmaz, Kathy. *Grounded Theory: Objectivist and Constructivist Methods. In The Handbook of Qualitative Research*, edited by Norman K. Denzin and Yvonna S. Lincoln, pg. 15. Thousand Oaks, CA: Sage, 2000.

In text, the citations would look like this:

Organizational theorists generally agree regardless of its source, leadership requires power or the ability to influence behavior.[1]

Anderson[2] points out. . . .

Smircich and Morgan[3] suggest that framing the meaning of a team requires the acquiescence to power among other team members.

Common Grammatical Errors   ▼

The final thing you need to pay attention to when writing your literature review is grammar and punctuation. Some students are naturally good writers, while other students simply are not. We have found that proper grammar and punctuation separates the "A" papers from the "B" and "C" papers, so we've included this section to give some tips to those of you who need them. You want to make sure your paper is correct in regard to grammar and punctuation. In this chapter, we do not intend to teach you basic grammar, but we want to help you avoid common errors that students often make in their papers.

Remember that all sentences must have a subject (noun) and a verb. A sentence without a subject and a verb is a fragment.

If you are writing a number between one and ten, spell it out. If you're writing a number over 10, use numerical figures (use "12," rather than "twelve"). If mixed numbers (between one and ten, and over 10) referring to the same type of object are in a single sentence, keep it consistent and use figures. Write fractions in figures (1½) unless they begin a sentence—numbers that begin a sentence are always spelled out. Write decimals in figures (.7).

Your subject and verb must agree. If one is singular, both must be singular; if one is plural, both must be plural. So, for example, "We are talking," but "She is talking."

You must keep your tenses consistent. This is a particular challenge when conducting literature reviews, because the tendency is to write using the tense of the paper we are reading, so if the tenses in our literature change, the tenses in our paper tend to change along with them. It's helpful to write in the present tense when reviewing literature ("Smith says that . . . ") and in the past tense when you're talking about research you have conducted ("We interviewed 100 people."). This is such a challenge that we recommend that when think you are finished with your paper, make one proofreading pass to specifically check your tenses. While you're at it, make another proofreading pass to check APA and another to check grammar and punctuation.

"Its" is possessive (its scarf means the scarf belongs to it), while "it's" is a contraction that means "it is."

Pronouns should agree with the nouns they are replacing, so for a nonhuman noun, you'd use the pronoun "that," while you'd use "who" for a human noun. ("The class that," but "The teacher who").

Use nongender biased word choices, so do *not* use *mankind* to refer to *humankind*, or *men* to refer to *men and women*. Avoid the generic *he* by alternating between *he* and *she*, using *he/she* or *she/he*, or switching to plural nouns and pronouns ("people and their . . . ").

So What?

Writing a good literature review requires good skills in synthesizing the literature, organizing your paper, giving proper credit to your sources in the citation style commonly accepted by your peers in your academic community, and effectively communicating your findings through proper grammar and punctuation. We suggest you treat each of these skills as a separate step in your writing process. Often, students spend the bulk of their time finding the literature and then throw together their findings at the last minute. Unfortunately, students' grades frequently represent this misallocation of time. Once you have found your literature, your work has really just begun. You need to read through the literature so that you can understand the claim to make. You then need to outline your paper, organizing the outline around that claim. Once you have an outline, you're ready to start writing. Many researchers suggest writing your introduction last—after you know what you're actually introducing. Some of us write the introduction first (sometimes it helps us to get started in the paper), but then rewrite it at the end, to make sure it fits with where our paper actually ended up going. This raises another suggestion—you should plan on making several *passes* through your paper. In other words, your paper should go through several drafts. Your first draft will simply get down the information as you fill in the details under each point of your claim. Your next draft will make sure your citations are complete. Your next draft will make sure your citations follow the correct style format exactly. Your next draft will check for grammar and punctuation, perhaps even specific elements for separate passes. For example, one of your authors, Christine Davis, struggles with keeping tenses consistent through my papers. I always take one editing pass to specifically check my tenses. You may know specific writing challenges you have—take the time for a separate editing pass for each one. Finally, we suggest you leave enough time for one final pass, after you've had a good night's sleep. Putting it aside for a few hours will let you come back to your paper with a more objective mind. You'll be surprised how you can identify areas in which you were unclear or disorganized when you look at it with fresh eyes. After all, you've gone to a lot of trouble to learn what there is to know about your topic. Take the time to effectively communicate it to others.

Glossary

American Psychological Association (APA) style
The editorial style most commonly used by social science and communication scholars, this style features a list of references and specifies the names and order of headings, among other elements. (Please refer to the *Publication Manual of the American Psychological Association* for the most up-to-date style rules and guidelines.).

Annotated bibliography
A list of separate summaries of various sources.

Chicago style
An editorial style sometimes used by communication scholars that is useful for providing detailed information about sources, and features footnotes and endnotes, among other elements. (Please refer to the *Chicago Manual of Style* for the most up-to-date style rules and guidelines.).

Modern Language Association (MLA) style
An editorial style sometimes used by communication scholars that features an alphabetical list of works

cited and brief parenthetical citations in the text, among other elements. (Please refer to the *MLA Handbook for Writers of Research Papers* and the *MLA Style Manual and Guide to Scholarly Publishing* for the most up-to-date style rules and guidelines.).

Plagiarism
The failure to properly cite sources, which results in taking credit for someone else's words or ideas.

References

American Psychological Association (2009). *Publication manual of the American Psychological Association* (6th ed.). Washington, DC: Author.

Booth, W. C, Colomb, G. G., & Williams, J. M. (1995). *The craft of research*. Chicago: University of Chicago Press.

Cegala, D. J, Socha McGee, D., & McNeilis, K. S. (1996). Components of patients' and doctors' perceptions of communication competence during a primary care medical interview. *Health Communication, 8*(1), 1–27.

Constantinides, H., St. Amant, K., & Kampf, C. (2001). Organizational and intercultural communication: An annotated bibliography. *Technical Communication Quarterly, 10*(1), 31–58.

Davis, J. P. (2007). *The Rowman & Littlefield guide to writing with sources*. Lanham, MD: Rowman & Littlefield.

McNeilis, K. S. (2001). Analyzing communication competence in medical consultations. *Health Communication, 13*(1), 5–18.

Query, J. L., & James, A. C. (1989). The relationship between interpersonal communication competence and social support among elderly support groups in retirement communities. *Health Communication, 1*(3), 165–184.

Pepper, G. L., & Larson, G. S. (2006). Cultural identity tensions in a post-acquisition organization. *Journal of Applied Communication Research, 34*(1), 49–71.

Rossman, M. H. (1995). *Negotiating graduate school: A guide for graduate students*. Thousand Oaks, CA: Sage.

Weidenborner, S., Caruso, D., & Parks, G. (2005). *Writing research papers: A guide to the process*. Boston: Bedford/St. Martin's.

Young, A., & Flower, L. (2001). Patients as partners, patients as problem-solvers. *Health Communication, 14*(1), 69–97.

UNDERSTANDING RESEARCH ETHICS

CHAPTER OUTLINE

1. Why Do We Care about Human Subjects Protection?
2. How Do We Follow Research Ethics and Ethical Guidelines?
   a. Respect for Persons and Informed Consent
   b. Nonmaleficence and Beneficence
   c. Justice
   d. Including Participants in Co-Constructed Research
3. Who Oversees Research Ethics? Institutional Research Boards (IRBs)
4. How Do We Maintain Ethics through all Research Phases?
5. So What?

KEY TERMS

Anonymity
Assent
Belmont Report
Beneficence
Confidentiality
Deception
Ethical research

Human subjects protection
Informed consent
Justice
Legitimation
Member checks
Nonmaleficence
Nuremberg Code

Participatory action research
Relational ethics
Representation
Research ethics
Respect for persons
Vulnerable populations

CHAPTER OBJECTIVES

1. To understand the standard, proper, and ethical way in which to conduct the many types of communication research
2. To understand how to conduct research that is respectful to participants, the research community, and society
3. To understand how to conduct research that has appropriate legitimation and representation and appropriately represents multiple voices

● ●

▼ # Why Do We Care about Human Subjects Protection?

research ethics
The specific principles, rules, guidelines, and norms of research-related behavior that a research community has decided are proper, fair, and appropriate.

ethical research
Research that is designed and conducted validly, reliably, legitimately, and representatively, and protects a research participant's rights.

human subjects protection
Ethical research rules that refer to the guidelines that are followed to ensure the protection of people (participants) being studied.

Nuremberg Code
The first set of principles outlining professional ethics for medical researchers, which forms the basis for today's research ethics codes. It specifically required voluntary consent among research participants and was the first international standard for the conduct of research.

Research ethics refer to the specific principles, rules, guidelines, and norms of research-related behavior that a research community has decided are proper, fair, and appropriate. In short, **ethical research** protects a participant's rights (Murphy & Dingwall, 2001), but it does more than that. Ethical researchers also do what they say they are doing, and they design and conduct research that is valid, reliable, legitimate, and representative. In this chapter, we will discuss the history of research ethics and human subjects' protection, provide examples of ethics breaches, discuss some major concepts behind research ethics, explain the role of Institutional Research Boards (IRBs), and teach you how to ensure that your research follows ethical guidelines. We'll discuss ethics from the points of view of both interpretive and positivist paradigms and specific applications of ethics in both qualitative and quantitative research.

The research ethics that most researchers in the world follow were written as a result of abuses and violations of ethical principles by many researchers over many years, worldwide. You might hear these rules referred to as **human subjects protection**, which refers to the guidelines we follow to make sure we are protecting the people we are studying (people whom we, in communication studies, typically call our "research participants"). Our field of communication studies also has its own ethical views, guidelines, and norms that are specific to the types of research we conduct, which we will discuss throughout this chapter.

The history of human subjects protection in research really begins with the Nazi medical war crimes during World War II, because these abuses were particularly heinous, including—in the name of research and science—conducting medical experiments on concentration camp prisoners such as injecting people with gasoline, live viruses, and poisons; forcing them to sit in ice water or freezing temperatures for hours; forced sterilization; depriving them of food and water; dissecting their brains; and burning them with bomb material. After the war, former Nazis were indicted before the War Crimes Tribunal at Nuremberg in 1946. One of the outcomes of this trial was the **Nuremberg Code**, which was the first set of principles outlining professional ethics for medical researchers and which forms the basis for today's research ethics codes. The Nuremberg Code specifically required voluntary consent among research participants and was the first international standard for the conduct of research (Annas & Grodin, 1995).

We'll discuss the ethical standards and principles for research more in a minute, but first let's take a look at some other examples of violations of rights of research participants in our own country.

The most famous violation might be the Tuskegee Syphilis Study, a long-term study of black males conducted in Tuskegee by the U.S. Public Health Services. This research is especially concerning, because although it began in the 1930s, it continued until 1972. The researchers studied over 400 black men with syphilis and 200 without syphilis. They were recruited without informed consent and were misinformed about what the procedures were that were done on them. Most appalling, they were not informed of the complications experienced by others in the study. (The death rate among those with syphilis was twice as high as among the control group.) In addition, in the 1940s, penicillin was found to be effective in treating syphilis, but the study continued and the men were not informed about the possible treatment, nor were they given penicillin. Investigation into this research abuse led to the U.S. government's oversight of ethics for federally supported research projects (Thomas & Quinn, 1991).

In 1963, studies were conducted at New York's Jewish Chronic Disease Hospital to understand whether the body's inability to reject cancer cells was due to cancer or rehabilitation. So, to test this, they injected live cancer cells into patients. The consent process did not tell people they were going to inject cancer cells, because the researchers didn't want to "unnecessarily frighten them." The researchers were later found guilty of fraud, deceit, and unprofessional conduct (Edgar & Rothman, 1995).

From 1963 to 1966, at the Willowbrook State School in New York, an institution for "mentally defective children," researchers wanted to study the natural history of infectious hepatitis, and newly admitted children were deliberately infected with the hepatitis virus. Parents gave consent, but since the hospital was only admitting patients who were in this program, this wasn't really freedom of consent because parents didn't have an alternate choice if they wanted treatment for their children (Krugman, 1971).

Don't think all research abuses and dilemmas have been in medical research. There are many examples of ill-treatment of research participants in social science research, as well. The most famous example may be the Milgram experiment, in which the researcher used bogus electric shocks to measure the extent to which people would submit to authority to inflict pain on another person. Since the shocks were not real, the ethical criticism was not about the physical pain seemingly inflicted on the recipient of the shock, but on the emotional pain and duress inflicted on the research participant, the person administering the shocks (Kelman, 1967).

In a study closer to what communication researchers might investigate, in 1955, researchers in Wichita studied jury deliberations to look at group decision making and negotiating. This study was also ethically criticized because participants were not told they were being researched, observed, and videotaped, and, as part of the social institution of the jury process, had reason to believe their communication was private and confidential (Kimmel, 1988).

Many qualitative and ethnographic social science researchers have been criticized for covertly observing people without their knowledge or consent. Humphrey's (1970) study of gay sex in public restrooms and Kotarba's (1979) study of sexual activity in a public jail visiting room are two examples. Even seemingly innocuous observations of people's day-to-day lives can be criticized if people don't know, or forget, they are being observed. Carolyn Ellis, for example, published her research of two Eastern Virginia fishing communities in her book *Fisher folk: Two communities on Chesapeake Bay* (Ellis, 1986). While she had obtained informed consent at the onset of her research, she spent so long in the field (several years) that many community participants claimed they

relational ethics
The value placed on the relationships between researchers and the people they are researching.

Belmont Report
This document serves as the cornerstone of ethical principles upon which federal regulations for the protection of human research participants are based.

respect for persons
Research participants should be treated as autonomous agents—that means they are independent, self-governing, and capable of making decisions for themselves as long as they are given sufficient information to make those decisions.

informed consent
This process assumes that the research participant is competent to consent—that, if he or she is given all relevant information, he or she will be able to comprehend the information and be able to agree to participate in a voluntary manner free from coercion.

had forgotten she was researching them and had begun to think of her as simply a friend. As Ellis states later in many writings on the subject (see Ellis, 2007, for example), her experience requires her, and us, to question **relational ethics**—the value placed on the relationships between the researchers and those they are researching. We'll discuss this in more detail later in this chapter.

In response to various research abuses in the United States, especially in medical research, the U.S. government, in 1979, wrote a document titled "Ethical Principles and Guidelines for the Protection of Human Subjects," commonly known as the **Belmont Report**. The Belmont Report serves as the cornerstone of ethical principles upon which federal regulations for the protection of human research participants are based. Our human subject protection guidelines are based on the three principles of the Belmont Report: respect for persons, beneficence/nonmaleficence, and justice (Murphy & Dingwall, 2001).

How Do We Follow Research Ethics and Ethical Guidelines?

Respect for Persons and Informed Consent

The first principle, **respect for persons**, says that research participants should be treated as autonomous agents—that means they are independent, self-governing, capable of making decisions for themselves as long as they are given sufficient information to make those decisions. This principle forms the basis for **informed consent**. In the consent process, people are to be given full information about the research, both risks and benefits, and allowed to make the decision for themselves if they will participate. A proper consent form should include the participant's right to withdraw from the study, the focus of the study and methods to be employed, statements surrounding confidentiality, and a signature of both the researcher and the participant (Creswell, 2007). The informed consent process assumes that the research participant is competent to consent—that, if he or she is given all relevant information, he or she will be able to comprehend the information and be able to agree to participate in a voluntary manner free from coercion. As part of the informed consent process, the researcher must disclose all relevant information to potential participants, including the purpose of the study; the nature of the research procedure; reasonable alternatives to the proposed intervention (if the intervention provides a service or treatment such as in medical research); and any risks, benefits, or uncertainties of the intervention. The process also insists that participants can change their mind and withdraw at any time, which can be more than a little nerve-wracking in long-term ethnographic research in which the entire research study could be thrown out if the participant changes his or her mind. However, withdrawing from research is always the participant's prerogative. We have included a sample consent form in the appendix of this textbook.

There are a few exceptions to required informed consent, however. If the research could not possibly be carried out with informed consent, and if the risk to participants is minimal, it might be ethical to waive informed consent. An example in a communication studies project might be one in which participants are being interviewed about illegal drug use. In this case, signing a consent form (and putting their name on a legal document if their participation implies admission to drug use) would be more harmful than a waiver of consent. Typically, the researcher would obtain verbal consent, but not signed consent. Sometimes, in an ethnographic research study, researchers are observing individuals in public places in which it would be impossible to obtain consent from everyone present. If the research was being conducted in a place sufficiently public that there is no reasonable expectation of privacy, consent is usually not required or obtained. Examples of this type of research might include studying anonymous chat room communication or observing nonverbal communication (from a distance) at a shopping mall. Of course, even if consent can be waived, this doesn't mean that the researcher is exempt from treating participants in an ethical manner.

There are also other types of communication studies research that are exempt from obtaining informed consent. Informed consent is, obviously, obtained from people who are research participants, typically defined as a living individual about whom a researcher obtains information through an interaction with the person. A research participant might also need to give consent to let the researcher have access to identifiable private information (i.e., medical records), or to let a third-party participant give information about him or her (e.g., if you are interviewing a doctor about a patient, the patient has to give consent to let the doctor talk about him or her) (Mertens & Ginsberg, 2008). In other words, when a communication scholar writes a rhetorical analysis of Barack Obama's latest speech, since Obama is a public figure, his speech is considered a public event, and if the researcher has not obtained that data through interaction with Obama, informed consent is neither possible nor necessary. Similarly, analysis of diaries or letters of a deceased historical figure does not require informed consent. However, analysis of letters from a person who is still alive might—or might not—require informed consent, as might a study of Internet blogs or videos posted to Facebook or MySpace, if that study uses information in a way that identifies the author of the blog or video. In fact, the proliferation of blogs and other Internet-based communication raises new ethical considerations. Many scholars now say that if information is posted to an online community that is password protected, it should be considered private rather than public information (Parry, 2011). Many communication scholars are currently debating the issues of consent, confidentiality, and anonymity in online environments, and not all agree on what Internet-based information is public and what information is not.

In fact, the use of online information as data is a hot button right now. A 2011 article in the *Chronicle of Higher Education* (Parry, 2011) reported on the use by Harvard sociologists of 1,700 Facebook profiles of students at their university. On the "pro" side, researchers say that the research they are doing can lead to important social information about culture and communication and that steps were taken to minimize the risk of privacy violations. On the "con" side, critics of this research say that deceptive practices were used to access the Facebook information in the first place (research assistants added in people who had set restrictive privacy settings but were their own "friends" so available to them), and when the researchers shared the database of information with other researchers, the students' privacy was not sufficiently protected. Outside people were able to figure out who some of the people were by comparing information from the Facebook profiles (hometown and major, for example) with the Harvard student database. Critics further say that the fact that people whose information was included were not informed of the project and didn't give consent is a breach of research ethics. Certainly, it's unclear whether information posted online in such settings is considered public or private information, but we suggest you always make your decision on the side of caution.

Therefore, we think there really is a bottom line issue here—if the information is publically available (published someplace, including online), and if there is not a reasonable expectation of confidentiality, you should obtain consent if possible, cite appropriately at all times, and maintain ethical standards when using the information. If the research participant can be identified by you, regardless of whether you keep that identification confidential, and if obtaining informed consent is possible, you should obtain it. If it's not possible to obtain consent, you must make sure risks are minimal and participants are treated ethically. Sometimes, this can be accomplished by using aliases, reporting information only in aggregate (combined with other people rather than individually), leaving out identifying information, or otherwise maintaining participant confidentiality when citing Internet-based communication. Of course, researchers must always abide by decisions on consent and exemptions from consent made by their Institutional Research Boards (IRBs).

Third-party information is frequently obtained in health communication research, in which a health-care professional might be asked questions about a patient. In this type of research, consent must be obtained from both the provider and the patient.

Sometimes, simply obtaining informed consent from participants isn't enough. As Ellis's study of fishing villages illustrates, when we are in the field for long periods of time, or when we are researching cultures in which we ourselves participate, we must also be attuned to our relationships with our research participants so that we don't use friendship to obtain information in ways that might be harmful or hurtful to them. As Ellis (2007) stated in musing about her experience, "the problem comes not from being friends with participants but from acting as a friend yet not living up to the obligations of friendship" (p. 10).

vulnerable populations
Persons with diminished autonomy; specifically children, people with cognitive impairments, older adults, people with severe health problems, employees, and students.

There are some potential participants who may not be able to fully decide for themselves if they want to take part in the research. These people are referred to in Human Subjects Protection terms as **vulnerable populations**, and they are defined as "persons with diminished autonomy" (NIH Office of Extramural Research, 2008). Children, people with cognitive impairments, older adults, people with severe health problems, employees, and students are vulnerable populations. Most of the characteristics are obvious, but why would employees and students be vulnerable populations? Both are susceptible to coercion—by employers or professors—to participate, and safeguards must be taken to make sure that their consent is truly optional. Some vulnerable populations, such as children, must be given additional protections in research, such as needing permission of a legal guardian overseeing their care in order to include them in research. However, researchers must give everyone, regardless of diminished autonomy, the opportunity to choose, to the extent they are able, if they want to participate in the research. This might mean that if you want to interview a person with Alzheimer's disease, you would first obtain legal consent from his or her guardian, then obtain **assent**—ask permission of the person with Alzheimer's to conduct the interview just prior to doing so.

assent
Permission obtained from vulnerable individuals allowing themselves to be included as participants in research studies.

There are specific ethical challenges in conducting ethnographic, autoethnographic, and narrative research among certain vulnerable populations. Many autoethnographers have written about relationships with friends or relatives who are deceased. Obviously, it is impossible to obtain consent or assent from a person who is no longer alive, and IRB rules would exempt such studies from IRB oversight since research subjects are not living participants. However, Ellis (2007) maintains that such writing should be held to even higher ethical standards. She reminds us that the dead cannot provide consent nor be libeled, and such research incites positive and negative emotions on behalf of the writer, as well as the audience. She suggests that writing about deceased friends or relatives serve as a memorial to them.

Nonmaleficence and Beneficence

Nonmaleficence (no harm should be done to participants) and **beneficence** (the outcome of research should be positive and beneficial) maintain that research is ethical if the "benefits outweigh the potential for harm" (Murphy & Dingwall, 2001, p. 340). The types of risk-benefit analyses used in biomedical research would be helpful, but this is usually not feasible in communication research. Sometimes, participants may experience emotional or psychological harm that cannot be measured or may be delayed. The greatest risk in ethnography, for example, comes after publication, as a result of what is and what is not printed (Cassell, 1978; Murphy & Dingwall, 2001; Wax & Cassell, 1979). Unlike studies in more quantitatively oriented social science research, anonymity may not be possible in ethnography. It is difficult to gauge a subject's possible feelings of shame or embarrassment due to self-disclosure. To combat this phenomenon, it has been suggested that subjects have an opportunity to share in production of a work or be able to provide a response to printed material. We will discuss this in more detail later in this chapter.

nonmaleficience
No harm should be done to participants.

beneficence
The outcome of research should be positive and beneficial.

The principle of beneficence refers to making efforts to secure the well-being of research participants, or to maximize the possible benefits of the research and minimize its possible harm. The key to this principle is, since all research has both risks and benefits, to make sure they balance. Benefits to research might include a monetary inducement for participation, a relationship with the researcher or other participants, knowledge or education gleaned from participation, or the opportunity to do good for society or receive the esteem of others. The community of science also believes that it is important to make sure that the research is sound and will make a sufficient contribution to the research community that it is worth any risks incurred by the study participant.

The principle of beneficence says that no individual shall be intentionally injured in the course of the research. In communication studies research, we typically don't inflict physical harm on participants, but our research might inflict emotional or social harm, such as embarrassment, shame, or stigma. Our research must always protect a participant's right to privacy through anonymity or confidentiality of responses, unless the participant gives permission to waive confidentiality. **Anonymity** means that no one, including the researcher, can connect the participant's responses with his or her identity. An example of anonymous research is a survey in which participants do not release their names or chat groups in which people don't use their real names. **Confidentiality** means that, although the researcher knows what each participant said (or can find out this information), the participant's identity is kept secret when reporting or writing up the findings. Sometimes, for example, participant confidentiality is ensured by providing aliases in the final report (Creswell, 2007). In all research, participants must be warned that, by many state and federal laws, a researcher must disclose information indicating a risk of harm to others (homicidal thoughts), a risk of harm to themselves (suicidal thoughts), or child or elder abuse. There may be instances in a research setting that require the interviewer/observer to report illegal activity divulged by a participant (Creswell, 2007).

There are times, especially when conducting qualitative research such as narrative or autoethnographic research, when anonymity and confidentiality are not possible or desirable. If this is the case, participants must be told this up front, and the researcher should follow two other related principles: Do no harm when publishing the results, and be attentive to causing discomfort in the study. There are times when a research finding *could* be reported but *must not* be reported if doing so could cause harm to a study participant.

Most researchers consider it highly unethical to deceive a participant for the purpose of gaining information, such as gathering information secretively (except when you are observing public behavior, as we discussed earlier) (Creswell, 2007). However, if an extreme instance makes it necessary to deceive the participants, you must lessen the adverse effects from the **deception** by, after the fact, dehoaxing them (tell them what you've done), debriefing them (discussing the research with them), and desensitizing them (if they have acquired negative information about themselves in the course of the research, make sure they know it is not true).

While we are rightly concerned about our research participants, we also might safeguard against potential harm done to researchers themselves. Researchers can also be harmed by improper boundaries between themselves and their participants, and many qualitative researchers report ethical uneasiness with the levels of interpersonal intimacy they develop with study participants whom they come to care about and feel protective of. Qualitative researchers also have to balance their own self-disclosure to participants in interview situations. Some researchers report feelings of vulnerability, guilt, and emotional

anonymity
No one, including the researcher, can connect a participant's responses with his or her identity.

confidentiality
The identity of participants is kept secret when researchers report or write up their findings.

deception
A violation of the right to informed consent that may sometimes mislead participants as to the study purpose.

exhaustion resulting from their time in the field. Other researchers not directly involved with participants, but studying data about sensitive or disturbing topics, report experiencing emotional problems resulting from their research (Dickson-Swift, James, Kippen, & Liamputtong, 2007). Dickson-Swift and colleagues (2007) suggest that researchers vulnerable to these challenges utilize a support network of colleagues and researchers with whom to debrief their experiences.

Justice

The last tenet of the Belmont Report is the principle of **justice**. This principle takes a slightly different point of view of research participants, because it looks at who is included as research participants and who is excluded. This principle says that all classifications of people (race, ethnicity, gender, age, etc.) should be equally subjected to risks and benefits of the research. Certainly, including only people of one race in research that subjects them to harm is not just. However, excluding people of a certain race in research that might help them is equally unjust. Risks and benefits should be distributed fairly and without bias, and people should be included or excluded in research only for reasons that have to do with the research question or hypothesis.

> **justice**
> *All classifications of people (race, ethnicity, gender, age, etc.) should be equally subjected to the risks and benefits of research, and people should be included or excluded only for reasons that have to do with the research question or hypothesis.*

Again, medical experiments provide the most obvious examples of ethical breaches in this area. Bayer and Tadd (2000) reviewed research protocols of 155 medical studies that were relevant to elderly people and found that over half excluded people over a certain age without justification, failing to test medical interventions on sections of the very populations for which they were intended! In social science research, similar breaches can occur. Becker-Blease and Freyd (2006) argue that many policy decisions on child abuse are made on insufficient information because researchers are reluctant to interview survivors of abuse, for fear of causing emotional harm. They suggest that researchers are inflicting even more harm on abuse survivors by inadequately studying this experience.

Another consideration related to justice is including participants with physical or cognitive impairments in research, especially those participants whose impairments may affect their communication abilities, such as in the case of people with brain damage or neurological disease (Paterson & Scott-Findlay, 2002). It's a challenge to appropriately include people with communication impairments in research while overcoming those very impairments in the data collection process. In such research, it is common for proxies, such as nurses and family members, to assist in facilitating an interview. While the service of a proxy can be helpful, the proxy's own bias in making decisions for the subject is often unavoidable. Informed consent procedures may need to be modified so the research participant can understand the instructions. Researchers may also need to be attuned to participant distress, participant fatigue, misrepresentation of research questions, and irregular or conflicting responses from the participant.

In regard to justice, when designing a study and analyzing and writing results, researchers are dissuaded from prioritizing the perspective of the elite or privileged while downplaying the views of the less fortunate (Guba & Lincoln, 1989; Marshall, 1985; Murphy & Dingwall, 2001; Sandelowski, 1986; Silverman, 1985). It is important to accurately depict all parties involved (Murphy & Dingwall, 2001).

Including Participants in Co-Constructed Research

legitimation
The question of who can represent another person in narrative writing.

representation
Fully understanding the lived experiences of research participants and including the multiple realities, interpretations, experiences, and voices emergent from all individuals and all angles.

member checks
The process of providing study participants with the research findings, and giving them the opportunity to voice agreement or disagreement with the research as reported.

Researchers, especially those following the interpretive paradigm (see Chapter 2), are also concerned about issues of **legitimation** (Who can speak for these people?) and **representation** (How can you speak for these people?). Representation refers to fully understanding the lived experiences of research participants and including the multiple realities, interpretations, experiences, and voices emergent from all individuals and all angles. One challenge is to ensure that the people and context studied are adequately and sufficiently represented, and that rigorous attempts are made to include their own voices and interpretations. Methods that directly include—and help researchers more fully understand—participants' voices and interpretations might include interactive techniques such as interactive interviewing, interactive focus groups, co-constructed narratives, or close observation over a long period of time (which we will discuss later in this book), which allow study participants to give their own accounts of their own experiences. Other advantages of coauthored methods include the possible avoidance of obtaining consent (since participants are also researchers), alleviation of concerns about offending subjects, and less likelihood of research participants changing their minds about participating (Denzin, 2003; Ellis, 2007).

Qualitative researchers should also ensure that they are representing the voice of their participants by conducting **member checks** at the conclusion of their study. Member checks consist of a process of providing study participants with the research findings and giving them the opportunity to voice agreement or disagreement with the research as reported.

Social science researchers have been increasingly concerned about the moral ethics of conducting research among traditionally marginalized and stigmatized groups of people in ways that might exploit or take advantage of them. Some feminist researchers argue that proper interpretation can only be achieved by cooperation between the researcher and participant. Many feminist ethnographers, and others, subscribe to methods of reciprocity in researcher–participant relationships (Murphy & Dingwall, 2001). The traditional researcher–participant relationship is one of hegemonic power, in which the researcher holds power over the people he or she is studying, simply by virtue of the fact that the researcher is in charge of the study, the methodology, the analysis, and dissemination of the findings. In addition, in more traditional forms of research, researchers, in essence, speak for the participants, in effect silencing their voice and assuming a professional stance in which the researcher's opinion of the participant's point of view might be presumed to be more valid than the participant's own opinions. In this context of "narrative privilege" (Adams, 2008, p. 180), researchers hold what's called "legitimate power" over non-researchers in their narratives. In other words, stories with stronger perceived cultural value—traditional researchers' stories—are considered to be more important or more valid than other types of stories—stories of people from marginalized groups. In addition, the narrative skills and ability traditional researchers have also hold legitimacy over people who cannot write or access textual forms.

More researchers are moving toward equalizing this power differential in their relationship with research participants by making a conscious effort to include the voice and feedback of all system of care participants, and by seeking to understand participants' own meanings and interpretations and using these interpretations of reality rather than their own. More recently developed methodologies represent multiple voices in a collaborative, co-constructed manner that let research participants have a say in how the research is conducted by exerting or influencing control over the conversations. **Participatory action research** is an example of one methodology that attempts to break down power relationships between the researcher and the researched by letting the stakeholders define the problem and work toward solutions; inviting participants to formulate the original questions, design the methodology, facilitate the sessions, and lead the analysis efforts; and moving the research into the community. In a study by Ozer and Wright (2012) participatory action research was used to examine whether student led participatory research increased autonomy in two urban secondary schools. It was suggested that this type of research led to unique interactions between students and adult faculty and expanded areas of student influence within these schools.

participatory action research
An example of one methodology that attempts to break down power relationships between the researcher and the researched by letting the stakeholders define the problem and work toward solutions; inviting participants to formulate the original questions, design the methodology, facilitate the sessions, and lead the analysis efforts; and moving the research into the community.

Who Oversees Research Ethics? IRBs

Most academic research is overseen by university IRBs (Institutional Research Boards). Simply put, IRBs act as gatekeepers to research conducted by researchers affiliated with their university. They have a three-fold purpose: to protect the university from legal repercussions of conducting research deemed unethical, to protect the university from financial (and legal) sanctions imposed by the federal government and other funders on research deemed unethical, and to protect research participants from unethical practices in research. IRB board members usually consist of a cross-section of university faculty, and might also include legal and administrative representatives. All faculty—and some student—research must be submitted to the IRB for approval before being conducted. Even if the IRB will consider the research to be exempt from human subjects protection, most university IRBs want to make that ruling themselves. Student research conducted as part of a class project is usually exempt from IRB oversight because the students are considered to be under the oversight of their professor. However, if the research may later be submitted for publication, since peer-reviewed journals usually require IRB oversight, IRBs usually recommend that it be submitted to them anyway. Student research conducted for thesis or dissertation purposes is usually required to be submitted to the IRB.

Even if you are not conducting research under the authority of a university, you might still be subject to IRB oversight. Hospitals, research institutes, community agencies, and other organizations that conduct research frequently have their own IRBs.

Often, IRBs approve research projects quickly and efficiently. Criticism with IRBs and the IRB process occur when they don't. IRBs, at times, require researchers to change their method or procedures, and some researchers see this as a threat to academic freedom and a form of censorship, especially since most university faculty are required to conduct and publish research (Lewis, 2008; Lincoln, 2000). Critics of IRBs and other research gatekeepers claim that such censorship serves to suppress more innovative forms of research (Lincoln, 2000; Lincoln & Cannella, 2004).

▼ **How Do We Maintain Ethics through all Research Phases?**

Ethical considerations in research do not stop when you are done with data collection—ethical researchers make ethical decisions at every stage of the research process, from study design to publication of findings. Booth, Colomb, and Williams (1995, pp. 255–256) address ethical decision making in all stages of the research process in their "7-commandments" of ethical research. They say that ethical researchers:

1. Do not steal by plagiarizing or claiming the results of others.
2. Do not lie by misreporting sources or by inventing results.
3. Do not destroy sources and data for those who follow.
4. Do not submit data whose accuracy they have reason to question.
5. Do not conceal objections that they cannot rebut.
6. Do not caricature those with opposing views or deliberately state their views in a way they would reject.
7. Do not write their reports in a way that deliberately makes it difficult for readers to understand them, nor do they simplify that which is legitimately complex.

To borrow from the NRA's (National Rifle Association) familiar saying about gun control: "Research doesn't harm, researchers do." Research findings, both qualitative and quantitative, can be manipulated, misinterpreted, and misrepresented. Despite the desire of quantitative positivist researchers to remain objective, researchers of all paradigms should admit that it is impossible to remain completely objective in any research. Quantitative researchers address this dilemma by designing studies that are as objective as possible. Qualitative researchers, in contrast, address it by admitting their subjectivity, and taking that into account when analyzing their results (Hewitt, 2007). All researchers use rigorous, acceptable, analytical methods to determine what their data means. Quantitative researchers use appropriate statistical and systematic techniques to analyze their data. Qualitative researchers take into account interpretation and context as they acknowledge their role in the construction of knowledge (Hewitt, 2007).

So What?

In summary, it is our responsibility as a researcher to ensure that the study is properly designed, scientifically sound, and yields valid results; we do what we say we're going to do; the study is approved by IRB and conducted according to protocol; informed consent is appropriately obtained; the rights and welfare of the participants are monitored throughout the study; the risks and benefits of the research are positively balanced; participant anonymity and confidentiality are appropriately maintained; and all participants—including those from underprivileged and marginalized populations—have an opportunity to have their voices and interpretations fully represented. The bottom line: Researchers are accountable and must show respect to colleagues in their profession and society at large.

Glossary

Anonymity
No one, including the researcher, can connect a participant's responses with his or her identity.

Assent
Permission obtained from individuals allowing themselves to be included as participants in research studies.

Belmont Report
This document serves as the cornerstone of ethical principles upon which federal regulations for the protection of human research participants are based.

Beneficence
The outcome of research should be positive and beneficial.

Confidentiality
The identity of participants is kept secret when researchers report or write up their findings.

Deception
A violation of the right to informed consent that may sometimes mislead participants as to the study purpose.

Ethical research
Research that is designed and conducted validly, reliably, legitimately, and representatively, and protects a research participant's rights.

Human subjects protection
Ethical research rules that refer to the guidelines that are followed to ensure the protection of people (participants) being studied.

Informed consent
This process assumes that the research participant is competent to consent—that, if he or she is given all relevant information, he or she will be able to comprehend the information and be able to agree to participate in a voluntary manner free from coercion.

Justice
All classifications of people (race, ethnicity, gender, age, etc.) should be equally subjected to the risks and benefits of research, and people should be included or excluded only for reasons that have to do with the research question or hypothesis.

Legitimation
The question of who can represent another person in narrative writing.

Member checks
The process of providing study participants with the research findings, and giving them the opportunity to voice agreement or disagreement with the research as reported.

Nonmaleficence
No harm should be done to participants.

Nuremberg Code
The first set of principles outlining professional ethics for medical researchers, which forms the basis for today's research ethics codes. It specifically required voluntary consent among research participants, and was the first international standard for the conduct of research.

Participatory action research

An example of one methodology that attempts to break down power relationships between the researcher and the researched by letting the stakeholders define the problem and work toward solutions; inviting participants to formulate the original questions, design the methodology, facilitate the sessions, and lead the analysis efforts; and moving the research into the community.

Relational ethics

The value placed on the relationships between researchers and the people they are researching.

Representation

Fully understanding the lived experiences of research participants and including the multiple realities, interpretations, experiences, and voices emergent from all individuals and all angles.

Research ethics

The specific principles, rules, guidelines, and norms of research-related behavior that a research community has decided are proper, fair, and appropriate.

Respect for persons

Research participants should be treated as autonomous agents—that means they are independent, self-governing, and capable of making decisions for themselves as long as they are given sufficient information to make those decisions.

Vulnerable populations

Persons with diminished autonomy; specifically children, people with cognitive impairments, older adults, people with severe health problems, employees, and students.

References

Adams, T. E. (2008). A review of narrative ethics. *Qualitative Inquiry, 14*(2), 175–194.

Annas, G. J., & Grodin, M. A. (1995). *The Nazi doctors and the Nuremberg Code: Human rights in human experimentation.* New York: Oxford University Press.

Bayer, A., & Tadd, W. (2000). Unjustified exclusion of elderly people from studies submitted to research ethics committee for approval: Descriptive study. *BMJ [British Medical Journal], 321,* 992– 993.

Becker-Blease, K. A., & Freyd, J. J. (2006). Research participants telling the truth about their lives: The ethics of asking and not asking about abuse. *American Psychologist, 61*(3), 218–226.

Booth, W. C., Colomb, G. G., & Williams, J. M. (1995). *The craft of research.* Chicago: University of Chicago Press.

Cassell, J. (1978). Risk and benefit to subjects of field-work. *American Sociologist, 13,* 134–143.

Creswell, J. W. (2007). *Qualitative inquiry & research design* (2nd ed.). Thousand Oaks, CA: Sage.

Denzin, N. (2003). *Performance ethnography: Critical pedagogy and the politics of culture.* Thousand Oaks, CA: Sage.

Dickson-Swift, V., James, E. L., Kippen, S., & Liamputtong, P. (2007). Doing sensitive research: What challenges do qualitative researchers face? *Qualitative Research, 7*(3), 327–353.

Edgar, H., & Rothman, D. J. (1995). The Institutional Review Board and beyond: Future challenges to the ethics of human experimentation. *The Milbank Quarterly, 73*(4), 489–506.

Ellis, C. (1986). *Fisher folk: Two communities on Chesapeake Bay.* Lexington, KY: University Press of Kentucky.

Ellis, C. (2007). Telling secrets, revealing lives: Relational ethics in research with intimate others. *Qualitative Inquiry, 13,* 3–29.

Guba, E.G., & Lincoln, Y. S. (1989). *Fourth generation evaluation.* Newbury Park, CA: Sage.

Hewitt, J. (2007). Ethical components of researcher-researched relationships in qualitative interviewing. *Qualitative Health Research, 27*(8), 1149–1159.

Humphrey, L. (1970). *Tearoom trade: Impersonal sex in public places.* London: Duckworth.

Kelman, H. C. (1967). Human use of human subjects: The problem of deception in social psychological experiments. *Psychological Bulletin, 67*(1), 1–11.

Kimmel, A. J. (1988). *Ethics and values in applied social research.* Thousand Oaks, CA: Sage.

Kotarba, J. A. (1979). The accomplishment of intimacy in the jail visiting room. *Qualitative Sociology, 2*, 80–103.

Krugman, S. (1971). Experiments at the Willowbrook State School. *Lancet, 1*(7702), 749.

Lewis, M. (2008). New strategies of control: Academic freedom and research ethics boards. *Qualitative Inquiry, 14*, 684– 699.

Lincoln, Y. S. (2000). Institutional review boards and methodological conservatism: The challenge to and from phenomenological paradigms. In N. K. Denzin & Y. S. Lincoln (Eds.), *The Sage handbook of qualitative research* (pp. 165–181). Thousand Oaks, CA: Sage.

Lincoln, Y. S., & Cannella, G. S. (2004). Qualitative research, power, and the radical right. *Qualitative Inquiry, 10*(2), 175– 201.

Marshall, C. (1985). Appropriate criteria of the trustworthiness and goodness for qualitative research on educational organizations. *Quality and Quantity, 19*, 353–373.

Mertens, D. M., & Ginsberg, P. (2008). *The handbook of social research ethics.* Thousand Oaks, CA: Sage.

Murphy, E., & Dingwall, R. (2001). The ethics of ethnography. In P. Atkinson, A. Coffey, S. Delamont, J. Lofland, & L. Lofland (Eds.), *Handbook of ethnography* (pp. 339–351). London: Sage.

NIH Office of Extramural Research. (2008). Retrieved May 25, 2009, from http://phrp.nihtraining.com/users/login.php

Ozer, E. J. & Wright, D. (2012). Beyond school spirit: The effects of youth-led participatory action research in two urban high schools. *Journal of Research on Adolescence*, doi: 10.1111/j.1532-7795.2012.00780.x

Parry, M. (2011, July 15). Harvard researchers accused of breaching students' privacy: Social-network project shows promise and peril of doing social science online. *The Chronicle of Higher Education*, pp. A1, A8–A11.

Paterson, B., & Scott-Findlay, S. (2002). Critical issues in interviewing people with traumatic brain injury. *Qualitative Health Research, 12*(3), 399–409.

Sandelowski, M. (1986). The problem of rigor in qualitative research. *Advances in Nursing Science, 8*, 27–37.

Silverman, D. (1985). *Qualitative methodology and sociology.* Aldershot: Gower.

Thomas, S. B., & Quinn, S. C. (1991). The Tuskegee Syphilis Study, 1932 to 1972: Implications for HIV education and AIDS risk education programs in the black community. *American Journal of Public Health, 81*(11), 1498–1505.

Wax, M., & Cassell, J. (1979). Fieldwork, ethics and politics: The wider context. In M. Wax and J. Cassell (Eds.), *Federal regulations: Ethical issues and social research* (pp. 85–102). Boulder, CO: Westview.

PREPARING TO CONDUCT RESEARCH

PART **2**

RESEARCH QUESTIONS AND HYPOTHESES

6

CHAPTER OUTLINE

KEY TERMS

Conceptual definition

Fact pattern

Hypothesis

Null hypothesis

Operational definition

Research question

CHAPTER OBJECTIVES

1. To understand the purpose of research questions
2. To explain the different types of research questions
3. To understand research hypotheses
4. To learn how to evaluate research questions
5. To consider the boundaries of research questions and hypotheses

▼ # How Do You Design Good Quality Research through Appropriate Questions and Hypotheses?

If we do our job as instructors and mentors, by the time you graduate, you will know maybe the answers to some questions, but most importantly—how to ask good questions (Miller & Nicholson, 1976). In this chapter, you will consider the role of objectives, questions, and hypotheses construction in good research design. Your study objectives, the questions you ask, and the hypotheses you write are grounded in metatheory (see Chapter 2) and collectively contribute to your understanding of communication theory. In fact, this chapter will focus on research objectives, questions, and hypotheses and how they are driven by our metatheoretical consideration, and subsequently, how these research objectives, questions, and hypotheses drive the methodological choices we make in research design.

▼ # What Are the Functions of Theory, Research Objectives, Research Questions, and Hypotheses?

Recall from Chapter 2 that in the deductive paradigm, research questions and hypotheses derive from theory. Theory, research questions, and hypotheses allow us to organize and summarize information, while simultaneously focusing our attention on important questions or ideas. They also give us a framework for knowledge; and they function to explain, predict, and/or control. Specifically, theory, research questions, and hypotheses help to explain or make sense of reality, essentially answering the question of "Why?" (see Barnlund, 1968; Bross, 1953; Dance, 1982; Hall & Lidzey, 1970; Hawes, 1975; Kaplan, 1964; Kuhn, 1970; Littlejohn, 1996; and Poole, 1990). Questions and hypotheses also allow us to predict or forecast what will happen, essentially telling us what to be on the lookout for. In terms of control, once we understand how a process works, to some extent it allows us to control it. Ultimately, the primary function of research questions, hypotheses, and theory is heuristic, allowing us to generate new knowledge, learning, and understanding. Notice that under this paradigm, research questions and hypotheses are built on existing theory—either extending, testing, or explicating a theory. This type of research falls under the positivist paradigm, using deductive reasoning, and researchers who conduct research in this paradigm believe that reality is fixed, measurable, controllable, orderly, and objective.

Also recall that research can be conducted under the inductive model, in which researchers seek to answer more open-ended questions and end with, perhaps, a theory, or a deeper understanding of a phenomenon. This model of research falls under the interpretive paradigm, and researchers who subscribe to this metatheory tend to believe that reality is subjective, constructed, and chaotic. Note that theory—in terms of providing an organization or framework for knowledge, or understanding of reality—has its place in both paradigms and types of research.

Theories begin with either a **fact pattern** or a question. A fact pattern is a factual relationship occurring repeatedly. A good example of a fact pattern in Communication Studies is what we call *divergence* or *convergence*. Have you ever noticed how when you are in a conversation with someone you like, or perhaps someone you need to impress, you adjust your style of speaking to match hers? This is an example of convergence. What about when you are in a conversation with someone you feel dissimilar to or dislike in some way? Do you tend to match him? Research suggests you will maintain your own style of communicating. This is an example of divergence. This is the basis for Communication Accommodation Theory (CAT). Giles and his colleagues have studied CAT in a variety of contexts, including how we adjust our communication behaviors when interacting with the elderly (McCann & Giles, 2006). A researcher with a positivist bent might design a study to see if CAT affects the therapeutic value of medical communication. A researcher with an interpretivist bent might instead look at medical communication in a more open-ended sense, and might in the end use CAT to help explain what they found in their study.

fact pattern
A factual relationship occurring repeatedly.

Theories might also begin with a question—a search for an answer to why something happens. As Miller and Nicholson (1976) suggest, "People incessantly ask questions" (p. 10). Regardless of the reason why people ask questions, we are going to assume for our purposes here, questions are asked when people are sincerely searching for answers. This search for answers, via questions posed, is really at the heart of the process of inquiry, the search for understanding. In our case, we will focus on the process of communication inquiry, but that does not mean the process of writing and examining research questions we will discuss is inappropriate for other forums of inquiry. However, what is unique to our approach is our substantive vantage point; we are interested in human interaction via communication.

What Are Research Objectives? ▼

Research objectives represent the reasons you give for undertaking your own research project. They are the step between your research topic, your "I wonder if . . . " musing, and your research questions or hypothesis. When you are given an assignment to conduct a research study, the first thing you will do is determine your general area of inquiry. Several of the previous chapters mentioned several possible areas of inquiry in our field of study: organizational communication, health communication, interpersonal communication, mass media, or public relations. From your general area of inquiry, you would need to narrow your focus to a slightly more specific topic for your research. We suggest you start with something that interests you most—keeping it related to communication, of course. You should work on narrowing your topic until you have something specific enough to build a research study on it. Narrow it by adding modifying words and phrases to each of your topic ideas. For example, if you are interested in the general field of health communication, you might decide you are very interested in patient-provider communication. That's good, but not specific enough. Let's add some modifiers: What types of patients? How about terminally ill patients. What types of healthcare providers? How about physicians. What types of communication? How about giving the bad news about their terminal diagnosis. Ahh, so *now* we see it! You're interested in studying how physicians give terminal diagnoses to people with terminal illness. Now, *that's* a research topic!

Now, let's turn it into a research objective. Research objectives are your statements of what you want to get out of this research. For many studies, your research objective can be determined by filling in the blanks of this statement: "I am studying _____, because I want to find out [who/what/when/where/whether/how] _____ is, in order to understand _____" (see Booth, Colomb, & Williams, 1995). For the example above, your research objective may be stated as, "I am studying patient-provider communication, because I want to find out how physicians give terminal diagnoses to patients, in order to understand the different ways to break bad medical news." Notice that we added a new part: "in order to understand the different ways to break bad medical news." This last section answers a significance or "so what" element. All research studies should connect to a bigger picture in some way. In the example above, you might be developing a theory about terminal diagnosis communication, or you might be testing an existing theory within this specific context. You might be understanding something that's important to society, or you might be describing something that will have public policy implications, or you might be measuring something that will have financial ramifications. There are lots of ways your study should answer the "so what" question, but you should know—up front—the significance of your own research.

Research objectives are frequently turned into research questions or hypotheses, but qualitative researchers also frequently stop at the research objective stage when designing their qualitative study. Countless qualitative studies simply have one of these two objectives: to understand _____ or to describe _____. In some types of qualitative research, such research objectives are actually unstated. For example, in an autoethnographic narrative (we'll explain more about this in Chapter 14), Davis (2005) wrote a story about her experience with the last week of her mother's life. The unstated objective of that research was to describe that experience. Green's 2002 study of having a child with a disability is a good example of qualitative research that had the (unstated) objective to understand or describe an experience. In her paper, she says that:

> *This work offers a glimpse into the emotional and social experience of disability through the lens of my own experience of mothering a child with severe cerebral palsy. (p. 21)*

Johnson's 2002 essay (textual analysis) on the performance of black American gospel music by white Australian gospel choirs states his objectives in the abstract, as the objectives of his essay are to prove two points—his conclusions, in fact:

> *This essay examines how the medium of gospel music facilitates a dialogic performance of "blackness." This essay also addresses the politics of appropriation, highlighting the ways in which Australians explain their interest in and performance of gospel music and the ironies that underlie these explanations. (p. 99)*

What metatheoretical perspectives (see Chapter 2) do you think these researchers tend toward? Researchers "seeking to understand or describe" reality tend toward the interpretivist tradition. They are using the open-ended study objective (rather than the more specific research question and even more precise hypothesis, to be explained in the next section) to study a reality they believe to be chaotic and subjective.

How Do You Ask Research Questions?

What is a **research question**? Research questions are questions scholars ask about the way things work. Just as research can be basic or applied (see Chapter 1), research questions can be either basic or applied. In our field, most research questions are about the nature of communication or about the relationship between two variables. We'll talk more about variables in Chapter 7, but for now you should know that when you are stating a communication research question that relates two variables, at least one of the two variables must be a communication variable, because we are scholars of the process of communication.

research question
Questions scholars ask about the way things work.

While research *objectives* are used by communication researchers to design open-ended research about a topic, such as with some types of qualitative research, other communication researchers pose research questions when they want to find out certain information about a topic but don't know enough about a topic to make a prediction, or when they want to understand or describe communication behavior. When you ask a research question, it is simply a question, a curiosity, as though you really do not know what to expect, or what will happen. Research questions are good starting points for new areas of inquiry.

Fundamentally, a communication research question must be concerned with communication, must be empirical, which means it can be experienced and is practical and/or pragmatic, and must have some level of specificity. Typically, research questions ask about the *who, what, when, where,* and *how* of communication. They ask about: *Who* is impacted by, or involved in, this communication act; *what* does this communication act look like; *what* are the parts of the communication act; *what* are the categories of the communication act; *what* is the outcome of the communication act; *when* do the parts of the communication act occur; *where* does the communication act occur—what is the environment and context of the communication; *how* does this communication act relate to other things (society, community, power, culture, outcomes, etc.); and/or *how* does this communication act happen?

Consider some examples of research questions about the nature of communication. How much violence is depicted during Saturday morning cartoons? What persuasive techniques are used on late night infomercials? How do couples use touch to signal relationship status in public? All of these questions are concerned with some basic question about communication behavior.

Now consider some examples of research questions exploring the relationship between two variables (remember one must be a communication variable). Do children who watch a lot of cartoons behave more aggressively on the playground? Are couples who touch less in public as happy as couples who touch more in public? How have persuasive techniques in late night infomercials changed over time? Remember, research questions are simply questions that scholars are seeking answers to; there is not a statement or assertion of what will happen, just a question the research attempts to answer.

The research question is symbolized as the capital letters RQ, followed with a numeric subscript (RQ_1). The numeric subscript refers to the number of the research question in a particular study. In a complicated study, you may have several research questions and numbering allows us to easily keep track of what research question is being analyzed and discussed. Here's an example of a research question from a quantitative study conducted by Segrin, Powell, Givertz, and Brackin (2003):

> RQ_1: Do members of dating couples exhibit symptoms of depression that are indicative of emotional contagion?

And, here's an example of research questions from a qualitative study conducted by Davis (2009):

> RQ_1: What reality does hospice construct for patients and families through communication?

> RQ_2: How does hospice use communication to construct this reality?

Notice that the first stated RQ, for the Segrin et al. 2003 study reflects positivist tendencies, toward a reality that is observable and measurable, while the RQs for the Davis 2009 research reflect interpretivist tendencies, toward a reality that is constructed and subjective.

Types of Research Questions about Communication

Questions of Definition. One common type of research question is a question of definition. There is some debate as to whether questions of definition are research questions, because they are not empirical questions with a definitive answer. However, these types of questions are important to the process of communication inquiry, so we will discuss them here. In fact, in our field, we don't have to go far to recognize that, perhaps, this is the fundamental question of our field. How exactly do you define communication? Often in introductory communication courses, we debate all the possible forms and definitions of communication and what constitutes communication and what does not. In fact, most students of communication are familiar with Watzlawick, Beavin Bavelas, and Jackson (1967), whose statement, "one cannot not communicate" (p. 51) provides ongoing debate and ardor. In fact, because the name of our field is so difficult to agree upon, most textbooks as a matter of course (including ours) stipulate their own definition for the term *communication*, so as to alleviate some of the likelihood of misunderstanding. This is true for other types of questions that concern Communication Studies. Consider the question, "What communication patterns cause conflict in marriage?" Before you even address this question, you must agree upon the definition of *conflict*. Many scholars have attempted to define conflict in organizations and relationships (i.e., Gottman & Notarius, 2004; Pondy, 1967; Schmidt & Kochan, 1972).

We should note that questions of definition are an important part of the process of communication inquiry (Miller & Nicholson, 1976). We are always concerned with the way in which we define the concepts we desire to study. In fact, we will discuss this at length in Chapter 7. However, it is necessary to understand that if you are unclear about your definition, your research questions will suffer, and as a result your research design will encounter problems. Writing a good research question is more difficult and arduous than it seems at first glance. If you don't believe us, trying writing one!

Questions of Fact. Another common type of research questions are questions of fact. Much communication scholarship focuses on questions of fact, wherein you ask questions regarding what has or will happen. These questions concern what is going on in the world. For example, "Will your instructor give you a pop quiz next class period over your reading?" As you know, there is, in fact, an answer to that question that has yet to be determined. Interestingly, these types of questions can only be answered in the known external world. This should remind you of the metatheoretical considerations we discussed in Chapter 2. Doesn't it sound like an objectivist epistemology? These questions can be confirmed or disconfirmed, essentially locating an affirmative or negative answer; a simple yes or no. For example, "Do men interrupt in conversations more than women?" This is a question of fact, with a simple yes or no answer. As we pointed out earlier, the question itself drives the decisions scholars make about how to design and conduct research. If you return to your pop quiz example, how can you determine the answer to your question, in other words, how do you research the answer? Well, the easiest way is to attend the next research methods class period and observe whether your teacher administers a pop quiz. How could you find the answer to your question about who interrupts in conversations more, women or men? Well, again, observation would be a likely candidate. It is unlikely that you could ascertain the correct answer utilizing surveys, for instance.

So far, the questions of facts we posed are quite simple. We don't want to suggest all questions of fact are so simple, because they can be much more complicated. Take for instance, the following question: "Are fear appeals effective instruments of persuasion?" If you have already taken a persuasion course, you know this question is much more involved than it initially appears. Other message components must be considered as potential caveats to this question: message source, previous knowledge, beliefs, and attitudes, as well as personality. So, while this question is a question of fact, a simple yes or no answer is essentially impossible.

Here are two other examples of research questions—these are ones posed in a qualitative study. This research (Kramer, 2004) uses ethnography (see Chapter 14) to look at the dialectical tensions in group communication in a community theatre group. Kramer asks:

RQ₁: What dialectical tensions are experienced by community theater group members as they communicate to produce a group performance?

RQ₂: How do members of a community theater group manage the dialectical tensions through their communication?

Note that both of these questions are questions of fact, even though they are very much open-ended questions based in the interpretivist tradition.

Here is another way to look at research questions. How many observations are necessary to make a valid conclusion about the answer? In the pop quiz example, you need only attend class on the next occasion to answer the question. With the questions about who interrupts more, whether fear appeals work in health messages, or how members of a theater group manage dialectical tensions, the number of observations necessary increase exponentially. So, again, you begin to see that the question you ask drives the research design process, including what methodology is an appropriate choice.

Research questions can ask about a relationship of association ("Do families with a child with a disability experience closed communication?"), or about a relationship of causation ("Does depression in a relational partner affect the number of conversational turns in a communication act?"). We'll talk more about those relationships in the next section and in future chapters.

● ●

▼ What Are Research Hypotheses?

hypothesis
A statement a researcher makes about the relationship between a dependent and an independent variable.

A research hypothesis is used when the researcher knows enough about the topic under study to make a prediction. A **hypothesis** is a statement the researcher makes about the relationship between two variables (a dependent and independent variable). It is often predictive, specifying how two concepts are believed to be related. Most of you are already familiar with the common definition of a hypothesis—an educated guess. And that's exactly what a hypothesis is: an educated guess about what will happen in a relationship between variables.

This educated guess is based upon some previous knowledge and/or scholarship into related ideas. Frequently (since hypotheses fall under the deductive model), your hypothesis is based on a theory you found in your library research. Perhaps, for example, you want to study communication between hospice physicians and their patients. Your library research may have found Spiers's 2002 study on the interpersonal contexts within which care is negotiated between home care nurses and their patients. Spiers identified six communication contexts (territoriality, shared perceptions of the situation, an amicable working relationship, role synchronization, knowledge, and taboo topics) that affect the therapeutic value of the communication, and perhaps you think some of these contexts might be relevant to hospice communication as well. You might write a hypothesis based on this previous research: "When hospice physicians and patients share the same perceptions of the situation, communication is perceived by the patients as being more therapeutic."

The research hypothesis is symbolized by a capital letter H, followed with a numeric subscript (H_1). The numeric subscript refers to the number of the hypothesis in a particular study. In a complicated study, you may have several hypotheses and numbering allows you to easily keep track of what hypothesis is being analyzed and discussed. The symbol and numeric subscript is then followed with a statement concerning how you think the two variables will be related.

Here are some examples from Segrin et al. (2003):

H_1: There will be a negative association between depression and relational quality in dating relationships.

H_2: The poor relational quality associated with depression will be associated with increased loneliness.

Notice that both of these hypotheses have at least two variables: depression and relational quality, and depression and loneliness, respectively. Notice, also, that these Hs reflect positivist tendencies, studying a reality that is believed to be orderly, fixed, objective, observed, and measurable.

Consider these examples:

H_1: The more people watch soap operas, the more extramarital affairs they will have.

H_1: Adolescent males report greater enjoyment of slasher films than do adolescent females.

What are the two variables in each of these hypotheses? For the first hypothesis, the two variables are soap opera viewing and extramarital affairs; in the second hypothesis, the variables are gender and slasher film enjoyment.

Null Hypotheses

Technically, although statistically testing your research hypothesis to see if it's true, you are actually testing whether your hypothesis is *not* true. In other words, the research hypothesis is always contrasted with a **null hypothesis**, which simply says the research hypothesis is wrong. In other words, there is no (null) relationship between the variables that the research predicted. The null hypothesis, when written, is symbolized by a capital letter H, followed with a numeric subscript of zero (H_0). Consider the null hypotheses for the original hypothesis from Segrin, Powell, Givertz, and Brackin (2003):

null hypothesis
A statement that the research hypothesis is wrong. In other words, there is no (null) relationship between the variables that the research predicted.

H_1: There will be a negative association between depression and relational quality in dating relationships.

H_0: There will be *no association* between depression and relational quality in dating relationships.

And,

H_2: The poor relational quality associated with depression will be associated with increased loneliness.

H_0: The poor relational quality associated with depression will *not be associated* with increased loneliness.

Are you getting the idea? Simply substitute in the phrase "no relationship" or "no association" to turn a research hypothesis into a null hypothesis. What are the null hypotheses for these research hypotheses?

H_1: The more people watch soap operas, the more extramarital affairs they will have.

H_1: Adolescent males report greater enjoyment of slasher films than do adolescent females.

The correct answers are as follows:

H_0: There is no relationship between exposure to soap viewing and extramarital affairs.

H_0: Males and females do not report different enjoyment of slasher films.

Although you should be familiar with the concept of the null hypothesis, it is implied from the research hypothesis and is seldom written out in actual research studies. However, as we move toward analysis and statistics, it is imperative that you understand the concept.

Forms of Relationships in Hypotheses

Another important component of understanding research hypotheses is recognizing that the research question specifies the form of the relationship in the hypothesis.

There are two key types of relationship specified in a hypothesis: relationship of association ("associational relationship") and relationship of causation ("causal relationship"). A relationship of association implies that where one variable is found, the other also will be found. For example, the format for a relationship of association in a hypothesis would be: If A, then B (A and B are different variables). An example of a relationship of association would be "interpersonal conversation and friends go together." We're not implying that having friends causes conversation, or that conversation causes a person to have friends, or even that the *more* conversation you have the *more* friends you have. We're just hypothesizing that the two occur together. It's entirely possible that a third variable (high intelligence, perhaps) causes both of these two variables to occur. Or that they co-occur for another reason. We don't know enough to predict cause. We're simply predicting association—that if one happens, the other also tends to happen. If we word our earlier hypothesis as "H_1: People who watch soap operas have extramarital affairs," it is an example of an associational relationship.

A causal relationship implies that one variable causes a change in the direction of the other variable. The format for a relationship of causation in a hypothesis would be: An increase in "A" causes an increase in "B". It could also be: A decrease in "A" causes a decrease in "B"; an increase in "A" causes a decrease in "B"; or a decrease in "A" causes an increase in "B". Or, simply, it could be "A" causes "B". Note that many words can be used in our hypothesis to mean "cause"; results in, affects, creates, induces, and so on. If we word our earlier hypothesis as "H_1: Watching soap operas causes people to have extramarital affairs," this is an example of a causal relationship.

Possible forms of relationships include positive and linear relationship (as A increases, B increases), negative and linear relationship (as A increases, B decreases), and curvilinear relationships (U shape, inverted U shape, and other more complicated curves). A U curvilinear relationship implies that as A increases, B decreases for awhile, then B increases. (Perhaps the more you drink, the less inhibited you are up to a point; then if you drink enough, you will become more inhibited.) One of your authors (Christine Davis) once conducted research on children's mental health treatment team meetings and found that meeting communication was less dialogic (called "wraparound fidelity score" in the graph) as team leader experience rose—up to six to ten years of experience. Then, meeting communication became more dialogic as team leader experience rose past eleven years of experience.

An inverted U shape implies that as "A" increases, "B" increases for awhile then decreases. Davis once conducted research that found that the more people in attendance at children's mental health treatment team meetings, the more dialogic the meeting communication was up to a point—7 to 10 attendees, in fact. After 10 attendees, the dialogic nature of the meeting communication decreased.

If you consider the previous work cited in this chapter by Segrin and colleagues (2003):

> H_1: There will be a negative association between depression and relational quality in dating relationships,

this is predicting a negative and linear associational relationship, such that as depression increases, the quality of dating relationships will decrease; and

> H_2: The poor relational quality associated with depression will be associated with increased loneliness,

indicates a positive and linear associational relationship. In other words, they predicted more depression is related to more loneliness.

What about the form of the relationship in the following hypotheses?

> H_1: The more people watch soap operas, the more extramarital affairs they will have.

> H_1: Adolescent males report greater enjoyment of slasher films than do adolescent females.

In the first hypothesis, we have a positive and linear associational relationship, while the second hypothesis is a negative and linear associational relationship.

Now, what about those curvilinear relationships? An example of a communication study that considers a curvilinear relationship is the use of touch across relational stage. Guerrero and Andersen (1991) found that touch in public spaces follow a curvilinear relationship, such that couples that are either in the early stages or later stages of relationship development exhibit less touch than

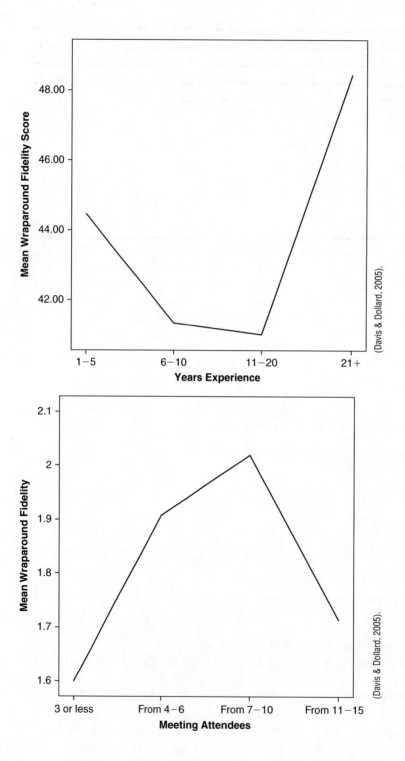

(Davis & Dollard, 2005).

(Davis & Dollard, 2005).

couples between these two stages. This is a curvilinear relationship—actually an inverted U.

Directional and Nondirectional Hypotheses

Another component of hypotheses that becomes increasingly important to you is whether the hypothesis is directional. Some hypotheses are written specifying the direction of the relationship. Consider stating, "People from the South speak more slowly than people from the North." This is an example of a directional hypothesis because of the specific nature of the relationship between the variables. If, however, you had said, "People from the North and South speak at different rates," you have not specified who you expect speaks faster or slower, thus you have not identified a direction. This is a nondirectional hypothesis. Again, both hypotheses are acceptable, but they should be based upon previous research and the researcher's best guess. Being able to identify a hypothesis as directional or not becomes important when we approach statistical analysis in subsequent chapters. Directional hypotheses are called *one-tailed*, because you know where you expect to find your result. This identifies which tail end of the distribution your result will be associated with—based upon what your hypothesis identifies. A nondirectional hypothesis tells you that you must consider a result that could occur on either end of your distribution—thus it is *two-tailed*. This is because you are unsure about where the result will occur.

How Do You Set Up Good Research Questions?   ▼

While there are many possible ways to critique a research question, you need to keep in mind that the best way to define what makes a good research question is based on utility, not a sense of correctness or incorrectness. In other words, is the research question helpful to use in advancing your understanding of a particular communication problem or issue? Does it allow you to effectively get at an important unanswered question in the field? If it does, then you have a successful research question. When we ask our students to write questions, they often struggle to write a solid research question. The number one mistake they make is writing a question that has already been answered. We suggest that they dig a little deeper, perhaps there's a new and interesting way to expand that area that they and other scholars have not considered. Another important tool for evaluating research questions is the concept of quality. In other words, that you have quality variables and the relationship among your variables. While we will talk later about types of validity (or accuracy), the question of validity begins to be answered when you write your research question and/or hypothesis.

Conceptual Definitions

While we will discuss variables more completely in Chapter 7, there are some core components that should be addressed here because they bear on whether you have an accurate research question and/or hypothesis. A quality research

conceptual definition
How the concept or variable that is being studied is defined.

* must be clear to the reader

question and/or hypothesis begins with a solid **conceptual definition**. A conceptual definition is how you define the concept or variable that you are going to study. Think of the concept as the pieces of the research question or the hypothesis. They are the nouns in the question or statement. For example, we like to ask our classes to define the word *violence*, something many of our mass media scholars are interested in pursuing as a variable. Remarkably, the definitions of this word vary a great deal from student to student. Some people see violence as an act or behavioral situation, while others more broadly define violence to include verbal attacks. We could likely debate the merits of each type of definition for a long time; however, that is not the point. Your conceptual definition must be clear and explain to other scholars what you consider violence to be. Most successful communication scholars will explore their variable's conceptual definitions somewhere within their literature review. Consider another example. Imagine that you believe people engage in matching behavior when they desire intimacy with another person. Your first consideration is to define, conceptually, what you mean by intimacy. What if you mean "romantic and sexual interest" when you talk about intimacy, and we mean "caring and giving concern" when we talk about intimacy? There are potentially as many conceptual definitions as there are people to define them. It is essential that you make sure you know what you mean when you talk about your concepts.

Operational Definitions

The second consideration you must make in determining whether you have a quality research question and/or hypothesis is how you define your variables operationally. An **operational definition** is how you plan to measure and/or observe the concept or variable of interest. In the violence example, you must specify how you plan to determine whether behavior in the television programs you watch is to be coded as violent. What do you count as violence? What are the categories you'll use? Do you code physical violence, the different types of physical violence, the outcome of the violence? Do you code the verbal violence? How will you do that exactly? Will it be just the verbal content that determines verbal violence, or will you also take into account nonverbal components of the message such as tone of voice, volume, and paralanguage?

operational definition
How the concept or variable of interest is measured and/or observed.

* a list of directions

Operational definitions are important as they minimize confusion within our scholarly field, provide an opportunity for others to replicate your work, and provide some *control* over the variable you study. What about the intimacy example? Obviously, it depends upon what conceptual definition you agree upon. Then based upon that definition, you need to create an operational definition that will determine what types of questions you ask or what you measure as you observe relational couples.

Both a solid conceptual definition and operational definition are necessary for a quality research question and/or hypothesis. Yet, the key is that conceptual and operational definitions need to match. A quality research question and/or hypothesis will be certain that they do. You can't write a conceptual definition about violence that includes verbal aggression and then not include it in your operational definition.

What Are the Boundaries of Research Questions and Hypotheses?   ▼

Another important consideration for both research questions and hypotheses is whether you wish to impose any boundaries upon them. In other words, under which conditions do you suspect your research question and/or hypotheses may be true? If you expect there to be boundaries, you need to specify this information in the question and/or hypothesis. If you don't expect there to be boundaries, there is no need to include this type of information in the question and/or hypothesis. Time, place, people, and situations could all be boundaries you place upon your questions and hypotheses. For example, do you suspect that the age of the individual matters? We generally assume that most research is based in current time, but is there a reason to consider that history or time might have some affect? Place, which could be culture and/or location, may matter a lot, depending on what the question and/or hypothesis is about. What about the situation? Is it possible that this communication behavior you are interested in only occurs in certain situations? We have a graduate student currently interested in the communication scripts that occur in a speed dating situation. This type of event—speed dating—is very different than any other type of dating situation. This must be included in the question.

Essentially, here you are considering, what are the limits on your research question? The key is to consider boundaries that might influence the process of inquiry. This can even be an opportunity to generate new research questions. Is there something specific about communication students at UNCC or Boston College that will influence the outcome of your study? If so, this may be a limitation to generalization and an example of how boundaries can influence your process of inquiry. It does not mean that you shouldn't ask the question; rather it means that you need to be aware of the level of specificity you offer. As you will see later, when we discuss each methodology, no one methodology is perfect; rather they are types of inquiry ripe with tradeoffs. What one method offers as its strength, another is its weakness. That is why we insist our students be exposed to a variety of methodologies because no one method is right for every study. In fact, we want you to consider how the question and/or hypotheses you write actually influence the methodology you should use, and the type of analysis you will conduct.

How Is Metatheory Related to Research Questions and Hypotheses?   ▼

While we detailed at length in Chapter 2 the important foundations of metatheory to understanding communication research methods, we always like to revisit the topic when we discuss research questions and hypotheses. This is because what we find most interesting about reading a variety of communication research questions and/or hypotheses is how much metatheory seeps out from beneath the question or hypothesis. What we mean is that even when students are still grappling with the abstract concepts of metatheory, once they begin writing research questions, it becomes a little more clear to them. Both your epistemological and ontological entailments drive how you write a particular question. In other words, you approach any question or hypothesis you write with certain assumptions about the world.

So What?

 In summary, your research objectives, questions, and hypotheses are driven by the way you see the world and the assumptions you make about reality; but they are also driven by your curiosities and interests, as well as the research other people have conducted, and the theories, concepts, and conclusions they have come to in your area of interest. In previous chapters, we have shown you how to begin your research search in the library—among the mounds and mounds of research that has come before you. In this chapter, we've shown you how to pull your unique research idea out of that history, find the important questions left to be explored, and formulate good, solid objectives, questions, and/or hypotheses that will result in good quality research. The next several chapters will help you further design your research study as we show you how every decision you make in the research process—from choosing your method to designing your study to analyzing your results—depends on the objectives, research questions, and/or hypotheses you set out to address.

Glossary

Conceptual Definition
How the concept or variable that is being studied is defined.

Fact pattern
A factual relationship occurring repeatedly.

Hypothesis
A statement a researcher makes about the relationship between a dependent and an independent variable.

Null hypothesis
A statement that the research hypothesis is wrong. In other words, there is no (null) relationship between the variables that the research predicted.

Operational definition
How the concept or variable of interest is measured and/or observed.

Research question
Questions scholars ask about the way things work.

References

Barnlund, D. C. (1968). *Interpersonal communication: Survey and studies.* Boston: Houghton Mifflin.

Booth, W. C., Colomb, G. G., & Williams, J. M. (1995). *The craft of research.* Chicago: University of Chicago Press.

Bross, I. B. J. (1953). *Design for decisions.* New York: Macmillan.

Dance, F. E. X. (1982). Essays in human communication theory: A comparative overview. In F. E. X. Dance (Ed.), *Human communication theory: Comparative essays* (pp. 286–299). New York: Harper & Row.

Davis, C. S. (2005). Home. *Qualitative Inquiry 11*(2), 392–409.

Davis, C. S. (2009). *Death: The beginning of a relationship.* Cresskill, NJ: Hampton Press.

Davis, C. S., & Dollard, N. (2005). Team process and adherence to wraparound principles in a children's community mental health care system of care. Tampa, FL: Louis de la Parte Florida Mental Health Institute, University of South Florida.

Gottman, J. M., & Notarius, C. I. (2004). Decade review: Observing marital interaction. *Journal of Marriage and Family, 62,* 927–947.

Green, S. (2002). Mothering Amanda: Musings on the experience of raising a child with Cerebral Palsy. *Journal of Loss and Trauma, 7,* 21–34.

Guerrero, L. K., & Andersen, P. A. (1991). The waxing and waning of relational intimacy: Touch as a function of relational stage, gender and touch avoidance. *Journal of Social and Personal Relationships, 8*(2), 147–165.

Hall, C. S., & Lidzey, G. (1970). *Theories of personality* (2nd ed.). New York: Wiley.

Hawes, L. C. (1975). *Pragmatics of analoguing: Theory and model construction in communication.* Reading, MA: Addison-Wesley.

Johnson, E. P. (2002). Performing blackness down under: The café of the gate of salvation. *Text and Performance Quarterly, 22*(2), 99–119.

Kaplan, A. (1964). *The conduct of inquiry.* New York: Harper & Row.

Kramer, M. W. (2004). Toward a communication theory of group dialectics: An ethnographic study of a community theater group. *Communication Monographs, 71*(3), 311–332.

Kuhn, T. S. (1970). *The structure of scientific revolutions.* Chicago: University of Chicago Press.

Littlejohn, S. W. (1996). *Theories of human communication* (5th ed.). Belmont, CA: Wadsworth.

McCann, R., & Giles, H. (2006). Communication with people of different ages in the workplace: Thai and American data. *Human Communication Research, 32*(1), 74–108.

Miller, G. R., & Nicholson, H. E. (1976). *Communication inquiry: A perspective on a process.* Reading, MA: Addison-Wesley.

Pondy, L. R. (1967). Organizational conflict: Concepts and models. *Administrative Science Quarterly, 12,* 296–320.

Poole, M. S. (1990). Do we have any theories of group communication? *Communication Studies, 41,* 237–247.

Schmidt, S. M., & Kochan, T. A. (1972). Conflict: Towards conceptual clarity. *Administrative Science Quarterly, 17,* 359–370.

Segrin, C., Powell, H. L., Givertz, M., & Brackin, A. (2003). Symptoms of depression, relational quality, and loneliness in dating relationships. *Personal Relationships, 10,* 25–36.

Spiers, J. A. (2002). The interpersonal contexts of negotiating care in home care nurse-patient interactions. *Qualitative Health Research, 12*(8), 1033–1057.

Watzlawick, P., Beavin Bavelas, J., & Jackson, D. D. (1967). *Pragmatics of human communication. A study of interactional patterns, pathologies and paradoxes.* New York: W. W. Norton & Company.

UNDERSTANDING VARIABLES

CHAPTER OUTLINE

KEY TERMS

Coextensive relationships	Interval level measurement	Reversible relationships
Conceptual fit	Irreversible relationships	Self-report
Confounding variable	Measurement	Sequential relationships
Contingent relationships	Multidimensional concepts	Social desirability
Dependent variable	Necessary relationships	Stochastic relationships
Deterministic relationships	Nominal level measurement	Substitutable relationships
Hawthorne Effect	Ordinal level measurement	Sufficient relationships
Independent variable	Ratio level measurement	Unidimensional concepts

CHAPTER OBJECTIVES

1. To understand the function of variables
2. To explore the relationships that occur between variables
3. To understand confound variables
4. To become familiar with the process of variable measurement

▼ What Is the Function of Variables in Communication Research?

According to Willard van Orman Quine (1953), "To be is to be the value of a bound variable" (p. 15). In this chapter, we will consider how variables function within communication research studies. We consider the types of variables, both independent and dependent, while revisiting the importance of how we define variables at the outset of our research. We also explore, in depth, the types of relationship between variables. Additionally, we discuss problematic variables, called extraneous variables, that we have to be on the lookout for as we design our research studies. Finally, we consider measurement theory, levels of measurement, and whether variables are unidimensional or multidimensional. Our focus continues to remain on how all of the decisions we make along the way, from the variables we choose, to how we define them, decide some of the subsequent research design we will consider, as well as the methodological choices we will make.

▼ What Is a Variable?

Variables can be any concepts that have the ability to take on more than one value. In other words, a single object cannot be a variable because it is incapable of taking on more than one value. In communication, we are interested in concepts that can vary. They can vary from person to person, vary in time, and vary in intensity. The key is that a variable varies. Remember that we have suggested that the variables of the study are the nouns in our research question or hypothesis.

Revisiting Conceptual and Operational Definitions

▼

Although we discussed the concepts of conceptual definitions and operational definitions in Chapter 6 when we discussed research questions and hypotheses, we need to revisit our discussion on that topic, as that is an important consideration you make when choosing what variables to study in your research.

Conceptual Definitions *

Remember that a conceptual definition is simply how you define the variable you plan to study. We used the example of defining the word *violence*, illustrating that we might all have a slightly unique definition of what counts as violence. The goal of a conceptual definition is to clearly delineate what you mean when you are identifying your variables of interest. It allows the reader of research and others who wish to study the same construct to know without a doubt what you mean when you study a particular variable. The conceptual definition is really the written definition of the variables of the study. The conceptual definition allows you to define an often broad, obscure concept in terms of related, similar (often more concrete) concepts.

Operational Definitions *

Operational definitions describe observable characteristics of a concept so that the characteristics can be measured or otherwise identified or represented. These definitions identify how the communication scholars plan to measure and/or observe the variable of interest. There are two types of operational definitions: measured operational definitions and experimental operational definitions. Both explore how you can measure a variable of interest, but they differ based on the methodological choices a scholar makes.

Measured Operational Definition.   A measured operational definition describes how a researcher can measure the existence or quantity of a variable—for example, intelligence measured with an IQ test, class performance with a letter grade, communication competence with Spitzberg's (1983) conversational skills rating scale, dialogic communication with discourse analysis, communicating power with a close textual analysis.

Experimental Operational Definition.   Experimental operational definitions specify how the researcher can manipulate a variable in an experiment to produce at least two values or levels of a concept. For example, a variable with an experimental operational definition would describe how we manipulate exposure to differing levels of media violence: *The Dark Knight* vs. *Mama Mia!*, or persuasive message presented by attractive vs. unattractive speaker—Randy Johnson vs. Michael Jordan.

So, if you plan to code violence in horror films, like Weaver (1991) did, you must delineate what you will count and how. In Weaver's study, "Each scene was coded for (a) duration (in seconds); (b) the number, gender, and dramatic role (i.e., protagonist vs. antagonist) of all characters; (c) the general type of action depicted; (d) the specific nature of each action; (e) the resolution, if any, of each action; and (f) the involvement of nudity" (p. 387). Here he identifies exactly what will be coded. He then becomes even more specific, "Acts of aggression, for example, were coded as involving verbal abuse, an attempted attack, or an attack on a person or persons" (1991, p. 387).

The goal of a well-written operational definition is as a guidebook to other scholars in your field. They allow others to replicate previous work, while additionally providing some control over what you will study. Operational definitions steer how you observe and measure your variable, thus functioning as guidelines for some of your methodological choice making. However, ultimately, the key of both conceptual and operational definitions is that they need to match. They define the variables of interest in any communication research study.

● ●

▼ ## Operationalizing: Matching Your Variables to Your Study

Conceptual Fit

One of the primary goals of this textbook and of communication research methods courses across the country is to teach you to be a critical consumer of research. In such, we are not interested in only teaching to be critical of the results of empirical work, but also of the methodological choices the researcher makes in building their work. While there is clearly no such thing as a perfect study, we expect you to learn how to evaluate the components of all communication research. It is important that you give consideration to how to evaluate operational definitions. The biggest concern in defining a variable, operationally, is in the **conceptual fit** between what is measured and what you set out to measure. This conceptual fit is really designed to be certain that the meaning of both your conceptual and operational definitions is preserved throughout the research process. One important question you can ask is: Is the operational definition adequate or complete; does it include all of the essential aspects of a variable? For example, we might ask our students if they are comfortable with us determining whether they are a good student from their G.P.A. Not surprisingly, not all students are comfortable with this one measure having tapped into all of the aspects that should be considered when evaluating the relative success of a college student. Please recognize that while you strive to be as thorough as possible, most operationalizations are incomplete. It is nearly impossible to capture the complete meaning of some constructs with a single variable. The second question you should ask is: Is it accurate? In other words, do you agree with how the research measured the variable? Does it make

conceptual fit
How closely your operational definition matches your conceptual definition.

sense? For example, you might ask whether hitting a Bobo doll (an inflatable child-size doll filled with sand and designed to be punched) is an accurate measure of aggression (see Bandura, Ross, & Ross, 1961; and Bandura, Ross, & Ross, 1963). Last, in evaluating both measured and manipulated operational definitions, the question you should ask is whether the researcher has made clear to us how the variable is measured or manipulated.

Measuring Variables

The last component of operational definitions we want to discuss has to do with the choices you make about the operational procedures for measured variables. There are three primary procedures you follow for measuring variables: self-report, other report, and observing behavior.

Self-Report.   **Self-report** procedures are familiar to most students. Think about the evaluation you make of professors and instructors at the end of each semester. Or perhaps, you find yourself consulting ratemyprofessor.com prior to enrolling in a class with a particular professor. These are good examples of self-report procedures, although, despite student's belief to the contrary, one of these two methods is more accurate than the other. However, that's an issue we best leave for our discussion of sampling in Chapter 8. Self-report procedures are good at measuring an individual's beliefs, attitudes, and values, or in finding out about behaviors (after the fact) we might not be able to observe directly.

SOCIAL DESIRABILITY BIAS IN SELF-REPORT DATA.   Remember, research methods are about making the best choices with the tools at your disposal and none of the operational procedures for measured variables is without limitations. Some limitations of self-report data collection are that it depends upon the participant's willingness to provide the information, as well as his ability to recall and reflect upon something that has already happened. The most significant weakness of self-report is an issue we call **social desirability**. Social desirability is the idea that if you are asking participants to answer questions that are sensitive in nature, people might feel swayed to present themselves in a particular light, regardless of whether it is indeed true. An example of this can be seen in Oliver and Hyde's (1993) meta-analysis of sexual behavior by gender. This study found significant gender differences for sexual behavior, with eight of the nine measures reflecting greater experience for males. While this seems reasonable, the authors themselves note in the discussion that because all the studies they reviewed used self-report data, what they had found evidence of then was "gender differences in reporting tendencies" (p. 45).

Other Report.   Another operational procedure for measured variables is an *other report*. In this method you ask others to report on the individual in question's behavior. The hope is that they may be more objective than an individual's self-report, eliminating your concern about social desirability.

LIMITATIONS IN OTHER REPORTS.   However, problems in asking people to rate others' behavior can include limited experience with the individual or limited prior exposure to her behavior. It is also possible that if a

self-report
This procedure is good at measuring individual's beliefs, attitudes, and values, or in finding out about behaviors we might not be able to observe directly.

✱ problem: people lie

social desirability
The idea that if participants are asked to answer questions that are sensitive in nature, they will undoubtedly feel swayed to present themselves in a particular light, regardless of whether it is indeed true.

significant other rates his partner's behavior, he may exhibit bias. In fact, one interesting finding from your author Heather Gallardo's dissertation indicated that individuals who rated their social skills as being high in a communication task tended to do the same for their partners (2002). In Bandura, Ross, and Ross's (1963) Bobo doll experiments, you might replicate them and measure children's aggression after viewing violent or nonviolent films by asking the classroom teachers to report on children's behavior.

Observing Behavior.   The third operational procedure you can use for measuring variables is observing behavior. For example, your author Christine Davis observes children's mental health treatment team meetings to assess communication in the meetings. Students often like to observe communication behaviors in research settings such as bars, shopping malls, or restaurants. Other communication researchers prefer to do their observations in laboratory settings. They might use an observation lab, which is a room set up like a living room (or conference room) with video cameras and/or one-way mirrors. Researchers give participants communication tasks (such as, "talk to each other on this subject") and observe them while they are carrying out the behavior.

The primary strength of observing behavior is its tendency to be more accurate than self-report or even observers' ratings. Imagine that we ask you to rate your communication competence in a communication task you complete with your significant other. Are you likely to be an objective judge of either your own skills in communication or even of our relational partner's skills? Perhaps. However, to guard against this, we often have trained researchers assess communication competence in strangers. They tend to be much more objective. However, observation is not without its own inherent limitations. You can only assess what people do—not why they may behave in a particular way, what they believe, or what they feel. Therefore, scholars must observe the behavior they believe best represents the concept of interest accurately. This can pose potential problems; it can sometimes be challenging to be certain that the behavior indicates what you think it does.

HAWTHORNE EFFECT BIAS IN OBSERVING BEHAVIORS.   Another potential limitation that occurs is the **Hawthorne Effect**. When you know others are observing you, do you change your behavior? Sure, most of us do alter our behavior slightly when we know that we are being observed. This is known as the Hawthorne Effect.

Hawthorne Effect
An effect where people alter their behavior because they know they're being observed.

Triangulation

As you can see, each type of operational procedure for measured variables has both strengths and limitations associated with it. As is often the case, there is no solution to the limitations presented. As such, one solution is to combine a variety of different methods for measuring the variable in question. This idea is called triangulation, and, as we suggest to our students, is the ideal way to measure many variables. Triangulation is defined as "the comparison of two or more forms of evidence with respect to an object of research interest" (Lindlof & Taylor, 2002, pp. 240–241). There are actually several different types of triangulation: you can triangulate *sources*—multiple interviewees, multiple field sites, multiple cases, multiple observations; *methods*—qualitative methods plus quantitative methods, observation plus self-report plus other-report; or *researchers*—multiple interviewers or observers (Lindlof & Taylor, 2002). However, not nearly enough scholars employ this technique in their research studies. Triangulation moves you closer to understanding the variable in question and enhances the validity of the findings. For example, you might study communication competence and triangulate the methods by measuring the variable in three different ways: self-report, other report (rating their conversational partner), and trained coders' observational ratings. Triangulation often yields interesting results and enhances study validity (see Chapter 9).

Measurement

Regardless of what method you use to gather the information to measure your variables (self-report, other report, or observing behavior), you might need to use a scale as a questioning device to obtain a fairly precise and consistent measurement. **Measurement** is a process of determining the characteristics and/or quantity of a variable through systematic recording and organization of observations. Often, when conducting research, you use a scale to assign numbers and/or symbols to the characteristics of variables. There are four levels of measurement, which you consider from least specific to most specific: nominal, ordinal, interval, and ratio.

measurement *

A process of determining the characteristics and/or quantity of a variable through systematic recording and organization of observations.

Nominal Level Measurement.   **Nominal level measurement** makes use of unordered categories, classifying the variable into qualitatively different and unique categories. These categories do not indicate any type of order or intensity of the degree to which a characteristic exists. Rather, they represent the potential categories of some variable of interest. For example, political party affiliation, religious affiliation, biological sex, and race are all variables measured at the nominal level. When unclear as to whether a scale is nominal, ask yourself whether there is some inherent order to the categories. If there is no order, the scale is nominal. There are two requirements for categorical representation: that each category must be mutually exclusive and the list of categories must be exhaustive. Mutually exclusive categories have no overlap. You should be able to place an observation into one and only one category. One of the places you have likely encountered a categorical system that lacked mutually exclusive categories is when you have purchased music. Ever try to figure out what genre your favorite artist fits into? Is a CD by Madonna likely to be found in Pop or Rock? Where do you look for a Taylor Swift CD, Country or Pop? In fact, Bacciga-lupo, Plaza, and Donaldson (2008) presented a paper at the recent Conference on Music Information Retrieval, suggesting that genre is a fuzzy classification system for music, supporting our notion that genre is an example of a nominal categorical system violating the necessary mutually exclusive requirement of a categorical system. Second, the category system must be exhaustive. In other words, each category must represent the variable fully; each observation must be able to be classified by the measurement scheme. One of the ways scholars ensure that their category system is exhaustive is to identify the last category

nominal level measurement *

This type of measurement makes use of unordered categories, classifying the variable into qualitatively different and unique categories. These categories do not indicate any type of order or intensity of the degree to which a characteristic exists, but it represents the potential categories of some variable of interest.

as *other*, thus ensuring that each observation will fit somewhere. For example, political party affiliation: democrat, republican, independent, other.

Qualitative research frequently uses nominal measurements. Stephanie Houston Grey (2002), for example, analyzed the discourse of Japanese survivors of the Hiroshima and Nagasaki bombings in World War II as narratives of Christian transformation and meaning, redemptive knowing, and cultural authenticity. In another example, Warren and Kilgard (2001) studied a performance of Nathaniel Hawthorne's "The Birthmark" to understand the concepts (variables) of *whiteness*, *power*, and *privilege*—all nominal variables.

In quantitative research, nominal measurement is often used as a strategy to describe the sample of the study. For example in their study on employee satisfaction with meetings, Rogelberg, Allen, Shanock, Scott, and Shuffler (2010) used nominal variables to describe participants' gender and organization type (publicly traded, privately held, private not for profit).

ordinal level measurement
This type of measurement has ordered categories or rank, and it can be determined whether an observation is greater than, less than, or equal to other observations. However, this type of measurement does not indicate how much the difference is; the amount separating levels is not known.

Ordinal Level Measurement. **Ordinal level measurement** is an ordered category or rank. Here we can determine whether an observation is greater than, less than, or equal to other observations, which cannot be determined from nominal level measurement. However, ordinal level measurement does not indicate how much the difference is; the amount separating levels is not known. The intervals between the numbers on the scale are not equal; thus, the difference between a rating of 2 and 3, and 4 and 5, on a five-point ordinal scale is not equivalent. Ordinal level measurement examples include television programs classified as high, medium, or low in violence; the top five college football teams; and the top ten finishers in a NASCAR race. Any measure that uses ranking is ordinal level measurement.

Ordinal level measurement is often seen in the corporate world in terms of performance evaluation. For example, most sales organizations often rank order their employees based on sales production. A life insurance company may hold a competition for life applications and rank a group of agents by number of applications in a month.

interval level measurement
This type of measurement specifies relative position and also establishes standard, equal distances between points on the scale.

Interval Level Measurement. **Interval level measurement** specifies relative position and also establishes standard, equal distances between points on the scale. Most rating scales used in research are interval level measurement scales. Teacher evaluations are a good example of interval level measurements. When you are asked to use a 5- or 7-point scale, most researchers assume people assume the distances between points on the scale are equal. A benefit of interval level measurement is that if the differences between the numbers are meaningful, calculations (such as addition and subtraction) can be done. However, remember that the zero point is meaningless, and as a result it is impossible to make proportional statements. In other words, take the IQ (intelligence quotient) test, which is considered an interval level measurement; while the points between numbers are thought to be equal, there is no such thing as an IQ of zero. As such, someone with an IQ of 150 is not twice as smart as someone with an IQ of 75. Another example of an interval level measurement scale is both the Fahrenheit and Celsius scales of temperature. The difference between 80 and 90 degrees is the same as the difference between 50 and 60; but 80 degrees isn't twice as hot as 40 degrees, because zero degrees does not indicate a total lack of temperature.

Interval measurement is pervasive throughout quantitative research methods, allowing us to study communication in marriage, patient satisfaction, employee dissent, and even communication strategies in a deceptive encounter. In fact, most any consumer survey you receive from the local grocery store, telephone company, voter attitude phone survey, or even the Nielsen television ratings uses interval level measurement.

Top Grossing Films in the USA (2007) An Example of an Ordinal Level of Measurement	
1. Spider-Man 3	$336,530,303
2. Shrek the Third	$322,719,944
3. Transformers	$319,246,193
4. Pirates of the Caribbean: At World's End	$309,420,425
5. Harry Potter and the Order of the Phoenix	$292,004,738
Retrieved September 16, 2008, from http://www.boxofficemojo .com/yearly/chart/?yr=2007	

Because interval level scales are so prominent in research, we should consider three types of interval level scales: Likert's method of summated ratings, Osgood's semantic differential, and the Thurstone scale. All three of these scales measure participants' feelings or attitudes. The key difference between them is the way they get at obtaining this information. We should take a second to note that not all researchers consider these three scales to be interval—some consider them to be ordinal scales. The determining factor is whether you believe that everyone sees the difference between 1 and 2 on a semantic differential, or *agree strongly* and *agree somewhat* on a Likert scale as the same. Most researchers in our field are willing to make that assumption and treat these scales as interval data.

LIKERT SCALE. The Likert scale is most common. You are probably already familiar with this interval scale, which measures participants' feelings or attitudes toward another person, issue, and event. The Likert scale is named after Rensis Likert (1932), an organizational psychologist who published a report detailing the use of this scale. Participants receive statements representing clear positions and are asked to indicate the extent to which they agree with each statement, usually on a 5- or 7-point scale (e.g., strongly agree, agree, neither agree nor disagree, disagree, strongly disagree). Often both positive and negative statements appear on the measure to be sure that participants are reading the questions, rather than responding without thought. Most human beings are quite patterned in their responses, so to avoid a response set, wherein they answer the same answer for each question, alternating the direction of a statement can alleviate this issue. Negative items are then reverse scored and scores are summed across the measure.

In their study on electronic multitasking in organization meetings, Stephens and Davis (2009, p. 71) utilized a Likert scale to measure the experience with technology variable. Participants were asked to rate their comfort with and skill with technology from "complete novice (1) to expert (7)."

Example of a Likert Scale

Listening Measure

Please indicate the degree to which each statement applies to you by indicating whether you:

Strongly Disagree = 1; Disagree = 2; are Neutral = 3; Agree = 4; Strongly Agree = 5

_____ **1.** I dislike speeches that don't interest me.

_____ **2.** Usually I can listen to a speech that doesn't interest me.

_____ **3.** I get restless and daydream when I listen to someone who doesn't interest me.

_____ **4.** I listen even when the information in a speech doesn't interest me.

_____ **5.** Listening to dull presenters about dull information makes me restless and causes me to daydream.

_____ **6.** I do listen to dull presenters about dull information.

_____ **7.** I don't usually listen to a presenter if there are distractions in the room.

_____ **8.** I do listen when there are distractions during a presentation.

_____ **9.** I listen to presentations that are not directed at me.

_____ **10.** I do not listen to presentations if they do not apply to me.

_____ **11.** If I have other things on my mind, I don't pay attention to a presenter.

_____ **12.** I listen to a presenter even if I have other things I'm thinking about.

_____ **13.** I usually will not listen to a presentation that does not have a clear agenda.

_____ **14.** I usually will listen even if a presentation has no clear agenda.

_____ **15.** I am accepting of a presenter who does not give continuous feedback.

_____ **16.** I am not accepting of a presenter who does not give continuous feedback.

_____ **17.** I listen to presenters who do not give continuous feedback.

_____ **18.** I will not listen to presenters who do not give continuous feedback.

_____ **19.** I will listen to a presenter who has different opinions than mine.

_____ **20.** I will not listen to a presenter who has different opinions than mine.

_____ **21.** I will listen to a presenter who does not explain his/her subject matter.

_____ **22.** I will not listen to a presenter if his/her subject matter is not defined.

SEMANTIC DIFFERENTIAL SCALE.   Osgood's semantic differential scale is another interval level measurement technique, which measures the meanings participants assign to some stimulus (e.g., groups, types of music, a person, an idea). This scale named after Charles Osgood (Osgood, Suci, & Tannenbaum, 1957) initially was used to measure the connotative meaning of concepts. This scale presents a stimulus at the top of a list of scales, wherein the scales are anchored at either end by pairs of polar-opposite adjectives (active-passive; warm-cold). Participants check a single point on the scale expressing their perception of the stimulus. A friend of one of your authors in graduate school was interested in the music used during public service announcements, and to pretest different types of music, we listened to five clips of music and rated them using a semantic differential scale (happy-sad; calm-anxious; relaxed-fearful, etc.). In a study by Uhlmann and Swanson (2004), they used a semantic differential scale to have participants measure their own and others' association of aggression. In other words, they reported where they fell on a scale from –3 to +3. The scale anchors were aggressive-peaceful, fighter -quiet, and combative-gentle (p. 45).

Example of a Semantic Differential Scale

Group Behavior Inventory, Friedlander (1966)

In this section, you are asked to judge the meaning of the concept Group Meeting (as it relates to _____ Department) in terms of each of the seven scales beneath it. Check one blank for each of the seven scales that best describes the meaning of the concept:

_____ DEPARTMENT GROUP MEETINGS

good								bad
weak								strong
active								passive
pleasant								unpleasant
deep								shallow
relaxed								tense
valuable								worthless

Ratio Level Measurement.   The most specific level of measure is the **ratio level measurement**, which not only has all of the characteristics of an interval scale, but also a true, meaningful zero point. Ratio scales also are assumed to be measured in equal intervals, and they can be mathematically measured, even to a decimal point or fraction of a point. Many variables have a true and meaningful measure of zero (e.g., age, heart rate, years at current address, the number of times you attended church in the last year, driving speed, income). As there is a true, meaningful zero point, you can make proportional statements: Someone who is

ratio level measurement
As the most specific type of measurement, it has all of the characteristics of an interval scale, but also a true, meaningful zero point.

50 is twice as old as someone who is 25 years of age. It is important to be able to identify whether a variable has been measured with a nominal, ordinal, interval, or ratio level of measurement, as the type of measurement level will determine the statistical techniques you can use to test your hypotheses and research questions.

Most often used in quantitative research studies communication scholars use ratio measurement to examine relationships with a participant's age or measure a type of behavior of the participant. Powell and Segrin (2004) used a ratio level to measure sexual behaviors asking such questions as, "How many times in the last month did you engage in vaginal intercourse?" They also gathered number of sexual partners over specific time frames; this too, would be a ratio level measure.

Is the variable measured or manipulated?

If the variable is measured: is it nominal, ordinal, interval, or ratio?

1. *Preferred news source* (self-report): newspaper, TV, magazine, other, none.

2. Length of acquaintance: Ask married people to report number of months they knew spouse prior to marriage.

3. Personal relevance of issue: Freshmen hear message advocating comprehensive exams for seniors; some told to begin next year, some told it will begin after they graduate.

4. Personal relevance of issue: Ask people to rate how personally important an issue is to them on a 7-point scale ranging from not at all important to very important.

5. Compliance-gaining strategies: Ask people to describe how they tried to gain compliance on one occasion, classify strategies.

6. Ask how successful the strategy was: not at all, somewhat, very.

7. Instruct people to use one of four different strategies to gain compliance from others in the context of collecting door-to-door for a charity.

8. Record amount of money donated to the charity.

Answer key: (1) measured, nominal; (2) measured, ratio; (3) manipulated; (4) measured, interval; (5) measured, nominal; (6) measured, ordinal; (7) manipulated; (8) measured, ratio.

Types of Variables

Now that we've discussed how to measure variables, let's review certain types of variables. There are two types of variables in communication research projects that follow an experimental design: independent and dependent variables. It is necessary that we know the differences between the two.

Independent Variables

independent variable
The variable that causes or determines the value in another variable.

An **independent variable** is the variable that won't take advice from any other variable in your study. It is often thought to predict or determine the value in another variable. For example, consider two variables: the number of cigarettes a person smokes and the probability of getting lung cancer. Both are variables because they can take on different values. One might have smoked zero cigarettes or might have smoked 3,000 in his or her lifetime. Even lung cancer is a variable because it can vary—you can have lung cancer, or not. Thus, the concept has more than one value, making it a variable. In this example, which one is your independent variable? If you guessed the number of cigarettes smoked, then you are correct. Consider another example. If we assume that your ratio of fat to lean is a function of how much you exercise, what is your independent variable? This seems a little trickier; reread and think it through. The amount of exercise is your independent variable, because it is thought to predict the value of your fat/lean ratio.

Dependent Variables

While we have been discussing these examples, there are other variables present—lung cancer and our ratio of fat/lean. In both of these cases, they are the **dependent variable**. The dependent variable is assumed to depend on or be predicted by another variable. In the examples above, cancer is presumed to be predicted by or dependent on the number of cigarettes smoked, while the ratio of fat/lean depends upon the amount of exercise one engages in.

dependent variable
The variable that is assumed to depend on or be caused by another variable.

Examples of Independent and Dependent Variables. Another way to think about the independent variable is that this variable is likely to be what the researcher manipulates or what the research manipulates, while the dependent variable is what the researcher measures. So, for the first example, you will measure whether the participant has cancer, while you select a variety of people (who undoubtedly smoke a variety of number of cigarettes). And in the second example, you select a variety of people who exercise to varying degrees, and measure their fat/lean ratio.

An unusual, yet effective way to think about independent and dependent variables comes from ballroom dancing. When two dancers are dancing, they are in a partnership. As Tony Prado, Owner of Queen City Ballroom in Charlotte, explained it: Both partners have a job to do—one, the male (think independent variable), is in charge of where the couple moves to on the floor; he is in the lead. However, his task depends upon the woman's ability (think dependent variable) to follow his lead. In this example, the independent variable (the male lead dancer) predicts—or determines—which direction the dependent variable (the woman) goes.

As one last example, let's imagine that you do a survey of current college students measuring both marijuana smoking and grades. Imagine that you find that the more pot an individual smoked, the lower his or her grades. What is the independent variable, and what is the dependent variable? In other words, what caused what? How many of you think that the amount an individual smokes is the independent variable, causing the student to have lower grades (dependent variable)? Is it possible that it works the other way around? Is it possible that an individual might have poor grades (independent variable) and as a result begins smoking more marijuana (dependent variable)? Here, there is no clear answer; it is up to the researcher to identify with his or her research question and/or

© steamroller_blues, 2010, Shutterstock, Inc.

hypotheses to decide for us. The research questions and/or hypotheses identify what variable is the independent variable and what variable is the dependent variable. In other words, you as the researcher determine which is the independent variable or the dependent variable when you set up your experiment.

Identify the independent and dependent variables for each of the following hypotheses:

1. People with high levels of exposure to television news will report greater satisfaction with life than people with low levels of exposure to television news.
2. Communicators with formal debate training will report higher levels of assertiveness than communicators without formal debate training.
3. When people are exposed to fear-arousing messages, as opposed to non-fear-arousing messages, they will report increased levels of anxiety.
4. The older one is, the greater will be the levels of stress perceived in one's life.
5. Children who stutter will have higher self-esteem than children who do not stutter.
6. Subjects reading persuasive messages by attractive sources will experience greater attitude change than subjects reading persuasive messages by unattractive sources.
7. Individuals with low communication apprehension will report significantly more positive parental behaviors and attitudes toward communication than individuals with high communication apprehension. [HINT: There are two dependent variables.]
8. Alcohol use and misuse would increase across adolescence.

Extraneous Variables

Sometimes a third (or more) variable will make finding the *true* relationship between the independent and dependent variables *cloudy*, because this additional variable is another possible cause (other than the independent variable) of the effect on the dependent variable. This is called an extraneous variable. An extraneous variable is one that is typically thought of as being unpredictable and uncontrolled by the researcher, or as being a variable that is not part of the research design.

confounding variable
An extraneous variable that muddies the relationship between the independent and dependent variables.

A **confounding variable** is an extraneous variable that, because of its relationship to both the independent and dependent variables, cannot be distinguished from the independent variable in the analysis. Another way to define a confounding variable is when the effects of two variables cannot be separated from each other. An example of this would be if a public speaking instructor not only asked students to practice their speeches an hour each day, but also suggested they visualize giving the speech before doing so. If the students were then rated as being better public speakers, there would be no way of knowing which of the two variables (practice or visualization) was responsible for the effect (better public speaking). These two actions likely had an effect on each other as well as on the dependent variable. Another example of a confounding variable, frequently used, is this: Imagine that you do a survey of various cities; you measure two variables—crime incidence and ice cream consumption. In this example, what are the dependent and independent variables? Do either one of these make sense to be dependent or independent? So, why is there a relationship between these two variables? The reason these are related variables in this instance is because both ice cream consumption and crime rates are dependent upon a third variable. This third variable is heat—hot weather causes more crime and also causes more ice cream consumption. Therefore, heat is the confounding variable, as it *muddies* the ability to detect the effect of the independent variable on the dependent variable. The relationship between the two variables, which is due to some confounding variable, is called a spurious correlation. When you design a research project and identify your variable, you need to attempt to anticipate potential confounds and eliminate them in the design of the study.

An Example of a Confounding Variable in "Much Ado about Nothing" from the Simpson's

Homer: Not a bear in sight. The Bear Patrol must be working like a charm.

Lisa: That's specious reasoning, Dad.

Homer: Thank you, dear.

Lisa: By your logic I could claim that this rock keeps tigers away.

Homer: Oh, how does it work?

Lisa: It doesn't work.

Homer: Uh-huh.

Lisa: It's just a stupid rock.

Homer: Uh-huh.

Lisa: But I don't see any tigers around, do you?

[Homer thinks of this, then pulls out some money.]

Homer: Lisa, I want to buy your rock.

[Lisa refuses at first, then takes the exchange.]

One of our favorite examples of a confounding variable is found in a newspaper article from June 11, 1984. The article, titled, "Ethel May Not Be Sexy, but She'll Do Better in Business than Cheryl," by Gary Dessler, reports on a master's thesis by Dorothy Linville, wherein she considered the question of whether the name of a woman would prevent her from landing management level positions. This particular research project utilized an experimental design. First, students rated the sexiness of 255 women's names on a scale of one to seven, with higher scores representing sexier names. Eight names receiving the highest scores were considered sexy, whereas the seven lowest scoring names were considered the least sexy. Keeping in mind that this study was done in the early 1980s, the sexy names were: Christine (M = 5.08), Candice (M = 4.92),

Cheryl and Melanie (M = 4.91), Dawn, Heather, Jennifer, and Susan (M = 4.83). Not sure whether we should point this out, but both female authors of this textbook have *sexy* names! We sure hope Ken doesn't feel left out. The least sexy names were as follows: Ethel (M = 1.00), Alma (M = 1.08), Zelda (M = 1.16), Florence, Mildred, Myrtle, and Esther (M = 1.15).

In the actual study, 100 college seniors and graduate students were asked to imagine being in the role of personnel managers. They received resumes of eight equally qualified women and were asked to rate them for management positions. Four of the resumes had low sexy names: Ethel, Myrtle, Mildred, and Esther; while four had high sexy names: Cheryl, Dawn, Jennifer, and Michelle. The results of this study indicated that men preferred hiring women with less sexy names for the management positions than did women. In fact, the article stated, "A new study finds that men are more likely to hire women with names they perceive as nonsexy for managerial positions, and give these women higher salaries. Women hiring other women are less influenced by the sound of a name" (Dessler, 1984). Is this really the conclusion one can draw based on the study as we have described it to you? What is the problem with the manipulation in this experiment, or in other words, what is the confounding variable? Think for a minute about who you know with a name like Cheryl, Dawn, Jennifer, or Michelle. Now, what about Ethel, Myrtle, Mildred, and Esther? Is it likely that these two groups of names come from two different generations? Therefore, there's a third variable going on here: perceived age of the applicant. Thus, it's highly possible that this is in fact age discrimination, not name discrimination. And that makes sense, right? The key is that in this case there was another variable besides the sexiness of the name; therefore, it is incorrect to attribute the results to the sexiness of the woman's name.

There are two other types of variables that also have an effect on the dependent variable: mediating variables and moderating variables. These differ from extraneous variables in that they are typically predicted and controlled by the researcher.

Mediating Variables. With a mediating variable, instead of hypothesizing that A causes B directly, you might hypothesize that A causes M (mediating variable), which in turn causes B. An example of this might be that low communication apprehension (A) might cause a student to speak out more in class (M), which in turn might cause the student to get a better grade in class (B). Thus, while it may appear that low communication apprehension causes the student to get a better grade, it's only because of the mediating effect of speaking out more in class.

Moderating Variables. A moderating variable is a third variable that has an effect on both A and B. An example of this might be that an individual's overall health (M, moderating variable) affects both the individual's communication competence with his or her health-care provider (A) and the individual's satisfaction with his or her health care (B). Thus, it may appear that the individual's communication competence with his or her health-care provider causes the individual to be more satisfied with his or her health care, but it's actually that the individual's overall health affects both. We know that mediating and moderating variables sound similar to a confounding variable, but here's the primary difference—in the experiment, the researcher controls for the mediating and moderating variables and does not control for a confounding variable.

••

The Different Types of Relationships between Variables

In Chapter 6, we discussed how variables might have associational or causal, and directional or nondirectional, relationships with each other. As you have a better grasp on understanding the relationships between independent variables and dependent variables, and even how to look out for confounding variables, you must now consider the different types of relationships between the variables within the hypotheses you read and write.

Reversible and Irreversible Relationships

First, relationships between variables can be reversible or irreversible. **Reversible relationships** can go either way. For example, think about the pot smoking example. Which comes first: pot smoking or grades? As you saw earlier, that relationship could go in either direction, thus it is a reversible relationship. Some are **irreversible relationships**, meaning the direction can only go one way. Think about the lung cancer and number of cigarettes smoked relationship. Can it go either way? No, thus it is an irreversible relationship.

Deterministic and Stochastic Relationships

Second, relationships between variables can be deterministic or stochastic. Relationships that are **deterministic** occur when the dependent variable must result from the independent variable. In communication studies, few relationships are deterministic; most are **stochastic**, which means probable. Again, think about the relationship between lung cancer and smoking. In fact, ask almost any smoker you know and he will tell you a tale of someone he knows who smoked like a fiend and died peacefully at an ancient age without ever getting lung cancer. That is because it is a probabilistic (stochastic) relationship, not deterministic. In other words, if a person smokes, she is more likely to get lung cancer (more probable), but smoking does not guarantee (determine 100%) lung cancer.

The above example is a classic case of what is sometimes referred to as an *individualistic fallacy*. When people fail to recognize the differences between stochastic and deterministic relationships, they may make inaccurate assumptions about the relationships between variables. It may very well be the case that the person in the example above knows someone who smoked his entire life and lived into old age in good health. There are always exceptions to rules.

reversible relationships
depending on the other
Relationships that can go in either direction or either way.

irreversible relationships
Relationships that can only go in one direction or one way.

deterministic relationships
Relationships that occur when the dependent variable must result from the independent variable.

stochastic relationships
Relationships that are probable.

But in the aggregate, smoking will still damage your health and shorten your life. Rejecting this notion is an example of individualistic fallacy, rejecting a stochastic relationship based on a single observation.

Sequential and Coextensive Relationships

Third, relationships between variables can be sequential or coextensive. In **sequential relationships**, the ordering of the variables is important and must occur sequentially, meaning chronologically or in order. The Bobo doll experiments are an example of relationships between variables that occur sequentially (Bandura, Ross, & Ross, 1961). They exposed children to violent or nonviolent cartoons, then allowed them the opportunity to play in a room complete with Bobo dolls as a measure of violent behavior. Here the relationship between viewing violence and violent behavior is sequential. On the other hand, if they are **coextensive relationships**, the variables within the relationship co-occur or happen simultaneously. For example, if we feel happy, we will also be smiling. Marital dissatisfaction and depression often co-occur within distressed marriages.

Sufficient and Contingent Relationships

Fourth, relationships between variables can be sufficient or contingent. In **sufficient relationships**, one variable is enough to bring about a second variable; whereas, if a third variable is needed, those are considered **contingent relationships**. Consider the following example: Is viewing violent television sufficient to cause violence or does viewing violent television cause violent behavior when: drugs are present, weapons are present, and violence is in the living environment? If other factors are involved, then the relationship is contingent. If other factors are not involved, the relationship between variables is sufficient.

Necessary and Substitutable Relationships

Fifth, relationships between variables can be necessary or substitutable. When one variable must be present for the second variable to be present, you have **necessary relationships**. If other forces might bring about the same effect, you have **substitutable relationships**. As you think about the following question, consider whether it is a necessary or substitutable relationship: Is unprotected sexual behavior necessary to contract human immunodeficiency virus (HIV)? No, HIV can be transmitted by other means, such as intravenous drug use; thus, a substitutable relationship. However, fire cannot occur without oxygen; therefore, the relationship between fire and oxygen is a necessary relationship. As communication scholars study human beings, it is highly unlikely that many of the variables you study will constitute a necessary relationship; rather most of the variables you study in communication are substitutable relationships.

---

sequential relationships
Relationships where the ordering of the variables is important and must occur sequentially, meaning chronologically or in order.

coextensive relationships
Relationships where the variables co-occur or happen simultaneously.

sufficient relationships
Relationships where one variable is enough to bring about a second variable.

contingent relationships
Relationships where one variable is enough to bring about a third variable, if needed.

necessary relationships
Relationships where one variable must be present for a second variable to be present.

substitutable relationships
Relationships where other forces might bring about the same effect as a necessary relationship

The Dimensions of Variables

Variables are concepts that can be described and understood from one dimension or more than one dimension. We're talking here about the complexity of the item you're measuring. Some items are not complex at all, and require only one question or series of questions to address. These are called unidimensional concepts. Other concepts require many different questions or ways to look at them. They are called multidimensional concepts.

Unidimensional Concepts

Some variables are **unidimensional concepts**; they contain only one dimension. A simple example of a unidimensional concept is education: What's the highest grade you've completed in school? An example of a unidimensional scale is the Neuliep and McCroskey (1997)'s classic Intercultural Communication Apprehension Scale, which measures cultural and ethnic communication apprehension on one dimension: the fear and anxiety a person associates with interacting with people from different cultural or ethnic groups.

unidimensional concepts
Variables containing only one dimension.

Multidimensional Concepts

On the other hand, **multidimensional concepts** are complex variables embodying more than one component or dimension. We're sure you're familiar with the concept of self-disclosure as a multidimensional concept (breadth and depth). Another example of a multidimensional concept is the SAT Reasoning Test (formerly Scholastic Aptitude Test and Scholastic Assessment Test). A college entrance exam testing writing, mathematics, and critical reading skills; each construct is measured through more than one measure and then a composite score is created from the combination of the three area scores. The variable sensation-seeking is also a multidimensional concept, including boredom susceptibility, disinhibition, experience seeking, and thrill seeking.

multidimensional concepts
Complex variables embodying more than one component or dimension.

So What?

This chapter has considered variables from every possible angle. Beginning with independent and dependent variables, we revisited the importance of the significance of how you choose and define your variables within research. We also considered some important variables to watch for: confounding variables. We explored the typology of relationships between variables. Considering measurement theory, you must remember that measurement levels, determines the type of statistical analysis that you can conduct. We discussed the difference between whether variables are unidimensional or multidimensional. Our goal in this chapter is to continue reinforcing the idea that within the research process, the decisions you make—from the variables you choose, define, and measure—determine the path you take, guiding the subsequent research methodology you choose from your toolbox.

Glossary

Coextensive relationships
Relationships where the variables co-occur or happen simultaneously.

Conceptual fit
How closely your operational definition matches your conceptual definition.

Confounding variable
An extraneous variable that muddies the relationship between the independent and dependent variable.

Contingent relationships
Relationships where one variable is enough to bring about a third variable, if needed.

Dependent variable
The variable that is assumed to depend on or be caused by another variable.

Deterministic relationships
Relationships that occur when the dependent variable must result from the independent variable.

Hawthorne Effect
An effect where people alter their behavior because they know they're being observed.

Independent variable
The variable that causes or determines the value in another variable.

Interval level measurement
This type of measurement specifies relative position and also establishes standard, equal distances between points on the scale.

Irreversible relationships
Relationships that can only go in one direction or one way.

Measurement
A process of determining the characteristics and/or quantity of a variable through systematic recording and organization of observations.

Multidimensional concepts
Complex variables embodying more than one component or dimension.

Necessary relationships
Relationships where one variable must be present for a second variable to be present.

Nominal level measurement
This type of measurement makes use of unordered categories, classifying the variable into qualitatively different and unique categories.
These categories do not indicate any type of order or intensity of the degree to which a characteristic exists but represent the potential categories of some variable of interest.

Ordinal level measurement
This type of measurement has ordered categories or rank, and it can be determined whether an observation is greater than, less than, or equal to other observations. However, this type of measurement does not indicate how much the difference is; the amount separating levels is not known.

Ratio level measurement
As the most specific type of measurement, it has all of the characteristics of an interval scale, but also a true, meaningful zero point.

Reversible relationships
Relationships that can go in either direction or either way.

Self-report
This procedure is good at measuring individual's beliefs, attitudes, and values, or in finding out about behaviors we might not be able to observe directly.

Sequential relationships
Relationships where the ordering of the variables is important and must occur sequentially, meaning chronologically or in order.

Social desirability
The idea that if participants are asked to answer questions that are sensitive in nature, people will undoubtedly feel swayed to present themselves in a particular light, regardless of whether it is indeed true.

Stochastic relationships
Relationships that are probable.

Substitutable relationships
Relationships where other forces might bring about the same effect as a necessary relationship.

Sufficient relationships
Relationships where one variable is enough to bring about a second variable.

Unidimensional concepts
Variables containing only one dimension.

References

Baccigalupo, C., Plaza, E., & Donaldson, J. (2008). *Uncovering affinity of artists to multiple genres from social behavior data.* Presented at the International Conference on Music Information Retrieval, Philadelphia, PA.

Bandura, A., Ross, D., & Ross, S. A. (1961). Transmission of aggressions through imitation of aggressive models. *Journal of Abnormal and Social Psychology, 63*(3), 575–582.

Bandura, A., Ross, D., & Ross, S. A. (1963). Imitation of film-mediated aggressive models. *Journal of Abnormal and Social Psychology, 66*, 3–11.

Beck, A. T., Ward, C. H., Mendelson, M., Mock, J., & Erbaugh, J. (1961). An inventory for measuring depression. *Archives of General Psychiatry, 4*, 53–63.

Dessler, G. (1984, June 11). Ethel may not be sexy, but she'll do better in business than Cheryl. *Miami Herald.* Retrieved September 16, 2008, from News Bank on-line database (America's Newspapers) on the website: http://infoweb.newsbank.com

Friedlander, F. (1966). Performance and interactional dimensions of organizational work groups. *Journal of Applied Psychology, 50*, 257–265.

Gallardo, H. L. (2008). *Social skill in sexual communication and sexual risk-taking in dating relationships.* Unpublished paper.

Grey, S. H. (2002). Writing redemption: Trauma and the authentication of the moral order in *Hibakusha* Literature. *Text and Performance Quarterly, 22*(1), 1–23.

Likert, R. (1932). A technique for the measurement of attitudes. *Archives of Psychology, 140*, 1–55.

Lindlof, T. R., & Taylor, B. C. (2002). *Qualitative communication research methods.* Thousand Oaks, CA: Sage.

Neuliep, J. W., & McCroskey, J. C. (1997). The development of a U.S. and generalized ethnocentrism scale. *Communication Research Reports, 14*(4), 385–398.

Oliver, M. B., & Hyde, J. S. (1993). Gender differences in sexuality: A meta-analysis. *Psychological Bulletin, 114*, 29–51.

Osgood, C. E., Suci, G., & Tannenbaum, P. (1957). *The measurement of meaning.* Urbana, IL: University of Illinois Press.

Powell, H. L., & Segrin, C. (2004). The effect of family and peer communication on college students' communication with dating partners about HIV and AIDS. *Health Communication, 16*, 427–449.

Quine, W. V. (1953). *From a logical point of view: Nine logico-philosophical essays.* New York: Harper and Row.

Rogelberg, S. G., Allen, J. A., Shanock, L., Scott, C., & Shuffler, M. (2010). Employee satisfaction with meetings: A contemporary facet of job satisfaction. *Human Resource Management, 49*, 149–172.

Spitzberg, B. H. (1983). Communication competence as knowledge, skill, and impression. *Communication Education, 32*, 323–328.

Stephens, K. K., & Davis, J. (2009). The social influences on electronic multitasking in organizational meetings. *Management Communication Quarterly, 23*, 63–83.

Thurstone, L. L. (1928). Attitudes can be measured. *American Journal of Sociology, 33*, 529–554.

Uhlmann, E., & Swanson, J. (2004). Exposure to violent video games increases automatic aggressiveness. *Journal of Adolescence, 27*, 41–52.

Warren, J. T., & Kilgard, A. K. (2001). Staging stain upon the snow: Performance as a critical enfleshment of whiteness. *Text and Performance Quarterly, 21*(4), 261–276.

Weaver, J., III. (1991, Summer). Are "slasher" horror films sexually violent? A content analysis. *Journal of Broadcasting & Electronic Media, 35*(3), 385. Retrieved August 28, 2008, from Communication & Mass Media Complete Database.

SAMPLING

KEY TERMS

Cluster sampling

Convenience sample

Data saturation

Extreme instance sampling

Generalizability

Maximum variation sampling

Network sampling

Nonrandom sampling

Proportional stratified sample

Purposive samples

Quota sampling

Random sampling

Refusal rate

Response rate

Sample size

Sampling frame

Simple random sample

Snowball sampling

Statistical power

Stratified sample

Theoretical construct sampling

Typical instance sampling

Unit of analysis

Volunteer sample

Chapter Objectives

1. To understand how we select the participants we include in our research
2. To know how to design the sample for a research study that is valid and representative
3. To be able to critique how representative a given sample is

▼ # How Important Is Sampling?

We cannot overstate how important sampling is to the quality, validity, and credibility of your research study. You may have the best study design, do the best possible job in writing a survey instrument or study protocol, do an outstanding job in coding or statistical analysis, but if all your effort is based on a poor sample, you are simply wasting your time. Proper sampling ensures that you are appropriately representing whomever you say you're representing (we'll talk more about this in a minute). By the way, this is called *external validity*—are your findings valid among the population you're studying? (We'll discuss this in more detail in Chapter 9.) For now, just know that *whom* you study is just as important as *how* you study them.

This chapter will give you an overview of the theory behind sampling and will help you tie different types of sampling to different metatheories and research paradigms. We'll also talk about the basic concepts behind appropriate sampling, then we'll teach you how sampling is done in both quantitative and qualitative research. We'll also discuss issues such as sample size and statistical power.

▼ # Sampling Theory

generalizability
Ensuring that a researcher's findings will apply to other people and situations that a study's sample supposedly represents.

Generalizability and Representation

First, let's explain a basic concept behind research design. In research, a *sample* of people is chosen to be included in the study as participants. This *sample* is expected to be *representative* of the entire *population* under study. Because you have chosen a *representative sample*, you can find out information about the *population* without having to actually interview the entire *population*.

Maybe you're asking what's wrong with interviewing the entire population. Do you know what it is called when you actually interview an entire population? It's a *census*. It's so difficult to do that, that the federal government only does it once every ten years. Few researchers can afford to take a census of their entire population. And, it's not necessary.

Unless you have an extremely small population, you would want to research a sample of your population. However, there is a trade-off in researching only a sample of your population: how well does that sample represent your population? Since you are not going to include everyone, the people you do include act as spokespersons for everyone else. In quantitative research, especially, this issue of representation is quite salient, as each study participant potentially represents the ideas or opinions of thousands of people. And in quantitative research, you are measuring and making predictions about those measurements, projecting them to your population. Obviously, if you are going to make predictions about your population based on the research you do of your sample, you want your sample to *accurately* represent your population in a measurable way. Representation is important in qualitative research also, by the way, but in a different way. We'll discuss that shortly.

So, let's talk about representation—how much of a problem is this? Wouldn't any group of people from your population represent your population? And how large should this group be? Five percent of the population? Fifty percent?

Let's look at an example. When your author Christine Davis was growing up, my parents had fairly conservative beliefs, while my sisters and I had fairly liberal beliefs. Suppose you wanted to survey us to determine how we felt about 10:00 PM Friday night curfews. And suppose you said my parents should represent our family—after all, they are the parents.

If you interviewed my parents, you would be talking to 40 percent of our family. Surely this is a large enough sample to be representative, right? Wrong!

If you had sampled my parents about their attitudes toward the curfew, you would probably have gotten 100 percent responses in favor of the curfew. Is this representative of the population? Let's take a census and compare:

- Mom—For
- Dad—For
- Cris—Against
- Kathy—Against
- Kelly—Against

The results of the census show that, in the population, only 40 percent were for the curfew, and 60 percent were against it.

Then why did the sample show such a big difference from the census? Why wasn't interviewing 40 percent of the population enough?

It might have been, *if* it had been a representative sample.

In both quantitative and qualitative research, in order to derive a representative sample, there are several steps you would take.

You would first define your population. Your population may be as broad as all adults over the age of 18, but you still need to state the definition. More likely, your population will have some parameters, such as Communication Studies undergraduates at your university (that's a pretty narrow definition), or all young adults between the ages of 18 and 24 (that's a fairly broad definition). If you're a rhetorical scholar, perhaps you study African American oratory. That's pretty wide open. In order to conduct a research project, you would need to define which orators, which years, which speeches you plan to study, and so on. Perhaps you're an ethnographer, and you want to understand how a particular mental health treatment team interacts (see Davis, 2006), or how a specific street gang communicates (see Siegel & Conquergood, 1990). That mental health team or street gang would be your population, but then your sampling would be more concerned with representing their meetings or interactions. For example, you might want to observe student activities on campus; and in this case, you're not sampling people, you're sampling observations (times of day, weeks, months, year, variety of locations, etc.). For example, you wouldn't only observe the library on Saturday morning during summer session—this likely is not representative of all student activities, and will likely produce very different data than observing the student center at lunchtime during fall semester. To be representative, you'd want to observe both, and probably more (more times, places, etc.).

Sampling Frame

sampling frame
A realistic version of your population; the ones you can identify and access.

Once you have defined your population, you have to determine how you will access them. The ones you have access to are called your **sampling frame**. For example, if your population consists of all Communication Studies undergraduates at your university, you might define your sampling frame as all Communication Studies majors currently enrolled in classes. This will capture most of your population, but not all. The sampling frame can be thought of as the realistic version of your population—the ones you can identify and access. Perhaps you want to study newspaper accounts of a particular event. You might define your sampling frame as the news stories available through the Lexis-Nexis database. If you're studying that medical team or street gang, your sampling frame might be the meetings or interactions you have access to.

Unit of Analysis or Sampling Units

unit of analysis
Sampling units.

Your next step will be to define your **unit of analysis** or sampling units. Most of the time, your unit of analysis will be individuals—individual students in our example above. Sometimes, however, your unit of analysis will be something other than individuals. For example, if you are studying couples' communication, your unit of analysis may be marital (or relational) dyads. If you are studying patient–provider communication, your unit of analysis may be patient–provider dyads. If you are studying group communication, your unit of analysis may be meetings, or groups themselves. Other units of analysis or sampling units might consist of sites, activities or events, times, or artifacts (documents, diaries, or texts). In a participatory action research study examining narrative as a method of transformation within emergency medicine, Eisenberg, Baglia, and Pynes (2006) defined their unit of analysis as an entire emergency room department, while their unit of analysis was observation of communication.

● ●

▼ # Sampling in Quantitative Research

Sampling Methods

You have now identified your population by defining it, by identifying your sampling frame, and by defining your unit of analysis. Now you need to determine what sampling method you will use to represent your population. The sampling method you choose depends a lot on your study objectives, hypothesis, or research questions. Let's define the different types of samples used in quantitative research.

Random Sampling. In quantitative research, in order to ensure that you have a representative sample, you sample *randomly*. This means that each person in the population (or, really, your sampling frame) has an equal chance of being interviewed as each other person. The laws of statistics and probability insure that, if you have a true random sample, it will be representative of your population. **Random sampling** is typically used by research in the positivist paradigm, because it helps ensure the objective reality being measured is being measured accurately. By the way, random samples are also called probability samples, because, based on probability theory, there is a probability (that you can measure) that the sample represents the population. Therefore, nonrandom samples are also called nonprobability samples.

Das, Kerkhof, and Kuiper (2008) used a fairly random sample for their study of the effectiveness of alternative fundraising messages. Here's how they described their sampling procedure:

> *Passersby in the vicinity of the university campus of a large city were asked if they were willing to participate in a survey about the work of the Leprosy Foundation. Upon agreeing, participants were asked to read one of eight fundraising messages.... (p. 166)*

What do you think makes this a random sample? What could the researchers have done to make it even more representative?

SIMPLE RANDOM SAMPLE. The first sampling method, therefore, is called a **simple random sample**. Professional researchers (such as market researchers) who have more sophisticated technology do this by creating computer-generated random telephone numbers. A computer generates random seven-digit combinations of numbers, and these numbers are called. This allows an equal chance that people with unlisted numbers will be called, as well as those with listed numbers. You can approximate this method yourself. Get a list of your sampling frame, perhaps a telephone book, or a list of every Communication major, or a course registration list. Pick every fifth name (or tenth, or twentieth, depending on the sample size you desire). Make sure you call people from the beginning of the book, the middle of the book, and the end of the book. You don't want Jonathan Abernathy to have a greater chance of being called than Benny Zimmerman. Another alternative is to generate a list of random numbers through your computer (e.g., Excel has a function to do this). Number your sampling frame, giving the first name on the list a number of one, and so on. If you want a sample size of 100, generate a list of 100 random numbers. Choose the 100 people from your sampling frame who correspond to the random numbers.

Here's an example of how this works in real-life research. Mannion (2008) studied the effects of caring for people with Alzheimer's disease on informal caregivers. She used a:

> *... random representative group of caregivers registered with the Alzheimer Society of Ireland, Galway, or the Western Alzheimer's Foundation. The sampling frame was the list of caregivers registered with these organizations. The technique for the study was simple random sampling, which involved an employee from both voluntary organizations randomly selecting numbers from the list of registered caregivers until the required number of subjects was chosen. (p. 33)*

random sampling
A sample in which everyone in your sampling frame has an equal chance of being included in the study.

simple random sample
A basic sampling method where a group of subjects (sample) are selected for study from a larger group (population), and each member of the population has an equal chance of being chosen at any point during the sampling process.

stratified sample
A type of sampling that uses a technique in which different subcategories of the sample are identified and then randomly selected.

STRATIFIED SAMPLE. Sometimes you want more detail by subgroup than simple random sampling provides. Let's say you're not just interested in Communication Studies students in general, but you want to be able to compare students in Interpersonal Communication classes with students in Public Speaking classes, and students in Mass Media classes. You would take a **stratified sample**. Interpersonal Communication students would be one stratum, Public Speaking students would be another stratum, and Mass Media students would be a third stratum. In this case, rather than sampling 100 students randomly, you might randomly sample 33 students in the first stratum, 33 in the second stratum, and 33 in the third stratum.

In a content analysis of newspaper radio schedules from 1930 to 1939 in three major Canadian cities to determine what percentage of the programming originated from the United States as opposed to Canada, MacLennan (2005) used a stratified random sample—taking three weeks' programming from each year. She had ten strata—each year was a stratum, and the strata had equal sample sizes (three weeks' programming in each).

proportional stratified sample
A type of sampling that uses a technique in which different subcategories of the sample are identified and then selected proportionate to their occurrence in the population.

PROPORTIONAL STRATIFIED SAMPLE. Let's say you want to represent students from Interpersonal Communication, Public Speaking, and Mass Media, but you want to represent them proportionally to their occurrence in the population. For example, perhaps 40 percent of your students are Interpersonal Communication students, while 45 percent are Public Speaking students, and 15 percent are Mass Media students. In this case, you would take a **proportional stratified sample**. Since 40 percent of the students are Interpersonal Communication students, then 40 percent of your sample (out of your sample of 100, or 40 students) would be Interpersonal Communication students; 45 percent (or 45 out of 100) would be Public Speaking students; and 15 percent (or 15 out of 100) would be Mass Media students.

For example, in order to study the optimal channel distribution (theaters, home video, video on demand) of movies and media, Hennig-Thurau, Henning, Sattler, Eggers, and Houston (2007) used a proportional stratified random sample to represent movie consumers in three major movie markets: the United States, Japan, and Germany. They drew three random samples of a total of 5,094 consumers in the United States (n = 1,701), Japan (n = 1,802) and Germany (n = 1,591), with the sample from each country proportionate to that country's overall population.

cluster sampling
A type of sampling method in which clusters, or groups (subsets of a population), are identified that are representative of the entire population, and are then sampled randomly within each cluster, letting each cluster represent the population.

CLUSTER SAMPLING. What if you can't get a sampling frame for your entire population? Let's say that you have defined your population as Communication Studies majors, but you can't access a list of all majors. You can, however, get several instructors to give you access to their class rosters. You could conduct what's called **cluster sampling**. In cluster sampling, you identify clusters, or groups (subsets of your population), that you think are representative of the entire population and sample randomly within each cluster, letting each cluster represent the population. In the example, you could use Dr. Smith's Public Speaking class as one cluster, and Dr. Jones' Interpersonal Communication class as another cluster. The trade-off for this method is obvious—if you cannot ensure that the clusters truly represent the population, you do not have a representative sample.

Hilari and Northcott (2006) used cluster sampling to understand the role of social support on communication difficulties (called *aphasia*) after a stroke. Their clusters were three different speech therapy and rehabilitation sites, and they sampled randomly within each cluster.

Sarrafzadegan et al. (2009) evaluated the effects of a lifestyle intervention on diet, physical activity, and smoking in communities in Iran. They used cluster sampling in which they targeted three counties, and randomly sampled within each county. The counties each served as a cluster.

Nonrandom Sampling.   Sometimes for logistical or convenience reasons, quantitative researchers use **nonrandom sampling** techniques. The most commonly used nonrandom samples in quantitative research are: convenience samples, volunteer samples, and snowball samples. While nonrandom sampling might be used by researchers with a positivist bent, they are used with an acknowledgment of the accuracy they're giving up by not using a random sample. Researchers from an interpretivist metatheoretical bent might be more comfortable with samples that are representative in ways that are different from orderly, fixed, predictable measurements.

nonrandom sampling
Sample that is not generalizable to the population; sample that is not a random sample.

CONVENIENCE SAMPLE.   A **convenience sample** is, simply, a group of people that is convenient to access—a Communication Studies class, for example, or patients of a particular doctor or medical clinic, or employees of a particular organization.

Samp and Haunani Solomon (2005) sampled 106 dating couples to analyze their dyadic communication before and after they received certain types of problematic messages. This is clearly an experimental design (see Chapter 12), a very positivist method, yet the authors used a convenience sample of students solicited from "undergraduate communication courses at a large Midwestern university" (p. 30). Students were given extra credit or $10 to participate. Samp and Solomon's analysis does not discuss the limitations of their sample choice, but we can think of several. First, their sample is only representative of those 106 dyads. It's not necessarily representative of all communication students in that university, because students who participated may be different than students who didn't. Even if that wasn't an issue, it's also only representative of couples with the same demographics as the people in their sample—18 to 31 years old, and in relationships from 1 to 70 months. What other limitations to the sample can you think of? Nonetheless, it's published in a key communication journal (*Communication Monographs*), and this method of sampling is common in academic studies.

convenience sample
A group of people that is convenient to access.

VOLUNTEER SAMPLE.   A **volunteer sample** is similar to convenience sampling—it consists of people who are willing to volunteer for a study, perhaps people who respond to a flyer you send out or post. Wilson, Morgan, Hayes, Bylund, and Herman (2004), for example, used a volunteer sample in a study to categorize mothers' child abuse potential based on observation of playtime interactions between mothers and children. They posted flyers advertising the study at two social service agencies, and when clients indicated an interest in participating, the researchers contacted them.

volunteer sample
Consists of people who are willing to volunteer for a study.

snowball sampling
This sampling method asks study participants to make referrals to other potential participants, who in turn make referrals to other participants, and so on.

SNOWBALL SAMPLING. **Snowball sampling** is the method of asking study participants to make referrals to other potential participants, who in turn make referrals to other participants, and so on.

Doerfel and Taylor (2004), for example, conducted a social network analysis (analysis of social networks) of Croatian organizations to understand how organizations and media in Croatia work together. They used snowball sampling to identify organizations to include in their sample. In their paper, they state:

Organizations for inclusion . . . were identified through interviews with USAID, IREX Pro-Media (1999), Soros, and the British Fund. These international donors identified active organizations in the 2000 parliamentary campaign that were also continuing to work on civil-society projects. (p. 381)

We think this was a very appropriate use of the nonrandom sample. Do you agree? Why?

Network sampling is using social or other networks (workplace, organizations, support groups, etc.) to locate and recruit participants.

network sampling
Using social networks to locate or recruit study participants.

Smith et al. (2008) sampled agricultural workers to assess brochures designed to inform them about the threat of hearing loss in their profession. They recruited participants through "seminars sponsored by the Michigan Farm Bureau . . . [and] through a pesticide certification meeting and by contacting the landscape departments of large organizations and local firms" (p. 204). This was network sampling—the networks being the Michigan Farm Bureau, the pesticide meeting, and the organizations and firms.

Research exploring the unique communication processes surrounding adoption within a family system requires creative use of both snowball and network sampling. Specifically, Harrigan and Braithwaite (2010) were interested in adoptions wherein it would be obvious to outsiders an adoption had taken place due to differences in racial characteristics, a visible adoption. Here they describe their sampling decision:

We used both network and snowball sampling procedures. Participants met three specific criteria. First, they were the age of majority in the state in which they resided. Second, they parented a visibly adopted child. Third, they self-identified as heterosexual. It is important to note that we do not deny the need for understanding salient communication in same sex families; instead adding this last criterion allowed us to focus on parents' communication regarding adoption and visible differences rather than same sex parenting. (p. 130)

ADVANTAGES AND DISADVANTAGES. The advantages of nonrandom samples are obvious—they are easier (and often less expensive) to obtain than random samples, so research projects can be facilitated. The dangers to such samples are many, however. Research that gives a great deal of information about a nonrepresentative sample can be useless or at least misleading. It's important to know who or what your sample is representative OF, and limit your conclusions to that population. Use of all samples must be done with the full knowledge of the limitations of the study.

Response Rate and Refusal Rate

Another factor in determining how representative your sample is of your population is the **response rate**. The response rate is the proportion of people actually included in your sample, relative to the number of people you attempted to include. In other words, it's the number of people who agreed to participate, versus the number of people who refused participation (called the **refusal rate**). The higher the response rate, the better, and you generally want your response rate to be 60 percent or better. The problem with low response rates is that, if a lot of people are refusing to take part in your study, people who agree may be different in some way than people who refuse. Perhaps people who agree have an ax to grind, or perhaps one (or both) of the groups have some sort of biased opinion. With a low response rate, you can't be sure that your sample is representative of your population. There are several things you can do about low response rates. The first set of suggestions involves ways to improve your response rate: Offer an incentive of some kind to get more people to agree to participate; follow up with people who refuse to participate to ask them again, hoping they'll change their mind the second time you ask; make your study easy to participate in (shorter surveys, for example), so they'll be less likely to refuse. The second suggestion is to determine if people who refused to participate have similar attitudes or characteristics than people who agreed. The only way to do this is to recontact a sample of those who refused and try to get them to answer a few questions from the original survey, so that you can compare their responses with people who completed the entire study.

Sample Size and Power

Now that you know who to talk to, how many of them do you talk to? How many is enough to represent your population?

Let's do an experiment. You can do this yourself. Take a jar of marbles—some are black and some are white. You want to know how many black marbles are in this jar. You don't want to take the time to count them, so you take a sample.

Let's also say that you can draw out random handfuls of marbles.

In the first handful, you pull out five marbles—two of them are black (40%). You put them back and shake up the jar. Now, you pull out ten marbles—five of them are black (50%). You put them back and shake up the jar. Now, you pull out twenty marbles—eleven are black (55%).

Each time you increase your sample size, the number of black marbles you find in your sample is closer to what the actual number really is in your population. (Because you counted the marbles before you started the experiment, you know that 60% of the marbles are black).

The larger sample you take, the more representative that sample is of the population. This is the "Law of Large Numbers."

So, you might wonder, what is large enough? That depends on what you want to do with the information after you get it.

Let's define two more terms: *confidence levels* and *margins of error*. You may have heard a television newscaster quote a political poll and say it had a 5 percent margin of error at a 95 percent confidence level. Statisticians talk about confidence levels of 80 percent, 90 percent, and 95 percent.

response rate
The proportion of people actually included in a sample, relative to the number of people that were attempted to be included.

refusal rate
The number of people that refuse participation in a study.

A confidence level of 95 percent means that, if you take 100 handfuls of marbles, 95 of those times you will come up with the same number of black marbles that are actually in the jar, within a margin of error, which we will define in a minute.

In other words, there is a 95 percent probability that your answer is pretty close to correct.

How close you are to correct is the margin of error. If you have a 5 percent margin of error, that means that your answer is within −5 or +5 percentage points of the true answer in the population.

In the case of your marbles, if you have a 5 percent margin of error, that means you count out between 55 percent and 65 percent black marbles.

If we tell you that at a 95 percent confidence level and a 5 percent margin of error, there are 60 percent black marbles in the jar, we are telling you that there is a 95 percent probability that there are between 55 percent and 65 percent black marbles in the jar.

Using a more real-life example, if we tell you that at a 95 percent confidence level and a 5 percent margin of error, your advertisement has 80 percent consumer recall, we are telling you that there is a 95 percent probability that your advertisement has consumer recall somewhere from 75 percent to 85 percent.

If you're right 95 percent of the time, that's not bad odds, is it? What confidence level you choose to use depends on what you are going to do with the information. For example, if your doctor is choosing a medicine to treat you for cancer, you surely want your doctor to choose a drug that was tested with a pretty high confidence level—99 percent, preferably (100% is impossible). If you are making a go/no-go decision on spending your life savings to open a business, you would probably want a fairly high confidence level. Other decisions only warrant an 80 percent confidence level—being right 80 percent of the time isn't always bad. In social science research, like the quantitative research Communication Studies scholars conduct, most studies are conducted at the threshold of 95 percent confidence level with a desired margin of error at ±5 percent.

So, you may ask: What does all this have to do with sample size? There are many factors that enter into the statistics of sample size, and they have to do primarily with the statistical power you want for your study. We'll talk a lot more about this in later chapters when we discuss statistics, but for now, you need to understand what statistical power has to do with **sample size**. **Statistical power** is defined as the probability your research will identify a statistical effect when it occurs. You want your sample size to be large enough to give your study the ability to do just that—to detect a statistical effect when it actually occurs. Statistical power is determined by a combination of sample size, confidence level, margin of error, and the data itself resulting from the research. The sensitivity of your research to identify this statistical effect can be increased by increasing your sample size. In other words, the larger your sample, the more statistical power your study has. However, there's a limit as to how large you can make your sample. For cost and other practical considerations, you want your sample to be just large enough to have the statistical power you need. To determine what that is, you conduct an *a priori* power analysis; to do this, you need to know your

sample size
The number of data sources that are selected from a total population.

statistical power
The probability that research will identify a statistical effect when it occurs.

desired confidence level, your desired margin of error, and the data proportions you expect to find in your study. Since you often won't know the data results you expect ahead of time, researchers use a general rule to calculate power and sample size. This rule assumes the largest sample size necessary to detect effect size. The chart below gives what that sample size rule would be for each of several combinations of confidence level and margin of error. For example, if you are conducting a study and plan to set a confidence level of 95 percent and want to be able to detect differences at an error factor of ±5 percent, you would want to have a sample size of 400. If you are content with detecting differences at an error factor of ±8 percent, you can lower your sample size to 150.

| | At a confidence level of: | | | |
	80%	90%	95%	99%
With an error factor of:	**Your sample size should be:**			
± 5%	160	275	400	665
8%	64	100	150	260
±10%	40	70	100	170

For you math lovers in the class (yes, we know there are a few!), the formula for determining these sample sizes is:

$$n = \frac{(s^2)pq}{B^2}$$

In this formula, p and q are the two proportions (percentages) you'll be conducting your study to determine. Thus, this really contains circular reasoning, since you need to know what those proportions will be to determine your sample size, but you don't know what they are until you conduct your study. You can be more precise in determining sample size if you base these numbers on a pilot study or on previous research. However, for the purposes of the chart above, we used the most conservative estimate of proportions—we estimated that the proportions would end up being 50–50. B refers to the error factor (±5%, etc.), and s refers to the number of standard deviations from the mean your confidence intervals are. We haven't discussed this yet and won't until we get into statistics later, but for now know that:

A confidence level of	Is this many standard deviations from the mean
80	1.28
90	1.645
95	1.96
99	2.58

So, if you want to determine the sample size for an error factor of 5 percent, a confidence level of 95 percent, and proportions that are 50–50, your formula would be:

$$n = \frac{(1.96^2)(.5)(.5)}{.05^2}$$

If you do the math, it comes to 384. We round to 400.

We said previously that there are many factors that enter into deciding the sample size. Strangely enough, the size of the population is not one of the factors that makes a big difference in the necessary sample size. Generally speaking, the size of your population is irrelevant to your desired sample size.

The only time the population size is important is if it is extremely small—so small that your sample size would be 5 percent or more of your population size (or when your population is less than 20 times larger than your sample). Then, there is a statistical correction for a small population. However, even this correction doesn't make much of a difference.

Again, for you math lovers, here's the formula for the correction:

$$\sqrt{1 - \frac{n}{N}}$$

You may remember from your statistics class that small n refers to your sample size and large N refers to your population size. So, let's say the earlier formula said you should have a sample size of 400, but your population size is only 4,000. If you apply those numbers to this formula for the small population correction, you'll end up with .95, which is the correction you should make to the sample size. Thus, .95 * 400 (the original sample size) is 380—and that's the sample size correction you would make.

You may have noticed that you can't use this formula if your population is smaller than your sample size, because you'll be trying to get the square root of a negative number and you can't do that. That's okay. First of all, if your population is that small, you may want to reconsider your desired confidence level and error factor, conduct a census, redefine your population, or consider a qualitative or case study method. Otherwise, you may feel better to note that Hamburg (1970), in his classic statistics textbook, states that "so long as the population is large relative to the sample, sampling precision becomes a function of sample size alone and does not depend on the relative proportion of the population sampled" (p. 290). In other words, it's what we said earlier—the size of your population is somewhat irrelevant to your desired sample size. Hamburg also notes that in the early days of statistics, researchers just arbitrarily sampled a percentage of their population—10 percent, for example. We don't generally recommend that, but you'll have to make some concession if your population is that small.

You may be saying to yourself it doesn't make sense that population size is irrelevant to your desired sample size. Well, it really does. The reason for this is that all populations, regardless of their size, fall into what is called a *normal distribution.*

This means that, in any population, 95 percent of the responses will cluster around the average response, with a certain variability.

This is true if the population is 100 people or one million people. Since the sample is attempting to represent this cluster of responses, it doesn't matter how large the population is. We are only interested in sampling enough people to represent the curve of responses, regardless of the size of the population.

· ·

Sampling in Qualitative Research   ▼

Sampling Methods

In qualitative research, you are also sampling to represent the population. However, you don't want to represent the population numerically or in a way that you can predict numbers or proportions. You want to represent the sample behaviorally, or in a way that you can describe or understand the population. While quantitative research typically involves large samples so you can make accurate predictions mathematically (little information about a lot of people), qualitative research typically involves small samples that you study in-depth (a lot of information about a few people). Qualitative researchers frequently also use convenience and volunteer samples, snowball and network sampling, but they also use other types of sampling methods.

Purposive Sampling.   Qualitative samples are often **purposive samples**— samples chosen for a particular purpose. For example, in health-care research, you might want to conduct a focus group among residents of a battered women's shelter who have been receiving services for at least six months, so you would specifically choose people who meet that purpose or criteria. You might purposely choose people because they can serve as *informants*→people who can give you inside information about the group you're studying.

purposive samples
Samples chosen for a particular purpose.

Karen Tracy (2007), for example, used a purposive sample in her case study of crisis communication in school board meetings. She studied meetings from one school board, but her unit of analysis was not school boards, it was meetings. Therefore, we need to see how she chose the meetings to analyze. She did not analyze all the meetings, but she analyzed three specific meetings, chosen because they "were the center of public attention" (p. 438). She also analyzed documents downloaded from the school board's website, as well as all relevant stories in the local newspapers during the time period under study. She determined relevance of documents and news stories based on how whether they discussed the crisis issue.

In order to examine the question of what men think about gender roles and issues surrounding work-life, Tracy and Rivera (2010) recruited thirteen male executive gatekeepers to interview. Other forms of sampling simply wouldn't have been appropriate to answer this question. Remember that your questions should help determine your methods, including the best choices for sampling.

Martin (2004) also observed meetings—workplace meetings—to investigate the use of humor among women in middle management positions. She conducted research at one field site (a zoo) and sampled women who fit the desired characteristics (they were middle managers). She also studied the people who report to them and their male peers as informants. Her paper clearly states the limitations of this sampling method:

It is important to realize that the findings from this study are limited to the site and informants from which they are derived. For example, the behaviors exhibited by managers at The Zoo cannot be assumed to apply to non-white women, who may confront additional or very different constraints around humor usage and who may face entirely different forms of organizational paradox. (p. 153)

Yet, even though the findings may not be generalizable in a positivist sense, how might an interpretivist feel about the representativeness of the sample?

Quota Sampling.   Perhaps you want to talk to people who have been receiving services at the battered women's shelter for less than six months and people who have been receiving services for more than six months. You might conduct five in-depth interviews among people who meet each of those criteria. If you did this, you would be doing **quota sampling**—assigning quotas of interviews/focus groups to different groups. You'll notice that quota sampling is similar to stratified sampling, but stratified sampling is a random sampling method while quota sampling is conducted with nonrandom samples.

For example, Duke and Ames (2008) conducted a study to understand unplanned pregnancies among women enlisted in the U.S. Navy. They conducted fifty-two in-depth interviews at seven naval facilities. They used quota sampling, and in order to adequately represent the different viewpoints involved, they assigned quotas by gender, occupation (sailors versus other personnel), and location.

Maximum Variation Sampling.   Qualitative researchers also use several other sampling methods to ensure that their samples represent their populations in ways that meet their study objectives. **Maximum variation sampling** is a method that selects study participants to find examples that represent a wide range of characteristics that are present in the population and are of interest to the research. This sampling method is based on the "law of requisite variety," which says that any research study should represent the variety of characteristics present in the population. If you're studying street gang interactions, you might want to observe a range of different types of meetings or interactions.

Tracy (2004), for example, observed and interviewed correctional officers and staff to analyze organizational discourse. She "studied both male and female officers who worked 8- and 12-hour shifts and who represented a variety of ethnic backgrounds but were primarily white, black, and Hispanic" (p. 126). Assuming these characteristics represent the range of characteristics at the correctional facility, she used maximum variation sampling.

Theoretical Construct Sampling.   **Theoretical construct sampling** selects study participants who have characteristics that represent theories on which the study is based. For example, a researcher might wish to study medical teams through the lens of systems theory, and might select such teams based on their systemic properties (e.g., teams that interact with each other a great deal).

---

quota sampling
A nonprobability (nonrandom) sampling technique that sets quotas for key categories to identify how many members of the sample should be put into those categories.

maximum variation sampling
A sampling method that selects study participants that represent a wide range of characteristics that are present in the population and are of interest to the research.

theoretical construct sampling
The selection of study participants who have characteristics representing theories on which a study is based.

Klossner (2008) conducted a study to understand socialization among students in an athletic training program. She used theoretical sampling, specifically recruiting second-year students because they were in the middle of their educational experience, and she theorized that they would be at the third phase of professional socialization and their point of enrollment would enable them to have reciprocal social interaction.

Typical and Extreme Instance Sampling.   **Typical instance sampling** would consist of sampling units (e.g., participants or meetings) who have characteristics typical of the population (e.g., a typical meeting), while **extreme instance sampling** would consist of sampling units who have characteristics quite different from the rest of the population (e.g., unusual interactions).

Davis (2009), in her ethnographic study of a hospice interdisciplinary team, sampled typical interactions between team members by attending various normal team meetings and healthcare visits.

Manatu-Rupert (2000), for example, used extreme instance sampling when she conducted a textual analysis of the depiction of black women in films by African American and non–African American filmmakers. She analyzed two films—Spike Lee's *She's Gotta Have It* and *Lethal Weapon*—chosen for their controversial representation of black women.

Sample Size and Data Saturation

Determining sample sizes for qualitative research is quite different than for quantitative research. Remember, again, you're not trying to measure or predict anything with qualitative samples; you're trying to understand, explain, or describe. For that reason, qualitative researchers are more concerned with the *level of depth* of information than the number of participants about whom they're getting the information. Qualitative researchers sample until they reach what is called **data saturation**—until no new information emerges. Researchers typically begin with a planned sample size (maybe ten to twenty-five interviews, maybe monthly meetings over twelve months, maybe six to twelve months of field observations), then adjust this size as they collect the data, adjusting the size up if they determine they need more information, and adjusting down if they determine they are reaching saturation earlier than expected.

Guest, Bunce, and Johnson (2006) conducted a project about social desirability bias in health research among women from two West African countries, in which they attempted to determine the ideal sample size required for saturation to occur. Their study yielded thematic saturation at twelve interviews, but this may or may not hold for other dissimilar studies. Recommended sample sizes vary depending on the type of qualitative research conducted. These variations will be discussed in more detail in Chapter 14.

typical instance sampling
Consists of sampling units who have characteristics typical of a population.

extreme instance sampling
Consists of sampling units who have characteristics quite different from the rest of a population.

data saturation
Sampling until no new information emerges.

So What?

Whether you're conducting qualitative or quantitative research, whether you're approaching your research from a positivist or an interpretivist paradigm, your sample will be representative of something, and as a good researcher, it's your job to make sure it's representative of what you intend to study. Sampling procedures range from random, parametric samples that are representative of the population in a measurable, predictive sense; to nonrandom, nonparametric samples that are representative of theories, behaviors, descriptions, or viewpoints. We'll talk in Chapter 9 about issues of validity, reliability, and credibility, but for now, know that a study is not valid, reliable, or credible if it doesn't represent whomever or whatever it's supposed to represent.

Glossary

Cluster sampling
A type of sampling method in which clusters, or groups (subsets of a population), are identified that are representative of the entire population, and are then sampled randomly within each cluster, letting each cluster represent the population.

Convenience sample
A group of people that is convenient to access.

Data saturation
Sampling until no new information emerges.

Extreme instance sample
Consists of sampling units that have characteristics quite different from the rest of a population.

Generalizability
Ensuring that a researcher's findings will apply to other people and situations that a study's sample supposedly represents.

Maximum variation sampling
A sampling method that selects study participants that represent a wide range of characteristics that are present in the population and are of interest to the research.

Network sampling
Using social networks to locate or recruit study participants.

Nonrandom sampling
Sample that is not generalizable to the population; sample that is not a random sample.

Proportional stratified sample
A type of sampling that uses a technique in which different subcategories of the sample are identified and then selected proportionate to their occurrence in the population.

Purposive samples
Samples chosen for a particular purpose.

Quota sampling
A nonprobability (nonrandom) sampling technique that sets quotas for key categories to identify how many members of the sample should be put into those categories.

Refusal rate
The number of people that refuse participation in a study.

Response rate
The proportion of people actually included in a sample, relative to the number of people that were attempted to be included.

Sample size
The number of data sources that are selected from a total population.

Sampling frame
A realistic version of your population; the ones you can identify and access.

Simple random sample
A basic sampling method where a group of subjects (sample) are selected for study from a larger group (population), and each member of the population has an equal chance of being chosen at any point during the sampling process.

Snowball sampling
This sampling method asks study participants to make referrals to other potential participants, who in turn make referrals to other participants, and so on.

Statistical power
The probability that research will identify a statistical effect when it occurs.

Stratified sample

A type of sampling that uses a technique in which different subcategories of the sample are identified and then randomly selected.

Theoretical construct sampling

The selection of study participants who have characteristics representing theories on which a study is based.

Typical instance sampling

Consists of sampling units who have characteristics typical of a population.

Unit of analysis

Sampling units.

Volunteer sample

Consists of people who are willing to volunteer for a study.

References

Das, E., Kerkhof, P., & Kuiper, J. (2008). Improving the effectiveness of fundraising messages: The impact of charity goal attainment, message framing, and evidence of persuasion. *Journal of Applied Communication Research, 36*(2), 161–175.

Davis, C. S. (2006). Sylvia's story: Narrative, storytelling, and power in a children's community mental health system of care. *Qualitative Inquiry, 12*(6), 1–24.

Davis, C. S. (2009). *Death: The beginning of a relationship.* Cresskill, NJ: Hampton Press.

Doerfel, M. L., & Taylor, M. (2004). Network dynamics of interorganizational cooperation: The Croatian Civil Society movement. *Communication Monographs, 71*(4), 373–394.

Duke, M., & Ames, G. (2008). Challenges of contraceptive use and pregnancy prevention among women in the U.S. Navy. *Journal of Qualitative Health Research, 18*, 244–253.

Eisenberg, E. M., Baglia, J., & Pynes, J. E. (2006). Transforming emergency medicine through narrative: Qualitative action research at a community hospital. *Health Communication, 19*, 197–208.

Guest, G., Bunce, A., & Johnson, L. (2006). How many interviews are enough? An experiment with data saturation and variability. *Field Methods, 18*(1), 59–82.

Hamburg, M. (1970). *Statistical analysis for decision making.* New York: Harcourt, Brace, & World.

Harrigan, M. M., & Braithwaite, D. O. (2010). Discursive struggles in families formed through visible adoption. *Journal of Applied Communication Research, 38*, 127–144.

Hennig-Thurau, T., Henning, V., Sattler, H., Eggers, F., & Houston, M. B. (2007). The last picture show? Timing and order of movie distribution channels. *Journal of Marketing, 71*, 63–83.

Hilari, K., & Northcott, S. (2006). Social support in people with chronic aphasia. *Aphasiology, 20*(1), 17–36.

Klossner, J. (2008). The role of legitimation in the professional socialization of second-year undergraduate athletic training students. *Journal of Athletic Training, 43*(4), 379–385.

MacLennan, A. F. (2005). American network broadcasting, the CBC, and Canadian radio stations during the 1930s: A content analysis. *Journal of Radio Studies, 12*(1), 85–103.

Manatu-Rupert, N. (2000). The filmic conception of the black female. *Qualitative Research Reports in Communication, 1*(3), 45–50.

Mannion, E. (2008). Alzheimer's disease: The psychological and physical effects of the caregiver's role. Part 2. *Nursing Older People, 20*(4), 33–38.

Martin, D. M. (2004). Humor in middle management: Women negotiating the paradoxes of organizational life. *Journal of Applied Communication Research, 32*(2), 147–170.

Samp, J. A., & Haunani Solomon, D. (2005). Toward a theoretical account of goal characteristics in micro-level message features. *Communication Monographs, 72*(1), 22–45.

Sarrafzadegan, N., Kelishadi, R., Esmaillzadeh, A., Mohammadifard, N., Rabei, K., Roohafza, H., Azadbakht, L., Bahonar, A., Sadri, G., Amani, A., Heidari, S., Malekafzali, H. (2009). Do lifestyle interventions work in developing countries? Findings from the Isfahan Healthy Heart Program in the Islamic Republic of Iran. *Bulletin of the World Health Organization, 87*, 39–50.

Siegel, T. (Producer), & Conquergood, D. (Director). (1990). [DVD]. *The heart broken in half.* Portland, OR: Collective Eye.

Smith, S. W., Rosenman, K. D., Kotowski, M. R., Glazer, E., McFeters, C., Keesecker, N. M., & Law, A. (2008). Using the EPPM to create and evaluate the effectiveness of brochures to increase the use of hearing protection in farmers and landscape workers. *Journal of Applied Communication Research, 36*(2), 200–218.

Tracy, K. (2007). The discourse of crisis in public meetings: Case study of a school district's multimillion dollar error. *Journal of Applied Communication Research, 35*(4), 418–441.

Tracy, S. J. (2004). Dialectic, contradiction, or double bind? Analyzing and theorizing employee reactions to organizational tension. *Journal of Applied Communication Research, 32*(2), 119–146.

Tracy, S. J., & Rivera, K. D. (2010). Endorsing equity and applauding stay-at-home moms: How male voices on work-life reveal aversive sexism and flickers of transformation. *Management Communication Quarterly, 24,* 3–43.

Wilson, S. R., Morgan, W. M., Hayes, J., Bylund, C., & Herman, A. (2004). *Communication Monographs, 71*(4), 395–421.

ENSURING VALIDITY, RELIABILITY, AND CREDIBILITY

9

KEY TERMS

Alternate form reliability

Concurrent validity

Construct validity

Convergent validity

Credibility

Criterion validity

Data triangulation

Discriminant validity

Evaluator apprehension

Face validity

History

Instrumentation

Inter-coder reliability

Item-total reliability

Maturation

Member checks

Peer reviewer

Predictive validity

Random error	Split-half reliability	Thick description
Reliability	Test-retest reliability	Validity
Reliability statistics	Testing	

CHAPTER OBJECTIVES

1. To understand the importance of validity, reliability, and credibility in social research
2. To know different techniques for ensuring validity, reliability, and credibility
3. To be familiar with validity, reliability, and credibility considerations in measurement and research
4. To understand validity, reliability, and credibility threats associated with research processes and procedures

reliability
The ability of a measure to produce the same results if replicated.

validity
Accuracy of a measure, in terms of measuring intended constructs or observations.

credibility
The believability of the research to the reader; how much the reader believes the research to represent participant's reality.

▼ # Thinking about the Quality of Your Observations

In Chapter 7, we discussed operationalizing your variables to make sure you are clear on the elements you are studying. In Chapter 8, we discussed sampling appropriately so that you are representing what/whom you need to be representing. Now, in this chapter, we bring you face-to-face with thinking about other aspects of your research design. Specifically, you must think about your measures and observations in terms of their relative quality. We call these considerations **reliability**, **validity**, and **credibility**.

What Is Reliable? What Is Valid? What Is Credible?

Why would you want to have the highest quality measures? Well, the answer to this question is pretty simple: The better your measures, the more confidence you can have in the conclusions you draw from your research, and the more confidence your audience has in your conclusions. If you think you are measuring one construct, and you are really measuring another, this will undermine your findings. Likewise, if you actually do measure the things you are interested in, but the measures sometimes work and sometimes do not, you will have difficulty in replicating your study—your findings will not be meaningful. And, if you write your analysis in such a way that readers do not believe your interpretations, your research will not be accepted.

When you think of the quality of your observations, measurement, and analysis, that's really the bottom line. You want to know that you really are measuring and representing the things you think you are measuring and representing; further, you want to know that if you did it a number of times, in a number of different ways, you would still be measuring and representing the same things.

Having a measure that replicates over and over again is necessary, but not sufficient, for good measurement. It could very well be measuring the incorrect concept and do a very good job of it. Measures have to be ~~reliable~~, able to produce the same results if replicated. But they must also be ~~valid~~, or accurate, in terms of measuring their intended constructs or observations. Both are necessary for good measurement. Your textbook author Christine Davis is always on some sort of a diet. She used to own a scale that changed the results every time she stepped on it. If she didn't like what the scale said, she'd just get off and keep trying until she found the results she wanted. Fun, maybe, but not at all reliable, and not particularly useful. However, if another scale consistently said she weighed 500 pounds, it would be reliable; but if you knew her, you'd know it wasn't valid.

The measure also needs to be representative of whatever you say you're representing. A scale that reports my weight may consistently report my weight, but it may or may not adequately represent my experience of being a person who fights her body weight. Finally, it needs to be *credible*. My scale may tell me I'm up a pound, but if my clothes are fitting more loosely, that may be a more credible report of my fitness or size.

As we will see, validity threats may be the greatest concern to a researcher in the positivist paradigm, who is trying to measure objective reality, simply because there are many things that can go wrong in that measurement. Reliability is typically a question of designing good measures. With validity, a number of factors can affect your procedures in such a way as to distort your observations. These factors may be related to your sample, the design of the items, the procedures you perform in your study, or problems with research participants. Interpretivists are more concerned with issues of representation and credibility—have I represented all viewpoints, have I adequately described the experience, have I sufficiently interpreted the results?

Sound simple? Actually, this is far more complex than you might think. In fact, there are scholars in Communication and other disciplines who brand themselves as *methodologists*, or sometimes *psychometricians*, who spend their careers investigating new ways of developing quality measures and improving the techniques used for their assessment. Entire books have been written on estimating reliability and validity. This chapter is only a brief description of a multifaceted phenomenon, but it is essential to understand as you begin to think about your own research.

● ●

Reliability ▼

Physical and Social Measurement

Measuring the length of a football field and measuring a person's closeness in a relationship are two very different things. Measurement in the physical sciences is quite different from measurement in the social sciences and humanities, mainly in its degree of precision. The basic units of measurement we use to assess things in the observable physical world—feet, inches, ounces, pounds, miles, degrees Fahrenheit, and so on—are standardized and are not likely to shift from measurement to measurement. A yard is always a yard, so if a football field is found to be 100 yards long, and you measure it again, chances are you will find it to be 100 yards long.

People, on the other hand, are different. The football field is just lying there motionless. People are in constant flux, paying varying degrees of attention, experiencing a myriad of thoughts and emotions that may affect their answers. Further, if you are working with people, then the concepts you are measuring are likely to be rather abstract, and you will have to use several measures that get at the construct in question. In other words, people sometimes change their responses from measure to measure, for reasons you haven't thought of, or perhaps even for no good reason at all.

Random Error

random error
A fluctuation in measurement.

This fluctuation in measurement is called **random error**. According to Nunnally and Bernstein (1994), one definition of reliability is freedom from random error. In other words, reliability refers to how repeatable a measure is from test to test. This could include how well it repeats when it is taken by different people, alternative instruments are used to measure the same thing, or when incidental variation exists in the measures to an extent that is not cause for concern (see the section below on reliability statistics).

Types of Reliability

There are several ways to check if your measures repeat over different time frames and groups of people. A few of them are described below.

test-retest reliability
A reliability method in which the same measure is given to the same people at two different times.

Test-Retest.   This is perhaps the simplest means of checking for reliability. In the **test-retest reliability** method, you simply give the same measure to the same people at two different times. If you don't expect a difference for any other reason, and the scores come out the same, then you can be fairly confident that you have a reliable measure.

Consider this example. You could administer an IQ test to a group of students in a college classroom. For each student, you produce an IQ score estimating his or her intelligence. You then come back the next day and administer the test again. You would expect the scores to be exactly the same, since the test items are the same and it is highly unlikely that a student has suddenly become more intelligent overnight. If the scores turn out pretty much the same, then you can say with some confidence that the measure is reliable.

Of course, this seldom actually happens. For the same reasons related to random error mentioned above, the scores in our IQ example would probably fluctuate a little bit. This does not necessarily mean that the student taking the test has become smarter overnight. Rather, it probably means that the measure is not perfectly reliable. If it is not perfectly reliable that's okay, most measures aren't. But the scores should be pretty close. In a few pages we will discuss just how close they ought to be in order to have confidence that your scale is reliable.

alternate form reliability
A reliability method to determine if the order in which the items in a measure are presented affect the ways in which people respond.

Alternate Form.   **Alternate form reliability** is a handy way to determine whether the order in which the items in your measure are presented affect the ways in which people respond. In this means of testing reliability, you start with a pool of people that you expect to score similarly on your instrument. You then take the same pool of items and rearrange them in different orders to create alternate forms of the same measure. If your measure is free from any reliability threats related to order of presentation, and your subjects are expected to score similarly, then the scores should be fairly similar across the different forms of the measure.

Perhaps the most common example of this takes place in the classroom. If you have ever taken a multiple-choice exam in a large classroom, then you have actually participated in an elaborate measure of your understanding of a particular knowledge base. Chances are your instructor developed different versions of the same exam, with the same items arranged in a different order in an attempt to discourage cheating. Let's say in a perfect world, you take this exam and everyone in the room has complete mastery over the material. If this is the case, then everyone should score very high on the exam, regardless of which form they have. If they do not, then the alternate form test has revealed that there may be reliability problems related to the order in which the questions were presented.

Split-Half. *male + female; equal number of both sexes* Of course, there are more sophisticated means of testing for reliability than simply giving the same test twice, or giving it to the same people with the items rearranged. While Communication researchers may use test-retest or alternate forms as a reliability test when developing a measure, they are much more likely to report more sophisticated techniques in their manuscript. These more sophisticated techniques are known as *internal consistency methods*, and the first of them is called **split-half reliability**.

In split-half reliability, you randomly divide your measure in half. Of course, good measures should have multiple items (as we have previously discussed). Using some kind of randomizing technique (rolling dice, random number table, etc.), you randomly select half of the items on the scale and move them to make a second scale. You, of course, need to make sure that your two scales are separate, but equal. For instance, if your initial scale includes items that measure three dimensions, both halves must also include items from each of three dimensions. Once you've split them, you now have two scales of items that were randomly selected from the scale you are actually using. *Correlation* is a statistical measure of similarity that refers to how closely related two variables are to each other, and you would expect these two new scales to be highly correlated; if they are, you can have confidence that your original scale is reliable. You could then repeat this random splitting over and over again, and the more often you produce this result the more confident you can be in the reliability of your scale and the notion that you do not have a bad item or two.

split-half reliability
A means of evaluating internal consistency of a scale that compares one randomly selected half of a scale from the other randomly selected half of the same scale.

Item-Total.   **Item-total reliability** is the second means of evaluating internal consistency. In this technique, you first create a score for each participant summing each of the items. You then correlate each of the individual items with this sum score. The correlation between any one item on the scale, and the total of all items in the scale, should be fairly high. This would indicate to you that all items in the measure are doing just about the same job of measuring your construct. If you have an item or two that have a substantially lower correlation

item-total reliability
A means of evaluating internal consistency of a scale that compares the total score for a scale with individual item scores for the same scale.

with the scale total, then they are probably not good items. You should remove them from the scale.

Inter-Coder.

inter-coder reliability
An indicator of how similarly coders are coding content, both in terms of identifying units of analysis and in the contextual labels they ascribe to those units.

Inter-Coder. There is another type of reliability that deals with the consistency of your measures, but does not look at how multiple subjects will respond to the same scale. Rather, it deals with how multiple people will rate something that they observe. This is known as **inter-coder reliability**. It is used most often to determine the extent to which those working on a research project will evaluate things in the same way. In Communication research, it is perhaps most common in qualitative coding, content analysis, or observational research. *Coding* refers to the analysis of data (usually textual data) by categorizing it into, usually, thematic categories. In content analysis, for example, you will likely have multiple coders counting and categorizing content in order to process the data in a timely manner. In observational research, you might have multiple observers watching the same phenomenon. In order to have confidence in the judgments that are being made by the coders or observers, you would first need to make sure that they were seeing things in roughly the same way. A rogue coder or inconsistency between coders or observers in their perceptions could cause serious problems with your data.

Consider this example. The National Television Violence Study (Wilson et al., 1997) examined a massive amount of TV content—almost 10,000 hours—and sought to identify not only how often violence occurred, but also certain contextual elements that might be worrisome. In order to code this enormous amount of television content, more than fifty undergraduate coders were trained over a period of months in the definitions of violence and risky portrayals with which they were concerned. While the content was being coded, each coder was given a reliability test every two weeks, in order to make sure all coders were still seeing things in the same way. Accomplishing this huge task in a timely manner required dozens of research employees. To get the job done and in a scientifically rigorous manner, repeated checks for inter-coder reliability were necessary. Today, the NTVS is often held up as the *gold standard* of content analysis, partly due to its ability to maintain inter-coder reliability across such a large group of research employees.

In a study by Jameson, Bodtker, and Linker (2010), they analyzed transcripts of workplace conflict mediation sessions to identify strategies used by mediators to engage others in emotional communication. Throughout this process they used inter-coder reliability to ensure transcripts were coded similarly. This is common in communication research studies.

Reliability Statistics

reliability statistics
Statistical tests that can show consistency between items, reflecting reliability of a scale.

Fortunately, there are **reliability statistics** that can be calculated and reported fairly easily. Since most of the techniques of assessing reliability deal with some calculation of consistency between items, researchers have developed a number of mathematical indicators of the reliability of a particular measure. Measures like a simple correlation coefficient, **r**, can be used to express split-half or item-total reliability fairly easily. Other internal consistency measures that are relied upon more frequently include: Cronbach's Alpha, the Kuder-Richardson formula (KR-20), and Cohen's Kappa. For identifying categories consistently, Scott's Pi (see Krippendorf, 1994) is commonly used to establish inter-coder reliability.

Cronbach's Alpha and KR-20 are used to measure the consistency of items in a list of items. Specifically, Cronbach's Alpha is an average of the correlations of pairs of items, using split-half reliability computed with a correlation coefficient. This is a highly regarded way to measure reliability in scales which measure attitudes, beliefs, or perceptions, when you are simply measuring the reliability of items in a scale. This measure is not appropriate for scales with right-wrong items, or when items should not have high intercorrelations between them (in which case a split-half reliability is not an appropriate measure) (Reinard, 2006). The KR-20 is used to provide estimates of internal consistency for scales when the items in the scale are scored as "passing" or "not passing," such as in a true-false comprehension test (Reinard, 2006).

Cohen's Kappa and Scott's Pi are used to determine agreement between coders or raters. An extension of Scott's Pi can be used when you are comparing the results of more than two coders. Both of these tests result in reliability coefficients that range from 0 to 1.00. In fact, all of these reliability statistics mentioned are based on correlations or coefficients that are designed mathematically to range between 0 and 1.00. A value of 1.00 indicates perfect agreement across all items in the measure, while 0 indicates no agreement at all. An acceptable reliability level is really kind of a subjective call; it depends on the degree of precision you wish to achieve with your measures. You may strive for perfect agreement, but most social researchers agree that perfect agreement is next to impossible when conducting research dealing with people. Unfortunately, people are not machines and, as this chapter points out, 100 percent precision is highly unlikely when examining human behavior. The conventional criterion is that a coefficient of about .70 is the minimum acceptable level of reliability, regardless of which coefficient you choose to use (Fleiss & Cohen, 1973; Krippendorf, 1994; Nunnally & Bernstein, 1994). Jameson et al. (2010), reported their intercoder reliability in the form of Cohen's Kappa at .91, a very solid agreement rating for several unique coders.

This text will not expect you to compute these reliability coefficients yourself, as you can compute each of them in SPSS and other major data analysis programs. Instead, it is more important that you know when it is appropriate to use each one.

Validity ▼

Now that we have discussed the different techniques researchers use to establish what measures perform consistently if given to the sample of people twice, you must deal with whether they are measuring what they are intended to measure. As stated earlier in this chapter, reliability is necessary, but not sufficient for good measurement; a measure can repeat itself with great reliability, yet tap into something completely different from what you think it measures.

Knowing What You Are Measuring

Validity, as a concept, is not nearly as cut and dry as reliability. To determine reliability, researchers typically pretest their measures to see if they hold together, and then conduct and report reliability coefficients to demonstrate the internal consistency of their measures. Validity is much more subtle. There is no magic coefficient that statistically indicates validity. Often, you have to design a study that includes one validity threat in order to avoid another. Validity is really a matter of the researcher's common sense in executing measurement and design decisions that make sense, given the research questions she is asking. The validity of the measures and observations in any study are subjective and debatable, and researchers often engage in debate over the validity of their findings.

✳ Face Validity

face validity
A type of validity consideration in which measures, or procedures, are looked at and questioned if they make sense at face value.

The most simple validity consideration is **face validity**. Face validity is simply looking at the measures, or looking at your procedures, and asking if it makes sense at face value. As simple as this seems, you would probably be amazed at how often social researchers design measures and studies that violate face validity.

Here's an example. Let's say you wanted to design a measure of deceptiveness. You go to the drawing board and come up with twenty items that you believe measure deceptiveness. You give it to a group of college freshmen and discover that, for the most part, they are not deceptive at all. In fact, they appear to be the most honest group of people you have ever come across in your life. You conclude that they are all very trustworthy.

Do you see a problem here? You just asked people to answer a self-report scale concerning how deceptive they are. If you were a deceptive person, why would you be expected to answer honestly? In fact, if you were someone who is prone to being deceptive, you would probably lie when responding to the items on the scale. So, honest people report that they are very honest, and deceptive people lie and report exactly the same thing. This is an example of poor face validity—before even administering the scale we should have known that it doesn't really measure deception. It didn't seem true "on the face of it." You really shouldn't have much confidence in your finding that everyone is honest because at face value it makes no sense.

Criterion Validity

criterion validity
A type of validity consideration that deals with how a particular measure holds up when compared to some outside criterion.

Another type of validity concern is **criterion validity**. Criterion validity deals with how a particular measure holds up when compared to other criteria, variables, or scales you think also measure or indicate the construct your scale intends to measure. Criterion validity can be broken out into two subcategories: predictive validity and concurrent validity.

predictive validity
How well a measure predicts that something that will happen in the future.

✳**Predictive Validity.** **Predictive validity** deals with how well a measure predicts that something that will happen in the future. You may design a measure that you believe gauges a construct that will predict future behavior; in this case, you'll want to know that it actually does. Probably the best-known examples of this are the standardized tests used in college and graduate school admissions.

When you took the SAT, you may have looked at the test items and wondered what in the world they had to do with anything. In actuality, the SAT and other standardized tests are remarkable pieces of psychometric research; across large populations, they predict performance in academic programs with tremendous precision. While there are always exceptions, on the whole, those who perform better on the SAT do better in college. The same goes for the GRE, the LSAT, and the MCAT, as those who do better on these exams do better in graduate school, law school, and medical school, respectively. This is why admission boards rely on them so heavily. Since they want the best prepared students they can get so their programs can be rigorous and train students well, they need to be able to predict success ahead of time. The predictive validity of standardized tests allows them to have confidence that they indicate academic preparation.

Concurrent Validity.   The other form of criterion validity is known as **concurrent validity**. Concurrent validity is simply a case of how well your scale measures up against another scale that has been demonstrated to measure exactly the same thing. You may have a number of reasons for developing a scale that is slightly different, such as making the scale situationally specific, or shortening the scale to eliminate subject fatigue. In any case, you would want to make sure that the new version of a scale correlates very strongly with the old version. This is known as concurrent validity. You would probably want to pretest the scale, giving the same subjects the new scale and the old one, and correlating the scores to make sure that they are fairly similar.

concurrent validity
How well a scale measures up against another scale that has been demonstrated to measure exactly the same thing.

Construct Validity

Another broad category of validity is known as **construct validity**. Construct validity deals with logical relationships between variables. If your measures really get at what they are supposed to get at, then you can make certain predictions about their relationship with other variables with which they ought to have certain relationships (Kerlinger, 1986). If these relationships hold, then you can have a certain amount of confidence that your measure is valid in terms of its relationship to other constructs. Construct validity can be more specifically broken out into convergent and discriminant validity.

construct validity
The extent to which your variables are logically related to other variables.

Convergent Validity.   You may develop a measure and expect it to correlate positively with some other construct. You expect two constructs to be related, though not exactly the same thing. Sound confusing? Here's an example.

Lannutti and Lachlan (2007) thought it might be a good idea to develop a scale measuring people's attitudes toward same-sex marriage, since it might be a slightly different construct than other related ones (such as homophobia). They developed a thirty-two-item scale tapping into the construct and found that it had strong reliability. Next, they expected it to correlate positively with a single item asking respondents if they would vote to approve a bill legalizing same-sex marriage in their state. Although attitudes toward same-sex marriage and willingness to vote in favor of it are not the same thing, logically they should be positively correlated. Sure enough, the researchers found that there was a strong correlation between favorable attitudes on the scale and willingness to vote yes on the hypothetical bill, thus they concluded that their measure had strong **convergent validity**.

convergent validity
When two measures you expect to be related are shown to be positively statistically related.

Discriminant Validity. Conversely, there are constructs with which you may expect your measure to be negatively related. Let's return to our same-sex marriage example from above. Lannutti and Lachlan (2007) also asked their participants to respond to a standardized test measuring homophobia. Logically, you would expect homophobes to not approve of same-sex marriage. Sure enough, the researchers found a strong, negative correlation between their new scale and the established scale measuring homophobia. While the constructs were not the same, they found the expected negative relationship between them; thus, they concluded that their measure had strong **discriminant validity**.

discriminant validity
When two measures you expect to be negatively related (opposite to each other) are shown to have a negative statistical relationship.

Validity and Reliability Examples

Okay, we've talked about valid and reliable measurement in an abstract sense, now let's see how this works in actual research. Let's take a look at Rittenour and Martin's (2008) work on the Communication Based Emotional Support Scale (CBESS). The CBESS is a unidimensional scale and was previously determined to be reliable by the researchers who initially developed it, Weber and Patterson (1996).

From "Convergent Validity of the Communication-Based Emotional Support Scale" by C. E. Rittenour & M. M. Martin. *Communication Studies Vol. 59, No. 2*, January 7, 2008. Reprinted by permission of Taylor & Francis Group, www.informaworld.com. ■

communicated within the confines of those relationships warrants scholarly attention to the accuracy of its measurement.

Recognizing that previous scales focused on social support, a construct that primarily focuses on who is giving support and how that support produces positive outcomes, Weber and Patterson (1996) developed the Communication Based Emotional Support Scale (CBESS). This scale focuses on emotional support, incorporating the messages themselves and their emphasis on communicating care or concern as well as the communication networks from which these messages were created. Weber and Patterson created items that addressed qualities of concern, compassion, sympathy, esteem, and helpfulness. Starting with 20-items, they produced a 13-item scale that was internally reliable ($\alpha = .93$). The CBESS was positively correlated with relational solidarity and relationship quality, supporting the validity of the measure.

Communication-based emotional support has been studied in numerous types of relationships, including dating partners, superiors–subordinates, friends, spouses, and online support groups (Avtgis, 2000; Campbell & Wright, 2002; Merolla, 2004; Weber & Patterson, 1996; Wright, 2002). The CBESS was positively related to trust, commitment, relationship satisfaction, attributional confidence, and perceived understanding while negatively related to evoking jealousy (Avtgis, 2003; Cayanus, Martin, & Weber, 2004; Weber, Johnson, & Corrigan, 2004). Campbell, Martin, and Weber (2001) found that when superiors frequently used avoidance strategies, subordinates reported less emotional support, whereas when superiors frequently used approach strategies, subordinates reported more emotional support. When applied to online-support groups' emotional support, when superiors frequently used approach strategies, sub-ordinates reported more emotional support. When online-support group superiors frequently used approach strategies, subordinates reported more emotional support. When applied to online-support groups, communication-based emotional support was negatively correlated with perceived stress, dominance, and formality and positively correlated with immediacy, similarity, receptivity, and equality among group members (Campbell & Wright, 2002; Wright, 2002). By correlating communication based emotional support with the aforementioned variables, these findings provide some construct validity and criterion-related validity of the scale. The purpose of this study was to further establish convergent validity by correlating the Communication Based Emotional Support Scale with other support scales.

As you can see from the excerpt from Rittenour and Martin's (2008) article, Weber and Patterson (1996) developed a thirteen-item scale that, they determined, had internal reliability of $\alpha = .93$, based on a Cronbach's Alpha (α stands for "alpha"). Remember earlier we said that reliability statistics range from 0.00 to 1.00, and researchers generally agree that anything over .70 has good reliability. Therefore, the CBESS appears to be a reliable scale. That means it measures whatever it measures consistently.

However, these data do little to tell us anything about the validity of the scale, or the extent to which it measures what it purports to measure. Rittenour and Martin report that Weber and Patterson found that "The CBESS was positively correlated with relational solidarity and relationship quality, supporting the validity of the measure" (p. 236). In other words, they're telling us that the measure has good convergent validity—we would think that emotional support would have a lot in common with relational solidarity and relationship quality. Therefore, this scale is valid. They also cited several other studies that correlated emotional support (using the CBESS) with perceived stress, dominance, and formality (it was negatively correlated, as you would expect, providing discriminant validity), and with immediacy, similarity, receptivity, and equality (it was positively correlated, as you would expect, providing convergent validity). They claim, correctly, that these correlations provide additional construct and criterion validity of the scale. However, they wanted to further test the validity of the scale. They wanted to know if the CBESS also measured similarly to other scales—they wanted to "further establish convergent validity by correlating the Communication Based Emotional Support Scale with other support scales" (p. 237).

The following scales were used to establish the convergent validity of the CBESS: the Perceived Social Support - Friend Scale (PSS-Fr; Procidano & Heller, 1983), which measures participants' perceptions of their own needs for support as fulfilled by friends;

Continued

From "Convergent Validity of the Communication-Based Emotional Support Scale" by C. E. Rittenour & M. M. Martin. *Communication Studies, Vol. 59, No. 2,* January 7, 2008. Reprinted by permission of Taylor & Francis Group, www. informaworld.com. ■

Continued

the friend subscale of the Multidimensional Scale of Perceived Social Support (MSPSS; Zimet, Dahlem, Zimet, & Farley, 1988), which measures participants' perceived social support from friends; the Social Support Behaviors Scale (SSB; Vaus, Riedel, & Stewart, 1987) that measures perceived emotional, socializing, practical assistance, financial assistance, and advice/guidance dimensions of support; and the friend subscale of the Scales of Perceived Social Support (Macdonald, 1998) that measures participants' perceived social support from friends.

Although other support scales omit the two qualities that the CBESS takes into account—the supportive messages themselves and the interpersonal relationships

Their hypothesis was:

H_i: Individuals' scores on the CBESS are positively related to their scores on the Perceived Social Support–Friend Scale, the friend subscale of the Multidimensional Scale of Perceived Social Support, the Social Support Behaviors Scale, and the friend subscale of the Scales of Perceived Social Support. (p. 237)

They administered the scales in a survey to convenience sample of 209 students. What did they find? Their hypothesis was supported; they did determine statistically significant correlations between the CBESS and the other scales.

Results

The hypothesis predicted a positive correlation between scores on the Communication Based Emotional Support Scale and scores on the Perceived Social Support -Friend Scale, the friend subscale of the Multidimensional Scale of Perceived Social Support (MSPSS), the Social Support Behaviors Scale (SSB), and the friend subscale of the Scales of Perceived Social Support (Macdonald, 1998). The hypothesis was supported. Results of two-tailed *Pearson Product-Moment* correlations indicated significant relationships between the CBESS and the following: the Perceived Social Support – Friend Scale ($r = .72$, $p < .01$), the friend subscale of the Multidimensional Scale of Perceived Social Support ($r = .61$, $p < .01$), the Social Support Behaviors Scale ($r = .71$, $p < .01$), and the friend subscale of the Scale of Perceived Social Support ($r = .75$, $p < .01$).

Results of *Pearson Product-Moment* correlations indicated the following positive correlations between communication based emotional support and the subscales of the Social Support Behaviors Scale: emotional ($r = .76$, $p < .01$), socializing

Therefore, they established additional construct validity for the scale.

What if you're not developing a scale, you just want to use a measurement scale in a study you're conducting? Let's look at one more example.

Keaten and Kelly (2008) examined the relationship between family communication patterns, emotional intelligence, and reticence. To measure those three variables, they used three previously developed scales: the Revised Communication Patterns Scale (Ritchie & Fitzpatrick, 1990), the Emotional Intelligence Scale (Schutte et al., 1998), and the Reticence Scale (Keaten, Kelly, & Finch, 1997). They wanted to conduct valid research, so they had to choose scales that were themselves valid and reliable. One of the first things Keaten and Kelly do when they describe their study methods to us is tell us the reliability and validity statistics of the scales they are using:

Measures

The questionnaire packet consisted of three instruments: (a) The Reticence Scale, (b) Emotional Intelligence Scale, and (c) the Revised Family Communication Patterns scale. The Reticence Scale (RS; Keaten, Kelly, & Finch, 1997) is a 24-item measure of reticence, employing a 5-point Likert scale (1 = Strongly Disagree to 5 = Strongly Strongly Agree). The RS measures six dimensions of reticence experienced in social situations: (a) feelings of anxiety ("I am nervous when talking"); (b) knowledge of conversational topics ("I know what to discuss"); (c) timing skills ("I say things at the time I want to say them"); (d) organization of thoughts ("I arrange my thoughts when talking"); (e) delivery skills ("I fluently say what I want to say"); and (f) memory ("I remember what to say when talking"). Scores for each of the six dimensions range from 1 to 21. Total scores range from 6 to 126; lower scores indicate lower levels of reticence, that is, less anxiety, fewer problems with knowledge, timing, delivery, and so on. The internal consistency of the RS has been consistently high (α > .90) in prior studies (Keaten et al., 1997, 2000; Kelly et al., 2002). In this study, reticence was treated as a unidimensional construct by combining scores of the six dimensions. Using Cronbach's alpha, the reliability for the RS was .91.

The Emotional Intelligence Scale (EIS; Schutte et al., 1998) consists of 33 statements based on the emotional intelligence model developed by Salovey and Mayer (1990) and is measured using a 5-point Likert scale (1 = Strongly Disagree to 5 = Strongly Agree). The EIS has been shown to have a good internal consistency and test-retest reliability (Schutte et al., 1998). Validation studies indicated that scores on the EIS correlated with 8 of 9 theoretically related constructs, including alexithymia, attention to feelings, clarity of feelings, mood repair, optimism, and impulse control. The Cronbach's alpha for the EIS was .85.

The Revised Family Communication Patterns scale (RFCP; Ritchie & Fitzpatrick, 1990) measured participants' perceptions of family communication behaviors. The scale is composed of 26 statements comprising two dimensions: conversation orientation and conformity orientation. Items are measured on a 5-point Likert scale (1 = Strongly Disagree to 5 = Strongly Agree). Ritchie and Fitzpatrick (1990) reported that the internal consistencies of both dimensions were acceptable (conversation orientation, α = .84; conformity orientation, α = .76) and test-retest reliability of the scale was satisfactory (conversation orientation, r = .81; conformity orientation, r = .80). In the present study, the alpha reliabilities were .91 for conversation orientation and .83 for conformity orientation.

From "Development of an Instrument to Measure Reticence" by J. A. Keaten & L. Kelly, *Communication Quarterly*, Vol. 45, No. 1, January 12, 1997. Reprinted by permission of Taylor & Francis Group, informaworld.com. ■

Problems with Participants and Procedural Concerns. To this point, we have discussed validity concerns that pertain directly to the measures we develop in our research. There are other threats to the validity of our research that deal less with the measures themselves and more with what you do with the measures. Sometimes things go awry in our procedures that make us wonder if we are measuring what it is we think we are measuring. Below we will discuss a number of these threats known as *internal validity* threats. They call our observations into question not because our measurement is bad, but because some other factor we have not accounted for is affecting the responses (see Campbell & Stanley, 1963; Cook & Campbell, 1979).

HISTORY. Let's say you ask a number of subjects to report how they feel about driving under the influence. You survey men and women separately; men take the survey on a Monday, while women take it on Thursday. You look at the two groups and see noticeable differences between them. In fact, it appears as though women are much more disapproving of driving while impaired, and you conclude that there are differences between men and women.

Then you read the newspaper. As it turns out, a high-profile celebrity was seriously injured in an alcohol-related car crash on Wednesday night. Now you may have a validity problem known as **history**; something totally unrelated to your study happened at a particular time and may have affected the responses. Are women really different than men in their disapproval of driving under the influence, or did this public event skew their responses? You don't know, and this limits the confidence you can have in your observations.

History can be a serious validity issue when conducting qualitative research (such as focus groups or observations), especially if you're studying naturalistic groups. Let's say you're conducting a focus group among employees in an organization to discuss how they feel about the company's latest health promotion campaign. Unbeknownst to you, a key employee was laid off the previous day. This could affect their reactions in the focus group, and you might mistakenly think their reactions are to the campaign rather than to the layoff.

MATURATION. Another problem that can emerge in terms of the validity of your observations deals with the fact that subjects can change over time, otherwise known as **maturation**. This is especially problematic in long-term studies that track people over the course of months or years. Over time, people change both physically and psychologically. This can affect their responses to the measures you are interested in.

Let's say you are testing a new curriculum regarding Public Speaking. You ask college freshmen to take an instrument measuring their level of communication apprehension during the first week of classes. You then require them to take a Public Speaking class freshman year. You come back at the end of the year and give them the same measure. You notice that they are much lower in communication apprehension, and you conclude that your Public Speaking class was a huge success.

There is just one problem with this conclusion; lots of other things happened over the course of that school year, too. Generally speaking, college

history
A validity issue where something totally unrelated to your study happened at a particular time, and may have affected the responses.

maturation
A validity issue dealing with the fact that subjects can change over time, which can affect their responses to the measures a researcher is interested in.

students become more comfortable with strangers over the course of their freshman year, because they are forced to deal with roommates, classmates, professors, teaching assistants, a new town, and many other social interactions they were not forced to engage in back home. In effect, they grew and changed in a very natural way over the course of a year, becoming more comfortable around new people. So how confident can you be in your data that would otherwise indicate that your Public Speaking class was the source of this change? Not very.

In fact, the difficulty in understanding people's behaviors over time is one reason to choose qualitative research such as ethnography as a method, so you can attempt to capture and understand how people, their environment, their personality, and their lives interact in complex ways.

TESTING.   Sometimes people respond differently when they see the same set of questions twice. If you are more familiar or more comfortable with a series of questions or items, you may respond differently. This threat is known as **testing**. Let's think back to our reliability example from a few pages ago, where we talked about creating alternate forms of the same exam. You could give a student one form of the exam, and then come back a week later and administer the test again. By simply comparing the scores, you might conclude that the student must have studied very hard that week, because their score on the test is much higher than it was the first time.

testing
A validity threat where if someone is more familiar or more comfortable with a series of questions or items, they may respond differently to them.

Think about it. If you could take any one of the exams in this class for a second time, would you do better on it? Probably. While it is certainly possible that you could become better versed in the material between time points one and two, it is also very likely that you will do better because *you know what the questions are going to be ahead of time*. This may be a bit of an extreme example, but it illustrates one instance in which completing an instrument multiple times may affect the results.

INSTRUMENTATION.   The flip side of testing as a validity threat is **instrumentation**. Instrumentation, as a threat, deals with differences that are observed at two different time points in which different instruments are used to assess the same construct. Let's use our exam example again.

instrumentation
A validity threat that deals with differences that are observed at two different time points in which different instruments are used to assess the same construct.

You decide to give a student another exam on a particular section of material. Since you are concerned about testing as a validity threat, you give the student a different exam that covers the same chapter. It is not simply a different form of the same exam, it is an exam that has entirely different items drawn from the same chapter. You give it to the student, and he does much better on this version. Since you have controlled for testing, you conclude that he must have mastered the material the second time, because after all, he did so much better and they are not the same items.

There is a very simple alternate explanation. The second exam was easier. In getting around testing as a threat, the use of different instruments means that the responses might differ simply as a function of measurement. So, which should you be more concerned with—testing or instrumentation? There is no easy answer, but it is a topic we will come back to when we discuss design.

Hawthorne Effect

Sometimes, you might be using valid and reliable instruments, but research participants engage in unpredictable behavior that threatens the validity of your observations or measures. The confidence that you can have in your findings may be inhibited by certain responses that participants have that are beyond your control. Broadly speaking, the tendency for participants to respond differently when they know they are being observed is known as the Hawthorne Effect. Hawthorne effects can come in many varieties, but basically, they are instances in which research participants change their behavior or responses for no other reason than the fact that they know someone is watching. This is why it is considered a standard of validity for qualitative researchers to spend long periods of time in the field, so that study participants become accustomed to being observed and studied.

evaluator apprehension
When research participants become nervous or otherwise unsettled by the fact that they are in uncomfortable surroundings, which may limit their ability to concentrate or cause them to respond differently.

There are other more specific types of validity problems associated with participants. Take for example **evaluator apprehension**. If you have ever participated in laboratory research, you can probably relate to this. You walk into a laboratory and are greeted by a stranger who begins to ask you to do things you don't understand ("Sit over here . . . fill this out . . . wait until I come back. . . ." etc.). You are aware that you are being evaluated and that there are things going on that you don't know about. Are you being watched? What is it that they are looking for? Is this going to freak me out?

This is evaluator apprehension. Research participants may become nervous or otherwise unsettled by the fact that they are in uncomfortable surroundings. This may limit their ability to concentrate or cause them to respond differently. Research participants may also respond differently if they decide that they know what you are looking for (whether they are right or wrong). If you bring participants into a laboratory, make them play *Grand Theft Auto*, then ask them questions about how aggressive they feel; they might figure out that you are studying aggression responses. Depending on whether they like you, they may change their responses to either give you what they think you are looking for, or the exact opposite. The propensity of subjects to figure out what you are doing, decide they don't like you, and give you dishonest answers is sometimes jokingly referred to as the "screw you" effect.

If you're conducting longitudinal research, you might lose participants during the course of a study. This is called *attrition*, and it can be a real problem. Participants move away, decide to drop out of the study, or get bored. Large attrition can raise the same concerns that low sampling response rates raise—do the people who participate have the same thoughts and opinions as those who drop out? The best way to address this is to minimize the chances of people dropping out. If you're conducting a study in which you interview people every six months, keep in touch with them in between those times. Send them post cards or just call them up to remind them the next wave of research is coming up. Pay them an incentive; some researchers increase the incentive as the study goes along to keep people engaged.

External Validity Threats

We've talked about internal validity threats—the possibility that you may not be measuring what you think you're measuring, either due to error in your measurement instrument, or errors in the way you're administering the study or in the way the participants are taking part in the study. There is also something called external validity threats, and this refers to how well your research represents your population. We discussed this at length in Chapter 8.

Ecological Validity Threats

The final type of validity concern we need to discuss is ecological validity. This refers to how well your study measures or reflects the real world. The term *in vivo* means to conduct research in a natural setting. Research conducted in vivo has high ecological validity. Qualitative research, such as ethnographic research in which the researcher goes "into the field" to study people in their natural habitat, typically has very high ecological validity. Quantitative research such as laboratory experiments or surveys in which people are asked to recall prior behavior typically has low ecological validity.

• •

Credibility

▼

In qualitative research, rather than thinking of *validity* and *reliability*, researchers refer to credibility: Is the research considered to be credible to the reader, and most importantly, do we believe that the research adequately represents participants' reality? (Creswell & Miller, 2000)

Member Checks

Qualitative researchers use several strategies to enhance the credibility of their research: member checks, data triangulation, thick description, and peer reviews are some examples. **Member checks** are opportunities for the researcher to test her findings, interpretations, and explanations within the culture she is studying. Member checks are conducted at the end of the study, before the analysis is finalized, and they are typically conducted through personal interviews, focus groups, or other forms of communication (e.g., emails) in which the researcher discusses preliminary findings with members of the culture under study. Member checks are usually conducted with some of your study participants, but sometimes they are not available, so member checks can also be conducted with others in the culture who were not involved in your research. Sometimes, member checks are conducted with both study participants and people outside your study to further add to the credibility of the research.

member checks
Obtaining feedback on your research findings from representatives of the population under study.

Data Triangulation

Another way to enhance credibility of qualitative research might be to employ **data triangulation**—conducting more than one form of data collection (e.g., observation and in-depth interviews and/or review of artifacts). Multiple forms of data collection can ensure multiple perspectives, and that's another way to enhance credibility—to make sure that all relevant perspectives are represented in the research. Richardson (2000) suggested that, rather than triangulation, qualitative researchers think of *crystallization*, like a prism in which multiple colors reflect from the whole. Crystallization, therefore, refers to conducting research in such a way that *all* perspectives, including the researchers' and all study participants', are fully fleshed out and reflected in the study.

Credible Data Gathering, Coding, and Writing

Another design issue related to credibility includes how long the researcher is in the field. Generally speaking, the longer the researcher is in the field, the more credible the research. Extended periods of fieldwork enhance the validity and credibility of qualitative research because long periods of observation yield trust, access to gatekeepers and informants, collaboration with participants, and rapport and allow the researcher time to check out their ideas and opinions. Most ethnographers, say Creswell and Miller (2000), spend from four to twelve months in a field site.

Credibility also depends on how well the data themes or categories are sufficiently saturated: Has everything been covered or are there themes that seem to have been left out? One other credibility consideration is whether the researcher writes the analysis in a persuasive manner (Creswell & Miller, 2000). In fact, Creswell and Miller suggest that reflexive writing in which researchers "self-disclose their assumptions, beliefs, and biases . . . that may shape their inquiry" (p. 127), along with rich, *thick description*, allow the reader to validate the findings for him or herself.

Peer Reviews

In some types of qualitative research, coding teams or research teams debrief and discuss the data, codes, and findings. A *peer reviewer*, say Creswell and Miller (2000), provides "support, plays devil's advocate, challenges the researchers' assumptions, pushes the researchers to the next step methodologically, and asks hard questions about methods and interpretations" (p. 129).

While qualitative researchers don't use the same validity and reliability terminology (or the same assumptions and frames of reference) as do quantitative researchers, qualitative research follows practices that ensure similar validity and reliability:

Qualitative Researchers Do	Qualitative Researchers Do
Internal validity	Use multiple sources of information; Discuss my analysis with my research collaborators and consultants; Conduct a member check of the analysis by discussing them with my research participants; Study my participants over time so that they will gain trust and comfort in the study and will behave in a natural manner as I observe and interview them.
Construct validity	Use multiple sources of information; Discuss my analysis with my research collaborators and consultants; Conduct a member check of the analysis by discussing them with my research participants; Compare the results with other studies looking at similar topics.
Divergent validity	Compare the results with other studies looking at similar topics.
External validity	Use multiple sources of information; Use multiple cases; Generalize to theory; Sample to represent population of interest.
Reliability	Study the participants over time; Use multiple cases and compare them in my analysis; Follow a consistent protocol for data collection, coding, and analysis; Use multiple sources of information; Discuss my analysis with my research collaborators and consultants; Conduct a member check of the analysis by discussing them with my research participants.

So What?

In this chapter, you have dealt with a number of issues pertaining to the quality of your measures, and the conclusions that can be drawn from your observations and measurements. In order to have confidence in your data, you must not only ensure the reliability of your measures, but also make sure that both the measures and the inferences drawn from them make sense in terms of validity, and make sure that these inferences are credible and representative. Good empirical research is that which is drawn from observations and techniques that are reliable, valid, and credible. Considering these factors before deciding upon a particular study design is critical in executing a quality study and generating useful knowledge.

Glossary

Alternate form reliability
A reliability method where the order in which the items in a measure are presented affect the ways in which people respond.

Concurrent validity
How well a scale measures up against another scale that has been demonstrated to measure exactly the same thing.

Construct validity
The extent to which your variables are logically related to other variables.

Convergent validity
When two measures you expect to be related are shown to be positively statistically related.

Credibility
The believability of the research to the reader; how much the reader believes the research to represent participant's reality.

Criterion validity
A type of validity consideration that deals with how a particular measure holds up when compared to some outside criterion.

Data triangulation
Conducting more than one form of data collection to enhance the validity and credibility of your results.

Discriminant validity
When two measures you expect to be negatively related (opposite to each other) are shown to have a negative statistical relationship.

Evaluator apprehension
When research participants become nervous or otherwise unsettled by the fact that they are in uncomfortable surroundings, which may limit their ability to concentrate or cause them to respond differently.

Face validity
A type of validity consideration in which measures, or procedures, are looked at and questioned if they make sense at face value.

History
A validity issue where something totally unrelated to your study happened at a particular time, and may have affected the responses.

Instrumentation
A validity threat that deals with differences that are observed at two different time points in which different instruments are used to assess the same construct.

Inter-coder reliability
An indicator of how similarly coders are coding content, both in terms of identifying units of analysis and in the contextual labels they ascribe to those units.

Item-total reliability
A means of evaluating internal consistency of a scale that compares the total score for a scale with individual item scores for the same scale.

Maturation
A validity issue dealing with the fact that subjects can change over time, which can affect their responses to the measures a researcher is interested in.

Member checks
Obtaining feedback on your research findings from representatives of the population under study.

Predictive validity
How well a measure predicts that something that will happen in the future.

Random error
A fluctuation in measurement.

Reliability
The ability of a measure to produce the same results if replicated.

Reliability statistics
Statistical tests that can show consistency between items, reflecting reliability of a scale.

Split-half reliability
A means of evaluating internal consistency of a scale that compares one randomly selected half of a scale from the other randomly selected half of the same scale.

Test-retest reliability
A reliability method in which the same measure is given to the same people at two different times.

Testing
A validity threat where if someone is more familiar or more comfortable with a series of questions or items, they may respond differently to them.

Validity
Accuracy of a measure, in terms of measuring intended constructs or observations.

References

Campbell, D., & Stanley, J. (1963). *Experimental and quasi-experimental designs for research.* Chicago: Rand-McNally.

Cook, T. D., & Campbell, D. T. (1979). *Quasi-experimentation: Design and analysis issues for field settings.* Boston: Houghton Mifflin Company.

Creswell, J. W., & Miller, D. (2000). Determining validity in qualitative research. *Theory into Practice, 39*(3), 124–130.

Fleiss, J. L., & Cohen, J. (1973). The equivalence of weighted kappa and the intraclass correlation coefficient as measures of reliability. *Educational and Psychological Measurement, 33,* 613–619.

Jameson, J. K., Bodtker, A. M., Linker, T. (2010). Facilitating conflict transformation: Mediator strategies for eliciting emotional communication in a workplace conflict. *Negotiation Journal, 26,* 25–48.

Keaten, J., & Kelly, L. (2008). Emotional intelligence as a mediator of family communication patterns and reticence. *Communication Reports, 21*(2), 104–116.

Keaten, J. A., Kelly, L., & Finch, C. (1997). Development of an instrument to measure reticence. *Communication Quarterly, 45,* 37–54.

Kerlinger, F. (1986). *Foundations of behavioral research.* Fort Worth, TX: HBJ.

Krippendorf, K. (1994). *Content analysis: An introduction to its methodology.* Beverly Hills, CA: Sage.

Lannutti, P. J., & Lachlan, K. A. (2007). Assessing attitudes toward same-sex marriage: Scale development and validation. *Journal of Homosexuality, 53*(4), 113–133.

Nunnally, J., & Bernstein, I. (1994). *Psychometric theory.* New York: McGraw Hill.

Reinard, J. C. (2006). *Communication research statistics.* Thousand Oaks, CA: Sage.

Richardson, L. (2000). Writing: A method of inquiry. In N. K. Denzin & Y. S. Lincoln, (Eds.), *Handbook of qualitative research* (pp. 923–948). Thousand Oaks, CA: Sage.

Ritchie, L. D., & Fitzpatrick, M. A. (1990). Family communication patterns: Measuring intrapersonal perceptions of interpersonal relationships. *Communication Research, 17,* 523–544.

Rittenour, C. E., & Martin, M. M. (2008). Convergent validity of the Communication Based Emotional Support Scale. *Communication Studies, 59*(3), 235–241.

Schutte, N. S., Malouff, J. M., Hall, L. E., Haggerty, D. J., Cooper, J. T., Golden, C. J., & Dornheim, L. (1998). Development and validation of a measure of emotional intelligence. *Personality and Individual Differences, 25,* 167–177.

Weber, K. D., & Patterson, B. R. (1996). Construction and validation of a communication based emotional support scale. *Communication Research Reports, 13,* 68–76.

Wilson, B. J., Kunkel, D., Linz, D., Potter, W. J., Donnerstein, E., Smith, S. L., Blumenthal, E., & Gray, T. (1997). Violence in television programming overall: University of California, Santa Barbara study. In *National Television Violence Study* (Vol. 1, pp. 3–268). Newbury Park, CA: Sage.

PART 3

RESEARCH UNDER
THE QUANTITATIVE PARADIGM

SURVEY RESEARCH

KEY TERMS

Cohort study

Cross-sectional survey

Evaluation research

Funnel format

Interview

Inverted funnel format

Longitudinal survey design

Market research

Panel study

Political polls

Researcher-administered questionnaires

Self-administered questionnaires

Survey design

Trend study

Tunnel format

CHAPTER OBJECTIVES

1. To become familiar with survey research
2. To understand survey measurement techniques
3. To examine common types of research design
4. To explore the advantages and disadvantages of interviews and questionnaires

▼ Why Surveys?

Comedian Dave Barry once quipped, "If you surveyed a hundred typical middle-aged Americans, I bet you'd find that only two of them could tell you their blood types, but every last one of them would know the theme song from 'The Beverly Hillbillies'" (*The Quote Garden*, n.d.). *Late Night* host David Letterman said, "*USA Today* has come out with a new survey—apparently, three out of every four people make up 75% of the population" (*The Quotations Page*, n.d.). No doubt about it—survey research is popular in everyday society. In this chapter, we consider one of the most common types of research methodologies: surveys. We will consider why surveys are immensely popular; examine common survey research design; explore survey measurement techniques, including questionnaire design; and, finally, scrutinize the pros and cons of different ways of administering surveys.

▼ Survey Research

survey design
A method of asking research participants questions that provides researchers with a method of information gathering from a large number of people over a relatively short period of time.

Survey design is perhaps the most familiar research method to most of us. When you fill out a teacher's evaluation at the end of the semester, a comment card at a restaurant, or even a profile on a dating website, you are completing a survey. Surveys are popular in both proprietary and scholarly research for a variety of reasons. First, survey design provides researchers with a method of information gathering from a large number of people over a relatively short period of time. This allows you to gather a representative sample from a population of interest to you. Second, surveys are relatively inexpensive to administer. With new Web-based applications, such as Survey Monkey (www.surveymonkey.com) and Survey Share (www.surveyshare.com), the survey creation process has become even easier and more accessible to many. Third, this methodology involves a relatively straightforward research strategy. You ask people questions and analyze their answers. Fourth, surveys can include both quantitative questions and qualitative (open-ended) questions. Finally, since you can easily provide and administer identical questions to many participants, a well-written survey questionnaire is a reliable measurement technique.

Applications of Survey Research

Surveys have been widely used in communication research in many different ways. Macias, Springston, Lariscy, and Neustifer (2008) conducted a content analysis of 54 communication-related journals published from 1990 to 2002 and found 565 studies used a survey methodology. Most survey research they found was conducted in the subfields of public relations, marketing, public opinion, advertising, and mass communication journals; however, 85 percent of the journals investigated had some survey research in them, indicating that most segments of our field use survey research at least some of the time.

You can use surveys to describe communication characteristics of participants for the purpose of theory building or generalizing about the population they represent. Other times, you utilize survey research to test theoretical predictions about the relationships between communication variables and other variables in a population of interest. You'll see in Chapter 11 that experiments in our field sometimes use surveys as part of their design. In addition, much communication research uses surveys to assess participants' attitudes, beliefs, and opinions, and to let participants retrospectively replay incidents, behaviors, and meanings.

Survey Research Measuring Attitudes.   If you're designing a communication campaign to promote a product, service, or behavior, you're going to want to do an audience analysis—to determine what your potential audience already thinks, feels, or believes about your topic. You'd likely conduct a survey to find that out. Communication researchers also assess attitudes in surveys to develop, test, or apply theoretical concepts for both applied and scholarly research.

For example, Salmon, Park, and Wrigley (2003) conducted a survey research study among corporate spokespersons from 100 public companies to understand perceptions of risk and bias toward optimism about the possibility of bioterrorism among corporate spokespersons. They tested five hypotheses:

H_1: Corporate spokespersons will tend to estimate their own organization's risk to be less than that of other organizations similar to their own.

H_2: Optimistic bias will be greater for referents that are more distant (e.g., other corporations in the United States) than for those that are proximate (other corporations in the state).

H_3: Corporate spokespersons who perceive their own organizations as low in vulnerability tend to show high optimistic bias.

H_4: Corporate spokespersons who perceive high severity of bioterrorism tend to show high optimistic bias.

H_5: Corporate spokespersons who perceive that their own organizations can control external events tend to show high optimistic bias.

A survey method was appropriate for these hypotheses because they were measuring participants' attitudes, beliefs, and perceptions. Salmon and colleagues (2003) used a purposive sampling method. They got a list (sampling frame) of the largest 100 privately and publicly held companies in the state from the Harris Michigan Industrial Directory (Carlsen, 2010). They called each company and got a list of 142 names of corporate spokespersons. They mailed out an introductory letter, then called each potential participant. If a participant refused, they called a second time five days later to see if the person had changed his or her mind. They ended up with a sample size of 72, which represents a 51 percent response rate.

Applying Weistein's concept of optimistic bias to risk perception, Salmon and colleagues (2003) designed their own measurements of bioterrorism awareness, perceived vulnerability, perceived severity, and perceived controllability using Likert-type scales. They used Weinstein's own measure of optimistic bias which was a 0–10 scale.

Based on their statistical analysis (which we'll discuss in Chapter 13), Salmon et al. (2003) determined that there is a relationship between optimistic bias and perceived vulnerability and perceived severity, but not between optimistic bias and perceived controllability. What do you think are the pros and cons to their use of the survey method? What internal validity issues might they need to consider? How about external validity issues? How about ecological validity issues? How can they address these validity issues in future research? What can they do with this information?

Survey Research Measuring Retrospective Behaviors. Some researchers use surveys to ask participants to report on retrospective, or past, behaviors. While asking participants to remember past events raises concerns about the accuracy of memory, this method does have the advantage of obtaining a recollection of an incident from the point of view of a participant. Here's an example of this use of surveys: Botta and Dumlao (2002) wanted to see if there was a relationship between conflict and communication styles between fathers and daughters and eating disorders in the daughters. They had many hypotheses and research questions, all pertaining to that general topic (conversation orientation, conformity orientation, pluralistic, laissez-faire, and protective all referring to family communication styles; compromising, collaborating, avoiding, accommodating, confronting, and avoiding all referring to conflict styles):

H_1: Conversation orientation as encouraged by the father will be a significant negative predictor of anorexic and bulimic behaviors.

H_2: Conformity orientation as encouraged by the father will be a significant positive predictor of anorexic and bulimic behaviors.

H_3: Being raised by a pluralistic father will be a significant negative predictor of anorexic and bulimic behaviors.

H_4: Being raised by a protective father will be a significant positive predictor of anorexic behaviors.

H_5: Compromising as a way to respond to conflict will be a significant negative predictor of anorexic behaviors and a significant negative predictor of bulimic behaviors.

H_6: Collaborating as a way to respond to conflict will be a significant negative predictor of anorexic behaviors and a significant negative predictor of bulimic behaviors.

H_7: Avoiding as a way to respond to conflict will be a significant positive predictor of anorexic behaviors.

H$_8$: Accommodating as a way to respond to conflict will be a significant positive predictor of anorexic behaviors.

H$_9$: Confronting as a means of responding to conflict will be a significant positive predictor of bulimic behaviors.

H$_{10}$: Avoiding as a means of responding to conflict will be a significant negative predictor of bulimic behaviors.

RQ$_1$: Is being raised by a protective father, a laissez-faire father, or a consensual father a significant predictor of bulimic behaviors?

RQ$_2$: To what extent do family communication styles as encouraged by the father moderate the influence of a strong drive to be thin on anorexic and bulimic behaviors?

RQ$_3$: To what extent do conflict resolution styles between father and daughter moderate the influence of a strong drive to be thin on anorexic and bulimic behaviors?

To measure family communication patterns, Botta and Dumlao (2002) used Ritchie's 1991 Revised Family Communication Patterns (RFCP) Instrument, a multidimensional Likert scale that has been shown to have high reliability—Cronbach's Alpha for conversation orientation was .91 and for conformity orientation was .86. To measure conflict styles, they used Rahim's Organization Conflict Inventory, a multidimensional Likert scale that also has been shown to have high reliability—avoidance conflict style (α = .85), collaborating conflict style (α = .89), compromising conflict style (α = .74), confronting conflict style (α = .80), and accommodating conflict style (α = .81). They measured eating disorders using two scales: Garner and Olmsted's Eating Disorder Inventory and Eating Attitudes Test, two Likert-type scales, both of which they report have high validity and reliability.

Botta and Dumlao (2002) used what appears to be a convenience sample. Here's how they described it:

> After signing the required consent forms, 357 students from a university in the Midwest and a university in the southeast completed questionnaires with established instruments to tap FCPs, conflict styles, and eating disordered behaviors along with other items that were part of another study. Because 90% of those with eating disorders are women (APA, 1994), men were excluded from analysis, reducing the sample to 220. The sample was further reduced to the 210 participants who were younger than 24 years of age (90.5% of whom were 18–21 years of age) to reduce error due to forgetting what communication within the family was like when the participants lived at home. (p. 207)

What are other methods they could have used to collect their information and address their hypotheses and research questions? Why do you think they chose surveys over other methods such as ethnography or experiments?

There are three additional applications of survey research we should also consider: political polls, evaluation research, and market research.

Political Polls.   One of the most common and readily available uses of surveys in the world today is in the form of **political polls**. It seems that every day leading up to an election, we are bombarded with a detailed account of who is

political polls
One of the most common and readily available uses of surveys. They provide a detailed account of who is leading whom in the run for a particular office during an election.

leading whom in the run for a particular office. Often political poll surveys are conducted over the phone. The key to political polls and the validity of their findings rests upon the basic research method strategies used, the quality of sampling and sample size, the response rate, and, as we will see shortly, even the types of questions asked.

Evaluation Research.   Another type of survey research that many of you are already familiar with is the use of survey data in **evaluation research**. Evaluation research is designed to assess the effectiveness of campaigns, programs, or products either before (or while) they are being developed or after their completion. The use of evaluation research for campaigns and programs allows practitioners and managers to develop more effective communication programs. A good example of evaluation research in organizational communication would be research designed to assess a new training program put in place in the organization. If you are a participant in the training, you might be asked to fill out a survey at the end so the trainer can assess his or her success. In health communication, you might be interested in evaluating the relative success of a smoking cessation program or a new exercise regimen. You could even evaluate the success of a nutrition campaign such as the "5 a day" campaign that encourages Americans to eat five fruits and vegetables a day. This type of evaluation research is often called summative research, as it traditionally takes place after the program has run its course or the campaign is ending (Center & Broom, 1983).

Another type of evaluation research is known as *formative research*; this is simply evaluation research that helps the campaign or program manager develop a campaign or program, or evaluate it while it is ongoing (Atkin & Freimuth, 2000; Center & Broom, 1983).

The benefit of these types of evaluation research is that they allow you to identify ways the current or future program or campaign can be refined and improved upon. The third type of evaluation research, *needs analysis*, is a mechanism for identifying problems experienced by a group of people by comparing what exists with what study participants want. For example, organizational employees might fill out a needs assessment survey to help management develop a new training program by comparing what existing training programs offer versus what employees want or need in a training program. This data is often used to guide in the development of communication interventions, such as skill training. Finally, the fourth type of evaluation research, *organizational feedback*, also utilizes survey design. Here, organizational members are asked to report on practices within the organization. You might be interested in surveying national insurance companies about the communication practices within their organization. You could use surveys to ask them about the use of different channels of communication, the quality of information provided, and even their preferred method of communication. The results can then be used for organizational improvement.

Market Research.   Another common example of survey design comes in the form of **market research**. This is research designed to study consumer behavior. The idea behind market research is that if you can determine what

evaluation research
Research that is designed to assess the effectiveness of programs or products during development or after their completion.

market research
Research that is designed to study consumer behavior.

people consume, how often, and why, then you can predict future consumption (or at least market researchers can). Market research may question consumer reactions to a new product, interest in new products, and preferences for products and services. This type of research evaluates how satisfied consumers are with products and services, as well as explores persuasive strategies for advertising, product pricing, and even packaging. The most obvious example of market research in your world is likely to be a discount or frequent shopper card on your key ring, or the survey invitations issued to you on the receipt you receive from a local discount store. It seems marketers have many opportunities to gather data about your consumer behaviors. Did you really think the shopper card is to help you save money? What types of information do companies gather from your frequent shopper card? What marketing decisions could they make with it?

Design Concerns

Sampling.   We discussed sampling in detail in Chapter 8, but let's review the types of sampling that is done in survey research. With surveys, because of the way they are administered, researchers potentially have the ability to conduct a truly random and representative sample. Regardless of the type of survey you are designing, your design concerns are similar. One of your first concerns related to survey research design is selecting survey participants. To do this, you must have a sampling frame. Recall that a sampling frame is ideally a list of all members of a population, or at least it is the list you let stand in for your population. In some instances, an actual list of the population may be impossible to come by. At one time, telephone directories might have been a good choice, yet, in today's world, this would be an incomplete sampling frame at best, because so many people use telephone numbers—cell phones, for example—that are not listed in directories. In fact, these days, we might argue that using a list of numbers from a telephone directory is only representative of, perhaps older, less technologically savvy people. This is why many survey researchers are moving to random digit dialing—letting a computer randomly generate telephone numbers within an area code and exchange. Using random digit dialing, you're not limited to only listed or land-line numbers, and, if you're looking for an overall population sample, your sample should be more representative. However you sample, remember that your sample should adequately represent your population as closely as possible. If you were interested in studying dating behaviors of college students at UMass Boston, UNC–Charlotte, and the University of Kansas, you could likely contact the registrars of each of the schools and obtain a list of potential participants (with Institutional Research Board approval, of course). This list would be your sampling frame. If you're interested in why people voted for a particular candidate in an election, it would not make sense to poll people who didn't vote. Therefore, a sampling frame of all people—regardless of whether they voted—would not be very representative of the population you're interested in studying. You'd be better off using a list of registered voters, at least eliminating those who definitely couldn't have voted.

Many types of sampling can be used with survey design: random sampling, cluster sampling, stratified sampling, purposive samples, and even volunteer samples. What defines the best choice for a particular study? That's right, it's the research question. The question(s) and/or hypothesis(es) determine the technique you choose. It should make sense. For a better discussion of this, please revisit Chapter 8 on sampling.

Cross-Sectional Design.   Another consideration and decision you make early in the research process when using survey methodology is whether a cross-sectional or longitudinal design is best for your study. A **cross-sectional survey** describes the characteristics of a sample representing a population at one point in time. Think of it as a picture. Your friend pulls out her camera phone and takes a picture. That's like handing out surveys to a group of people and having them fill them out once. Researchers frequently utilize cross-sectional survey research because it's easy to collect data from a large number of people in a short period of time. One researcher we know has, at times, been able to sample from the local jury pool. In just one afternoon, he collected nearly 500 surveys of a very wide sample of people, which was appropriate for his research question. The Salmon et al. (2003) study mentioned earlier that looked at perceptions of risk and optimistic bias among corporate spokespersons about the possibility of bioterrorism is an example of a cross-sectional study.

> **cross-sectional survey**
> *A survey design that describes the characteristics of a sample representing a population at one point in time.*

A cross-sectional design is great for describing the status quo—how things are right now. However, there are some cautions to keep in mind. First, it is important to keep in mind the particular point in time when the survey was conducted. A friend of ours went through the Institutional Research Board and was approved to collect data on her project late one September. She was interested in studying different types of messages on brochures regarding breast self-exams. As she began her project, she realized that October, when she collected the majority of her data, happens to be Breast Cancer Awareness Month. Is there any chance that this particular month for data collection affected the outcome of her study? Absolutely. Data can be misleading if the survey is conducted at an unrepresentative time.

An interesting example of the use of cross-sectional survey design comes from Lim and Teo (2009) who studied e-manners, or the level of respect communicated via email communication in the workplace. They measured 192 employees in the financial services industry in Singapore at just one point in time. However, they caution that their results limit their ability to determine cause and effect despite some significant relationships between variables.

Cross-sectional surveys assume the variables and processes being studied have reached stability, but many variables and processes are constantly changing. For example, marital satisfaction, television viewing behavior, and communication apprehension are variables that have the potential to change over time. By that same token, you can't take one measurement at one point in time and assume causality. Consider the hypothesis that video game violence leads to an increase in aggressive behavior. If you measure both of these variables and find a positive correlation between them, can you conclude that video game violence caused aggressive behavior in your sample? No, you cannot. Causal conclusions can never be drawn from cross-sectional data. It is a lot like the question of which came first—the chicken or the egg. Do you know whether exposure to video game violence came before or after exhibiting aggressive behavior? Not if you only measure at one point of time. While a reasonable person might likely argue that watching violence causes aggressive behavior, it is possible, isn't it, that individuals with aggressive tendencies could choose to play violent video games? It is also equally likely that some other variable, such as family discipline, affects both video game playing and aggressive behavior.

Another concern to keep in mind, which we discussed at length in Chapter 7, is that confounding variables could also account for the relationship. Recall, a confounding variable is some third variable that explains the change in the dependent variable better than the independent variable. The independent and dependent variable may appear to be linked, while in reality they simply vary together because of some confounding variable. Remember our crime and ice cream story in Chapter 7: Crime and ice cream consumption may appear to be related, yet, in reality, both are correlated with heat. You should always try to anticipate potential confounds and eliminate them from the study design.

Longitudinal Design.

In **longitudinal survey design**, you gather data from respondents at several points in time. This allows you to evaluate the impact of unusual or unique environmental events on a population and assess whether a population's beliefs, attitudes, and/or behaviors are enduring or stable over time. One of the greatest strengths of longitudinal design is to allow you to examine causal relationships. You add this feature to survey research with a longitudinal design by determining whether A comes before B in time. You can only do this with a minimum of two measurements over some time frame. There are three types of longitudinal research design: a trend study, a cohort study, and a panel study.

longitudinal survey design
A survey design that gathers data from respondents at several points in time.

TREND STUDY. In a **trend study**, measurement occurs at two or more points in time, from different samples selected from the same population. This type of study is designed to identify changes or trends (thus the name) in people's beliefs about the variable of interest. An example of a trend study is the Gallup polls used during a presidential election. The Gallup organization, a premier research firm in the United States, draws a sample from all eligible U.S. voters and asks whom they plan to vote for in the upcoming presidential election. Each week they poll another group of people (sample) from this population (all eligible voters). Remember, the samples Gallup is taking are not the same people; they are merely samples from the same population. Keep in mind, though, that as your goal is comparison over time, you should be sampling from the same general population, at least. What if you sample first from the Socialists of America, second from the Students for Democratic Government, and third from the Young Republicans? Clearly, you cannot compare how people's attitudes changed over time because your sample would be very different each time. Obviously, to compare trends you must have comparable representative samples. What do you think are the pros and cons to trend studies?

trend study
Measurement occurs at two or more points in time, from different samples selected from the same population. This type of study is designed to identify changes or trends in people's beliefs about a variable of interest.

cohort study

A study in which responses from specific subgroups of a population are identified and compared over time.

COHORT STUDY.   In a **cohort study**, responses from a specific subgroup of the population are identified and compared over time. In a cohort study, the key is that for some reason (relevant to your study) you are interested in studying a group of people that have some characteristic in common because of a historical marker of significance (i.e., lived through the Depression) or some other meaningful life event. For example, you might be interested in people born or graduated from high school in the same year. Simply put, a cohort is usually defined with respect to time or history.

Imagine for a moment you are interested in comparing how baby boomers talk about money and financial security over time. You decide to embark on a ten-year longitudinal study with a cohort design in which you measure attitudes and financial talk once every two years. You decide on a cohort study of baby boomers (individuals generally born from 1946 to 1964, who are currently between the ages 45 to 63). You sample persons 45 to 63 in 2009, another sample of individuals 47 to 65 in 2011, another sample of persons 49 to 67 in 2013, and so on. Although the specific set of people studied in each of these surveys would be different, each sample represents the cohort born between 1946 and 1964.

panel study

A study in which a sample is drawn from a population or universe and those same people or objects are measured at multiple points in time

PANEL STUDY.   In a **panel study**, responses are obtained from the exact same people over time. Essentially, you draw a sample from your population or universe and measure those same people or objects at multiple points in time. This is also known as repeated measurements. The most significant advantage of using a panel study is that it can help address the question of what variable comes first, allowing you to begin to assess causality, while simultaneously tracing change over time. While these are important advantages to this type of design, it is not without disadvantages that warrant consideration. One important disadvantage of a panel study is that as you continue taking measurements over time, you may lose subjects. This is known as a high attrition rate or as an issue of mortality. While you seldom lose participants to death in communication research, if you study health communication and illness, it can happen. More likely, however, is that participants will drop out of school, change address or contact information, or just become impossible to track down to measure at a subsequent wave of measurement. Another major concern with attrition or mortality in a panel study is that you may not end up with enough participants in your study, and/or participants that do participate in all points of measure may somehow differ from participants who drop out of the study.

Consider this example conducted by Segrin and Flora (2000) in their study of students transitioning to college. In this study, they measured social skills and psychosocial problems at two points in time: during the end of the senior year in high school (wave 1), and again at the end of the first semester in college (wave 2). They found that (1) social skills interacted with stressful life events to predict changes in depression and loneliness, (2) people with lower social skills were predicted to make the transition to college with the worst psychosocial problems, and (3) people with lower social skills were more vulnerable to development of psychosocial problems than people with higher social skills. This all certainly makes sense and is a great use of a panel longitudinal survey method. However, what limitations can you identify with this method? What if the people with the poorest social skills dropped out by the second wave of interviewing? Would that make both waves of interviewing equivalent?

Consider another example of survey design. You might decide you are interested in studying family communication between children and their parents, paying particular attention to conflict. Your research question is this: Do parents believe conflict with their children increases as children move from elementary school through middle school and high school? How could you study this using a cross-sectional design? How could you study this same question using a longitudinal design? In a cross-sectional design, you would put together a questionnaire including a measure of conflict and ask parents of children in third, seventh, and eleventh grades to complete your survey. Or you could give one questionnaire to parents of eleventh-grade kids and ask them to fill out the questionnaire for their children when they were in third, seventh, and eleventh grades. In a longitudinal panel design, you could use the same questionnaire with the measure of conflict to assess parents with children currently in third grade, and then collect the same measurement again as their children entered seventh grade, and again four years later when their children were eleventh graders. What do you think are the pros and cons of each approach?

Measurement Techniques

Survey measurement techniques are what we call self-report. We talked about this in Chapter 7. Typically, in a survey you are asking the participants to tell you what they think or feel, and they are reporting on themselves. Do you think this is a good strategy? The obvious answer is it depends upon what you want to know. We will first consider some strategies for enhancing the strength of self-report data, before considering the disadvantages of self-report techniques. Self-report data can provide a clear and valid picture of some phenomenon of interest to the researcher.

To enhance the likelihood of obtaining valid self-report data, it is important that you clearly delineate why the study is important. Most questionnaires or surveys will include a statement on their cover sheet and their consent form detailing at least an abbreviated version of the main purpose of the study. While it may not be desirable to tell participants everything about the study purpose, they need to be given at least a general idea of what you're doing. It is also essential that participants be informed of whether their data will be kept in confidence or will be anonymous. As we discussed in Chapter 5 on ethics, it is important that the data is protected as though it was the researcher's own private information. Participants should be encouraged to give complete and accurate information when possible. We will discuss questions at length later, but participants should not be asked to respond to items that are irrelevant to them or their situation. You should also ensure that you consider the audience of the questionnaire before writing the statements and/or questions.

Self-report surveys are great for recording self-perception, covert or hidden behavior, beliefs, attitudes, opinions, and values. They might also be useful for questions of a personal nature, anything that might be considered private information. Self-report is also a strong technique for recording emotion or feelings; however, keep in mind that these have to be conscious thoughts and feelings you are interested in measuring.

As research questions ultimately guide your methodological choices, it is helpful to know what self-report surveys are particularly unsuccessful at measuring. First, self-report is a poor choice for unconscious behaviors and feelings or difficult to remember events. Surveys are also a weak choice as a method of gathering data about abilities, skills (think communication competence), and socially undesirable behaviors.

▼ Constructing a Survey Questionnaire

Writing Survey Questions

In designing survey questionnaires, one concern is how best to construct the questions. The first issue is the type of questions you can ask in a survey, which depends upon the research question asked and/or hypotheses stated. You can ask questions about experience or behavior: How often do you talk with your mother? You can ask questions about opinions or values: Is television too violent? You may ask questions about feelings or attitudes: Do you like your new research methods textbook? You might ask questions about knowledge: How many drinks can you consume before your blood alcohol level goes over .10? You can ask questions about background or demographics: How old are you? What is your major? Where are you from?

Strategies for Questions.   While the initial criteria for writing and deciding upon what questions to ask in a research study come from the research questions or hypotheses, there are additional strategies for what questions work best. First, recent and important events are remembered more easily. For example, if you ask people to report on their television viewing behavior, asking them to report the previous day or week's behavior will produce more accurate data than asking about the distant past. People can recall past serious issues, but not past minor issues. For example, you may not be able to recall whom you communicated with last Friday; yet most of you remember the first person you talked with following the news of the attacks on New York and Washington, D.C., on September 11, 2001. Another important strategy is that certain unpleasant and ego-threatening incidents tend to be reported inaccurately. In other words, parents underreport children's misbehavior; college students underreport unsafe sexual behavior.

1.   Questions should be clear.
     Creating good questions, at first glance, seems like an easy task; yet upon the first attempt, you will find this is a complex task and warrants much deliberation. Some guidelines can make the task easier. First and foremost, questions should be clear, using simple language participants can easily understand. Your word choice is dependent upon your audience. Just as you have been trained to consider your audience in public speaking, you need to give thought to your audience when writing a question for a survey. If you are surveying

adolescents or engineers, the words you choose will differ. It is common for words to have multiple meanings, so you need to be sure that the interpretation you are thinking of is clear to the participants. For example, think about the word "drugs." Suppose you ask the question "Have you ever taken drugs?" What would people think you were asking about? On many research projects you might be talking about illegal substances, such as marijuana; however, in some health communication studies, you might be talking about prescription drugs. The key here is to be clear! If there is any doubt about what your question is asking, you need to write a better question.

2. Questions must be about only one issue.
    A second important guideline to follow when writing research questions is that the questions you write must be about only one issue. Questions that contain more than one issue are called double-barreled questions. Why should it matter if you ask questions containing more than one concept? To answer this question, an example will be useful. Imagine that you ask the following question: "Do you like the education and social life at UNC–Charlotte?" In reality, a "Yes" tells you that the participant likes both the education and social life at UNC–Charlotte, while a "No" tells you that the participant dislikes both the education and social life at UNC–Charlotte. However, are these the only two possible answers? No. One might like the education and dislike the social opportunities at UNC–Charlotte, or one might dislike the education and like the social life at UNC–Charlotte. In any event, if you ask a double-barreled question, you can never be certain what the participant intended when he or she answered the question. This will affect both the reliability and validity of the survey, compromise the measure's integrity, and thus impact the overall study.

3. Questions should avoid biased wording.
    Another guideline for good question construction is to avoid using wording that leads participants to particular outcomes. The actual wording of the question can dramatically change the outcome. Some common examples of this include starting questions and/or statements with phrases like "Wouldn't you agree . . ." or "Isn't it true . . ." A related guideline for question construction is to avoid language that is emotionally charged, as this can bias answers. A great example of emotionally charged language can be seen in the abortion debate. No matter what side you identify with, the language both sides use to talk about their perspective is emotionally provocative. Let's consider the debate language. Pro-choice groups equate legal abortion with free choice and a woman's control over her own body. They talk about being *pro-choice*, while they see the other side as being *anti-choice*. Similarly, pro-life groups equate legal abortion with murder, using phrases such as *pro-life* and *pro-abortion*. All of these terms, regardless of your own personal beliefs, are emotionally charged and if used in a survey will likely result in difficulty in getting an unbiased response.

4. Questions should avoid making assumptions.
   The fourth guideline for question construction is to avoid making assumptions about your participant. So, while we suggested earlier you need to consider your audience when writing questions, here you want to move a step beyond that by asking participants questions that are relevant to them, and asking questions only when participants are informed about the topic. Do you take your pet to the vet for yearly exams? This question assumes the person answering the question has a pet. What do you think of proposition 301? This question assumes the person answering the question knows what proposition 301 is about. Neither of these questions will provide accurate or reliable answers with the wrong participants. The solution to this problem often comes in the form of filter questions, which can assist in *filtering* out individuals who lack the appropriate knowledge or lack the appropriate conditions to adequately answer the question at hand.

5. Questions should avoid offending participants if possible.
   Be careful how you phrase sensitive questions. Examples of sensitive topics are age and income. Suppose you ask such questions as "How old are you?" and "How much money do you make?" You will probably get an answer like "None of your business!" The best way around this is to list groupings of ages and income levels to follow your questions, such as: "In which of the following age categories do you fit?" and "In which of the following categories was your total household income before taxes last year?"

Types of Questions

Before we leave the discussion of questionnaire writing, let's talk briefly about different types of questions. There are basically two types of questions: *closed-ended* questions and *open-ended* questions. A closed-ended question is one where you only give the respondent certain possible answers that his response must fit into—for example, a "yes/no" question, or the question "In which of the following age categories do you fit? Under 21; 21–34; 35–49; 50–64; or 65 and over." Closed-ended questions are suited for eliminating interviewer interpretation, eliminating coding and editing interpretations, making recording of the data easier as the interview is being conducted, and ensuring consistency in interviewing. When you are using scales or similar measurement tools that we discussed earlier, you are usually using closed-ended questions.

Sometimes closed-ended questions are not appropriate, however. What would happen with the closed-ended question "Do you believe the United States ought to enter into a treaty with Iran to eliminate long-range nuclear warheads?" Some people may simply say "yes" or "no." But others may wish to elaborate: "It depends on—if they will honor it, if they will allow independent inspections, and if they are willing to cease production now until the treaty is signed." In other words, "yes" and "no" may not be a sufficient choice of answers for some participants, and you'll need to allow for expanded answers. So, you would go to an open-ended question.

Open-ended questions are suited when you need to measure a participant's level of knowledge, or playback of something, or detailed explanation of an opinion. Examples of open-ended questions are "Why do you say that?" and "What do you remember about _____?" and "What are your impressions of _____?"

Although we are not talking about *in-depth qualitative* interviewing (see Chapter 15), open-ended questions require some amount of probing and clarifying. A common weakness of inexperienced interviewers is poor probing. After the participant has seemingly finished what he or she is going to say, you would need to probe. For example, you may need to ask: "What do you mean by that?" or "What else do you remember?" or "Why do you say that?" A probe of "Do you remember anything else?" usually results in a "no." But if you ask, "What else do you remember?" often you will get more responses. It is also very important to probe for clarity. There is nothing more frustrating than reading over a questionnaire later and thinking, "I wonder what he or she meant by that." If you don't ask when he or she is there in front of you, you'll never know what he or she meant.

Structure and Arrangement of Questions

Of course, many researchers use already published and validated scales to build their questionnaires, instead of writing their own questions. Most questionnaires in academic survey research are a combination of existing scales with newly written questions. However, whether compiling a questionnaire from existing scales or creating a completely new questionnaire, you have to make choices about the best way to structure and arrange your questions. The three commonly used question formats are: tunnel, funnel, and inverted funnel formats.

Tunnel format. In the **tunnel format**, questions tend to be similar in terms of breadth and depth throughout the questionnaire. They are organized by similarity and vary little in terms of depth.

Funnel format. In a **funnel format**, the questions begin with broad, often open-ended questions followed by narrow, more closed-ended questions. Think of this as a format moving from general to specific.

Inverted funnel format. Finally, the **inverted funnel format** is the polar opposite of the funnel format. It generally begins with more closed-ended, narrow questions moving throughout the questionnaire to the most open-ended, broad questions. Think of this format as moving from specific to general.

How to Choose the Right Format.   As we have suggested throughout the book, the preferred questionnaire structure is the one best suited to your research question and/or hypotheses. Just as the questions determine the type of methodology that is best, the same components assist you in determining the most appropriate format for your question. For example, your author Heather Powell Gallardo studied the negotiation of sexual risk taking in college dating couples. When she wrote her questionnaire, she considered suggestions from research experts on related topics who suggested an inverted funnel design is best for this topic, as the topic of sex can be taboo or very personal. Therefore,

tunnel format
A type of question format in which questions tend to be similar in terms of breadth and depth throughout a questionnaire. Questions are organized by similarity and vary little in terms of depth.

funnel format
A type of question format in which questions begin with broad, open-ended questions followed by narrow, more closed-ended questions.

inverted funnel format
A type of question format that generally begins with more closed-ended, narrow questions moving throughout the questionnaire to the most open-ended and broad questions.

with an inverted design, she started with low-risk, closed-ended questions before moving on to more personal questions about sexual partners, protection methods, and safe sex practices. Interestingly, she has learned over time that those more sensitive questions are most likely answered when she embeds them within the middle of the questionnaire rather than at the end. The first time she asked such questions, she did leave the open-ended most ego-threatening measure of sexual behavior to the end and discovered that many participants skipped that section of the survey.

Some survey question guidelines recommend that demographic questions should come first or last in a survey; however, there is much debate about what is best and why. Although it will vary by the type of organizational format you choose, the best choice is always to let your research question, hypotheses, and subsequent design help you determine the best option for your particular study. Regardless of what organizational format you choose, it is best to arrange questions about the same topic together, with transition statements between topic areas.

If you have ever answered a survey and thought, "I think I already answered that question," it may be that you have indeed answered a similar question—often one written that is the opposite of the first. For example, in McCroskey's (1982) Personal Report of Communication Apprehension Scale, one item states, "Ordinarily I am very tense and nervous in conversations," while another statement asks you to respond to the following, "Ordinarily I am very calm and relaxed in conversations." These items are written to minimize the tendency people have to start answering without much thought. This is called a *response set*. Reversing the polarity of some of the items on scales as you write is a good technique for avoiding a response set when participants complete your survey.

Survey Administration

When administering a questionnaire, researchers have choices to make about how best to deliver the material to the individual participating in the study or completing the questionnaire. This is known as questionnaire administration and we have three options: researcher-administered, self-administered, and interviews. In their content analysis of survey research in communication, Macias and colleagues (2008) found that the most common method of administration of surveys, by far, was mail (self-administered) surveys, used in 54 percent of research reviewed. Interviews over the telephone or in-person each were used in 11 percent of research reviewed. Web and fax surveys were rarely seen (only in 1% of studies reviewed).

researcher-administered questionnaires
A researcher is present when a participant completes a survey.

Researcher-Administered. In **researcher-administered questionnaires**, the researcher is present when the participant completes the survey questionnaire, usually in a group setting. When a person fills out her own survey instrument, regardless of whether the researcher is present at the time, the instrument is called a *questionnaire*. Researcher-administered surveys allow the researcher the opportunity of answering any questions participants may have. Another primary benefit to researcher-administered questionnaires is that when administering questionnaires to a large group of people at one time, data collection is quick and efficient. However, the disadvantage to administering a survey in such a setting is that participants sometimes feel less anonymous, as the researcher is present. Another disadvantage of administering a survey to a group of people is that groups can sometimes bias an individual's own responses. We may answer the survey differently if we feel that the information can be tied to us or if we feel that there is the chance someone in the group may find out about our responses.

Self-Administered.   In the past, most **self-administered questionnaires** were either handed out and sent home or mailed; however, the advent of technology allows us to collect data in a self-administered questionnaire via the Internet. Macias et al. (2008) found that, on average, self-administered surveys via mail yielded a 42 percent response rate, via email yielded a 30 percent response rate, and via fax yielded a 66 percent response rate. Mailing and allowing participants to take paper surveys home tends to decrease the response rate. In other words, the number of individuals who complete and return the surveys is less than if we had used researcher-administered questionnaires. For example, imagine that you are studying how stress impacts college student communication with roommates and you are using a longitudinal design. In the past, you might have sent home a packet with a questionnaire for both a student and her roommate to complete and return to the communication department. What are the odds that the surveys will be returned? More than likely, they will be excavated at the end of the semester, when the student cleans out the backseat of her vehicle before returning home for break. That will affect the outcome of your survey and diminish your response rate. Some researchers provide incentives to increase response rate. What incentives motivate you to respond to a survey request? Scholars may use extra credit, money, and/or gift cards to entice you to participate in their study and thus to increase their response rate. Sometimes, incentives appeal to some groups more than others and therefore can call into question the representativeness of the sample.

> **self-administered questionnaires**
> *Surveys that are completed individually, with no researchers or other people present.*

In their study on intensive care unit communication between physicians and nurses, Manojlovich, Antonakos, and Ronis (2012) were interested in communication's impact on patient outcomes. One part of their research design distributed surveys to 866 registered nurses; they collected 462, a response rate of 53.3 percent. Pretty good based on our discussion above. However, recognize that we don't know why the other 46.7 percent chose not to participate. This is certainly something to consider.

A key advantage to self-administered questionnaires over researcher-administered questionnaires is that individuals completing the survey tend to be more honest in their answers as neither researchers nor others are present. This protects an individual's sense of privacy, ensuring their data is anonymous. However, one of the trade-offs you make in self-administered questionnaires is that researchers are not present to answer any questions that may arise, so participants may guess at what you are asking them.

There are also pros and cons to conducting Web-based self-administered surveys. One large consideration for Web-based research is the representativeness of a sample that is able to access a questionnaire on the Web. There are still many people who don't have Internet access, or who are not comfortable with being on the Internet and thus might be less likely to complete a Web-based survey. Some research suggests that response rates for Web surveys are low, relative to other methods such as paper questionnaires (Couper & Miller, 2008). You can maximize representation of your sample by offering alternative modes of administration (Web and paper), but research suggests this also does not positively affect response rates (Couper & Miller, 2008). On the other hand, if your population is technologically savvy, a Web-based survey might be more attractive to them, and it is easier for you to work with since the data is already entered into a database ready for your analysis.

Interviews.   When the researcher asks the study participant the survey questions and records the responses, this is called an **interview**, and the researcher is called an *interviewer*. Interviewing can take place in person or over the phone. The survey instrument used in an interview is often called an *interview guide*, *interview protocol*, or *survey*. Essentially, what we are talking about here is a *quantitative* survey methodology, which differs from qualitative interviewing (which we cover in Chapter 14), and as such, utilizes a different set of rules. Macias and colleagues (2008) found that interviews conducted in person yielded on average a 79 percent response rate, the highest of all the methods they studied, and telephone interviews yielded a 61 percent response rate on average.

The first concern in this type of survey is the validity of interview data. Here, the validity of the data depends highly on how participants view the interviewer, as well as how effectively the interviewer manages the interaction. It is important to be capable of recording participant's answers unobtrusively, as well as knowing how to expand a person's answer with additional questions—also known as probing and clarifying.

The key to good quality interviews is the skill and training of the interviewers. There are, in fact, several validity threats related to interviewer issues. Interviewers can inadvertently create personal attribute effect (when characteristics of the researcher—gender, for example—influences people's behavior) or unintentional expectancy effect (by influencing participants by letting them know the behaviors they desire, such as by smiling or frowning). When conducting an interview, it's important that you don't predispose a participant to answer in some set manner. When you write your questionnaire or survey protocol, disguise your questions so the respondent does not continually try to outguess you or anticipate the answer you want. Unskilled interviewers can damage the validity of a well-designed survey. They can bias participant's responses, they may record responses incorrectly, and they can misrepresent the goals and questions of the survey. All of these create problems with the validity of the research at hand. Often, these types of interviews are conducted by multiple interviewers; therefore, it is necessary that all interviewers are carefully trained to follow a written protocol, which

interviews
A research practice with individual participants, or groups of participants, to obtain responses to survey questions by direct questioning.

details what questions will be asked in what order and how the entire interview will be conducted. Interviewers should be knowledgeable about the research, familiar with the interview questions, practice interviewing, and be skilled at building rapport with participants.

It is important that an interview gets off to the right start. Most people decide within the first few seconds whether they are willing to participate; therefore, the tone of the initial meeting and greeting with the researcher sets the tone for the rest of the interview process. A good interview should begin when the researchers introduce themselves to potential participants and identify the research entity they represent. They should identify the general research topic, explain any selection criteria for the study, and explain the time commitment participants must make. Finally, their role in the introduction of the interview is to convince the participant that his or her contribution is important to the research.

Interviews can be conducted either face-to-face or via telephone. We suspect future textbooks will have to consider survey designed interviews that will be conducted via instant messaging and other similar online forums. The beauty of a face-to-face interview is that it provides nonverbal data and demographic information; however, we sacrifice time, expense, and a decrease in privacy and anonymity. As Opdenakker (2006, para. 3) points out, "Face-to-face interviews allow synchronous communication of time and place." As you have seen throughout this text, there is no perfect design; there is always some trade-off. That is true of telephone interviews, too! Using a telephone interview structure is less costly and time consuming and simultaneously increases privacy and anonymity; however, it sacrifices nonverbal data that cannot be collected. Yet, it has the added advantage of providing the opportunity to interview people over vast geographic distances. Telephone interviews can be difficult. A relatively new barrier to collecting data via the telephone is the "Do Not Call" list. This is a national registry where individuals can request to have their number listed, so solicitors and telemarketers are prohibited from calling. This severely limits the proportion of the population who is available via telephone, which brings the representativeness of a random telephone sample into question. An additional barrier to collecting data via the phone is that it is easy for individuals to make an excuse, avoid the call (thanks to caller ID), or even hang up in the middle of an interview. In addition, since cell phone numbers are typically not available via traditional directories, researchers must make additional effort to obtain a good cross-section of all numbers. However, telephone interviews are advantageous in that they do allow for "synchronous communication of time and asynchronous communication of place" (Opdenakker, 2006, para. 3).

There are both advantages and disadvantages to using interviews (researcher asking the questions and recording the answers) in place of questionnaires (in which participants fill out the instrument themselves). Interviews usually have a higher response rate than questionnaires. This is particularly true of self-administered questionnaires when the researcher is not present while the questionnaire is being completed. Another benefit of interviews, when compared to traditional survey design, is that you can minimize the number of "don't know" responses. The facilitator or interviewer can use a probe, asking the question in a different way. Interviews also allow us to guard against misunderstandings. The interviewer or facilitator can clarify what she is asking. This provides more flexibility to your design, allowing for a deeper understanding.

In addition to recording verbal data when interviewing, an important advantage is that the interviewer can observe, as well as ask questions. Things such as race, age, and nonverbal communication cues can all be noted by the interviewer.

One example of face-to-face interviewing is the use of the Oral History Interview (OHI; Buehlman & Gottman, 1996; Buehlman, Gottman, & Katz, 1992; Krokoff, 1984). The OHI provides a useful tool for investigating perceptions about marriage as evidenced by how the couple communicates about their marital experience. The OHI is a structured interview that asks couples a series of open-ended questions about their relationship story; that is, the couple's dating and marital history, their philosophy of marriage, and how their marriage has changed over time (Buehlman & Gottman, 1996).

As a graduate student, interviewing for an oral history relational study, your author Heather Powell Gallardo interviewed a college-age dating couple using the OHI. As she interviewed this particular couple, their answers didn't seem to add up. They answered the questions, but there was something strange about the way they acted. After talking with another research assistant at the lab, who had watched the interview from the control room, she called the director of the study and let him know the concerns. When asked later, the couple admitted that they had never been in a relationship and just participated for the incentive (extra credit), even though there were alternative ways to earn the same incentive. Had she just had them fill out a self-administered questionnaire, it is unlikely she would have discovered their cheating, negatively impacting the validity of the study.

Thus far, we have detailed the strengths of interviewing over questionnaire survey techniques; however, it is not without disadvantages. One major drawback to interviewing is that it can be very expensive and time intensive. While time and expense can be overcome, a more substantial problem with interviews is that they may be subject to problems associated with social desirability. Remember social desirability is the idea that we may fudge our answers to present ourselves in a positive light. As such, participants are often inclined to provide answers they think we want to hear—regardless of whether they are true. Face-to-face interviews are most affected by social desirability compared to other methodological options available to use. Some argue that interviewers, through the use of rapport, try to increase honest answers, whereas others argue that social desirability is still a major concern.

When interviewing, we need to be certain that the interviewing is conducted in a consistent manner each time, regardless of who is interviewing the participants. Remember survey designed interviews follow a detailed protocol and while it is necessary to probe respondents for more complete answers, interviewers must follow the protocol consistently. This differs from qualitative interviewing techniques.

Relative Pros/Cons of Different Survey Methods

Here is a summary of the three main different methods of administering surveys:

Mail Surveys (Self-Administered)		
When to Use	**Pros**	**Cons**
When you want to save money; When self-selection bias and low response rate is not a problem; When you want to show participants something; When you don't have many/any open-ended questions; When the questions will be self-explanatory and easy to understand; When you have a large population so you can mail out many surveys (to account for low response rates); When you have ample time to conduct survey (to wait for questionnaires to be returned).	It is relatively inexpensive; It is relatively easy to do because you don't need trained interviewers to conduct the surveys.	Mail surveys generally have very low response rates (few people send them back). As a rule of thumb, for most mail surveys, you can expect a response rate anywhere from 2%–30%. This low response rate can cause: Bias (Do the people who returned the surveys have the same attitudes as those who didn't? Many researchers would say "no.") Invalid responses, because of too few people answering the questions; An inability to reach conclusions from the study because of the low return. It takes a long time to conduct a mail study, because you must allow time for mailing of materials and waiting for the return of the materials. Sometimes, you can wait weeks for the return of the surveys. Mail surveys do not allow you to "screen out" respondents. You are at the mercy of whoever opens the envelope and sends back the survey. You can ask for "only males between the ages of 18–24" to answer the survey. However, you have no control that this is who will actually do so.

How to Conduct Mail Surveys:

1. Define your population and sampling frame. Obtain a representative sampling frame.

2. Determine your desired sample size.

3. Determine your expected response rate (look at previous research or conduct a pilot study). From this, determine how many questionnaires you'll need to mail out. Be sure to account for wrong addresses and people who don't qualify for the study, as well as people who simply refuse or decline to participate.

4. Write your questionnaire. For a mail survey, all instructions must be "idiot proof"—crystal clear. The shorter the survey, the better your response rate will be.

5. Write a cover letter to be mailed with the survey. This letter should explain the purpose of the survey. It should ask for the respondent's assistance in this study. Think of a good reason why the person should help you. The more motivation you can give the respondents, the greater your response rate will be.

(Continued)

6. Make sure all your materials look as professional as possible. Letters on letterhead and envelopes with letterhead help response rates.

7. Always enclose a self-addressed, stamped envelope for return of questionnaire. No respondent is going to use his or her own money to return a survey to you. Have the envelope contents weighed at the post office to ensure that you have enclosed enough postage. Sending surveys out with "Postage Due" will not help your response rate.

8. Consider enclosing some type of incentive for filling out the survey: a $2 bill enclosed in each envelope works well. A promise to send $10–$25 when completed questionnaire is received also helps, but that requires the respondent to attach his or her name to the survey, which some are reluctant to do. Another incentive for some studies is to offer respondents a copy of the results.

9. Wait two weeks after mailing of materials. If not enough materials have been returned, do a second mailing to get more surveys.

10. Analyze the results.

Web-Based Surveys (Self-Administered)		
When to Use	**Pros**	**Cons**
When you want to save money; When self-selection bias and low response rate is not a problem; When you want to show participants something that you can reproduce digitally; When you don't have many/any open-ended questions; When the questions will be selfexplanatory and easy to understand; When you have a large population so you can invite many potential participants (to account for low response rates); When you are in a relative hurry, since participants can fill out a survey online and you get the results instantly.	It is relatively inexpensive; It is relatively easy to do because you don't need trained interviewers to conduct the surveys; Data is already entered and ready to be analyzed.	Web surveys have lower response rates than telephone or researcher-administered surveys. This lower response rate can cause: Bias (Do the people who returned the surveys have the same attitudes as those who didn't? Many researchers would say "no.") Invalid responses, because of too few people answering the questions; An inability to reach conclusions from the study because of the low return. Web surveys do not allow you to guarantee who actually answers the survey.

How to Conduct Web-based Surveys:

1. Define your population and sampling frame. Obtain a representative sampling frame.

2. Determine your desired sample size.

3. Determine your expected response rate (look at previous research or conduct a pilot study). From this, determine how many participants you'll need to invite. Be sure to account for wrong contact information and people who don't qualify for the study, as well as people who simply refuse or decline to participate.

4. Write your questionnaire and put it online, using a survey tool such as SurveyShare, Survey Monkey, or Zoomerang. All instructions must be "idiot proof"—crystal clear. The shorter the survey, the better your response rate will be.

5. Find a good way to invite participants, either in person or written. Personal invitations are more effective than cold mailings. When you invite them, explain the purpose of the survey. It should ask for the respondent's assistance in this study. Think of a good reason why the person should help you. The more motivation you can give the respondents, the greater your response rate will be.

6. Make sure all your materials look as professional as possible. Letters on letterhead and envelopes with letterhead help response rates.

7. Consider offering some type of incentive for filling out survey, but make sure that participants understand that an incentive mailed to them does not mean that you can connect their responses to their name.

8. Wait two weeks after inviting participants. If not enough surveys have been filled out, send a second invitation to get more surveys.

9. Analyze the results.

Telephone Surveys (Interviews)		
When to Use	**Pros**	**Cons**
When you want a more random, projectable sample; When you have more money to spend (than for mail surveys); When you need to probe open-ended (discussion) questions; When you want to complete a large number of interviews in a relatively short period of time; When you want to project the sample to the universe; When you have nothing to show respondent/nothing he or she has to see; When you need to "screen out" who you want to interview.	Sample is more reliable, less problem with bias; Usually fairly high response rates; Can usually be done in a fairly short period of time; Responses are better because interviewers can probe for clarity and complete responses; Allows you to "screen out" respondents/ determine if you do or do not want to talk to respondent.	More expensive; Ideally, requires trained interviewers.

How to do Telephone Surveys:

1. Based on your RQ or H, determine who you want to talk to—determine if you want to set any special requirements (such as age, sex, product usage).

2. Find a sampling frame and obtain your sample.

3. Determine your expected response rate (look at previous research or conduct a pilot study). From this, determine how many people you'll need to call. Be sure to account for wrong phone numbers and people who don't qualify for the study, as well as people who simply refuse or decline to participate.

4. Write survey.

5. Determine who will do the interviewing.

6. Train interviewers (if you are not doing all the data collection yourself).

7. Conduct interviews. Make sure that you make calls at all times of day, at all days of week, to eliminate bias.

8. Analyze the results.

Here's a sample survey questionnaire with the brochure we used to explain the study to potential participants. It's designed to be a self-administered survey and was provided to participants over the Internet via a Web-based service called Survey Share. Participants were recruited via network sampling through students in a research methods class. The Likert scale included in the questionnaire was derived from a validated, reliable scale of mental health literacy (Epps et al., 2007; Massey et al., 2008). Note the skip patterns in questions 15, 21, and 22, in which participants are instructed to only answer those questions if they are currently receiving mental health services. Also note the skip pattern in Q. 40, in which participants are told that if they have never received mental health services to skip to Q. 43. The consent form is part of the survey, and participants are told that if they fill out the survey, consent is presumed to be given.

"Study of Mental Health Attitudes, Knowledge, and Beliefs"
INFORMATION FOR POTENTIAL STUDY PARTICIPANTS

PROJECT OBJECTIVES

The "Study of Mental Health Attitudes, Knowledge, and Beliefs" project is designed to help us understand what the general public knows, thinks, and believes about mental healthcare patients and providers. The information we learn from this study will be used for research to help mental health providers understand how to most effectively communicate with patients and the general public.

THE RESEARCHERS

The data will be collected and analyzed by researchers at the University of North Carolina at Charlotte.

RECRUITER NAME:

PARTICIPATION

For this research, we are inviting you to fill out an online survey. This should take no more than 15 minutes of your time. We will be asking you questions about what you think, believe, and know about mental illness.

PAYMENT AND STUDY TERMINATION

You will not be paid for filling out the survey. However, the Research Assistant student recruiting you will receive course credit for recruiting you. Once you have opened the Web page and submitted the ID number of the student recruiting you, the student has received credit, regardless of whether you continue filling out the survey.

Participation in this study is completely voluntary. Once you are taking part in the study, you can terminate your participation at any time.

CONFIDENTIALITY

The results of this study may be published. However, since your name will not be input anywhere on the survey, there is no way that identifying information about you would be included. We are bound by professional confidentiality agreements.

To Participate

If you are interested in participating in this study, please go to the following website: **http://www .surveyshare.com/survey/take/?sid=48210**

Please make a note of the ID number of the student who recruited you so he or she will get credit for your participation:

Once you are on the Web site, simply follow the instructions.

FOR MORE INFORMATION ABOUT THIS RESEARCH PROJECT, PLEASE FEEL FREE TO CONTACT:

DR. CHRISTINE DAVIS, DEPT. OF COMMUNICATION STUDIES, UNC–CHARLOTTE

Thank you for your interest in participating in this study.
To continue, you MUST be 18 years old!!!!!

Please give us the code number of the student who recruited you for this project: _____. The student has now been given credit for this assignment regardless of whether you continue with the survey.

Answering these questions should take you about 15 minutes. If you decide not to answer them, that's okay. Since you will not write your name anywhere on the survey, your responses will be completely confidential and anonymous. We will not know what you said, or even whether you filled out a survey.

Informed Consent Information:

The purpose of this study is to understand the attitudes, knowledge, and beliefs people have toward mental illness. The Primary Investigator (PI) of this project is Dr. Christine S. Davis, Dept. of Communication Studies at the University of North Carolina at Charlotte. If you have any questions or concerns, feel free to contact her at: 704-687-6638 or csdavis2@email.uncc.edu

You may participate in this study if you are at least 18 years old. You will be asked to fill out an anonymous survey to indicate your agreement with statements concerning your attitudes, knowledge, and beliefs about mental illness. The survey should take no longer than 15 minutes to complete.

The project may involve risks that are not currently known. However, there are no known risks or benefits to study participants. Your information will be anonymous. Since the instructor, study PI, or the student who recruited you for this study will not know who is filling out the survey and who is not, the student's grade will not be affected by your either filling it out or not. There is a benefit to society in that the knowledge we are gathering will help us learn how to develop more effective healthcare messages.

If you choose not to fill out the survey, that is okay. By your entering the student's ID # at the beginning of this Web page, the student who recruited you has already been given credit, regardless of whether you continue with the survey. You are a volunteer. The decision to participate in this study is completely up to you. If you decide to fill out the survey, you may stop at any time. All data collected by the investigator will not contain any information that will link the data back to you or your participation in this study. The following steps will be taken to ensure this anonymity: Your name will never be entered on any of the survey materials.

UNC Charlotte wants to make sure that you are treated in a fair and respectful manner. Contact the university's Research Compliance Office (704-123-9999) if you have questions about how you are treated as a study participant. If you have any questions about the actual project or study, please contact Dr. Christine Davis, 704-123-9999, xxx@uncc.edu

By continuing and filling out the survey, you are agreeing with the following statement: I have read the information in this consent form. I have had the chance to call or email the study PI with any questions about this study, and if I have, those questions have been answered to my satisfaction. I am at least 18 years of age, and I agree to participate in this research project. I understand that I can call or email the study PI to request a copy of this consent information.

Thank you for your participation!

1. Where do you get (or have you gotten) any information you have about mental health or mental illness?

[CHECK ALL THAT APPLY]

Case manager/family support coordinator	
Child welfare (DCF) worker	
Juvenile justice (DJJ) worker	
School: teacher, social worker, counselor, psychologist, other	
Counselor/therapist/social worker/psychologist/psychiatrist	
Medical doctor/pediatrician/nurse/brochures or other materials from my doctor/health-care provider/doctor's office	
Clergy members (pastor, priest, rabbi, imam, etc.)	
Family members	
Friends/neighbors/people I know socially/coworkers	
Human resources people at my job	
Media: television/movies/magazines/newspapers	
Internet	
From my own (or my child's) personal experiences	
Trainings/workshops for parents of children with mental, emotional, and behavioral disorders	
Other [PLEASE WRITE IN]	

The following questions are about your opinion, beliefs, and knowledge about mental health and about mental healthcare services. If you have never received mental health-care services (or do not currently receive any mental health-care services), please answer how you THINK you would feel if you ever had to receive mental health-care services.

When you're thinking of mental health-care providers and services, please think of counselors, therapists, psychologists, psychiatrists, social workers, school guidance counselors or psychologists, and school special education teachers or special education counselors.

PLEASE PUT AN "X" IN THE BOX THAT INDICATES YOUR LEVEL
OF AGREEMENT WITH EACH OF THE FOLLOWING STATEMENTS:

	Agree Strongly	Agree Somewhat	Neither Agree nor Disagree	Disagree Somewhat	Disagree Strongly
2. I am capable of solving my problems.					
3. Any mental, emotional, and/or behavioral problems I may have can be successfully treated.					
4. I can control my behavior.					
5. Mental health treatments I may need to have are under my control.					
6. I have the right to receive any mental health *testing* I need (psychological, mental, or physical, etc.).					
7. I have the right to ask for mental health care help when I need it.					
8. I have the right to ask for all available mental health services in the community that I need.					
9. I have the right to *choose* what mental health services I will have.					
10. Having mental, emotional, and/or behavioral problems would *not* make me any less valuable to society.					
11. Mental, emotional, and/or behavioral problems in children or adolescents are ILLNESSES (not discipline issues).					
12. People with emotional, mental, and/or behavioral problems are still like everyone else.					
13. My opinions are important, regardless of any emotional, mental, and/ or behavioral problems I may have.					
14. Normal people can be mentally ill.					
15. [ANSWER IF YOU ARE CURRENTLY RECEIVING MENTAL HEALTH SERVICES] I understand any changes my mental health-care providers want me to make.					
16. I know what mental health resources and services are available for me if I need them.					

(Continued)

	Agree Strongly	Agree Somewhat	Neither Agree nor Disagree	Disagree Somewhat	Disagree Strongly
17. I know how to access all the mental health resources, services, and treatments available for me that I might need.					
18. I understand both the risks and the benefits of the alternative mental health-care treatments.					
19. I understand how to make an appointment with a mental health-care provider if I need to.					
20. I understand how to obtain mental health-care information I may need.					
21. [ANSWER IF YOU ARE CURRENTLY RECEIVING MENTAL HEALTH SERVICES] I understand how to juggle my mental health-care provider appointments and my other activities.					
22. [ANSWER IF YOU ARE CURRENTLY RECEIVING MENTAL HEALTH SERVICES] I understand how to fit my mental health-care treatments into my life.					
23. If necessary, I would be able to decide when I need to get a second opinion on my mental health care.					
24. If necessary, I would be able to decide whether the mental health-care treatments or services provided to me have worked well enough.					
25. I am able to decide when I need mental health help, assistance, or services.					
26. I am able to know when I need to make mental, emotional, and/or behavioral changes in my life.					
27. If necessary, I would be capable of asking my mental health-care providers questions.					
28. If necessary, I would be capable of expressing concerns to my mental health-care providers.					
29. If necessary, I would be capable of negotiating with my mental health-care providers to reach treatment or service solutions that are best for everyone.					

	Agree Strongly	Agree Somewhat	Neither Agree nor Disagree	Disagree Somewhat	Disagree Strongly
30. If necessary, I would be capable of asking for mental health-care help, services, treatments, and resources, in a way that gets me what I need.					

The following questions are for classification purposes:

31. What is your gender?
  a. Female
  b. Male

32. What is your race?
  a. American Indian or Native American
  b. Another race _____
  c. Asian or Pacific Islander
  d. Black or African American
  e. Multiracial _____
  f. White

33. Are you Hispanic?
  a. No
  b. Yes

34. What is your marital status?
  a. Divorced
  b. Living as married
  c. Married
  d. Never married
  e. Separated
  f. Widowed

35. What is the highest education level you have completed?
  a. Less than high school
  b. High school graduate or GED
  c. Vocational, technical, trade, or business school beyond the high school level
  d. Some college, but no degree
  e. Associate or Bachelor's degree
  f. Some graduate school
  g. Master's degree or higher
  h. Other (Please specify) _____

36. What best describes your work, school, or volunteer situation over the past year?
    a. Employed full time
    b. Employed part time
    c. Homemaker
    d. In the armed forces
    e. Other (e.g., volunteer worker, disabled) _____
    f. Resident of institution
    g. Retired
    h. Student
    i. Unemployed, looking for work
    j. Unemployed, on lay-off from job

37. Your health insurance is provided by:
    a. None
    b. Medicaid
    c. Medicare
    d. Private insurance (insurance through employer or purchase own)
    e. School insurance
    f. Other [WRITE IN] _____
    g. Don't know

38. Into which of the following age categories do you fall?
    a. 18–24
    b. 25–34
    c. 35–44
    d. 45–54
    e. 55–64
    f. 65+
    g. No answer

39. What mental health diagnoses have you ever been given?
    a. None
    b. Adjustment Disorder
    c. ADHD
    d. Depression
    e. Disruptive Disorder
    f. Other major psychiatric disorder
    g. Other: _____

40. In your entire life, how many years total have you received mental health-care services?
    a. Never received mental healthcare services (SKIP TO Q. 43)
    b. Less than one
    c. 1–4
    d. 5–9
    e. 10–14
    f. 15–19
    g. 20+

41. Are you receiving mental health-care services currently?

    a. Yes

    b. No

42. From whom have you ever received mental health-care services?

    a. Counselor

    b. Therapist

    c. Psychologist

    d. Psychiatrist

    e. Social worker

    f. School guidance counselor or psychologist

    g. School special education teacher or special education counselors

    h. Other: _____

43. Have you or anyone in your family ever experienced any of the following?

	Yes	No
a. Crime convictions	____	____
b. Physical abuse/violence	____	____
c. Psychiatric hospitalization	____	____
d. Running away	____	____
e. Sexual abuse	____	____
f. Substance abuse	____	____
g. Suicide attempts	____	____

So What?

Surveys will continue to be popular; technology is contributing to their prevalence in assessing many different types of research questions and hypotheses, and there are many uses and advantages to this research method. We have examined survey design and many considerations a scholar must make when designing a questionnaire. You should know the difference between a cross-sectional and longitudinal design and when each is the appropriate study design. Survey designed interviews have an important function in the assessment of many communication issues. Finally, we compared the uses, advantages, and disadvantages of using interviews and self-administered questionnaires. All methods and procedures have pros and cons and appropriate and inappropriate uses. The bottom line is—your research question or hypothesis drives what you do and how you do it.

Glossary

Cohort study

    A study in which responses from specific subgroups of a population are identified and compared over time.

Cross-sectional survey

    A survey design that describes the characteristics of a sample representing a population at one point in time.

Evaluation research

Research that is designed to assess the effectiveness of programs or products during development or after their completion.

Funnel format

A type of question format in which questions begin with broad, open-ended questions followed by narrow, more closed-ended questions.

Interview

A research practice with individual participants, or groups of participants, to obtain responses to survey questions by direct questioning.

Inverted funnel format

A type of question format that generally begins with more closed-ended, narrow questions moving throughout the questionnaire to the most open-ended and broad questions.

Longitudinal survey design

A survey design that gathers data from respondents at several points in time.

Market research

Research that is designed to study consumer behavior.

Panel study

A study in which a sample is drawn from a population or universe and those same people or objects are measured at multiple points in time.

Political polls

One of the most common and readily available uses of surveys. They provide a detailed account of who is leading whom in the run for a particular office during an election.

Researcher-administered questionnaires

A researcher is present when a participant completes a survey.

Self-administered questionnaires

Surveys that are completed individually, with no researchers or other people present.

Survey design

A method of asking research participants questions that provides researchers with a method of information gathering from a large number of people over a relatively short period of time.

Trend study

Measurement occurs at two or more points in time, from different samples selected from the same population. This type of study is designed to identify changes or trends in people's beliefs about a variable of interest.

Tunnel format

A type of question format in which questions tend to be similar in terms of breadth and depth throughout a questionnaire. Questions are organized by similarity and vary little in terms of depth.

References

Atkin, C. K., & Freimuth, v. (2000). Formative evaluation research in campaign design. In R. E. Rice & C. K. Atkin (Eds.), *Public communication campaigns* (pp. 125–145). Thousand Oaks, CA: Sage.

Botta, R. A., & Dumlao, R. (2002). How do conflict and communication patterns between fathers and daughters contribute to or offset eating disorders? *Health Communication, 14*(2), 199–219.

Buehlman, K. T., & Gottman, J. M. (1996). *The oral history interview and the oral history coding system.* Mahwah, NJ: Erlbaum.

Buehlman, K. T., Gottman, J. M., & Katz, L. F. (1992). How a couple views their past predicts their future: Predicting divorce from an oral history interview. *Journal of Family Psychology, 5,* 295–318.

Carlsen, F. L. (Ed.). (2010). *Harris Michigan Industrial Directory.* Austin, TX: Harrisinfosource.

Center, A. H., & Broom, G. M. (1983). Evaluation research. *Public Relations Quarterly, 28*(3), 1–3.

Couper, M. P., & Miller, P. v. (2008). Web survey methods: Introduction. *Public Opinion Quarterly, 72*(5), 831–835.

Epps, C. S., Armstrong, M., Davis, C. S., Massey, T. O., McNeish, R., & Smith, R. B. (2007). *Development and testing of an instrument to measure mental health literacy.* Tampa, FL: Louis de la Parte Florida Mental Health Institute. University of South Florida.

Krokoff, L. (1984). The anatomy of blue-collar marriages (Doctoral dissertation, University of Illinois at Urbana-Champaign, 1984). *Dissertation Abstracts International.*

Lim, V. K. G., & Teo, T. S. H. (2009). Mind your E-manners: Impact of cyber incivility on employees' work attitude and behavior. *Information & Management, 46,* 419–425.

Macias, W., Springston, J. K., Lariscy, R. A. W., & Neustifer, B. (2008). A 13-year content analysis of survey methodology in communication related journals. *Journal of Current Issues and Research in Advertising, 30*(1), 79–94.

Manojlovich, M., Antonakos, C. L., & Ronis, D. L. (2012). Intensive care units, communication between nurses and physicians, and patients' outcomes. *American Journal of Critical Care, 18,* 21-30.

Massey, O. T., Davis, C. S., Smith, R. B., Armstrong, M., & Vergon, K. S. (2008). *Refinement of an instrument to measure mental health literacy among caregivers and providers and a qualitative examination of interventions to enhance mental health literacy.* Tampa, FL: Louis de la Parte Florida Mental Health Institute. University of South Florida.

McCroskey, J. E. (1982). Oral communication apprehension: A reconceptualization. In M. Burgoon (Ed.), *Communication yearbook* (Volume 6, pp. 136–170). Beverly Hills: Sage.

Opdenakker, R. (2006). Advantages and disadvantages of four interview techniques in qualitative research. *Forum Qualitative Sozialforschung/Forum: Qualitative Social Research,* 7(4) <Electronic version>. Retrieved March 18, 2009, from http://www.qualitativeresearch.net/index.php/fqs/article/view/175/392

The Quotations Page. (n.d.). Retrieved June 15, 2009, from http://www.quotationspage.com/quote/706.html

The Quote Garden. (n.d.). Retrieved June 15, 2009, from http://www.quotegarden.com/tv-turnoff-week.html

Salmon, C. T., Park, H. S., & Wrigley, B. J. (2003). Optimistic bias and perceptions of bioterrorism in Michigan corporate spokespersons, Fall 2001. *Journal of Health Communication, 8,* 130–143.

Segrin, C., & Flora, J. (2000). Poor social skills are a vulnerability factor in the development of psychosocial problems. *Human Communication Research, 26,* 489–514.

11

QUANTITATIVE ANALYSIS OF TEXT AND WORDS: CONTENT AND INTERACTION ANALYSIS

CHAPTER OUTLINE

KEY TERMS

Chance agreement

Cluster sampling

Content analysis

Context units

Distributional structure

Interactive structure

Inter-coder reliability

Random sampling

Recording units

Sampling units

Scott's Pi

Sequential structure

Stratified sampling

Systematic sampling

Unitizing

Chapter Objectives

1. To understand what content analysis is and when it should be used
2. To understand how to select and unitize content
3. To understand how to train coders
4. To know how to analyze and interpret content analysis data

▼ # Exploring Quantitative Content Analysis

The February 11, 2006, edition of *The Charlotte Observer* (Germain, 2006) reported on a study of gender balance in top-grossing G-rated films from 1990 to 2004. The researchers, sponsored by the advocacy group Dads & Daughters, reported that male characters outnumbered females 3 to 1, with 28 percent of speaking characters being female and 17 percent of people in crowd scenes being female. What type of research did they conduct to determine this imbalance? A quantitative content analysis.

To this point, we have discussed measuring and evaluating human behavior using quantitative techniques for such surveys and experiments. We have discussed the ethics associated with conducting research involving human subjects, ensuring good measurement of human behavior, appropriate sampling techniques, and making sense of self-report data, among others.

Communication researchers may be interested in other forms of data, however, that may not be derived from the reports or testing of research participants. While survey data can be informative, sometimes it's not appropriate given the research question or hypothesis—sometimes communication researchers would rather observe behaviors and make judgments about their observations independent of participant feedback. Still other times, communication researchers may be concerned with the nature of messages themselves, as opposed to how certain subjects may react to them.

content analysis
A quantitative methodology that allows researchers to quantify content, including the content of participant responses or the content of media texts.

In either of these instances, quantitative **content analysis** may be an appropriate analytic technique. As a methodology, content analysis allows researchers to quantify content—whether that means the content of participant responses or the content of media texts. Quantifying the nature of content can answer numerous questions relevant to making sense of meaning.

Why Analyze Content?

There are two major circumstances under which it might make sense to conduct a content analysis. The first of these is most closely associated with mass media research. There is a long history in media research of attempting to quantify the nature of media content in terms of news themes, information presented, content that some may consider problematic, and so on. But why would someone want to make quantitative assessments of content?

Media researchers often talk about the *three-legged stool* of media effects research; the legs represent surveys, experiments, and content analysis. Of course, we have plenty of research linking media use with particular outcomes. Some have argued that violent television may make people more aggressive, that the consumption of political news leads to the polarization of attitudes, or that watching sexualized content may change one's opinions of their partners. Experimental and survey media research has even identified particular contexts that may make people more or less susceptible to these effects. Repeated violence may lead to desensitization toward aggression, for example, while sexual content may be especially worrisome when combined with issues of power or dominance. One can easily think of anecdotal examples of this kind of content, but the social relevance of these findings can be ascertained only by answering the following question: "Exactly how often does this content really appear?"

For the media effects researcher, this is where content analysis comes in: by providing evidence that media content shown to have effects on audiences in the lab exists in the real world. Take for example the National Television Violence Study (NTVS) (Wilson et al., 1997). Wilson and colleagues assembled a thorough review of the experimental research on television violence and identified numerous contextual features that mitigate the impact of violent content on aggressive attitudes and behaviors. These included the demographic attributes of perpetrators and victims, whether violence was rewarded or punished, whether it was repetitive in nature, whether there were weapons involved, and whether there were representations of blood and gore (just to name a few). They also came up with a definition of what they considered constituted an act of violence and looked at how often violent interactions took place and if any of these contextual features were commonplace. In analyzing thousands of hours of television content, they found that violence was fairly commonplace on network and basic cable and that the types of violence shown problematic in experimental research were also fairly common. Thus, they showed evidence that the content found troublesome in the laboratory was readily available and offered evidence that the same kinds of effects might be happening in the real world. As an aside, given the rigorous unitizing, sampling, and coding techniques they used, the NTVS is often held up as the *gold standard* in content analytic media research.

Content Analysis Versus Interaction Analysis

There is another very good time to analyze content. Instead of analyzing media messages, you may want to record the behaviors or interactions of participants and analyze the content. This type of analysis—often called interaction analysis—uses techniques similar to those of traditional content analyses, but looks instead at recordings of individuals or groups and how they may behave and exchange information. Interaction analysis is often used in conjunction with experimental research. While experimental procedures examining interpersonal interactions can produce data reflecting the feelings, attitudes, and opinions of the participants, having an unobtrusive measure of the nature of the interaction may also be very valuable to a researcher. In this way, communication researchers may be able to make quantitative assessments of both interpersonal interactions and group dynamics in relatively unobtrusive ways that may get around the biases of the individual respondent.

In 2008, Stephens and Mottet conducted an experiment to test the effects of Web-based communication on training. They tested trainer-initiated interactions against trainee-initiated interactions in terms of their effect on instructional outcomes, including perceived credibility, goodwill, trust, vocal variety, competence, satisfaction, and learning. In order to measure the interactions (which served as the independent variable of their study), they conducted an interaction analysis. They operationalized two different levels (high and low) of interactivity with the two different groups controlling and initiating the interactivity (either the trainer or the trainee). Thus, they measured four conditions (see p. 241): high trainer-controlled interactivity where the trainer asked the trainees to participate in polls during the training event, low trainer-controlled interactivity where there was no request for trainee participation, high trainee-controlled interactivity where trainees were allowed to chat with one another prior to the Web conference, and low trainee-controlled interactivity where trainees did not chat with one another.

There are similar methodological considerations in both traditional content analysis and in interaction analysis. Both techniques involve the selection of content, unitizing, coding, and analysis. In either case, making quantitative assessments of the nature and frequency of a particular kind of content is the end goal. This chapter will outline some of the basic logic behind content analysis, and lay out the basic methodological procedures and considerations associated with this type of inquiry.

▼ Content Structure

Distributional Structure

Baxter and Babbie (2004) identify three basic types of content structure that can be elaborated on from content analysis. The first of these, **distributional structure**, deals with the number or frequency with which certain interactions take place in a certain timeframe. Smith et al. (2003; 2004), for example, attempted to figure out how often acts of violence take place in popular video games. They sampled sixty popular video games and counted the number of times an act of violence took place. After adjusting for the ten-minute snippets of data they examined, they concluded that acts of aggression took place across their sample at a rate of *about thirteen acts of violence per hour on average—or more than three times* the frequency of violence on television found in the NTVS. This is an example of a statement concerning distributional structure; it answers the question of how often something happens.

Interactive Structure

Interactive structure, more applicable to interaction analysis, deals with the pattern of response types that may vary throughout an interaction. This type of analysis then becomes a case of analyzing who says what and to whom. By considering the nature of messages that are uttered, and considering

distributional structure
A type of content structure that deals with the number or frequency with which certain interactions take place in a certain timeframe.

interactive structure
A type of content structure that deals with the pattern of response types that may vary throughout an interaction.

who the senders and recipients of these messages are, the communication researcher can make numerous observation and claims about the relationships that are being established, reinforced, or undermined in a particular set of interactions.

Sequential Structure

Finally, there are questions of **sequential structure**. Typically, these types of questions have been associated with interaction analysis. They normally deal with an examination of the sequences of utterances, in order to make more sense of what is going on (Hirokawa, 1988). So, for example, examining an interpersonal exchange to evaluate how often a comment is followed by a slight, or how often a relational message is met with resistance, may be informative in painting a picture of the nature of the interaction. More recently, sequential analysis has found its way into traditional content analysis also. Lachlan and colleagues (2009) looked at the violence in professional wrestling telecasts and were particularly concerned with the extent of violence in a given interaction. They used sequential analyses to determine that violence acts in this genre are almost always met with acts that are over-retributive in nature. As a result, fairly benign insults lead to full-scale bloodbaths in only a few exchanges, a pattern of violence, they claim, that is rather alarming.

sequential structure
A type of content structure that normally deals with an examination of the sequences of utterances in order to make more sense of what is going on.

•••

Content Analysis Logic   ▼

Content analysis, as a methodology, is unique in the degree to which the findings and the interpretation of those findings are related to the procedural decision of the researcher (Krippendorf, 1980). This is because, to an extent, the researcher must *create* the data. The data are derived from a number of decisions the researcher must make concerning exactly what it is he or she wants to look at, where it might be found, and how it ought to be examined. The explicitness of these decisions and procedures must be clearly articulated in order for a reader to approach a content analysis with any sense of scientific scrutiny. Therefore, it is essential that the content analysis researcher make procedural decisions that make sense given the content under consideration and the questions that he wishes to answer.

As we walk through this decision-making process, it should become clear that content analysis is a different method than survey or experimental techniques. While other quantitative approaches have hard and fast rules regarding best procedures, the content analyst is often left to make judgment calls concerning exactly how to approach the content in question, what to look at, how to look at it, and how to make sense of the data. The first major issue that the content analyst must face, before proceeding any further, is the issue of what exactly it is that will be examined. This is a decision-making process called unitizing.

Interested in research on speech acts in computer-mediated communication, Carr, Schrok, and Dauterman (2012) analyzed status messages on Facebook. The abstract for their article explains:

A total of 204 status messages created by 46 participants were captured 3 times daily over 14 consecutive days. Content analysis of these data revealed that status messages were most frequently constructed with expressive speech acts, followed by assertives. Additionally, humor was integrated into almost 20% of these status messages. These findings demonstrate differences in how users express themselves in alternate media. Findings address implications for self-presentation in social networks and theoretical implications for computer-mediated communication research. (p. 176)

▼ Unitizing

unitizing
The process of deciding exactly what it is that should be observed.

Unitizing (Krippendorf, 1980) is the process of deciding exactly what it is that should be observed. This is not as easy as it seems. Are you primarily concerned with individual interactions? Individual scenes? Programs on the whole? Once you have made this determination, how do you define your units of analysis conceptually? What exactly defines a *scene*? Or an *interaction*? These are decisions the content analyst must consider carefully.

Sampling Units

sampling units
The units that are sampled from a larger population of content that you wish to examine.

The first unitizing decision that must be made by the content analyst is deciding upon **sampling units**. Sampling units are a determination of what type of content—in a broad sense—will be sampled or drawn from a population of similar content units. Confused yet? Don't be. Let's take our wrestling example from above. Lachlan and colleagues (2009) wanted to look at violence in professional wrestling, so they decided that their sampling units would consist of episodes of *Monday Night Raw* and *WWE Smackdown*. While similar content could be found in other wrestling shows, they decided that these two shows were most representative of unedited, first-run wrestling content. They also decided that recording an intact season of each show would be a good idea, just as a snapshot of what was going on within the telecasts. To sum up the sampling unit, it is where you are going to go for your content.

Recording Units

recording units
The individual parts of a sampling unit the researcher is examining.

Recording units are a bit more complicated. According to Holsti (1969), recording units are the individual parts of a sampling unit that you may wish to quantify and report on. Let's return to our wrestling example. Lachlan and colleagues (2009) decided to look at individual violent interactions in their analysis, in order to figure out whether violence escalated from interaction to interaction. To do this, they adopted the NTVS definition of a violent interaction, which is "any overt depiction of a credible threat of physical force or the actual use of such force intended to physically harm an animate being or group of beings. Violence also includes certain depictions of physically harmful consequences against an animate being/s that results from unseen violent means" (Smith et al., 1998, p. 30). Within each of their recording units (episodes of *Raw* and *Smackdown*), they identified individual violent interactions using this definition. They looked at each of these interactions to see what they contained in terms of context units.

Context Units

Context units are the types of content or contextual features that may appear in an individual recoding unit. So, you may be able to identify a certain number of interactions that appear in a given sampling unit. You may then decide to look at the specific features of each of these interactions. These are known as context units.

Returning once again to our previous example, Lachlan and colleagues (2009) identified a number of context units within each of the recording units they identified. After identifying individual interactions as recording units, they then looked at each of these violent interactions and made a number of contextual judgments for each one. These included the number of acts of violence within each unit, the motive for violence, whether there were weapons and what types, and several others. The authors then combined their observations to make statements about the frequency with which violent actions occur (recording units) and the frequency with which violence escalated in terms of the number of acts committed from interaction to interaction (context units).

context units
The types of content or contextual features that may appear in an individual recording unit.

Sampling   ▼

Like any quantitative procedure, issues of sampling become apparent when we are trying to figure out just how much we are going to examine and where it will be drawn from. As stated above, we talk about sampling units as the units that are sampled from a larger population of content that you wish to examine. Examining every issue of the *New York Times* would be a nearly impossible task; however, examining a sample of issues drawn from a particular timeframe may allow the content analyst to draw conclusions about the population in question, just as a sample of research participants may allow the experimentalist to draw conclusions about his or her population of interest. In other words, almost any research team would be overwhelmed by looking at an entire population of content, so content analysts, like behavioral researchers, almost always draw samples from larger populations of content.

Random Sampling

Random sampling involves the selection of a certain number of sampling units, at random, from the entire population of available sampling units. So in our *New York Times* example, your population of interest might be all issues from the 2008 calendar year. Instead of wading through over 300 issues of the paper, you could randomly select thirty from the calendar year using dice, a roulette wheel, a random number generator, or so on.

Stratified Sampling

Stratified sampling uses a technique in which different subcategories of the sample are identified and then randomly selected. To use a very simple example, you may want to sample twenty-eight issues of the *New York Times*, but want an even distribution of days of the week. You would randomly sample four Mondays, four Tuesdays, four Wednesdays, and so on, to evenly distribute the sample across days of the week. Another example of this is commonly found in television content analysis, where a *composite week* is often assembled. For example, Kunkel and colleagues (1999) randomly selected television content across different time slots and different days of the week, in order to assemble a sample of television content representing one week of programming, but drawn from numerous different weeks.

Systematic Sampling

systematic sampling
A type of sampling that is similar in logic to random sampling, but involves designating a timeframe ("k") and selecting every kth *sampling unit within the population.*

Systematic sampling is similar in logic to random sampling, but involves designating a timeframe ("k") and selecting every *kth* sampling unit within the population. In our *New York Times* example, one could select every eleventh issue of the *Times* for a given calendar year. This would allow for a sample that was drawn over the course of an entire year, but should be robust to any problems associated with sampling entirely from a particular day or a narrower timeframe that may not be representative of the year on the whole.

Cluster Sampling

Cluster sampling refers to the sampling of an entire group of sampling units. This is usually the case in which an entire population list is difficult or impossible to assemble. In this case, a group that has logical or natural boundaries is typically selected.

Take for example the Smith, Lachlan, and Tamborini (2003) content analysis. Smith and colleagues wanted to sample video game content. The problem was that they had no idea where to turn for a complete list of all available games. If they did have such a list available, they had no idea how to make sense of an appropriate sampling frame, since no one had attempted to quantitatively analyze video games before. So they felt their best course of action was to come up with a sample based on sales data. They sampled the top twenty selling games for each of the three major systems that were available at the time. While not a perfect sample by any stretch of the imagination, it at least allowed them to make statements about the games people were buying. Thus, without a true population list to draw from, a cluster technique was used to derive a sample that made sense.

▼ # Reliability

Once a sample has been assembled, the content analyst is left with the task of making sense of the data that has been collected. This typically involves turning to the recording and context units and making sense of them. Content analysis will first unitize the data by identifying the individual recording units (interactions, scenes, etc.) and then affix certain context categories to each recording unit. The frequency of these units, and the contextual elements associated with them, are later tallied for statistical analyses.

There is just one major problem with the process of identifying recording units and the content within them—time. Content analysts often have to analyze enormous amounts of data. The NTVS researchers, for example, had to unitize and code over 2,000 hours of television content. Further, if an individual researcher is responsible for unitizing and coding all of the content, she runs the risk of her own biases affecting the coding.

Coder Training ✳

The solution is to assemble a team of independent coders. Content analysts will typically develop a coding protocol (Riffe, Lacy, & Fico, 1998). This is a document that details the operational definitions of everything in the study, including the sampling frame, the unitizing criteria, and the contextual definitions. They will then typically recruit and train a group of coders to make and record these decisions across multiple sampling units, breaking up the mass of content that has been harvested into easy to analyze chunks.

Inter-coder Reliability ✳

What's critical in this process is making sure that all coders are analyzing content according to the definitions and criteria spelled out in the coding protocol. Content analysts will often meet with their coders numerous times, both in groups and in individual settings, and practice coding content that will not be included in the study itself. Typically, researchers will meet with their coder teams over and over again until they meet an acceptable level of agreement. This level of agreement, known as **inter-coder reliability**, is an essential component of the content analysis process. Inter-coder reliability is an indicator of how similarly the coders are coding the content, both in terms of identifying units of analysis and in the contextual labels they ascribe to those units.

inter-coder reliability
An indicator of how similarly coders are coding content, both in terms of identifying units of analysis and in the contextual labels they ascribe to those units.

Content analysts will typically train and retrain their coders until they reach an acceptable level of agreement across all coding categories. They will conduct reliability tests on these runs until it becomes apparent that the coders are examining the same content consistently. There are a number of ways of assessing reliability. The first is exact agreement. Let's say we have two coders. They are looking at ten newspaper clippings and evaluating whether each article contains a picture above the fold. This gives us a total of twenty judgments that the two coders have to make.

Coder A:	Y	N	Y	Y	Y	Y	N	Y	N	Y
Coder B:	Y	Y	Y	Y	N	Y	N	Y	N	Y

In this instance, sixteen of the twenty judgments made by the coders match. In terms of exact agreement, we might report an exact agreement of 80 percent between the two coders.

Of course, there is also the possibility that some of these could be due purely to chance. Since there are two response options and two coders, you would expect to get agreement due to chance one out of every four times, or 25 percent of the time. There are inter-coder reliability statistics that control for this kind of **chance agreement**. We discussed some of them in Chapter 9, but let's review them here. **Scott's Pi**, for example, is computed as follows:

chance agreement
The likelihood the two coders will agree on their coding judgments simply by chance.

Scott's Pi
A statistical test measuring statistical reliability between coders.

$$Pi = \frac{\text{observed agreement} - \text{expected agreement}}{1 - \text{expected agreement}}$$

So in this case:

$$\frac{.80 - .25}{1 - .25} = \frac{.55}{.75} = .73$$

Similarly, Krippendorf's alpha (Krippendorf, 1980) uses a mathematical adjustment for chance agreement. But what exactly do these coefficients mean? If you remember back to our earlier discussion of reliability in measurement, you'll recall that .70 is generally accepted as the minimum level of acceptable reliability for scales. The same benchmark applies to inter-coder reliability in content analysis. While content analysts more typically report inter-coder reliability above .80, .70 is generally considered to be the minimum mark for having an acceptable level of reliability between coders.

• •

▼ An Example of the Content Analysis Process

Let's return to our Smith et al. (2003, 2004) content analysis for a few minutes and walk through the process of designing and executing a content analysis. Consider this an *inside look* at one particular study. In the fall of 1999, these researchers and a few others at Michigan State University decided to launch a series of studies looking at the content and effects of violent video games. They were particularly interested in whether they could find any evidence that playing video games makes people respond aggressively when provoked. Of course, this question is only relevant if video games are, on the whole, fairly violent. Further, past research on media and violence has demonstrated that certain contextual features might be more likely to elicit aggressive responses. So when violence is presented as justified, committed by liked or attractive characters, goes unpunished, involves weapons, or is presented in an unrealistic manner these features can have particularly damaging effects on audiences.

In order to address some of these issues, Smith et al. (2003, 2004) decided to come up with a content analysis that took a snapshot of the world of video games in terms of the frequency and context of violence. They were then faced with the problem of where to look. Generating a list of all available games for the three major platforms at the time (PlayStation, N64, and the Sega Dreamcast) would have produced an overwhelming amount of data. Taking a random sample from this list seemed like a bad idea, as well; what if they randomly selected games that no one played? In the end, the researchers decided to go with a systematic sample, selecting the top twenty selling games for each platform in order to get at the games people were actually playing.

The researchers were then faced with their second unitizing issue: recording units. They decided to look at the content on two levels, both by identifying individual scenes of violence and by making appraisals of certain games on the whole. Thus, from a unitizing standpoint they decided that there would be two levels of analysis: individual scenes and games on the whole. These were their recording units.

Context units then became the next consideration. As mentioned above, there are a number of contextual features that they believed might moderate the relationship between game playing and aggressive responses. So they decided that at the level of individual violent scenes, a number of context units would be identified. These included reasons for violence, the weapons used to enact violence, the type of violent act, the number of acts in a violent exchange, the depicted harm to the victim, the harm that would be likely in real life, and a number of characteristics of the perpetrator and victim.

The researchers then asked a number of research assistants to play these games from the *beginning* of the game, playing for a total of ten minutes. At this time, the audio and video signal was routed through a VCR and recorded for later use. In a short amount of time, they had their content; in fact, they had ten hours of it. Now they were faced with how to make sense of it all. Since the NTVS had recently received praise from scientists and policy makers alike, they decided to borrow heavily from their coding structure. The first thing that was necessary was to establish exactly what constituted a violent exchange. Borrowing from NTVS, they declared that in this study violence would be defined (operationalized) as "any overt depiction of a credible threat of physical force or the actual use of such force intended to physically harm an animate being or group of being[s]. Violence also includes certain depictions of physically harmful consequences against an animate being/s that results from unseen violent means" (Smith et al., 1998, p. 30). This is the first example of an *operational definition* in this study: a hard and fast definitional criterion for what is or is not. The researchers then went on to develop similar operational definitions for their context units. For example, for level of harm depicted, mild harm was defined as "an instance in which the victim makes a verbal or nonverbal depiction of harm without physical depiction," as opposed to extreme harm, which was described as instances in which "high bloodshed, severed limbs, visible entrails, or large-scale disfigurement" was depicted.

Realizing that the coding process would be time consuming and tedious, they then hired a number of research assistants to help with the coding. Over a period of a few weeks, the coders were trained to identify these features consistently. In order to train the coders, the researchers had to create a *codebook*, a brief list of the definitions used in the coding scheme. Below is the actual codebook used in the study:

Codebook for V2 Content Analysis—Fall 1999

Level 1 Data (Individual Acts)

1. Game: game number
2. System: gaming system (PS, N64, or DreamCast)
3. Rating: game rating (E, T, KA, or M)
4. Typ: type of violent act (behavioral act, credible threat, behavioral consequence)
5. Por: portrayal of *player* (first person) or *character* (character is pictured)

Reasons for Violence (coded as y/n):

6. Prolife: protection of life
7. Proprop: protection of property
8. Retal: retaliation
9. Anger: anger
10. Gain: personal gain
11. Mental: mental instability
12. Other: other/unknown
13. Means: the means through which the act is carried out
    -natural: natural means (punching, kicking, slapping, etc.)
    -unconventional: use of atypical instruments (frying pans, bowling pins, etc.)
    -handheld firearm (a pistol)
    -heavy weaponry: heavier firearms or weapons (machine guns, bazookas, flamethrowers, etc.)
    -bombs: an explosive or incendiary device
14. Numacts: number of acts in the interaction
15. Depharm: the degree of harm depicted
    -none: no harm is depicted
    -mild: character makes a verbal or nonverbal indication of harm, but not physically depicted
    -moderate: bloodshed, visible bruising, or visible injury
    -extreme: high bloodshed, severed limbs, visible entrails, or large-scale disfigurement
16. Likharm: how harmful this act would be if it occurred in real life
    -same as above
17. Sexaslt: does the interaction contain a sexual assault (y/n)

Victim and Perpetrator Demographics:

18. Victype: victim type (human, nonhuman, animal, etc.)
19. Vicgroup: victim grouping (single, multiple, unseen)
20. Vicsize: number of victims in group, if applicable
21. Vicsex: sex of the victim
22. Vicage: age of the victim
23. Viceth: ethnicity of victim
24. Vicgood: victim portrayed as good (y/n)
    -good: place needs of others ahead of themselves
    -bad: place own needs ahead of those of others

25. Vicphys: level of physical attractiveness of victim
    -victim is highly, moderately, or not attractive according to contemporary community standards
26. Vicprovk: sexual provocativeness of victim
    -high: victim is portrayed in such a way as to arouse game player
    -neutral: victim is not
27. Perptype: type of perpetrator
28. Perpgroup: grouping of perpetrator(s)
29. Perpsize: size of perpetrator group
30. Perpsex: sex of perpetrator
31. Perpage: age of perpetrator
32. Perpeth: ethnicity of perpetrator
33. Perpphys: physical attractiveness of perpetrator
34. Perpprvk: sexual provocativeness of perpetrator

Level 2 Data (Game Level)
1. Game#: game number
2. System: game system (PS, N64, DreamCast)
3. Rating: game rating
4. Type: game type (sports, racing, adventure, etc.)
5. Vthreats: number of verbal threats in the game segment
6. Pthreats: number of physical threats
7. Acts: number of behavioral acts
8. Cons: number of behavioral consequences
9. Total: total number of violent acts
10. Rewards: any rewards for violence (material rewards, praise, etc.)
11. Punish: punishment for engaging in violence
12. Range: close-up or long shot
13. Gore: graphicness of depicted gore
    -same as depicted harm above
14. Humor: humor associated with violence (y/n)

The coders were instructed to study this manual very closely. The research assistants underwent four weeks of intensive training to master all of the definitions and coding procedures. During this training, the coders participated in three reliability tests designed to assess the consistency of their coding judgments. Using an adjusted reliability formula for multiple coders, coders were trained to the point where Scott's Pi was found to be over .79 for all variables, indicating an adequate level of reliability. After the third training session the coders were turned loose on the sample and coded the video game recordings.

Each coder went through the tapes and identified individual violent acts. For each violent exchange that was identified, the coder used a *code sheet* to indicate the various features of each scene. Here is the actual code sheet that was used in the study:

To give you an idea of how time consuming content analysis can be, the study had a total of 1,389 acts of violence across the sixty games. In other words, the coders filled out this sheet *almost 1,400 times.* After coding all of the acts of violence in a particular game, they were then asked to fill out a final coding sheet indicating the overall nature of the game—their second recording unit.

Coding Sheet for Level 1 (Individual Acts of Violence)

Game: _____

System: _____

Type of Interaction: ___ Verbal threat ___ Physical threat ___ Act ___ Consequence

Portrayal: ___ Character ____ Player

Reasons: ____ Protection of own life	**Means:** ____ Natural
____ Protection of property	____ Unconventional
____ Retaliation	____ Nonfirearm
____ Anger	____ Handheld firearm
____ Personal gain	____ Heavy weapon
____ Mental instability	____ Bomb
____ Other/Unknown	

Number of Acts in Interaction: _____ 1 _____ 2–9 _____ 10–20 _____ 20+

Depicted Harm: _____ None _____ Mild _____ Moderate _____ Extreme

Likely Harm: _____ None _____ Mild _____ Moderate _____ Extreme

Sexual Assault: _____ Yes _____ No

	Victim:	**Perpetrator:**
Type:	___ Human	___ Human
	___ Animal	___ Animal
	___ Supernatural being	___ Supernatural being
	___ Anthropomorphised animal	___ Anthropomorphised animal
	___ Anthropomorphised supernatural being	___ Anthropomorphised supernatural being
	___ Robot/Nonorganic	___ Robot/Nonorganic
	Victim:	**Perpetrator:**
Grouping:	___ Single	___ Single
	___ Multiple	___ Multiple
	___ Unseen	___ Unseen
Group Size:	___ 1	___ 1
	___ 2	___ 2
	___ 3–9	___ 3–9
	___ 10–99	___ 10–99
	___ 100+	___ 100+

Sex:	___ M ___ F ___ Can't tell	___ M ___ F ___ Can't tell
Age:	___ Child ___ Teen ___ Adult ___ Elderly ___ Can't tell	___ Child ___ Teen ___ Adult ___ Elderly ___ Can't tell
Ethnicity:	___ Caucasian ___ African ___ Hispanic ___ Native American ___ Asian/Pacific Islander ___ Middle Eastern ___ Can't tell/Nonhuman	___ Caucasian ___ African ___ Hispanic ___ Native American ___ Asian/Pacific Islander ___ Middle Eastern ___ Can't tell/Nonhuman
Good/Bad:	___ Good ___ Bad ___ Can't tell/Neutral	___ Good ___ Bad ___ Can't tell/Neutral
	Victim:	**Perpetrator:**
Physical Attractive-ness:	___ High ___ Average ___ Low ___ Can't tell	___ High ___ Average ___ Low ___ Can't tell
Sexual Pro-vocativeness:	___ High ___ Neutral ___ Can't tell	___ High ___ Neutral ___ Can't tell

The researchers now had data concerning 1,389 individual acts of violence and the nature of sixty different games. They next began to pull the data apart to look at patterns of association between the variables. The details are perhaps a bit beyond the scope of this chapter, but the long and short of it is that the results showed that games for mature audiences feature violence more

Coding Sheet for Level 2 (Scene Level Variables)

Game: _____

System: ____ PlayStation2 ____ X-Box

Rating: ____ E ____ T ____ KA ____ M

Violent Acts:	____ Verbal threats
	____ Physical threats
	____ Behavioral acts
	____ Behavioral consequences
	____ **TOTAL**

Rewards:	____ None
	____ Praise from others
	____ Self-praise
	____ Material rewards

Punishments:	____ None
	____ Condemnation from others
	____ Self-condemnation
	____ Physical restraint
	____ Physical violence

Reasons:	____ Protection of own life	**Means:**	____ Natural
	____ Protection of property		____ Unconventional
	____ Retaliation		____ Nonfirearm
	____ Anger		____ Handheld firearm
	____ Personal gain		____ Heavy weapon
	____ Mental instability		____ Bomb
	____ Other/Unknown		

View.ing Range:	____ Close-up	**Humor:**	____ Present
	____ Long shot		____ Absent
	____ Not shown		

Blood and Gore:	____ None
	____ Mild
	____ Moderate
	____ Extreme

frequently (4.56 acts/minute) than those for general audiences (1.17/minute). When compared to general audience games, mature games were more likely to feature child perpetrators, graphic violence, the use of guns and other weapons, and violence that was depicted with unrealistic consequences.

So What?

What have you learned from this chapter? Well, content analysis is a powerful tool for making sense of information exchanges that exist in the social world. These can come in the form of mediated information (content analysis) or interpersonal exchanges (interaction analysis). But in either case, you can use these analytic techniques to make empirical assessments of the nature of information exchange.

In this particular chapter, we have discussed the use of content and interaction analyses, and what types of research questions are best lent to these methodologies. We have examined different types of content, and the logic behind content analysis that leads to the production of data. We have explored techniques for sampling, unitizing, and evaluating the reliability of content data. Finally, we have walked through the logistics of the content analysis process, from initial conceptualization through data collection and analysis. It is our hope that this chapter illustrates the techniques and utility of content analysis in making sense of the social world. The chapter is also a logical segue into our next chapter, which deals with how to use surveys and quantitative observations to perform experiments.

Glossary

Chance agreement
The likelihood the two coders will agree on their coding judgments simply by chance.

Content analysis
A quantitative methodology that allows researchers to quantify content, including the content of participant responses or the content of media texts.

Context units
The types of content or contextual features that may appear in an individual recording unit.

Distributional structure
A type of content structure that deals with the number or frequency with which certain interactions take place in a certain timeframe.

Interactive structure
A type of content structure that deals with the pattern of response types that may vary throughout an interaction.

Inter-coder reliability
An indicator of how similarly coders are coding content, both in terms of identifying units of analysis and in the contextual labels they ascribe to those units.

Recording units
The individual parts of a sampling unit the researcher is examining.

Sampling units
The units that are sampled from a larger population of content that you wish to examine.

Scott's Pi
A statistical test measuring statistical reliability between coders.

Sequential structure
A type of content structure that normally deals with an examination of the sequences of utterances in order to make more sense of what is going on.

Systematic sampling
A type of sampling that is similar in logic to random sampling, but involves designating a timeframe ("k") and selecting every *kth* sampling unit within the population.

Unitizing
The process of deciding exactly what it is that should be observed.

References

Baxter, L. A., & Babbie, E. (2004). *The basics of communication research.* Belmont, CA: Wadsworth.

Carr, C. T., Schrok, D. B., & Dauterman, P. (2012). Speech acts within Facebook status messages. *Journal of Language and Social Psychology, 31(2).* doi: 10.1177/0261927X12438535.

Germain, D. (2006, February 11). Few females in G-rated films: 3-TO-1 gender imbalance found in study of 101 popular movies. *The Charlotte Observer (NC)*, 5E.

Hirokawa, R. Y. (1988). Group communication and decision making performance: A continued test of the functional perspective. *Human Communication Research, 14*, 487–515.

Holsti, O. (1969). *Content analysis for the social sciences and humanities.* Reading, MA: Addison-Wesley.

Krippendorf, K. (1980). *Content analysis: An introduction to its methodology.* Newbury Park, CA: Sage.

Kunkel, D., Cope, K. M., Maynard-Farinola, W. J., Biely, E., Rollin, E., & Donnerstein, E. (1999). *Sex on TV: Content and context.* Menlo Park, CA: Kaiser Family Foundation.

Lachlan, K. A., Tamborini, R., Weber, R., Westerman, D., Davis, J., & Skalski, P. (2009). The spiral of violence: Violent reprisal in professional wrestling and its dispositional and motivational features. *Journal of Broadcasting and Electronic Media, 53*(1), 56–75.

Riffe, D., Lacy, S., & Fico, F. G. (1998). Analyzing media messages: *Using quantitative content analysis in research.* Mahwah, NJ: Lawrence Erlbaum.

Smith, S. L., Wilson, B. J., Kunkel, D., Linz, D., Potter, J., Colvin, C. M., & Donnerstein, E. (1998). Violence in television programming overall: University of California, Santa Barbara study. In *National Television Violence Study (Vol. 3).* Thousand Oaks, CA: Sage.

Smith, S. L., Lachlan, K., & Tamborini, R. (2003). Popular video games: Quantifying the amount and context of violence. *Journal of Broadcasting and Electronic Media, 47*, 58–76.

Smith, S. L., Lachlan, K. A., Pieper, K. M., Boyson, A. R., Wilson, B. J., & Tamborini, R. (2004). Brandishing guns in American media: Two studies examining how often and in what context firearms appear on TV and in popular video games. *Journal of Broadcasting and Electronic Media, 48*(4), 584–606.

Stephens, K. K., & Mottet, T. P. (2008). Interactivity in a Web conference training context: Effects on trainers and trainees. *Communication Education, 57*(1), 88–104.

Wilson, B. J., Kunkel, D., Linz, D., Potter, W. J., Donnerstein, E., Smith, S. L., Blumenthal, E., & Gray, T. (1997). Violence in television programming overall: University of California, Santa Barbara study, *National Television Violence Study* (Vol. 1, pp. 3–268). Newbury Park, CA: Sage.w

EXPERIMENTS

12

KEY TERMS

Baseline

Between-subjects design

Control group

Experimental group

Factorial design

Induction

Preexperimental designs

Posttest

Pretest

Quasi-experimental designs

Random assignment

Social experiment

True experimental designs

Within-subjects design

CHAPTER OBJECTIVES

1. To understand what experiments are
2. To understand the questions that can be addressed with experiments
3. To understand different types of experiments
4. To understand how different experiments address different validity threats

● ●

▼ # What Is an Experiment?

In Chapter 1, we talked about some of the general conceptions and misconceptions people have about social research and about how the natural sciences may be more salient to them. In particular, we talked about how people can quickly think of examples of research in medicine, engineering, computer science, and so on, while they may have a more difficult time coming up with examples of social research.

To a certain extent, the same could be said for experiments. When you hear the word *experiment*, no doubt certain imagery enters your mind, perhaps of your tenth-grade science class, mixing and matching chemicals over a Bunsen burner; maybe even thoughts of odd-looking characters wearing lab coats and goggles.

Social researchers also frequently perform experimental research, although usually without the white coat and the Bunsen burner. Communication scientists have relied upon experimental procedures since the birth of the discipline to answer a variety of questions concerning the ways in which people use and respond to information. Experimental designs have been used to address how people respond to interpersonal interactions, mediated information, workplace dynamics, and interactions with computers. Of course, this raises the question of exactly what a social experiment is, by definition.

Bonito, Ruppel, and de Mainvilliers (2001) examined stimulated recall under a variety of conditions in group participation. Groups of participants worked on a task and then watched a videotape of their performance. Through random assignment, participants were assigned to one of four different viewing conditions based upon whether they could see themselves in the video playback and whether they rated themselves regarding their participation in the task.

social experiment
A procedure in which researchers take human subjects, do something to them, and observe the effects of what they did to them.

By definition, a **social experiment** is a procedure in which researchers take human subjects, do something to them, and observe the effects of what they did to them (Baxter & Babbie, 2004). This chapter will discuss some of the nuances associated with this seemingly simple procedure, including the use of subjects, random assignment, inductions, control groups, and multiple measures. More importantly, it will discuss how you can use these design elements to build confidence in your findings by ruling out particular validity threats.

Independent and Dependent Variables

Experimental researchers deal with independent and dependent variables. We use these terms to describe causes and effects. A variable is anything that can be measured or observed by the researcher. The independent versus dependent distinction is related to the researcher's involvement in the observation.

First, let's explain some concepts about variables in experiments. Remember that—for all research—variables can be measured through self-report, measured through other-report, or measured through observation. In an experiment, the independent variable can also be "manipulated" (we'll say more about this in a minute).

So, if—in your experiment—you are measuring a variable to determine beliefs, attitudes, or opinions, or to collect retrospective information about behavior or meaning, you would measure that variable using a SURVEY. If, in your experiment, you are measuring a variable to analyze the content of media messages, you would measure that variable using a *content analysis*. Finally, if you are measuring a variable to analyze the content of an interpersonal message, you would measure that variable using an *interaction analysis*. So, to recap, surveys can be used as a stand-alone method or as a way to measure a variable in an experiment. The same is true for content and interaction analysis. Depending on your RQ or H, they can either be used as stand-alone methods or to measure one or more variables in an experiment.

What Are Independent Variables? By definition, an independent variable is any observation that is controlled by the researcher. So, for example, you may want to test the effectiveness of an antismoking public service announcement (PSA). You develop two types of PSAs, one that uses a fear appeal to attempt to scare people into compliance and one that does not. You then show the fear ad to one group of people and the non-fear ad to another group.

In this instance, the independent variable is the type of ad that is being shown. While the researcher will make the observation that a particular group saw one ad or the other, it was the researcher who decided which group would see which and what those messages would look like. Any differences in the responses of the participants might be attributable to this decision. This leads us to our next way of thinking about independent variables: They are causes. Independent variables are the things that are manipulated by the researcher in order to produce a particular outcome.

What Are Dependent Variables? Dependent variables, on the other hand, are effects. They are observations made by the researcher that are not directly controlled by the researcher, but may be attributable to decisions surrounding the independent variable. In our example above, let's say the people who saw the fear appeal ad report that they are less willing to take up smoking. In this case, the dependent variable is willingness to take up smoking. It is the assumed result of a change in the independent variable.

Why do we call it a dependent variable? Because it is dependent on the independent variable. In short, independent variables are causes, while dependent variables are effects, or consequences.

Good Questions for Experiments

If you remember in Chapter 1, we talked about how social scientists use hypotheses to build theory, making educated guesses about the social world, and then testing those guesses through observation. In Chapter 6, we further discussed the formation of research questions and hypotheses, and how these may inform the selection of particular types of research design. As a classification of research design, experiments lend themselves best to particular types of questions. They are very useful for answering micro-level questions concerning responses to information. In particular, they lend themselves well to questions of *causation*.

As we will see, this is because most experimental designs involve some kind of pretest; by examining someone before you expose her to a stimulus, then examining her again, you can argue to a certain extent that what you did to her may have caused any changes that you observe. So, if you are trying to answer a question such as: "Do video games *cause* people to respond more aggressively?" or "Does attractiveness *cause* people to disclose more information?" then an experimental design might be the way to go. Experiments are not particularly useful for descriptive purposes (since they are limited in the scope of phenomena they can address), nor are they particularly useful for drawing non-causal associations. They are, however, very useful for establishing causal relationships between independent and dependent variables.

Of course, it is not quite that simple. As we discussed in Chapter 9, there are a myriad of internal validity threats that can undermine a simple "X causes Y" statement. Non-spuriousness (making sure the independent variable is the only cause for the observed effect on the dependent variable) also becomes an issue, as it may be difficult to rule out alternate explanations for what you observe. Different types of experimental designs may be more or less effective at dealing with these concerns. In this chapter, we'll discuss different designs, what they might look like, and how well they may address these concerns and problems.

▼ ## Understanding Experimental Notation and Language

Before discussing different types of designs, it may be useful to first describe the notation that is often used when describing experimental procedures. We can identify three basic elements in an experimental design: observation, induction (or manipulation), and random assignment.

Observation

If you are reading the shorthand that scientists use to describe experimental designs, you will, at the very least, see a capital "O." This symbol is used to represent an *observation*. In communication research, this is typically some kind of written, spoken, or observed behavior or attitude. It is the basic building block of experimental design, which is after all a series of observations.

Induction

induction
What is done to a participant in an experiment.

You may also see a capital "X." This symbol is used to convey some kind of **induction**—an induction is what you *do* to the participant. So, in our video game example from above, this may be the part of the design where you make someone play a certain type of game. In a persuasion experiment, it may be a certain kind of argument that is delivered to the participant. In a television violence study, it may be a short film clip that you show. In any case, this is what you do to the participant, the independent variable, the effect of which you are concerned with.

Inductions are often incorrectly labeled as a *manipulation*. Technically, it is only a manipulation if it actually works. The act of doing something to a participant, regardless of whether it affects them in any way, is more accurately referred to as an induction. In some fields, especially health communication, this is sometimes called an *intervention* or *treatment*.

Random Assignment

You may also encounter a capital "R" in experimental notation. This refers to the **random assignment** of participants to different groups within your design. In a true experimental design, you would want to assign people at random to different groups. Why? Well, if we were concerned about ruling out spuriousness, you would want all the groups in your study to be as similar or comparable as possible. Similar or comparable how, you might ask. It depends on your study, but certainly if you're studying health literacy you might want the two groups to have an equivalent distribution of education, and perhaps health status and experience with health-care providers. If you're studying employee productivity, you might want to make sure both groups are equivalent in terms of work experience and training. If you're studying the politeness level of communication on e-mail versus voice mail (see Duthler, 2006), you might want to make sure participants in both groups have equivalent distributions in terms of their relationships with the communication recipients. If you randomly assign people to groups—if everyone has an equal chance of being in a particular group, then (theoretically) they should be roughly the same. Of course, sometimes it is not logistically possible to have true random assignment. In these cases, you will sometimes see lines between conditions indicating that participants were not randomly assigned.

Terminology

There are also some key terms you should know in reading and understanding experiments. We just told you that you randomly assign participants to different groups. One of the groups is the group to whom you give the induction—this is called the **experimental group**. If you have more than one type of induction, you might have more than one experimental group. Ideally, you also have another group to whom you give no induction—this is called the **control group**. It's a group against which you can compare the experimental group. When you compare multiple experimental groups, this is known as a **between-subjects design**. When you only look at an experimental group, you call this a **within-subjects design**.

In many experiments, we measure the dependent variable both before and after exposure to the induction. The measurement before the induction is called a **pretest**, or **baseline** measurement. The measurement after the induction is called a **posttest**.

random assignment
The assignment of people at random to different groups in an experimental design

experimental group
The group of participants to whom you give the induction.

control group
A group that does not receive induction in an experiment.

between-subjects design
Designs comparing multiple groups.

within-subjects design
Designs looking at the same group multiple times.

pretest
An examination of someone before you expose him or her to a stimulus in order to argue, to a certain extent, that what was done to the subject may have caused any changes that are observed. Also called baseline measurement.

posttest
An examination or measurement conducted after administration of the induction.

▼ # Designs and Validity

If you remember in Chapter 9, we discussed a number of threats to validity that have to be taken into consideration when designing research. If you recall, there are a number of *internal validity* concerns that are relevant to the research process. These include history, or when something outside of the procedure takes place that skews your observations. Subjects may change over time, a process known as maturation. Testing describes the phenomenon in which participants respond differently as they become accustomed to your measures. Instrumentation refers to problems associated with using different measures to get at the same idea, and how well they measure the same things.

Fortunately, one of the advantages of the experiment is that in addition to allowing for causal statements, you can design studies in different ways to address each of these concerns. As we will see in the following descriptions, you can determine which of these issues concerns you the most, and design your study accordingly to rule it out as an internal validity threat. There is even one seldom-used design that rules out all of them. While no experimental design can ever rule out all plausible alternative explanations, thinking about internal validity concerns and designing a study appropriately can at least help you have more confidence in your findings.

▼ # Preexperimental Designs

One Shot Case Study Design

The simplest possible design in this research family is known as the One Shot Case Study (Campbell & Stanley, 1963). In this design, there is only one group. You give participants some sort of induction and observe the results. For example, you could bring a group of participants into the lab and show them an ad for blue jeans. You could then pose a series of questions asking them about their likelihood to purchase the jeans. Since they seem to feel favorably toward the jeans, you conclude that the ad must have worked.

$$X \quad O$$

Do you see any problems here? There is no pretest, so you have no idea where the participants stood before seeing the ad. It is literally impossible to determine if your ad actually affected the results, since there is no measure of prior attitudes toward the product. The results could have come from anywhere: long-standing disposition toward the product, something that happened outside the laboratory, instrumentation that leads them in a certain direction, and so on. In this design, you really can't have much confidence in the results at all. As you can see, this experimental design does lend itself to validity concerns, but it does offer a point of departure from which we can observe means of ensuring against validity threats and providing results in which you can have more confidence.

Campbell and Stanley (1963) label these as **preexperimental designs**, since they do not involve a true control group. In other words, there is no pretest and posttest, and in this case there is no control group. If your experimental group changes and your control group remains the same, then you can say with some confidence that your induction *worked* (or at least effected the change).

preexperimental designs
Experimental designs that do not involve a true control group; no pretest, posttest, or control group.

One Group Pretest Posttest Design

Here is another example of a preexperimental design that lacks a control group:

$$O_1 \quad X \quad O_2$$

This is known as the One Group Pretest Posttest Design. It is a slight improvement over the One Shot Case Study. It still does not have a control group, so it is not possible to make comparisons between participants that did or did not receive the induction. But at least you can draw comparisons within this group of people in terms of where they stood before and after the induction. In our blue jeans example, you could ask people how they felt about the jeans, then show them the ad, then ask them again. You could then at least say that this group of people—whoever they are—did or did not feel more inclined to buy them.

Static Group Comparison Design

The final preexperimental design is the Static Group Comparison Design. This design looks just like the One Shot Case Study, except that you (kind of) add a control group:

$$X \quad O_1$$
$$O_2$$

Note that now, in addition to participants who get the induction, then take a posttest, you have added another group that takes the posttest without getting the induction. You can then compare those who get the induction to those who don't.

Returning to our example, you now have a second group: one that does not see the ad or take the pretest, but are simply asked about the jeans. Of course, there are still problems with this design. You can't really tell if people in the experimental group got used to your measures. If you run these groups at different time points, you can't tell if something outside the procedure affected the results. Most importantly, you don't know if these two groups felt differently about the jeans to begin with.

• •

Quasi-Experimental Designs

This brings us to our next family of designs: the **quasi-experimental designs**. This term is used by Campbell and Stanley (1963) to describe designs that use pretests and posttests in more complicated ways, but that still lack random assignment. These designs are a marked improvement over the

▼ **quasi-experimental designs**
Experimental designs that use pretests and posttests in more complicated ways, but still lack random assignment.

preexperimental, and while not perfect by any stretch, they are commonly used by communication researchers.

Time-Series Design

The first of these is the Time-Series Design:

$$O_1 \; O_2 \; O_3 \qquad X \qquad O_4 \; O_5 \; O_6$$

This design is geared primarily to rule out history and maturation as validity threats. As you can see, you have several pretests, an induction, and several posttests. In our example, we could ask a group of people how they feel about the jeans several times over the course of a few weeks. We could show them the ad, then measure their attitude several more times over the course of a few weeks. Looking at the results, we could tell if the participant's attitudes were already shifting before seeing the ad, or perhaps find evidence that something happened outside the lab that would influence the results. There isn't really a control group, but we can at least detect other threats.

Nonequivalent Control Group Design

Here is another quasi-experimental design, and one that is actually used quite commonly: the Nonequivalent Control Group Design:

$$\begin{array}{ccc} O_1 & X & O_2 \\ O_3 & & O_4 \end{array}$$

For logistical reasons related to random assignment, communication researchers often use this design. As you can see, we now have a true control group; these are people that get both the pretest and posttest, but not the induction. If we are to rule out a number of validity threats, it should be the case that people in the test group change from pretest to posttest, but those in the control group should remain exactly the same. This helps control against instrumentation, testing, and maturation as design threats. It does not do too much to address history, and there may be selection problems since there is no random assignment, but at least three major threats are controlled for.

Multiple Time-Series Design

In order to improve this design to account for history, we can add multiple measures and produce the following, the Multiple Time-Series Design:

$$\begin{array}{ccc} O_1 \; O_2 \; O_3 & X & O_4 \; O_5 \; O_6 \\ O_7 \; O_8 \; O_9 & & O_{10} \; O_{11} \; O_{12} \end{array}$$

As you can see, this design combines the advantages of the last two. We now have controls in place for testing, instrumentation, and maturation, and we have added a history safeguard by collecting pretest and posttest measures at different times. It is still not a perfect design, though. The lack of random assignment is still a concern.

True Experimental Designs

Fortunately, there is another class of design that, by definition, introduces random assignment: true experimental designs. Campbell and Stanley (1963) define **true experimental designs** as those that randomly assign participants to both experimental and control groups. Through random assignment, the subject-related concerns we articulated in Chapter 9 should be pretty much taken care of. If everyone in your population has an equal chance of being in any group, then problems like evaluator apprehension, Hawthorne Effects, and selection problems should not be a concern. Over a large enough group, if these problems are present then they are at least equally distributed.

true experimental designs
Experimental designs that randomly assign participants to both experimental and control groups.

Pretest Posttest Control Group Design

One classic example of this type of design is the Pretest Posttest Control Group Design:

$$R \quad O_1 \quad X \quad O_2$$
$$R \quad O_3 \quad \quad O_4$$

Note that this looks a lot like the Nonequivalent Control Group Design we discussed earlier, but that it simply adds random assignment. In doing so, it takes care of subject-related problems. Many classic experimentalists rely heavily on this design, as it rules out most validity threats, but is still fairly economical in design.

Heimendinger and colleagues (2005) used this design in a study to test four alternative messages designed to increase fruit and vegetable consumption among callers to the National Cancer Institute's (NCI) Cancer Information Service (CIS). They conducted a baseline interview when the callers initially called CIS. They then randomly assigned each study participant to one of three experimental conditions (different messages promoting fruit and vegetable consumption) or to a fourth group, a control group which received a different message (unrelated to fruit and vegetable consumption). Finally, they did posttest interviews with all participants both five months and twelve months later. Here's something else to note about this study—the researchers used a survey interview format to gather the information pre and post intervention. Their surveys included several scales, including some Likert scales to test reactions to the messages.

Posttest-Only Control Group Design

Similar to the Pretest Posttest Control Group Design is the Posttest-Only Control Group Design:

$$R \quad X \quad O_1$$
$$R \quad \quad O_2$$

Here's a real-world example of this design used in communication research. In 2001, Lee and Guerrero wanted to see how people interpreted different types of interpersonal touch. They set up an experiment in which they video-taped dyads in an interaction that was ended with one of nine types of touch (handshake, clasping hands, soft touch on the forearm, arm around the shoulder, arm around the waist, soft touch on the cheek, tapping the shoulder in a condescending manner, push against the shoulder, and no touch). In their paper, they refer to this videotape as a *stimulus material*, another name for intervention or induction. One hundred ninety-three students were randomly assigned one of the touch videotapes. After watching the video, students were asked to rate their impressions of the interaction. From this experiment, Lee and Guerrero determined that different types of touch lead to different interpretations in terms of affection, romantic attraction, flirtation, and love, but not in terms of trust or happiness. They also found that face touch was interpreted to be the most intimate type of touch. Their design was limited by validity concerns about consistency across the videotaped dyads (since their videos used two women and two men with various ethnic combinations), reactions to touch initiated by women versus men, and reactions to the ethnic mix of the dyads. Since their experimental design did not account for these possible affects, they tested for them statistically. Again, note that the dependent variables were measured using Likert scale measurements in a survey interview format.

In their study on whether there is a difference between which type of communication is presented first—computer-mediated communication (CMC) or face-to-face (FTF) in diverse teams, Triana, Kirkman, and Wagstaff (2012) used an experimental design with twenty-five teams of four people each (three men and one woman) receiving the CMC first, then FTF. Another twenty-five teams communicated first utilizing FTF, then CMC.

As you can see, these designs also involve random assignment, although the absence of pretest measures may undermine your confidence in the results to a certain extent.

Solomon Four-Group Design

Finally, there is a true experimental design that controls for all of the commonly identified internal validity threats. Those that study experimental methodology hold this design as the gold standard in experimental methodology. It is known as the Solomon Four-Group Design:

$$R \quad O_1 \quad X \quad O_2$$
$$R \quad O_3 \quad \quad O_4$$
$$R \quad \quad X \quad O_5$$
$$R \quad \quad \quad O_6$$

Note that this design involves four different groups. There is a test group that receives both a pretest and posttest. There is a posttest-only experimental group, which should allow comparisons to evaluate testing and instrumentation as threats. There is a true control group, which can be used to rule out maturation and history as potential threats. The capacity to rule these out is further improved with the addition of a posttest-only control group. Random assignment should take care of any subject-related problems.

You may be reading the description of this design and wondering two things. First, you may be wondering why we have just walked though nine different designs to arrive at one that controls for everything. Next, you may be wondering why all experimental researchers don't just use the Solomon Four-Group. If this design is so effective at ruling out validity threats, then why wouldn't everyone use it?

Take a look at the design for a minute. You will notice that of the four groups, only one gets a pretest, an induction, and a posttest. This is the group that you would use to test your hypotheses. The other three groups simply exist as checks against validity threats. This makes the design a bit cumbersome and impractical at times.

Let's return to our blue jeans ad from a few pages ago. Suppose you wanted to use the Solomon Four-Group to test the effectiveness of the ad. You randomly sample 200 people from your population, then you randomly assign those 200 people to each of your four conditions. How many people do you actually get to test the ad on?

Fifty. Yes, that's correct. In this particular example, you would have to run (test) 200 research participants in order to obtain the results of fifty. While you could have strong confidence in your results, you would have to spend time, money, and resources collecting data from 150 people that you can't use to test your hypothesis. This lack of economy then increases multiplicatively. If you wanted to gauge the responses of 250 people, you would have to run 1,000 to get 250.

Communication researchers, like all social researchers, do not have unlimited resources. Given the parameters in which they operate—balancing budgets, lab time, student labor, and participant availability—they can seldom use this near perfect design. They are much more likely to think about their research problems, consider the validity threats they are most concerned about, and choose a less complex design, accordingly. In truth, the Nonequivalent Control Group design and the Pretest Posttest Control Group design are much more commonly used and do an adequate job of ruling out validity threats for the purposes of the communication researcher.

Factorial Design   ▼

There's another *wrinkle* to conducting experiments. We've discussed experiments in which the induction either is or isn't. People either see the ad, or they don't. You may have noticed from our real-world examples it's also possible for the induction to have different levels or types. Or, alternatively, you might want to test more than one induction or independent variable at a time. Remember our example earlier of the Lee and Guerrero (2001) study testing reactions to different types of dyadic touch. Their independent variable had nine different levels, or types. Recall that we mentioned they didn't control for extraneous variables (gender, ethnicity, initiator of the touch) in their design so they had to attempt to measure the effect of these extraneous variables

factorial designs
Analyses that involve multiple independent variables.

when they computed their statistics in their analysis. Another way they could have accounted for these extraneous variables was by using a **factorial design**. They could have made these extraneous variables additional independent variables and then tested for them. Let's set up a factorial design for this experiment, and let's simplify it by testing only two of their independent variables, or factors: type of touch, gender of toucher—person initiating the touch (you'll see in a minute why we are only testing for two of the factors). As we've stated, their type of touch had nine levels. Gender of toucher has, obviously, two levels (male/female). This would have given them a 9×2 factorial design (read "nine by two") in which each possible combination of these two factors and levels would be shown to the different groups. You can multiply these numbers to tell you how many groups you would need to test all combinations of these factors (in this example, they would have needed 9×2, or 18, groups to test these factors. If they had tested all possible extraneous variables, they might have ended up with 900+ groups!). Here's how this 9×2 design would be notated:

$$
\begin{array}{ccc}
R & X_{11} & O \\
R & X_{12} & O \\
R & X_{21} & O \\
R & X_{22} & O \\
R & X_{31} & O \\
R & X_{32} & O \\
R & X_{41} & O \\
R & X_{42} & O \\
R & X_{51} & O \\
R & X_{52} & O \\
R & X_{61} & O \\
R & X_{62} & O \\
R & X_{71} & O \\
R & X_{72} & O \\
R & X_{81} & O \\
R & X_{82} & O \\
R & X_{91} & O \\
R & X_{92} & O \\
\end{array}
$$

This notation tells us that we'd have eighteen groups, randomly assigned, each of whom will be exposed to a different experimental condition. Group one will view a videotape that includes level one of the touch (handshake) and level one of the toucher's gender (male). Group two will view a videotape that also uses the handshake but for whom the toucher is female. Group three will view a videotape that has the dyadic partners clasping hands, in which the toucher is male. Group four will view a videotape that has the dyadic partners clasping hands, in which the toucher is female, and so on, through all eighteen groups. Of course, participants in each group would be administered the same interview after viewing the video. Using this design, we can easily determine which independent variable, and which combination of independent variables, affects the dependent variable.

Communication-related studies frequently use a factorial design. Here's an example of one: Haumer and Donsbach (2009) conducted a study to see how a politician's nonverbal behavior influences his or her image. Using a mock television interview format, they tested viewers' reactions to politicians' communication. They had three independent variables, or factors: nonverbal behavior styles of the politician (active or passive), television host's reactions to the politician (negative, positive, or neutral), and television audience's reactions to the politician (negative, positive, or neutral). This gave them a $2 \times 3 \times 3$ factorial design. Their dependent variables (the effects they expected the independent variables to influence) were the viewers' perceptions of the politician's problem-solving competence, leadership abilities, integrity, and personal qualities. They, again, measured the dependent variables using Likert scale questions in an interview format. They had eighteen groups ($2 \times 3 \times 3$) with twenty participants in each. Each group viewed a different video, representing all eighteen possible combinations of the three factors. Note that this is a post-only design, as they did not conduct a pretest prior to administration of the intervention.

Field and Natural Experiments

As we've shown you throughout this chapter, when we talk about experimental designs, we almost immediately think of laboratory experiments. There are other kinds of experiments that can take place outside of the laboratory. A *field experiment* takes place in a naturalistic environment, but nonetheless involves the manipulation of independent variables and some of the design concerns we have already voiced. *Natural experiments* also generally take place in naturalistic environments, but they do not involve variable manipulation—they simply involve analysis of naturally occurring variables. While field and natural experiments may not be as precise as laboratory experiments in terms of control, they are nonetheless valuable in evaluating causal relationships. In fact, they both have one major advantage over laboratory experiments—they have much higher ecological validity. Thus, external validity versus control is a major consideration when deciding whether to do your experiment in the field or in a laboratory.

Here's an interesting example of a field experiment. Argo, Dahl, and Morales (2008) used a field experiment to see how attractiveness affects consumer consumption. Rather then set up a laboratory experiment, which they could have done (can you think of how they might have designed that?), they conducted an experiment in an actual retail shopping environment. They hypothesized that the attractiveness of a person touching a product affects the level of interest another consumer has in purchasing that product. Simply stated, the research was conducted in a university bookstore, and the researchers set up a *confederate* sales clerk (an actor who was in on the experiment) and a *confederate* shopper and had the shopper confederate only handle a T-shirt. They compared shopper attractiveness to interest in purchasing the T-shirt. Note the independent variable (shopper attractiveness) and dependent variable (purchase intent).

In a classic example of a natural experiment, the 1986 research of Holak and Reddy used the 1970 ban against cigarette advertising on television and radio as an independent variable (pre-ban, post-ban). Since the real world had already administered the induction, they were able to test the effect of the television and radio advertising ban on cigarette pricing, advertising spending, and product demand (dependent variables) and found that the ban affected all three of those variables.

Of course, a field experiment such as this one lacks the kind of control one could have in the laboratory. In fact, field experimentalists are often left to make sense of data where they have to decide what constitutes an independent or dependent variable. Complex designs, such as those we described above, are seldom utilized simply because the researchers don't have much control over the environment. They do, however, allow for consideration of causal relationships in more naturalistic settings.

So What?

So what have we uncovered? We have discussed how communication researchers use experimental designs to answer research questions, and in particular we have discussed how micro-level, causal research problems lend themselves well to these types of designs. We then went on to discuss different types of research designs, and how you can build confidence in your findings by using design to strategically address particular internal validity threats. We have discussed the differences between laboratory and field experiments. And finally, we have discussed the ways in which the data derived from an experimental design can be analyzed and interpreted.

Of course, there is a major validity concern related to experimental designs that cannot be overlooked: the problem of external validity. While experimental designs are very useful for demonstrating causal relationships between independent and dependent variables, the extent to which these procedures mirror real-life behaviors may be problematic. This is especially the case with laboratory research. When you go home after class today, you may turn on the television. It is highly unlikely that a stranger will ask you to fill out a survey first, then ask you to fill one out again when you are done. When you talk to a friend, no one subsequently asks you to report how disclosive you found him or her to be. While experiments are very effective at establishing relationships between independent and dependent variables, the extent to which these findings generalize into real life situations is questionable. Future chapters will detail some research methods that deal more with the experience of communication, as opposed to linear relationships between causes and effects. Again, we will see that the proposition of different questions begs the use of different methods.

Glossary

Baseline

An examination of someone before you expose him or her to a stimulus in order to argue, to a certain extent, that what was done to the subject may have caused any changes that are observed. Also called pretest.

Between-subjects design

Designs comparing multiple groups.

Control group

A group that does not receive induction in an experiment.

Experimental group

The group of participants to whom you give the induction.

Factorial designs

Analyses that involve multiple independent variables.

Induction

What is *done* to a participant in an experiment.

Preexperimental designs

Experimental designs that do not involve a true control group; no pretest, posttest, or control group.

Pretest

An examination of someone before you expose him or her to a stimulus in order to argue, to a certain

extent, that what was done to the subject may have caused any changes that are observed. Also called baseline measurement.

Posttest

An examination or measurement conducted after administration of the induction.

Quasi-experimental designs

Experimental designs that use pretests and posttests in more complicated ways, but still lack random assignment.

Random assignment

The assignment of people at random to different groups in an experimental design.

Social experiment

A procedure in which researchers take human subjects, do something to them, and observe the effects of what they did to them.

True experimental designs

Experimental designs that randomly assign participants to both experimental and control groups.

Within-subjects design

Designs looking at the same group multiple times.

References

Argo, J. J., Dahl, D. W., & Morales, A. C. (2008). Positive consumer contagion: Responses to attractive others in a retail context. *Journal of Marketing Research, 45*, 690–701.

Baxter, L. A., & Babbie, E. (2004). *The basics of communication research*. Belmont, CA: Wadsworth.

Bonito, J. A., Ruppel, E. K. & de Mainvilliers, I. G. (2011). Evaluating participation in small groups: Stimulated recall, self-ratings, and their effects on task-relevant judgments. *Communication Methods and Measures, 5*, 28–47.

Campbell, D., & Stanley, J. (1963). *Experimental and quasi-experimental designs for research*. Chicago: Rand-McNally.

Duthler, K. W. (2006). The politeness of requests made via email and voicemail: Support for the hyperpersonal model. *Journal of Computer-Mediated Communication, 11*(2), article 6, http://jcmc.indiana.edu/vol11/ issue2/duthler.html

Haumer, F., & Donsbach, W. (2009). The rivalry of nonverbal cues on the perception of politicians by television viewers. *Journal of Broadcasting & Electronic Media, 53*(2), 262–279.

Heimendinger, J., O'Neill, C., Marcus, A. C., Wolfe, P., Julesburg, K., Morra, M., Allen, A., Davis, S., Mowad, L., Perocchia, R., Ward, J. D., Strecher, V., Warnecke, R., Nowak, M., Graf, I., Fairclough, D., Bryant, L., & Lipkus, I. (2005). Multiple tailored messages are effective in increasing fruit and vegetable consumption among callers to the Cancer Information Service. *Journal of Health Communication, 10* (Supplement 1), 65–82.

Holak, S. L., & Reddy, S. K. (1986). Effects of a television and radio advertising ban: A study of the cigarette industry. *Journal of Marketing, 50*(4), 219–227.

Lee, J. W., & Guerrero, L. K. (2001). Types of touch in cross-sex relationships between coworkers: Perceptions of relational and emotional messages, inappropriateness, and sexual harassment. *Journal of Applied Communication Research, 29*(3), 197–220.

Triana, M. d. C., Kirkman, B. L., & Wagstaff, M. F. (2012). Does the order of face-to-face and computer-mediated communication matter in diverse project teams? An investigation of communication order effects on minority inclusion and participation. *Journal of Business and Psychology, 27*, 57–70.

WRITING, ANALYZING, AND CRITIQUING QUANTITATIVE RESEARCH

13

CHAPTER OUTLINE

1. Now That I Have My Quantitative Data, What Do I Do with It? Statistical Analysis of Quantitative Data
   a. Know Your Variables, Research Questions, and Hypotheses
   b. Describing or Summarizing Your Variables
      i. Measures of Central Tendency
      ii. Frequencies and Visual Representation of Data
      iii. Measures of Dispersion
   c. Comparing Groups to See if They Are the Same or Different
      i. Nominal Data
      ii. Ordinal Data
      iii. Interval or Ratio (Scale) Data
   d. Testing for Relationships (Association) between Two or More Variables
      i. Nominal Data
      ii. Ordinal Data
      iii. Ratio Data

2. Specific Uses of Statistical Analysis
   a. Content Analysis
   b. Survey Research
      i. t-Test Example
      ii. Regression Example
   c. Experiments
      i. Chi Square Example
      ii. Analysis of Variance Example

3. Writing Quantitative Findings
   a. General Information about Quantitative Writing
   b. Elements of Paper
      i. Introduction and Literature Review
      ii. RQs or H
      iii. Method
      iv. Results
      v. Discussion

4. Evaluating and Critiquing Quantitative Research

5. So What?

KEY TERMS

Central tendency	Mean	Negative correlation
Confidence level	Measures of dispersion	Negatively skewed
Correlation	Median	Platykurtic distribution
Correlation coefficient	Mesokurtic peak	Population parameters
Inferential statistics	Mode	Positive correlation
Leptokurtic peak	Multiple regression	Positively skewed

Range	Skewness	Stepwise regression
Regression	Standard deviation	Variability
Significance testing	Statistical significance	Variance

CHAPTER OBJECTIVES

1. To understand how research questions, hypotheses, and variable type translate into appropriate statistical analysis methods
2. To understand how to conduct appropriate and accurate statistical analyses
3. To understand how to interpret statistical results
4. To understand how to read and understand statistical findings
5. To understand how to write, evaluate, and critique quantitative research reports

▼ # Now That I Have My Quantitative Data, What Do I Do with It? Statistical Analysis of Quantitative Data

Know Your Variables, Research Questions, and Hypotheses

Just as your study method, sampling procedure, and data collection protocol all depend on your Research Questions (RQs) and/or Hypotheses (Hs), so does your data analysis. Thus, the first question you should ask yourself in determining how to analyze your findings is, "What did I set out to find or answer?" It's likely you set out to find or answer one of the following:

A. What do these people feel, believe, and think about "x"?

B. What does the rhetoric, language, text, visuals, and so on contain?

C. What does the communication between these people contain?

D. Does "A" cause "B"?

E. Are "A" and "B" related to each other?

F. Is "A" different from "B"?

Interestingly, pretty much all of the RQs and Hs you might have stated for your quantitative research could likely be summarized into one of three analytical goals: (1) to summarize or describe variables, (2) to compare two or more groups of people to see if they are the same or different, and (3) to see if two or more variables are related to each other. You'll use one or more statistical procedures to address these goals. What statistical procedures you use to address each of these goals depends entirely on what types of data you are testing. Remember in Chapter 7 when we discussed types of variables, we said that there are four levels of variables: nominal, ordinal, interval, and ratio.

Nominal is the most basic level and it refers to categorical data (male, female). Ordinal is the next lowest level and it also refers to categories, but ordinal categories have an order to them, although the order does not refer to degrees or measurement of difference. An example of an ordinal category would be a preference ranking. You and I might both prefer Japanese cars over American cars, but the distance from my first preference to my second preference will likely not be identical to the distance between your first and second preferences. Interval is the next level and while these categories have an order, they also have equal degrees of distance between the points. Recall that Likert scales are usually treated in the social science field as interval data (although purist researchers sometimes argue that Likert scales don't have identical distances for all raters). Ratio data is the highest level of data and it refers to measureable data; measurements on scales that have an absolute zero. When we think of ratio scales, we usually think of health- or medical-related things, such as height or weight. In our field, we might ask for demographic information that is ratio data, such as age, years of school completed, or household income. Why is this distinction important? Because the statistical procedure you choose depends entirely on what you want to accomplish with it and the type of data you are working with.

To compute all of these statistics we're going to discuss in this chapter, you could compute them by hand, but—good news—researchers (almost) never do. We're going to illustrate how you can use a well-known statistical program—SPSS. We need to introduce this idea with a caveat. The great thing about SPSS is that it's very easy to compute statistics using it. The terrible thing about SPSS is how easy it is to compute statistics with it. It's very easy for somebody who doesn't really know what he or she is doing to misuse the program. Before using SPSS or any other statistical analysis program, you must be familiar with your data, your study H or RQs, and your analytical goals so that you compute the *correct* statistics. Remember the saying, "garbage in, garbage out." SPSS will compute (almost) anything you ask it to—but it is up to you to make sure the analysis you report makes sense. We also want to give you one additional caveat. We are not attempting to introduce you to all possible statistical procedures you might encounter in communication research journals, just the most commonly used ones and the ones you are most likely to use in your Communication Research Methods course. In some cases, there are many alternative statistical tests you could use in a given situation. We have attempted to reduce the complexity of this chapter by giving you our recommendation to the most used, most popular, or most appropriate test in most situations. We are also not attempting to teach you everything you need to know about the theory, mathematics, and equations underlying each of the statistical methods we will be discussing. Most students who are taking this course have previously taken a course in statistics. In addition, for most students, it's much more important to understand when to use a particular statistical test and how to interpret the results than to know more advanced information on statistical tools. Finally, there are many very good statistics books available, and we encourage interested students to refer to them. Our favorite is Reinard's (2006), which focuses on statistics as they are used in communication research. In addition, the Babbie, Halley, and Zaino (2007) workbook on using SPSS in data analysis is a helpful addition to a statistics library.

Okay, let's introduce you to SPSS. The first thing you'll need to do in using SPSS is to set up your variables. When you open SPSS, you'll be opening what looks like a blank spreadsheet-type page. This is your *data view*. In order to set up your variables, you'll need to click on the tab (see the bottom of the page) for *variable view*.

Let's set up the data for a very simple survey. For now, you can set up the variables without having any data collected yet, so let's just look at the survey.

Mental Health Literacy Attitudes Survey

1. How many children do you have? _____

2. I'd like to know how much you agree with each of these statements. For each one, please tell me if you agree strongly, agree somewhat, are neutral, disagree somewhat, or disagree strongly.

	Agree Strongly	Agree Somewhat	Neutral	Disagree Somewhat	Disagree Strongly
a. My child, family, and I have many strengths that enhance our health and well-being.					
b. I am sure that my child will be able to support him or herself when he or she grows up.					
c. I am capable of solving my or my family's problems.					
d. I am capable of being a good parent to all my children.					
e. I can survive any problems my child and family are going through.					

3. In which of the following categories does your total household income before taxes fall?
   a. $0–$15,000
   b. $15,001–30,000 _____
   c. $30,001–$45,000 _____
   d. $45,001–$60,000 _____
   e. $60,001–$75,000 _____
   f. $75,001–$90,000 _____
   g. $90,001+ _____

Q. 1 (how many children do you have?) asks for ratio data. SPSS categorizes interval and ratio data together and codes it as *scale* data. We'll name this variable *children*, the data type of *numeric*, and way over on the right, the measure is *scale*. Q. 2 (the Likert scale for attitudes), as we know about Likert scales, is interval data. The last question could have been ratio data but we asked it as discrete categories. The categories have an order to them, and they would have equivalent distance except for the last category ($90,001+). Let's call it an ordinal scale. Here's how this data setup would look:

	Name	Type	Width	Decimals	Label	Values	Missing	Columns	Align	
1	Children	Numeric	8	2	#Children	None	None	8	Right	Sca
2	Q2A	Numeric	8	2	Strengths	{1.00, Disagre	None	8	Right	Sca
3	Q2B	Numeric	8	2	Support	{1.00, Disagre	None	8	Right	Sca
4	Q2C	Numeric	8	2	Solving	{1.00, Disagre	None	8	Right	Sca
5	Q2D	Numeric	8	2	GoodParent	{1.00, Disagre	None	8	Right	Sca
6	Q2E	Numeric	8	2	Survivor	{1.00, Disagre	None	8	Right	Sca
7	Income	Numeric	8	2	Income	{1.00, 0-15 ...	None	8	Right	Ord

Notice you have to define your variable labels for questions 2 and 3.

Now you're ready to input your data. We assigned numbers to the category labels in Qs. 2 and 3. So, for Q. 2, we said we would code "Strongly Agree" as a 5, "Agree Somewhat" a 4, "Neutral" a 3, "Disagree Somewhat" a 2, and "Disagree Strongly" a 1. Therefore, when you input the responses to those questions, you'll need to input the numbers corresponding to the answers. So, if someone answered Q. 2A with "strongly agree," you'll input a number 5. Here's what a sample input for 5 participants might look like:

	Children	Q2A	Q2B	Q2C	Q2D	Q2E	Income	var	var	var
1	3.00	4.00	1.00	5.00	5.00	2.00	1.00			
2	1.00	5.00	5.00	4.00	5.00	4.00	1.00			
3	4.00	4.00	3.00	3.00	4.00	5.00	2.00			
4	2.00	2.00	4.00	2.00	3.00	5.00	5.00			
5	2.00	1.00	2.00	2.00	2.00	3.00	3.00			

This, by the way, is your data set. Now, let's talk about how you can analyze it.

Describing or Summarizing Your Variables

Descriptive statistics describe your findings in an easily understandable way. In describing your findings, you'll typically be describing two things about your data: its **central tendency**, and its **variability**.

Measures of Central Tendency. Measures of central tendency are called summary statistics, and they give us a number that represents the *typical* number in an array (distribution) of data. If you are working with nominal (categorical) data, you'll be looking for the **mode**. The mode is the most frequently occurring value in a data distribution. In our content analysis example that opened Chapter 12, we noted that researchers found that more men were depicted in G-rated movies than women. In other words, *men* was the modal category. Sometimes we have a tie between modes—a data distribution with two modes is *bimodal*, a distribution with three modes is *trimodal*, and a distribution with more than three modes is *multimodal*. The **median** is the appropriate measure

---

central tendency
Also called summary statistics. It is a measure that represents the "typical" number in an array (distribution) of data. Depending on the type of data you are working with, this can be the mode, median, or mean.

variability
Contrasted with central tendency, variability refers to the differences in our data, how wide the range is, and how far a given value might be from the measure of central tendency. Variability is another word for dispersion.

mode
The appropriate measure of central tendency for nominal data. The mode refers to the most frequently occurring value in our distribution. For example, a sample of communication studies students at UNC Charlotte might reveal that there are more female students than male students. Since the value "female" occurs more often in our data set, this value would be the mode.

median

A measure of central tendency that represents the exact center point of our data set when it's put in numerical order. Median is the appropriate measure of central tendency for ordinal data. For example, a data set consisting of scores of 1, 3, 5, 9, 17 would have a median of 5, since it is the center point of our array. Median can help control for outliers in our data sets as in the above example. Even though 17 is an extreme value, 5 is still our median. If there is an even number of participants the two middle numbers will be "tied" and will be averaged together to get the median. The median is also sometimes used for higher levels of data than ordinal because it controls for outliers.

mean

A measure of central tendency; the arithmetic average, computed adding the scores together and dividing by the total number of score.

of central tendency for ordinal data. This is the exact center point of a data set when it has been put in numerical order. For example, if five study participants rated their interest (on a scale of 1 to 10) in getting a dog as: 8, 2, 6, 7, 9; we could put their ratings in numerical order (2, 6, 7, 8, 9) and determine the median—the center point—to be 7. In an array of data with an even number of participants, two scores will be *tied* for the middle score and they would be averaged; thus, a data array of 2, 4, 6, 7, 8, 9 would have a tie between 6 and 7; the median would be 6.5. The median is also sometimes used for higher levels of data than ordinal because it controls for outliers. When we compute a mean (or arithmetic average), extreme scores can skew our measure. Since the median doesn't mathematically consider extreme scores (except to put them in order), it is much less likely to be skewed by outliers. This is why governmental and many other public polls and surveys report *median* income rather than *mean* income; people in extreme poverty or wealth are less likely to skew the data so that the measure is a more accurate report of the population as a whole. The last measure of central tendency is **mean**, and it is typically used for interval and ratio data. The mean is the arithmetic average and is computed adding the scores together and dividing by the total number of scores.

Frequencies and Visual Representation of Data. While the measure of central tendency is an efficient way to summarize your data, a data set has much more information than that one number implies. So, researchers also use other measures to give information about the data distribution. For nominal or ordinal data, we might want to know the frequency of mentions, or observations, of each category. So, in our content analysis example, the researchers didn't simply say that *male* was the modal category; they also noted that, among the speaking characters in the movies, 28 percent were female and 72 percent were male. You might use a frequency table to show the frequency counts. You also might summarize the data array using a chart or graph. A pie or bar chart is most appropriate for nominal data, while a bar chart is best for ordinal data. Interval or ratio data could be depicted with a bar or a line chart.

Here's a frequency chart for our data:

#Children				
	Frequency	**Percent**	**Valid Percent**	**Cumulative Percent**
Valid 1.00	1	20.0	20.0	20.0
2.00	2	40.0	40.0	60.0
3.00	1	20.0	20.0	80.0
4.00	1	20.0	20.0	100.0
Total	5	100.0	100.0	

Measures of Dispersion. In addition to showing or depicting a summary of description of the data array, you might want to know more about the distribution of the scores. If you know the mean age of study participants is

20.4, you might want to know if most participants clustered around that mean (were all about that same age), or if their ages varied a lot. You might want to compute a **measure of dispersion**. The **range** is the simplest measure of dispersion, and it simply refers to the distance between the highest and lowest scores, computed by subtracting the lowest score from the highest score. Thus, you might report that the mean age of participants was 20.4 and the range was 20.1, telling us that the ages ranged from about 10 to about 30. The **variance** is a measure that lets us know how "on average, how far from the mean are the data?" (Reinard, 2006, p. 65). Specifically, the variance is the average distance of scores from the mean, squared. You might hear the variance also referred to as the average of the sum of the squares, because it's computed by squaring the deviation scores (how much each score deviates from the mean) and adding them, then averaging them (trust us on this mathematical computation). What does this mean, really? A high variance tells us that many of the scores are far away from the mean, and a low variance tells us that many scores are close to the mean. Since the variance is expressed in terms of the square of the scores, we translate it back into the original unit of measurement by taking the square root of the variance. This is called the **standard deviation**. For interval and ratio data, the mean and standard deviation are the two summary statistics most commonly reported.

All descriptive statistics can be computed in SPSS using the *analyze* command, and choosing *descriptive statistics*, then *descriptive*. The *options* box will let you select whichever descriptive statistics you choose to run.

measures of dispersion
Measures that represent the distribution of scores in a data array. Dispersion can be thought of as statistics that represent differences in our data, whether it's the overall distance between the high and low scores (range), an average of how far the scores are from our mean (variance), or the standard deviation or square root of that variance.

range
A measure of dispersion that refers to the difference between the highest and lowest values in a data set. Calculated by subtracting the lowest score from the highest score. A data set with values between 1 and 29 would have a range of 28.

variance
A specific measure of dispersion that represents the average of how far our data is from our mean. Mathematically it is calculated by squaring the average distance of scores from the mean. It could also be referred to as the average of the sum of the squares, because it's computed by squaring the deviation scores.

standard deviation
One of the most commonly reported summary statistics for interval and ratio data. A measure of dispersion that represents the typical amount an entry deviates from the mean. Mathematically, it's the variance (the square of the average distance of scores from the mean) translated back into the original unit of measure by calculating the square root.

mesokurtic peak
Indicates a distribution of scores that represents a normal curve.

platykurtic distribution
Indicates a flat distribution of scores (farther away from the mean than in a normal distribution). This type of distribution has a low peak, representing the fact that a relatively small number of scores are in the middle of the distribution. Platykurtic graphs also have a wide range, which represents a large amount of variance in scores.

positively skewed
More scores tend toward the left side of the graph, or lower than the mean.

negatively skewed
More scores are on the right side of the graph—or higher than the mean.

We see the mean number of children reported by people in our data set is 2.4, and the standard deviation is 1.14. This standard deviation isn't really very large, and you might recall from the data set that the individual scores mostly clustered around the mean of 2.4.

Descriptive Statistics			
	N	**Mean**	**Std. Deviation**
#Children	5	2.4000	1.14018
Valid N (listwise)	5		

By the way, you may recall from your statistics class that (approximately) all of the measures in a data set for a "normally distributed population (or sample)" occur within three standard deviations from the mean (+ or –), 95 percent occur within two standard deviations from the mean (+ or –), and 68 percent occur within one standard deviations from the mean (+ or –). You may also recall, this describes a *normal curve*, or a *bell-shaped curve*. A normal curve has what's called a **mesokurtic peak** or mesokurtic distribution.

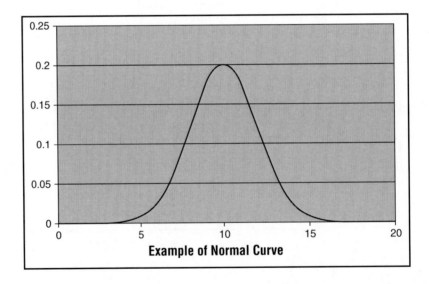
Example of Normal Curve

In our data, SPSS tells us our kurtosis is negative (–.178), indicating a flat distribution of scores (farther away from the mean than in a normal distribution), called a **platykurtic distribution**. It's also **positively skewed**, which means more scores tend toward the left side of the graph, or lower than the mean. (A **negatively skewed** value would mean that more scores are on the right side of the graph—or higher than the mean).

Descriptive Statistics					
	N	Skewness		Kurtosis	
	Statistic	Statistic	Std. Error	Statistic	Std. Error
#Children	5	.405	.913	−.178	2.000
Valid N (listwise)	5				

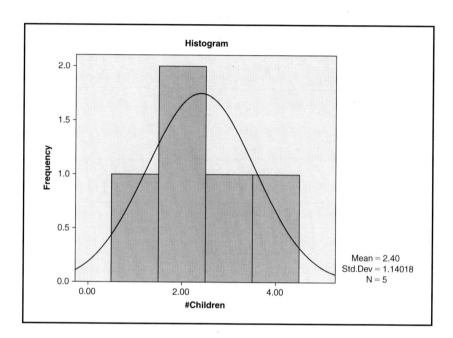

leptokurtic peak
Indicates a more peaked distribution of scores than a normal distribution (closer to from the mean than in a normal distribution). This type of distribution has a higher peak, representing the fact that a relatively larger number of scores are in the middle of the distribution. Leptokurtic graphs also have a smaller range, which represents a smaller amount of variance in scores.

skewness
Either positive (lower than mean) or negative (higher than mean), is the uneven, sloping, or unsymmetrical graph of scores. Refers to the condition that occurs when more scores ten to be higher than the mean (negative skewness), or lower than the mean (positive skewness).

Interestingly, our *income* data has a positive kurtosis (.536), indicating a distribution of scores that has stronger consistency around the mean than in a normal distribution, in what's called a **leptokurtic peak** or, leptokurtic distribution. This data also has a positive **skewness** value.

Descriptive Statistics					
	N	Skewness		Kurtosis	
	Statistic	Statistic	Std. Error	Statistic	Std. Error
Income	5	1.089	.913	.536	2.000
Valid N (listwise)	5				

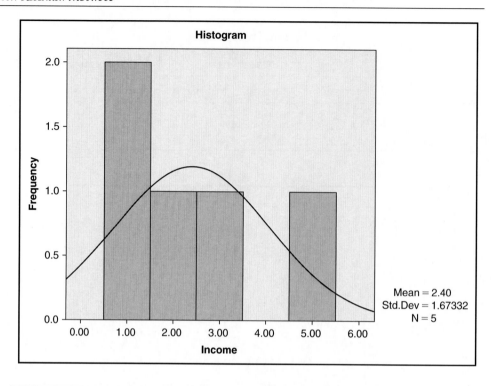

What Type of Data Do You Have?	Summarize Data
Nominal	*Measures of central tendency:* Mode *Visual displays:* Frequency table Pie chart Bar chart
Ordinal	*Measures of central tendency:* Median *Visual displays:* Frequency table Bar chart
Interval/Ratio (Scale)	*Measures of central tendency:* Median Mean *Measures of dispersion:* Range Variance Standard deviation *Visual displays:* Bar chart Line graph

Comparing Groups to See if They Are the Same or Different

Okay, summary statistics are fine and you will see them reported in journal articles as researchers describe the sample or explain a finding. However, they're not why you went to the trouble of conducting your research. You conducted your research to answer a question or test a hypothesis. You might have conducted your research to see if two groups of people are the same or different on a characteristic or variable. We need to take a minute to explain *sameness* or *difference* in statistical terms. When we talk about statistical difference, we want to know if an observed (or measured) difference is due to *chance*, or due to a *real* difference. Remember our null hypothesis discussion from Chapter 6. The null hypothesis says that there is no difference. We are always testing for the null; always hypothesizing there is no difference. Why? Well, remember we rely on samples that represent the population. But, of course, samples can't represent the population 100 percent—we estimate the population characteristics (**population parameters**) based on the sample characteristics, and samples are subject to *sampling error*. You can never know for sure that a difference is due to a *true* difference rather than sampling error, so there's no way to test for that. However, you can test that there's *no* difference (the null hypothesis). Is this confusing? Remember eighth-grade geometry? You can't prove a theorem; you just continue to try to disprove them. It's the same principle. You can't prove there's a difference without conducting a census, which you decided not to do in the first place, so instead you try to prove the null hypothesis, which disproves your difference. If you can't disprove it, then it's likely to be true. How likely? Researchers talk in terms of the *probability* of there being a *true* difference. They call this a measure of **statistical significance**. This is called **significance testing**, and the types of statistics you use to do this are called **inferential statistics**, because you're inferring things about the population based on the sample.

Let's review some terms we discussed in Chapter 8 on sampling and sample size. Remember **confidence level** and margin of error? Our sample represents our population to a certain extent. The *confidence level* refers to the probability that I'm *close to correct* when I infer population characteristics based on my sample. How close I am to correct is the margin of error. Remember the marble experiment? A confidence level of 95 percent means that if I take 100 handfuls of marbles, 95 of those times, I will come up with the same number of black marbles that there actually are in the jar, within a margin of error. In other words, there is a 95 percent probability that my answer is pretty close to correct. If I have a 5 percent margin of error that means that my answer is within –5 or +5 percentage points of the *true* answer in the population. When we are conducting inferential statistics, we are estimating this margin of error. Not to confuse you, but margin of error is often called *confidence intervals*, and it's reported in SPSS as a *confidence coefficient*. It's found under "Analyze," "Descriptive Statistics," "Explore."

For our "number of children" variable, the mean was 2.4 and—at a 95 percent confidence level—the confidence interval ranges from .984 to 3.81, which means that there is a 95 percent probability that the *true* mean in the population is between .984 and 3.81.

population parameters
Population characteristics based on the sample characteristics.

statistical significance
The probability of there being a "true" difference between scores of a data set, as opposed to a perceived difference that may occur, but might in reality be simply "overlapping" of margins of error.

significance testing
Testing to determine the probability of there being a "true" difference between scores of a data set. Involves testing a null hypothesis in order to prove it, and therefore disprove the difference.

inferential statistics
The type of statistic used when gathering information about a population based on the sample. The type of statistics used with significance testing.

confidence level
Refers to the probability that I'm "close to correct" when I infer population characteristics based on my sample. How close I am to correct is the margin of error.

Descriptives		
		Statistic
Mean		2.4000
95% Confidence Interval for Mean	Lower Bound	.9843
	Upper Bound	3.8157

What does this have to do with statistically significant differences? Let's say we have a second sample: Perhaps we spoke to another group of five people and their mean on this question was 2.9 and their confidence interval ranged from .83 to 4.15. We need to know if 2.4 versus 2.9 is a *true* difference (a statistically significant difference) or a difference due to chance (or sampling error). Let's draw a diagram of our two populations. The shaded areas represent their two confidence intervals. You can see that, even though their means are different, their confidence intervals have some overlap. Therefore, we cannot be certain that the two means are different. If the means of each sample are anywhere in their shaded areas, it's entirely possible that we could sample two means that are identical. We've proven our null hypothesis—it's possible there's no difference between the two groups.

You can see that one way to determine if there is a difference between the means of two groups is to compute their confidence intervals and see if there is any overlap. There are, however, easier ways to do this. You can compute statistical tests that test for differences.

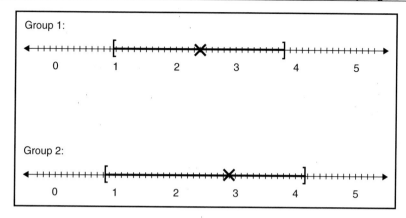

Nominal Data. If you have a nominal variable and want to see if there is a difference between categories of this variable, you would use a one-sample Chi Square. This statistic is notated by the Greek symbol: χ^2. For example, we added a variable "experience with mental illness" to our survey data and we see that 60 percent of our sample has some experience with mental illness, while 40 percent do not.

Experience with Mental Illness				
		Frequency	**Percent**	**Valid Percent**	**Cumulative Percent**
Valid	No experience	2	40.0	40.0	40.0
	Some experience	3	60.0	60.0	100.0
	Total	5	100.0	100.0	

What we do not know at this point, however, if there is a *true* statistically significant difference between the 60 percent and the 40 percent. Since this is nominal data, the appropriate statistical test is a one-sample Chi Square. In SPSS, you access this test through "Analyze," "Non-parametric tests," "Chi Square."

Note that the expected values setting should be left on "all categories equal," since we have no reason (prior research, for example) to believe that all categories would not be equal. Thus, what we're testing in this statistical test is whether there is a difference between equal categories (50%–50%) and the proportions we observed in our sample (40%–60%). Here's the output of our statistical test:

Test Statistics	
	Experience with Mental Illness
Chi-Square(a)	.200
Df	1
Asymp. Sig.	.655

SPSS reports our significance level as .655, but you need to know in SPSS the significance is really reported for the *null* hypothesis. The value above (.655) is what's called the *p* value—the probability that the null hypothesis is true. The smaller the *p* value, the more likely the null hypothesis is *not* true, and the more likely our test hypothesis is true and there is a statistical difference.

What does this mean? Recall that our standard significance level is 95 percent, or 95 percent probability, and we said that a significance level of 95 percent means that there is a 5 percent probability ($p = .05$) that the difference is due to chance, or there is a 95 percent probability that the difference is a *true* difference. A *p* value of .65 means that there is a 65 percent probability that the null hypothesis is true, or that the difference is due to chance, which is much higher than our threshold of 5 percent. Therefore, we accept the null hypothesis that there is no difference. Another way to read this output table is to say that at a significance level of 95 percent, the *p* value stated above would have to be .05 or smaller (between .00 and .05) for us to say there is a statistically significant difference. Obviously, it's not, so we say that our research has found no difference in experience with mental illness.

What if we have a nominal variable (gender, for example) as our independent variable and we want to see if this differs on a nominal variable (whether subjects have experience with mental illness, for example) as our dependent variable? Let's write a hypothesis: There is a difference by gender in terms of experience with mental illness. This, by the way, is a two-tailed hypothesis because we're not implying directionality. If we instead were to hypothesize that men have more mental illness experience than women, we'd be making a one-tailed hypothesis. Since we have no prior research on which to base a one-tailed hypothesis, we're making a two-tailed one. Since our dependent variable is nominal, we'd use a two-variable Chi Square. In SPSS, you'll find this under "Analyze," Descriptive Statistics," and "Crosstabs."

Under "Crosstabs," you'll indicate the rows (groups) and columns (variables) you're testing, then select "Statistics" to say you want to compute a Chi Square.

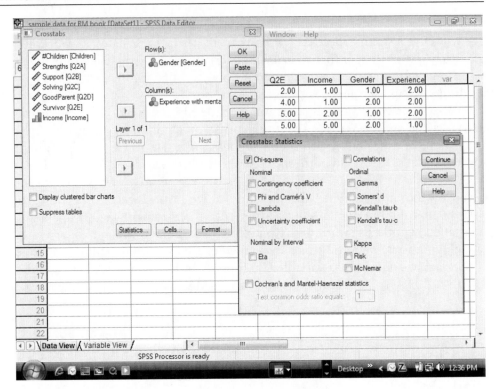

Normally, for nominal data, we look at the Pearson Chi Square *p* value. In our results, the *p* value for the two-sided Pearson Chi Square is .136. Since it is not between 0 and .05, we accept the null hypothesis that there is no difference between men and women on experience with mental illness. (An aside—if any cell has a zero value, we use the Fisher's Exact Test instead of the Pearson Chi Square. In this case, Fisher's Exact Test is .4 so we'd still accept the null.)

Chi-Square Tests					
	Value	**df**	**Asymp. Sig. (2-sided)**	**Exact Sig. (2-sided)**	**Exact Sig. (1-sided)**
Pearson Chi-Square	2.222(b)	1	.136		
Continuity Correction(a)	.313	1	.576		
Likelihood Ratio	2.911	1	.088		
Fisher's Exact Test				.400	.300
Linear-by-Linear Association	1.778	1	.182		
N of Valid Cases	5				

The Chi Square tests are nonparametric tests. Nonparametric tests are appropriate when your data is not continuous (that is, when your variables are not interval or ratio) and when you cannot assume you have a normal distribution of data (Reinard, 2006). Some have also suggested their use with very small samples, since normal distributions can generally not be assumed with samples smaller than twenty.

Ordinal Data.   What if we want to determine if there are statistically significant differences between groups on ordinal variables? Perhaps you want to know if men differ from women on their income. In our study, income is an ordinal variable because we asked people to indicate the income group to which they belong rather than give us their exact income. To compare two groups on an ordinal variable, we would use another nonparametric test—the Mann-Whitney U Test—which is a test that looks at the equality of two distributions. In SPSS, you would find this test under "Analyze," "Nonparametric Tests," "2-Independent Samples." Note that they want you to define your independent variable groups. For our gender variable, we coded "men" a "1" and "women" a "2."' That's what you would put for your definition of the groups.

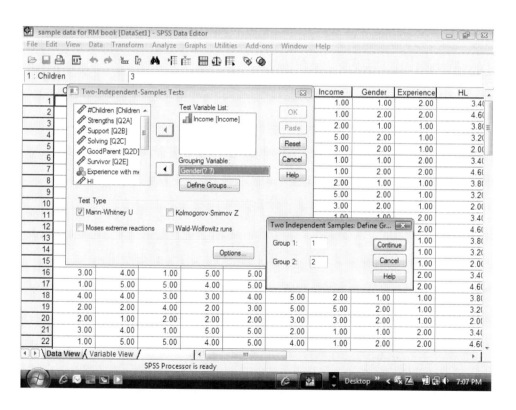

From our SPSS output, you can see there is not a statistically significant difference between men and women on income.

Test Statistics(b)	
	Income
Mann-Whitney U	1.500
Wilcoxon W	4.500
Z	–.889
Asymp. Sig. (2-tailed)	.374
Exact Sig. [2*(1-tailed Sig.)]	.400(a)
(a) Not corrected for ties	
(b) Grouping Variable: Gender	

If you are determining if there is a difference between three or more groups on an independent variable (that is an ordinal variable), you would use the Kruskall-Wallis Test. If you're looking for differences between what's called *matched* or *related* groups (such as pre-post test), you'd use the Wilcoxon Matched Pairs Signed Ranks Test if you have two groups and the Friedman Two-Way Analysis of Variance for more than two groups. All of these can be found in SPSS under "Analyze," "Nonparametric Tests."

Interval or Ratio (Scale) Data. When you have interval or ratio data, when your sample was randomized, when you have a normal distribution and equal variances in your population, you can use parametric statistics. You should know that most of the time, if a scholar has interval or ratio data, she presumes the other assumptions and uses parametric statistics, especially if her sample sizes are sufficiently large. This is because the Central Limit Theorem states that the larger the sample size, the more it approaches a normal distribution—if the population itself has a normal distribution (Reinard, 2006).

If I want to see if there is a difference between two groups (males and females, for example) on an interval or ratio independent variable (health literacy, for example), we would use an Independent Samples t-test. In our sample data, we computed a *health literacy* measure by determining the mean of the individual five health literacy questions. We will now see if males and females differ on health literacy. In SPSS, we would go to "Analyze," Compare Means," "Independent Samples T-Test."

The SPSS output first tells us if the two groups we are testing have equal variances, because that makes a difference in how we will interpret the results. Since there is not a statistically significant difference between the variances ($p = .286$), we'll look at the p-value for the two-tailed t-test when equal variances is assumed ($p = .756$). Clearly, we will accept the null hypothesis that there is no difference between men and women on health literacy.

Independent Samples Test						
		Levene's Test for Equality of Variances		t-test for Equality of Means		
		F	Sig.	t	df	Sig. (2-tailed)
HL	Equal variances assumed	1.681	.286	.340	3	.756
	Equal variances not assumed			.429	2.271	.705

If we had related groups—again, a pre-post test—we wanted to compare on interval or ratio data, we would use a Paired t-Test, also found in SPSS under "Analyze," "Compare Means." If we wanted to see if three or more groups were different on one interval or ratio variable, we would use a one-way Analysis of Variance (ANOVA). If the p-value indicates a statistically significant difference between the groups, we would follow with what's called a post-hoc test to determine exactly where the difference is. We'd use the most powerful and most popular post-hoc test, the Tukey HSD post-hoc test because it compares all pairs of means (Gravetter & Wallnau, 1986; Reinard, 2006; Williams, 1968). HSD stands for "honestly significant difference," and it computes a value that represents the minimum difference between means necessary for significance, then it compares each pair of means with that minimum difference. To compute a one-way ANOVA in SPSS, go to "Analyze," Compare Means," and "One-way ANOVA."

What Type of Data Do You Have?	Test for Differences between Groups
Nominal (Nonparametric)	*Analyze the distribution of the independent or dependent (nominal) variable:* Chi Square *Compare 2 or more (nominal) independent or dependent categories:* 2-variable Chi Square
Ordinal (Nonparametric)	*Analyze the differences between 2 groups on ordinal variable:* Mann-Whitney U Test *Analyze the differences between 3 or more groups on ordinal variable:* Kruskall-Wallis Test *Examine the differences between related (ordinal) scores:* Wilcoxin Sign Test (2 groups) Friedman 2-Way ANOVA (3 or more groups)
Interval/Ratio (Scale)	*Estimate parameters of interval/ratio variable:* Estimate confidence levels and margin of error *Examine differences between 2 unrelated groups on interval/ratio variable:* Independent samples t-test *Examine differences between 2 related groups on interval/ratio variable:* Paired t-test *Compare 3 or more groups on their distribution on one interval/ratio variable:* One-way analysis of variance (ANOVA) followed by a TUKEY post-hoc test

Testing for Relationships (Association) between Two or More Variables

The last thing you might want to do with your data is to see if there is a statistical relationship between variables. When we say there is a relationship between variables, we are simply stating that when one occurs, the other tends to occur also. **Correlation** is the statistical test designed to test for linear relationships between variables when you have interval or ratio variable, and we'll discuss this in detail in a few pages. Because of this, people frequently refer to relationships between variables as *correlations* between variables.

Remember from Chapter 6, there are several types of relationships you can hypothesize and/or find: a positive linear relationship (when "A" goes up, "B" goes up), a negative linear relationship (when "A" goes up, "B" goes down), a curvilinear relationship (when "A" goes up, "B" goes up for a while, then as "A" continues to go up, "B" goes down—or some variation on that). The statistical tests you use to see if there is a relationship between variables are called *Tests of Association*.

Nominal Data. If both of your variables are nominal variables, or if one of your variables is nominal and the other is ordinal, we recommend you use a Cramer's V. This can be used when there are either two or more than two categories for your variables, and it also adjusts for sample size. In SPSS, you'll find this test the same place you found the two-variable Chi Square, under "Analyze," "Descriptive Statistics," and "Crosstabs." As a matter of fact, Cramer's V is one of the options under the Chi Square function. It may appear that this statistic is the same as Chi Square, but while the Chi Square statistic only told us if there was a statistically significant difference between the two groups (male and female) on the independent variable (experience with mental illness), the Cramer's V statistic also gives us a value that indicates the strength of the relationship between the two variables, if there is one.

correlation
The statistical test designed to test for linear relationships between variables when you have interval or ratio variables. When one variable occurs, the other variable tends to be present as well.

Chi-Square Tests					
	Value	**df**	**Asymp. Sig. (2-sided)**	**Exact Sig. (2-sided)**	**Exact Sig. (1-sided)**
Pearson Chi-Square	.139(b)	1	.709		
Continuity Correction(a)	.000	1	1.000		
Likelihood Ratio	.138	1	.710		
Fisher's Exact Test				1.000	.700
Linear-by-Linear Association	.111	1	.739		
N of Valid Cases	5				
(a) Computed only for a 2 x 2 table					
(b) 4 cells (100.0%) have expected count less than 5. The minimum expected count is .80.					

Symmetric Measures		Value	Approx. Sig.
Nominal	Phi	−.167	.709
by Nominal	Cramer's V	.167	.709
N of Valid Cases		5	
(a) Not assuming the null hypothesis.			
(b) Using the asymptotic standard error assuming the null hypothesis.			

The values of Cramer's V range from 0 to 1. A 0 value indicates there is no association between the two variables and a 1 indicates there is a high association between the two. Since our significance supported the null hypothesis it should not surprise us that the value for Cramer's V is very low also.

Ordinal Data. If both of your variables are ordinal, or if one of your variables is interval/ratio and the other is ordinal, we recommend you use the Spearman's Rho (also called Spearman Rank Order Correlation). It is subject to less error than other statistics (Williams, 1968), although Kendall's tau (Kendall's Coefficient of Concordance) is preferred when you are testing interrater reliability on ordinal variables. In SPSS, Spearman's Rho and Kendall's tau can both be found under "Analyze," "Correlation," and "Bivariate Correlation."

correlation coefficient
The correlation coefficient is indicated by the Greek letter r (pronounced "rho"). It is a number that represents the extent that variables are related or go together and the magnitude of their relationships. Correlation cannot identify causation. Just because two variables are related or vary together, we cannot determine whether one causes the other. Range from +1.0 to −1.0. +1.0 indicates a positive relationship. −1.0 indicates a negative relationship. 0 indicates no relationship between the variables in question.

Correlations			Income	HL
Spearman's rho	Income	Correlation Coefficient	1.000	−.718
		Sig. (2-tailed)	.	.172
		N	5	5
	HL	Correlation Coefficient	−.718	1.000
		Sig. (2-tailed)	.172	.
		N	5	5

Note that in our example, the *p*-value for the statistical significance of the relationship between income (ordinal variable) and health literacy (ratio variable) is .172, which means we accept the null hypothesis.

There is also one additional piece of information to notice on this output table: the correlation coefficient. A **correlation coefficient** is indicated by the Greek letter *r* (pronounced "rho"). It is a number that represents the extent that variables are related or go together. It is important to note, however, that correlation does not have the capacity to distinguish between which variable comes first. In other words, correlation cannot identify causation. Just because two variables are related or vary together, we cannot determine whether one causes the other.

Correlations can range from +1.0 to –1.0. A +1.0 would indicate a perfectly positive relationship, a –1.0 indicates a perfectly negative relationship, and a 0 is indicative of no relationship between the variables in question. A correlation coefficient represents two pieces of information about any relationship: (1) the direction of the relationship, and (2) the magnitude of the relationship. The sign of the correlation, either positive or negative, indicates the direction of the relationship. If we have a **positive correlation**, this indicates that the two variables in question vary in the same direction. As one variable increases, so does the other variable, or as one variable decreases, so does the other variable.

positive correlation
Occurs when both variables vary in the same direction.

Consider an example. We could measure intelligence scores like IQ scores as well as reading ability. Would you predict a relationship between these two variables? Our hypothesis might be: As reading scores increase, so do IQ scores. This would be a hypothesis of association. Remember that the null hypothesis to this hypothesis is that there is no relationship between reading scores and IQ scores. So, using correlation we could test our hypothesis. This relationship predicts a positive relationship, as we predict scores will vary in the same direction—both increasing in this case. However, it is possible to have a positive relationship where both values decrease together.

On the other hand, a **negative correlation** occurs when one variable increases, while the other variable decreases, thus indicating two variables that vary in opposite directions. Consider another example: Reading ability and the time it takes to read a passage. In this case, we would hypothesize that the better your reading ability, the less time it will take you to read a passage. Here one score is increasing (reading ability) and the other variable is decreasing (time to read a passage), thus a negative correlation.

negative correlation
Occurs when one variable increases, while the other variable decreases, thus, indicating two variables that vary in opposite directions.

A correlation coefficient also represents the magnitude of the relationship. If we take the absolute value (drop the sign in front of the number) of the correlation coefficient, the actual numerical value indicates the strength of the relationship. Remember that correlation coefficients range from –1.0 to +1.0, so if we drop the sign, the strength of the relationship is captured by the numerical value's closeness to 1.0. The larger the absolute value, the stronger the relationship. Essentially, this means that all of the variation in one variable is shared by the other variable. Thus, numbers closer to 1.0 are stronger than numbers closer to 0. Another way to think about this is that the stronger the relationship, the more the correlation coefficient deviates from zero, which essentially leads to the null hypothesis. The null hypothesis of correlation is simply that there is no meaningful association between two variables. In regard to the correlation coefficient, the null hypothesis is correlation = 0.

One of the most important considerations to make in being a critical consumer of research methods is to ask yourself how you interpret r. First you must answer the question of whether the statistic is significant; this can be identified by the significance column produced in SPSS. Second, what is the direction of the relationship (positive or negative)? What does that tell us about our variables and how they vary? The numerical value also communicates to us the magnitude or the strength of the relationship. This is generally subjective and may take into account special knowledge of the variables involved. However, there are some general guidelines from three different sources summarized in Reinard (2006, p. 95) that we'll replicate for you here:

Koenker (1961)	Losh (2004, citing G. Lutz)	J. Cohen (1988)
.80 to 1.00: Highly dependable relationship	1.00: Perfect	Above .371: Large
.60 to .79: Moderate to marked relationship	.76 to .99: Very strong	
.40 to .59: Fair degree of relationship	.51 to .75: Strong	
.20 to .39: Slight relationship	.26 to .50: Moderate	.243 to .371: Medium
0 to .19: Negligible or chance relationship	.11 to .25: Weak	.10 to .243: Small
	.01 to .10: Very weak	
	0: No relationship	

Ratio Data. We've explained the correlation coefficient to you when we discussed using Spearman's Rho correlation for ordinal data. For ratio data, you would use the Pearson Product Moment Correlation, which was, by the way, developed by Karl Pearson, an English mathematician. It, in effect, considers the relationship of two continuous (interval or ratio-level) variables, and was the first statistic to consider the effect size (Rodgers & Nicewander, 1988).

A Pearson Product-Moment correlation would be appropriate to see if there is a relationship between the number of children a person has and their level of health literacy. In SPSS, go to "Analyze," "Correlation," and "Bivariate Correlations." Remember to tell it if you're doing a one-tailed or two-tailed test.

Correlations		HL	#Children
HL	Pearson Correlation	1	−.092
	Sig. (2-tailed)		.882
	N	5	5
#Children	Pearson Correlation	−.092	1
	Sig. (2-tailed)	.882	
	N	5	5

In our example, the *p*-value for significance is .882, so we accept the null hypothesis. In addition, we see that the correlation coefficient is −.092, virtually zero, again telling us there is virtually no association between the two variables.

If you want to test for relationships between many variables at one time, you can compute a correlation matrix, which is one big table that gives you the correlation coefficient for all possible combinations of variables. To compute this, you simply select multiple variables under "Correlation."

Correlations		Strengths	Support	Solving	GoodParent	Survivor
Strengths	Pearson Correlation	1	.289	.783	.957	.023
	Sig. (2-tailed)		.638	.109	.011	.970
	N	5	5	5	5	5
Support	Pearson Correlation	.289	1	−.243	.121	.728
	Sig. (2-tailed)	.638		.694	.846	.164
	N	5	5	5	5	5
Solving	Pearson Correlation	.793	−.243	1	.912(*)	−.559
	Sig. (2-tailed)	.109	.694		.031	.327
	N	5	5	5	5	5
GoodParent	Pearson Correlation	.957(*)	.121	.912(*)	1	−.176
	Sig. (2-tailed)	.011	.0846	.031		.776
	N	5	5	5	5	5
Survivor	Pearson Correlation	.023	.728	−.559	−.176	1
	Sig. (2-tailed)	.970	.164	.327	.776	
	N	5	5	5	5	5
(*) Correlation is significant at the 0.05 level (2-tailed).						

In this example, we computed a correlation matrix to see if there was a relationship between the different beliefs questions. There was a statistically significant relationship between beliefs in strengths and in being a good parent ($p = .01$) and beliefs in being able to solve problems and being a good parent ($p = .03$). The correlation coefficient (r) for the strengths/good parent relationship is .957 and for problem-solving/good parent is .912, both of which are awfully strong relationships whichever guideline you use.

Finally, there's one more thing you might want to look at as you look at relationships between interval or ratio variables: prediction, or **regression**. Sometimes you want to take what you know about the relationship between "A" and "B" and use it to predict what new "B" values might occur given new values of "A" (Babbie, Halley, & Zaino, 2003; Williams, 1968). Regression looks at the pattern in a data distribution to make predictions about future patterns. The term refers to a *line of best fit* and is based on an algebraic equation (regression equation) that takes into account the regression line, the slope (the angle of the line), and intercept (the point at which the line intersects the y-axis). The regression procedure finds the *line* that best fits your data distribution. We can construct a scatterplot of our HL/children correlation that approximates the overall relationship between the two variables. In SPSS, you would go to "Graphs" to create this plot. From "Graphs," go to "Scatter/Dot," then select "Simple Scatter." You assign your dependent variable (in our case, Health Literacy) to the y-axis and your independent variable (in our case,

regression
For interval or ratio, data, the procedure that looks at the pattern in a data distribution to make predictions about future patterns. This procedure finds the "line" that best fits your data distribution. This is also known as prediction. It is another way to look at relationships between interval or ratio variables. The term refers to a line of best fit *and is based on an algebraic equation (regression equation) that takes into account the regression line, the slope (the angle of the line), and intercept (the point at which the line intersects the y-axis).*

number of children) to the x-axis. Now you have a graph that shows how your data distribution plots. Now, let's overlay the *best fit* regression line to visually see the relationship between the two variables. Double click on your graph and a chart editor will open. Under "Elements," select "Fit Line at Total." Here's what we come up with for our data:

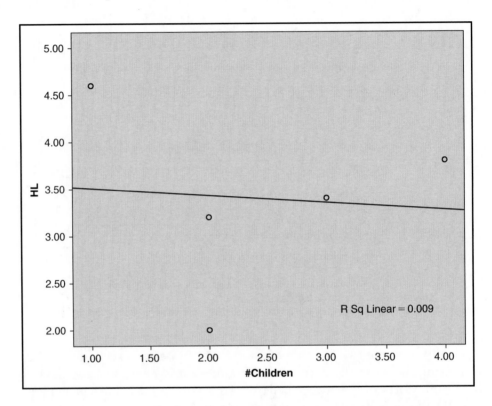

multiple regression
Represented by the symbol R, this predicts the dependent variable's value from two or more independent variables. Used when testing curvilinear effects that can't be tested with linear correlation methods and for testing the effects of extraneous variables.

Stepwise selection
A method of inserting independent variables into an equation for multiple regression. Each independent variable is subjected to a significance test, starting with the smallest p value, and then proceeding to the next smallest and so on, until there are no more variables with statistically significant probabilities.

You might notice that the slope is almost flat. In addition, the dots are pretty far away from the regression line. That makes sense, given our correlation data, which showed us that there was no statistically significant relationship between the two variables and the *r* was –.092. The closer the dots are to the regression line, generally speaking, the stronger the association between the variables. In our case, the data points are pretty widely scattered throughout the graph, indicating the weakness of the association. You can, however, visually see the slight negative relationship between the two.

Researchers often use what's called **multiple regression** (symbolized by *R*) to predict the value of a dependent variable from two or more independent variables. Multiple regression is used when you want to test curvilinear effects that can't be tested with linear correlation methods and when you want to test interaction effects—the effect of additional or extraneous variables on your dependent variables. Researchers often use **stepwise selection** (also called stepwise regression) to insert their independent variables into the equation. In stepwise regression, the statistics program subjects each independent variable to a significance test. In the first modeling step, the variable with the smallest *p* value is used first for the model. In the next step, the variable with the next smallest p is used, and so on, until there are no more variables with statistically significant probabilities.

To illustrate this, let's add two more variables to our sample data. Let's hypothesize that in addition to the number of children, we think number of doctor's visits and age of participant might be associated with health literacy. We've also added additional cases (participants) so we have a large enough sample size to compute this data. Using SPSS, we went to "Analyze," "Regression," and "Linear." Under "Method," we chose "Stepwise." The first thing we find is that "Age" and "Number of doctor's visits" are the only variables that were entered in the stepwise method; the other variable (number of children) was removed from the model.

Variables Entered/Removed(a)			
Model	**Variables Entered**	**Variables Removed**	**Method**
1	Age	.	Stepwise (Criteria: Probability-of-F-to-enter <= .050, Probability-of-F-to-remove >= .100).
2	No. Doctor's Visits	.	Stepwise (Criteria: Probability-of-F-to-enter <= .050, Probability-of-F-to-remove >= .100).
(a) Dependent Variable: HL			

We next see a fairly strong ($r = .988$) and statistically significant ($p = .00$) association between "Age," "Number of Doctor's Visits," and "Health Literacy." We also see that most of that association occurs with "Age," and very little of the additional association occurred with the addition of the "Number of Doctor's Visits" variable to the model.

Model Summary(c)								
Model	**R**	**R Square**	**Change Statistics**					**Durbin-Watson**
			R Square Change	F Change	df1	df2	Sig. F Change	
1	.987(a)	.973	.973	1755.429	1	48	.000	
2	.988(b)	.976	.002	4.632	1	47	.037	3.364
(a) Predictors: (Constant), Age								
(b) Predictors: (Constant), Age, No. Doctor's Visits								
(c) Dependent Variable: HL								

ANOVA(c)						
Model		**Sum of Squares**	**df**	**Mean Square**	**F**	**Sig.**
1	Regression	35.042	1	35.042	1755.429	.000(a)
	Residual	.958	48	.020		
2	Regression	35.128	2	17.564	946.439	.000(b)
	Residual	.872	47	.019		
	Total	36.000	49			

(a) Predictors: (Constant), Age

(b) Predictors: (Constant), Age, No. Doctor's Visits

(c) Dependent Variable: HL

We can see one final piece of information, and this may be the most interesting statistical finding yet. Partial correlation refers to the correlation with the dependent variable when the effects of the other variables are excluded. Note that the correlation between "Age" and "Health Literacy" is strong by itself, while the correlation between "Number of Doctor's Visits" and "Health Literacy" is not as strong by itself. This illustrates the interaction effects of the two variables working together.

Coefficients(a)						
Model		**t**	**Sig.**	**Correlations**		
				Zero-order	Partial	Part
1	(Constant)	−1.620	.112			
	Age	41.898	.000	.987	.987	.987
2	(Constant)	−.223	.824			
	Age	24.516	.000	.987	.963	.557
	No. Doctor's Visits	2.152	.037	.816	.300	.049

(a) Dependent Variable: HL

What Type of Data Do You Have?	Test for Relationships between Variables
Nominal	Cramer's V
Ordinal	Spearman's Rho
Interval/Ratio (Scale)	*Test for a statistically significant relationship between variables: 2 variables:* Pearson-Product Moment Correlation *3 or more variables:* Correlation Matrix *Predict outcomes:* Regression analysis

Specific Uses of Statistical Analysis ▼

Content Analysis

In this section, we're going to show you how scholars have used different statistical methods in quantitative research and how they report their findings. First, let's look at some Content Analysis examples. The process of generating content analysis data is a lengthy one. As we showed you in Chapter 12, once you reach an acceptable level of reliability among coders, you go through the previously selected sampling frame and code the content to be included in the analysis.

In order to make sense of all of this, content analysts tend to provide extremely detailed discussion of both their methods and their findings. In crafting their method sections, content analysts will typically begin with a discussion of the sampling frame that was employed in the study, including the rationale for why this particular sample was used. They will then go on to discuss the recording units in the study, sometimes referred to as the unitizing process; again, they will typically offer a rationale as to why particular units of analysis were selected for inclusion in the study. They will then offer definitions and rationale for including the particular context characteristics they associate with individual recording units.

Reporting the findings of the analysis is pretty straightforward. As in most quantitative endeavors, content analysts begin their reports by developing a series of hypotheses or research questions relevant to the subject matter under consideration. Often, a simple set of descriptive analyses reporting the frequency of the occurrence of certain content units serves to accomplish this goal. Other times, more sophisticated statistical analyses are necessary, particularly when looking at the ways in which different content characteristics distribute throughout each other, or *hang together*.

Gordon and Berhow (2009) used quantitative content analysis to examine websites of universities to determine which types of universities used more dialogic features and if dialogic features in websites were associated with factors such as student retention and alumni giving. You can see from the excerpt from their journal article that they reported descriptive statistics—means, standard deviations, and frequencies (percentages) in great detail.

The mean dialogic score found across all universities types was 24.3 (n = 232, s.d. = 7.3). Results ranged from a high of 53.2 to a low of 6.8. Several of the most frequently observed features were related to the "usefulness of information" principle: All websites studied included pictures of students/campus and contact information. The two least frequently observed features associated with this principle were streaming video (26%) and streaming audio (7%).

Associated with the "ease of interface" principle, 95 percent of websites featured a search option and links organized by audience. Ninety-four percent featured links to admission information on their homepage. Breadcrumbs, a system that allows user to track one's depth into the page, appeared in only 20 percent of websites.

Related to the principle "generation of return visits," 96 percent of websites observed had a calendar of events, and 70 percent gave users the option of requesting more information by e-mail or mail. The least frequently observed features were RSS feeds and podcasts.

Items related to the "dialogic loop" principle had the some of the lowest scores among the categories. The most frequently observed dialogic loop feature was opportunity for user response, observed on 38 percent of the websites. Links for contacting admissions and sign-ups for an appointment or tour were observed 31 percent and 30 percent of the time. The least frequently observed feature, opportunity for voting, appears in 4 percent of websites.

Institutional type (national versus liberal arts) was examined in relation to dialogic score. National universities had a mean dialogic index score of 23.1 (n = 124. s.d = 6.8); liberal arts universities had a mean dialogic index score of 25.7 (n = 108, s.d. = 7.6). A t-test revealed that the differences between the two mean dialogic index scores were statistically significant, $t(229)$ = 2.80, $p \leq .05$. However, the practical difference between 23.1 and 25.7 on a 100-point scale is not impressive.

However, liberal arts colleges featured links for contacting admissions counselors more than twice as often as national universities, 45 percent and 19 percent respectively. Liberal arts colleges also more frequently featured online chats (17%), links to "about" information pertaining to the school (89%), FAQs (49%), blogs (21%), and self-explanatory image maps (90%). National universities were observed as more frequently featuring lists of majors and minors (66%), lists of clubs and activities (90%), and portal technology (44%) than liberal arts colleges. National universities utilized site maps (82%) more often than liberal art colleges.

Tier 3 institutions had the highest mean dialogic index score of the four tiers (m = 26.03, s.d. = 6.79), followed by Tier 1 institutions (m = 25.07, s.d. = 7.92) and Tier 2 (m = 24.25, s.d. = .95). Tier 4 had the lowest mean dialogic index scores (m = 21.73, s.d. = 6.52). A post hoc Bonferroni's test revealed that a meaningful difference did exist between the Tier 3 and Tier 4 mean dialogic index scores (df = 4.31; $p \leq .01$)

The four principles composing the dialogic index score were examined by institution tier. Tier 3 institutions had the higher frequencies of dialogic features compared to Tier 1, 2, and 4 in all four principal categories. Tier 4 had the lowest frequencies of dialogic features in all four principle categories.

They then moved into more sophisticated statistical analysis to answer their research questions:

> *A post hoc Bonferroni's test revealed that a meaningful difference did exist between the Tier 3 and Tier 4 mean dialogic index scores (df = 4.31; p ≤ .01). . . . Pearson correlations were run between mean dialogic index score and each institutional variable (undergraduate enrollment, alumni giving, endowment, and retention rates). Some small correlations were found between two of the institutional variables, alumni giving (r = .180, p ≤ .05) and retention rate (r = .146, p ≤ .05). (Gordon & Berhow, 2009, p. 151)*

They evidently used an Analysis of Variance among the four tiers of institutions to see if there was a difference between the groups on the dialogic scores. When the ANOVA told them there was, they used a post-hoc test. We had recommended the Tukey test; they used the Bonferroni's test—an equally valid test. The post-hoc test found that the statistically significant difference found by the ANOVA was between Tiers 3 and 4. They then used the Pearson Product Moment Correlation to see if there was a relationship between the dialogic scores and undergraduate enrollment, alumni giving, endowment, and retention rates. They found that there was a statistically significant correlation between alumni giving and retention rate, and correctly noted that, based on the correlation coefficients, these were relatively small associations.

Survey Research

t-Test Example. Salmon, Park, and Wrigley (2003) conducted a survey research study among corporate spokespersons from 100 public companies to understand perceptions of risk and bias toward optimism about the possibility of bioterrorism among corporate spokespersons. They tested five hypotheses:

H_1: Corporate spokespersons will tend to estimate their own organization's risk to be less than that of other organizations similar to their own.

H_2: Optimistic bias will be greater for referents that are more distant (e.g., other corporations in the United States) than proximate (other corporations in the state).

H_3: Corporate spokespersons who perceive their own organizations as low in vulnerability tend to show high optimistic bias.

H_4: Corporate spokespersons who perceive high severity of bioterrorism tend to show high optimistic bias.

H_5: Corporate spokespersons who perceive that their own organizations can control external events tend to show high optimistic bias.

Their measurements of bioterrorism awareness, perceived vulnerability, perceived severity, perceived controllability used Likert-type scales, and Weinstein's measure of optimistic bias was a 0–10 scale.

They analyzed their data using a paired t-test and an independent samples t-test to test for differences between groups. Specifically, the groups they tested for their first hypothesis (H_1: Corporate spokespersons will tend to estimate

From "Optimistic Bias and Perceptions of Bioterrorism in Michigan Corporate Spokespersons, Fall 2001" by Charles Salmon, Hyun Soon Park, & Brenda Wrigley, *Journal of Health Communication, Vol. 8, No. 1.* Reprinted by permission of Taylor & Francis Group, www.informaworld.com. ∎

their own organization's risk to be less than that of other organizations similar to their own) were their organization versus another organization. The groups they tested for their second hypothesis (H_2: Optimistic bias will be greater for referents that are more distant (e.g., other corporations in the United States) than proximate (other corporations in the state) were distant organizations versus proximate organizations.

The groups they tested for their third hypothesis (H_3: Corporate spokespersons who perceive their own organizations as low in vulnerability tend to show high optimistic bias) were those who perceived their organizations as low in vulnerability versus those who perceived their organizations as high in vulnerability. The groups they tested for their fourth hypothesis (H_4: Corporate spokespersons who perceive high severity of bioterrorism tend to show high optimistic bias) were those who perceived low severity of bioterrorism versus those who perceived high severity of bioterrorism. Finally, the groups they tested for their fifth hypothesis (H_5: Corporate spokespersons who perceive that their own organizations can control external events tend to show high optimistic bias) were those who perceived their organizations can control external events versus those who perceived their organizations cannot control external events.

From "Optimistic Bias and Perceptions of Bioterrorism in Michigan Corporate Spokespersons, Fall 2001" by Charles Salmon, Hyun Soon Park & Brenda Wrigley, *Journal of Health Communication, Vol. 8, No. 1*, reprinted by permission of Taylor & Francis Group, www.informaworld.com. ■

Optimistic Bias about Bioterrorism

On a scale from 1 to 10, respondents estimated the likelihood of vulnerability to bioterrorism to be 1.61 (SD = 1.76) for their own company, 2.64 (SD = 2.21) at a company like their own in Michigan, and 3.76 (SD = 2.77) at a company like their own in the United States. To assess the presence of optimistic bias in comparative risk judgments, a one-sample t-test was conducted. The results were significant at the .001 level and Hypothesis 1 was supported (for own company vs. similar Michigan company, t(69) = −5.01, p < .001; for own company vs. similar company in U.S., t(68) = −7.31, p < .001).

Next, to assess whether distance affects optimistic bias, a comparison was made of the mean difference between optimistic bias of respondents' own company vs. a company like their own in Michigan vs. a company like theirs in the U.S. A paired samples t-test was conducted and Hypothesis 2 was supported at the .001 significance level [t(68) = 6.78, p < .001]. That is, distance is positively related to the magnitude of optimistic bias.

Perceived Vulnerability

Corporate spokespersons who perceive their organizations low in vulnerability (M = −1.40, SD = 1.93) tend to show higher optimistic bias than those who perceive high vulnerability (M = −.53, SD = 1.25) to bioterrorism [t(67) = −2.27, p < .05]. Corporate spokespersons who perceive their own organizations low in vulnerability (M = −2.64, SD = 2.77) tend to show higher optimistic bias than those who perceive high vulnerability (M = −1.53, SD = 1.83) to bioterrorism [t(66) = −2.00, p < .05]. Thus, Hypothesis 3 was supported.

In the example above, you see they tested Hypotheses 1 and 2 using a one-sample t-test for Hypothesis 1 and a paired t-test for Hypothesis 2. Can you explain why they used those particular statistical tests?

Regression Example. Here's another example of analysis of survey data: Botta and Dumlao (2002) wanted to see if there was a relationship between conflict and communication styles between fathers and daughters and eating disorders in the daughters. They had many hypotheses and research questions, all pertaining to that general topic (conversation orientation, conformity orientation, pluralistic, laissez-faire, and protective—all referring to family communication styles; compromising, collaborating, avoiding, accommodating, confronting, and avoiding—all referring to conflict styles):

H_1: Conversation orientation as encouraged by the father will be a significant negative predictor of anorexic and bulimic behaviors.

H_2: Conformity orientation as encouraged by the father will be a significant positive predictor of anorexic and bulimic behaviors.

H_3: Being raised by a pluralistic father will be a significant negative predictor of anorexic and bulimic behaviors.

H_4: Being raised by a protective father will be a significant positive predictor of anorexic behaviors.

H_5: Compromising as a way to respond to conflict will be a significant negative predictor of anorexic behaviors and a significant negative predictor of bulimic behaviors.

H_6: Collaborating as a way to respond to conflict will be a significant negative predictor of anorexic behaviors and a significant negative predictor of bulimic behaviors.

H_7: Avoiding as a way to respond to conflict will be a significant positive predictor of anorexic behaviors.

H_8: Accommodating as a way to respond to conflict will be a significant positive predictor of anorexic behaviors.

H_9: Confronting as a means of responding to conflict will be a significant positive predictor of bulimic behaviors.

H_{10}: Avoiding as a means of responding to conflict will be a significant negative predictor of bulimic behaviors.

RQ_1: Is being raised by a protective father, a laissez-faire father, or a consensual father a significant predictor of bulimic behaviors?

RQ_2: To what extent do family communication styles as encouraged by the father moderate the influence of a strong drive to be thin on anorexic and bulimic behaviors?

RQ_3: To what extent do conflict resolution styles between father and daughter moderate the influence of a strong drive to be thin on anorexic behaviors and on bulimic behaviors?

From "How do Conflict and Communication Patterns between Fathers and Daughters Contribute to or Offset Eating Disorders" by Renee Botta & Rebecca Dumlao, *Health Communication, Vol. 14, No. 2,* January 4, 2002. Reprinted by permission of Taylor & Francis Group, www.informaworld.com. ■

To measure family communication patterns, conflict styles, and eating disorders, Botta and Dumlao (2002) used Likert scales. To analyze the data, they used a regression analysis because they had interval data (Likert scales) and they wanted to predict outcomes—to see if the independent variables (communication and conflict patterns) could predict (have a predictive relationship with) the dependent variable (eating disorders).

The hypotheses and research questions were tested using hierarchical regression with anorexic and bulimic behaviors as the two criterion variables and the two FCP dimensions, the four conflict resolution styles, a drive to be thin, and the interactions as predictor variables.

H1 was supported for anorexic behaviors, but not for bulimic behaviors. Conversation orientation was a significant negative predictor of anorexic behaviors ($\beta= -.137$, $p = .046$) predicting 2 percent of variance, $F(3,206) = 1.05$, $p = .046$. Young women who do not appear to have a base of experience for talking things through with their fathers are more likely to engage in anorexic behaviors. Conversation orientation was not a significant predictor of bulimic behaviors ($\beta = -.073$, $p = .289$).

H2 was not supported for anorexic behaviors or for bulimic behaviors. Conformity orientation was not a significant predictor of anorexic behaviors ($\beta = .066$, $p = .374$). Conformity orientation was not a significant predictor of bulimic behaviors ($\beta = .052$, $p = .482$).

H3 was supported for anorexia. Young women from pluralistic families ($M = 1.85$, $SD = .64$) are less likely to be symptomatic of anorexia than those from other family types ($M = 2.08$, $SD = .76$), $t = -2.11$, $p = .036$. Fathers who encourage open communication while not encouraging conformity seem to provide a family environment that limits the development of anorexia. H3 was not supported for bulimia. Young women from a pluralistic family ($M = 1.91$, $SD = .60$) are no less likely to be symptomatic of bulimia than those from other family types ($M = 2.05$, $SD = .72$), $t = -1.36$, $p = .176$.

H4 was not supported. Protectives ($M = 2.05$, $SD = .71$) are no more likely to be symptomatic of anorexia than those whose fathers encourage other styles of family communication ($M = 1.99$, $SD = .73$), $t = 0.66$, $p = .511$). Fathers who do not encourage open communication while encouraging conformity do not seem to produce daughters who are more likely to engage in anorexic behaviors.

Results for RQ1 reveal young women with a laissez-faire father ($M = 2.07$, $SD = .82$) are no more likely to be symptomatic of bulimia than those of other fathers ($M = 1.99$, $SD = .65$), $t = 0.24$, $p = .813$. Young women with a protective father ($M = 2.05$, $SD = .73$) are no more likely to be symptomatic of bulimia than those with other fathers ($M = 1.99$, $SD = .65$), $t = 0.64$, $p = .521$. Young women with a consensual father

The excerpt above shows the results from their regression analysis. They used hierarchical regression, which is a method in which the researcher adds variables in a specified sequence, based on hypotheses or prior knowledge. You may notice they report their findings in terms of *beta weights*, indicated β, which represent standardized regression coefficients (Reinard, 2006).

Experiments

Chi Square Example. When we're discussing experiments, in thinking about our analyses, we must first think about the distinction between our independent and dependent variables. In the case of experimental designs, we are almost always looking to see if scores on some dependent variable change from group to group. Frequently, we will want to compare the mean of our dependent variable across these groups. Boster et al. (2009) conducted a field experiment to test a compliance gaining technique called *dump-and-chase* (DAC), which uses strategic persistence as a tactic. They tested the technique against other possible techniques. Their journal article reports on two different experiments conducted; we'll take a look at the first one. They randomly selected sixty pedestrians and approached them with a request using one of three compliance strategies: the test strategy, DAC; another compliance gaining strategy, called *door in the face* (DITF); and a placebo strategy (PI). which, like the two test conditions, also makes a request but gives an irrelevant reason for the request. Interestingly, they don't actually state a hypothesis or RQ, but a study objective: "The primary goal of this study is to test its effectiveness as a compliance-gaining technique relative to other techniques of known effectiveness" (p. 222).

Their independent variables are the compliance gaining techniques, nominal variables. Data on gender was also collected as additional independent variables. Their dependent variables are the participants' compliance with the request. The example below shows the results of their statistical tests, the Chi Square test of independence in which they tested to see if the three groups differed in terms of compliance. They found that, in fact, the DAC group had statistically significantly higher compliance than the other two groups.

Compliance rates for the target request are presented in Table 2. Overall, the three compliance rates differed from one another, χ^2 (2, $N = 60$) = 6.72, $p < 0.05$. A focused comparison indicated that the DAC technique resulted in a substantially higher compliance rate than did the DITF technique, χ^2 (1, $N = 40$) = 6.67, $p < 0.05$, $r = 0.41$, $OR = 6.00$. Additional focused comparisons showed that both the DAC and PI conditions, χ^2 (1, $N = 40$) = 0.90, *ns*, $r = 0.15$, $OR = 1.83$, and the

Used with permission of Taylor & Francis Group, from "Dump-and-Chase: The Effectiveness of Persistence as a Sequential Request Compliance Gaining Strategy" by F.J. Booster et al, *Communication Studies, Vol. 60, No. 3, 2009;* permission conveyed through Copyright Clearance Center, Inc. ■

Table 2 Target Compliance Rate: Experiment 1

Compliance	Condition		
	DAC (%)	**DITF (%)**	**PI (%)**
Complied	12 (60)	4 (20)	9 (45)
Did Not Comply	8 (40)	16 (80)	11 (55)

Analysis of Variance Example. In research looking at the effects of whether a person considers specific or abstract content and persons (when he thinks of violent video games) on his perceptions of the games, Ivory and Kalyanaraman (2009) set up a 2 × 3 factorial design between-subjects experiment. They tested two levels of content abstraction ("the most violent game with which you are familiar," and "games in general") and three levels of person abstraction ("other students in the United States," "other students on this campus," or "the person currently sitting nearest me") among 122 undergraduate students. They had three hypotheses, predicting that:

H₁: Perceptions of the effect of violent video games on aggression will differ by who they think is being effected—highest for people in the general U.S. population, next highest for other students at their campus, and lowest for specific persons in their class.

H₂ₐ: Perceptions of the effect of violent video games on aggression will differ by type of game—highest for a specific game and lowest for violent games in general.

Or, the inverse of H2a:

H₂ᵦ: Perceptions of the effect of violent video games on aggression will differ by type of game—highest for violent games in general and lowest for a specific game.

Perceptions were measured using several nine-point Likert scales.

To test their first hypothesis, that perceptions on violent video games' effects on aggression to be highest for the general U.S. population, lower for other students on their campus, and lowest for individually selected, specific persons, they used a between-subjects ANOVA because they were testing differences between three or more groups. Their independent variable was "subject abstraction," which had three levels—"general U.S. population" was Level 1, "other students" was Level 2, and "individual specific students" was level 3. Their dependent variable was "content abstraction," which had two levels of abstraction—"the most violent game with which you are familiar" was Level 1, and "games in general" was Level 2. Their ANOVA results indicated a p value of <.001, thus they reported a statistically significant difference between the three groups. Their reported statistics were: $F(2,116) = 8.54$, $p < .002$, $\eta^2_p = .128$. Remember that their hypothesis said that the perceived aggression would be highest for the group of "people in the general U.S. population," and it was ($M = 4.50$, $SD = 1.81$). They said it would be next highest for other students at their campus, and it was ($M = 3.43$, $SD = 1.85$). They predicted it would be lowest for specific persons in their class, and it was ($M = 2.93$, $SD = 1.72$). Thus, they rejected the null hypothesis (that there was no difference) and accepted their test hypothesis, H1.

By the way, the F statistic they're reporting from their ANOVA is a statistic that refers to a probability distribution. SPSS reports this statistic and automatically finds the critical value of F that determines statistical significance. In their reporting of the findings ($F(2, 116) = 8.54$, $p<.001$), the 2 refers to the degrees of freedom between groups, and the 116 refers to the degrees of freedom in total. The 8.54 is the between-groups F statistic. Of course, the p-value is the probability of accepting the null hypothesis. Since you're not computing these by hand, you won't be using these numbers directly in the F formula, but you do report them as SPSS gives them to you. Their next information ($\eta^2 = .128$), is somewhat similar to a correlation coefficient, and refers to the effect size of each individual independent variable and a measure called *eta squared*. Their statistic means that 12.8 percent of the variance is contributed by each variable that contributes a significant difference (Reinard, 2006).

Recall that they set up a 2 × 3 factorial design, so they will be comparing six groups. To analyze this, they would have used a two-way ANOVA. Notice that, rather than reporting one F test, there are two different F tests reported. They report the *main effect* (the effect of one independent variable by itself) for content abstraction and report the direction of the difference ("specific game" condition has lower effects and "games in general" condition has higher effects). They also report interaction effects, or the effect of the two independent variables (content abstraction and person abstraction) interacting with each other (which they report was not statistically significant). In short, they found differences among those who considered different content abstractions, but found that consideration of person abstraction plus content abstraction did not make a difference over content abstraction alone. Note that they also found a statistically significant main effect for person abstraction, and their interaction analysis found that consideration of content abstraction plus person abstraction did not make a difference over person abstraction alone.

Writing Quantitative Findings ▼

General Information about Quantitative Writing

The preceding examples may make you think that writing up your research findings is a confusing process, but actually, writing quantitative research papers is pretty straightforward. Let's answer the first questions students always ask about papers: How long should it be? Typically, quantitative research reports are about twenty to twenty-five pages long, not counting title page, abstract page, references, or tables or figures.

The second question students might ask is: How do I write it? Your writing style will be relatively formal, much more formal than our writing in this textbook. You don't necessarily have to use the *one says* language (which admittedly is very hard to read and comprehend), but you do need to use formal English and proper grammar. It depends on the journal to which you're submitting the paper, but you might use the term "this research shows," or, alternately, "these researchers found," or "we found." Some journal editors cringe at giving *research* human characteristics (by being able to show us something), but others think that "we found" is too informal. Whichever level of formality you use, keep it consistent throughout your paper. Of course, as with any other paper you write, journals (and professors) expect your language to be free of any language that would be considered sexist or discriminatory in any way. Therefore, if you're referring to men and women, use the plural form or say "he or she" (or "she or he").

In quantitative research, you write with certainty. Remember, quantitative researchers are measuring objective reality, and if your study has been properly and appropriately conducted, you can write with the certainty of that objective reality. In quantitative reports, you might read phrases such as "the hypothesis was not supported," or "variable A is positively related to variable B," or "the preferred method is overwhelmingly. . . ." Unlike qualitative research reports (see our next section of the textbook), quantitative researchers are unlikely to use phrases such as "seems to," "indicates that," or "tends toward." Quantitative researchers are much more positive than that in reporting their objective reality.

Elements of Paper

Introduction and Literature Review.   You'll start your paper with an Introduction. Usually, your Introduction will begin by telling us about the problem to be solved, the question to be answered, or at least the general topic you're looking at. In the Introduction, you might tell us your RQ or hypothesis, or at least begin to build the argument for that. You'll explain why you chose to study this topic (this is more a discussion of the research building to this topic rather than your personal interest). You also want to answer the "so what" question by giving us data that convinces us of the relevance and significance of the topic. This is probably the most important part of your Introduction.

You might have a separate Literature Review, if you are building the case for your research on a good body of previous research or theory. If you are writing a shorter paper, or if there is very little prior research to report, your Literature Review might be part of your Introduction.

We discussed both of these sections of the paper in detail in Chapter 4, so we'll refer you to that chapter for more information.

RQs or H.   Your Introduction should flow right into your RQ or H section. If you properly built your argument from the beginning of your paper, you have stated in the Introduction: "This is the general topic area of my research"; in the Literature Review: "This is what's known about my research topic, and these are the theories and concepts on which I am building my project"; in the RQ/H section then: "Therefore, this is why I want to ask this question or test this hypothesis."

Sometimes, your H or RQ section is actually part of your Literature Review, if they are tightly based on the argument you are building in that section. In the example below, Salmon, Park, and Wrigley (2003) did just that in their paper on optimistic bias and corporate reactions to bioterrorism.

From "Optimistic Bias and Perceptions of Bioterrorism in Michigan Corporate Spokespersons, Fall 2001" by Charles Salmon, Hyun Soon Park & Brenda Wrigley, *Journal of Health Communication, Vol. 8, No. 1,* reprinted by permission of Taylor & Francis Group, www.informaworld.com. ■

Harris & Middleton, 1994; Klar, Medding, & Sarel, 1996; Perloff, 1987; Weinstein & Klein, 1996; Whaley, 2000). Optimistic bias has been reported repeatedly to be greatest when subjects compared themselves to general others such as typical or average group members of the same age and gender (Taylor & Lobel, 1989; Weinstein & Klein, 1996; Wood, Taylor, & Lichtman, 1985).

However, more specific targets of comparison are proposed to have a different influence on optimistic bias. When participants are asked to compare their potential vulnerability with that of others, the illusion of invulnerability tends to be greater when people compare themselves with a close friend or an average college student than with their closest friend or family members (Chapin, 2000; Harris & Middleton, 1994; Klar et al., 1996; Perloff, 1987; Perloff & Fetzer, 1986). Therefore, as psychological distance increases (e.g., my closest friend, students in my class, students in my college, other students in the U.S., etc.), the degree of optimistic bias also tends to increase (Chapin, 2000). Perloff (1993) ascribed differential levels of optimistic bias to the difference in distance that may also reflect the heterogeneity and size of the audience or group (Perloff, 1993).

Based on the above discussion, the following research questions and hypotheses are proposed:

H_1: Corporate spokespersons will tend to estimate their own organization's risk to be less than that of other organizations similar to their own.

H_2: Optimistic bias will be greater for referents that are more distant (e.g., other corporations in the U.S.) than proximate (other corporations in the state).

Perceived Vulnerability, Susceptibility, and Controllability

According to prior research, optimistic bias is reportedly less a function of demographics such as age, gender, race, or education than of such psychological

Method. Your next section is where you describe—and justify—what you did and how you did it. When readers critique your research, it is the Methods section that will make or break their judgment. In this section, you will first tell us the population you are attempting to represent and how your sampling design ensured this representation. Explain your sampling design in detail—who you talked to and why they were selected; how you selected your sample; your sample size and justification for that size; when you collected your data and what data collection method you used; where you collected your data and how might that have affected validity and reliability; who specifically did the data collection, and how they were trained; and how reliability was insured. The participants should be described in enough detail that the reader can visualize them. If there was attrition, tell us the number of subjects who dropped out, the reasons for the attrition, and information about the dropouts, if available.

See below for a great example of a Method section from the Botta and Dumlao (2002) research.

From "How do Conflict and Communication Patterns between Fathers and Daughters Contribute to or Offset Eating Disorders" by Renee Botta & Rebecca Dumlao, *Health Communication, Vol. 14, No. 2,* January 4, 2002. Reprinted by permission of Taylor & Francis Group, www.informaworld.com. ■

METHOD

Participants

After signing the required consent forms, 357 students from a university in the midwest and a university in the southeast completed questionnaires with established instruments to tap FCPs, conflict styles, and eating disordered behaviors along with other items that were part of another study. Because 90% of those with eating disorders are women (APA, 1994), men were excluded from analysis, reducing the sample to 220.

The sample was further reduced to the 210 participants who were younger than 24 years of age (90.5% of whom were 18–21 years of age) to reduce error due to forgetting what communication within the family was like when the participants lived at home.

Control Variables

Ethnicity was entered as a control variable due to differences in the rate of eating disorders among ethnic groups (e.g., Neff, Sargent, McKeown, Jackson, & Valois, 1997). Self-reported ethnicity resulted in 85.7% European American, 7.6% African or Caribbean American, 3.3% Latin American, 1.9% Asian American, 1.0% Native American, and 0.5% for whom their ethnicity was not indicated.

Family Communication

Ritchie's (1991) Revised Family Communication Patterns (RFCP) Instrument uses 16 items, each with a 5-point Likert scale ranging from 1 (strongly disagree) to 5

You'll also need to define your variables—all of them—all the ones you included in your RQ or H. In your Introduction and Literature Review sections, you should have given us the conceptual definition of your variables and might have also shown us how other researchers have operationalized the same variables. Now it's time to tell us how, in your specific study, you operationalized your variables. Make sure all variables are clearly defined. Spell out for us which are independent and which are dependent.

Be specific about how you measured your variables—describe the scales or questions in detail so we could replicate them if we wished. If a published instrument was used, tell us the reliability and validity prior researchers (or scale developers) found with it, describe the scale in detail, and cite the appropriate reference(s). If an unpublished instrument was used, describe the traits that it was designed to measure, its format, and the possible range of scores. The whole instrument should also be reproduced in the Appendix of your paper. In addition to describing your measurement scales or instruments, all other details about your method—experimental procedures and other relevant information about how you conducted the study—should be described in sufficient detail so that the study can be replicated. The example below shows us how a relatively complex experimental design was explained in Boster and colleagues' 2009 study of compliance gaining strategies.

Used with permission of Taylor & Francis Group, from "Dump-and-Chase: The Effectiveness of Persistence as a Sequential Request Compliance Gaining Strategy" by F.J. Booster et al, *Communication Studies, Vol. 60, No. 3, 2009;* permission conveyed through Copyright Clearance Center, Inc. ∎

Procedure

The 20 observations made in each message condition were divided equally across the four different locations (on a university campus, outside of a shopping mall, on the sidewalk of a suburban commercial district, and on the sidewalk of an urban business district). Furthermore, the 20 observations per condition were divided equally across three time periods (10:00am–1:00pm, 1:00pm–4:00pm, and 4:00pm–7:00pm). After selecting a location and time, the experimenter (E) followed the described sampling plan and selected an S. The E, observing unobtrusively, telephoned the identity of the S and compliance-gaining message condition to the C who was waiting out of sight and ready to approach the S. The C then approached the S, making eye contact, gesturing with the wave of a hand, and saying, *"Excuse me."* The C then delivered the assigned compliance-gaining condition. If the S complied with the request, the C entered the building, returned in 10 minutes and retrieved the bicycle before riding away to prepare for the next S. If the S did not comply with the C's request, the C rode away and prepared for the next S. In all cases, the S was debriefed and consent was obtained using an IRB-approved procedure.

Instrumentation

After the request, the E recorded the sex of the S and whether or not the S complied with the C's request. The C kept mental record of how many chases were used in the DAC condition and if the concession was presented in the DITF condition. The C reported these results to the E when preparing for the next S.

Results. Which brings us to the *meat* of your paper—the Results section. This is the statistics-heavy section. You might begin by telling us how you analyzed your variables. Remember, you're justifying this based on your RQs or Hs and the type of data you are working with, so make that clear in this section. Organize the Results section around the research hypotheses (or purposes or questions) stated in the RQ/H section; describe the analysis and results for the first hypothesis, then describe them for the second hypothesis, and so on. Say something such as, "for RQ_1, I analyzed the data using. . . ." Tell us what statistics you used and any other details we need to decide whether to agree with your findings. Standard statistical procedures need only be named; you do not need to show the formulas. Point by point, tell us what you found. You might say, "for H_1, I found these statistical results which supported (or did not support) the null hypothesis." Give us your percentages and numbers, results of your statistical tests, and a brief interpretation of those results. Raw scores are usually not reported; only the statistics based on them are reported. Present descriptive statistics first, usually starting with measures of central tendency and variability (or, for categorical data, starting with frequencies and percentages). See below for an example of the Results section in the Botta and Dumlao (2002) study on fathers' communication and eating disorders.

From "How do Conflict and Communication Patterns between Fathers and Daughters Contribute to or Offset Eating Disorders" by Renee Botta & Rebecca Dumlao, *Health Communication, Vol. 14, No. 2*, January 4, 2002. Reprinted by permission of Taylor & Francis Group, www.informaworld.com. ■

The hypotheses and research questions were tested using hierarchical regression with anorexic and bulimic behaviors as the two criterion variables and the two FCP dimensions, the four conflict resolution styles, a drive to be thin, and the interactions as predictor variables.

H1 was supported for anorexic behaviors, but not for bulimic behaviors. Conversation orientation was a significant negative predictor of anorexic behaviors ($\beta = -.137$, $p = .046$) predicting 2% of variance, $F(3,206) = 1.05$, $p = .046$. Young women who do not appear to have a base of experience for talking things through with their fathers are more likely to engage in anorexic behaviors. Conversation orientation was not a significant predictor of bulimic behaviors ($\beta = -.073$, $p = .289$).

Watch your language as you present your results. You do not *prove* a hypothesis; your data or findings *support* or *do not support* your hypothesis (Reinard, 2006). Organize large amounts of data in tables and give each table a number and descriptive title (i.e., caption). In the text, describe the main conclusions to be reached based on each table and point out highlights that the reader may otherwise overlook. You do not need to discuss each entry in a table. Statistical figures (i.e., drawings such as histograms) should be professionally drawn and used sparingly in journal articles. Statistical symbols should be italicized. Use the proper case for each statistical symbol. Numerals that start sentences and that are less than 10 should usually be spelled out.

Discussion.   After you give us the results of your statistical testing and analysis, you then discuss them. This section is where you get to show off your analytical prowess and good mind for interpretation. In this section, discuss the highlights of the results. If there is room, give us either a brief summary of the study or a longer summary of what you did. Restate your hypotheses and tell us if they were supported by the data.

Take us back to the Introduction and Literature Review and remind us (yourself included) why you conducted this study in the first place. There was a reason you wanted to find something out. Now that you know whatever it is you found out, what does it *mean*? What does it mean for you? For society? For practice or policy? For the larger body of knowledge? What are the implications of the results? It is appropriate here to speculate of their meaning. Where is your data consistent and inconsistent with the literature you cited earlier? What does that mean?

Below is a good example of a Discussion section from the Salmon, Park, and Wrigley (2003) study of optimism bias and bioterrorism. Note how they tied the results to the events going on at the time and discussed how the timing of the study likely affected the results.

From "Optimistic Bias and Perceptions of Bioterrorism in Michigan Corporate Spokespersons, Fall 2001" by Charles Salmon, Hyun Soon Park & Brenda Wrigley, *Journal of Health Communication, Vol. 8, No. 1*, reprinted by permission of Taylor & Francis Group, www.informaworld.com. ■

Discussion

This is the only known study to document levels of awareness of the threat of bioterrorism in U.S. corporate spokespersons at the time of the September and October 2001 terrorism attacks. The findings indicate that levels of awareness of bioterrorism at that time were extremely low. The vast majority of corporate respondents were unaware of prior biological attacks in the United States, as well as differences between chemical and biological weapons, a distinction that has profound implications in terms of crisis response: biological organisms mutate and are potentially contagious, making them potentially far more hazardous to corporate security personnel. The finding that half of the respondents were still not aware of a bioterrorism event in the U.S. by Phase 2 of the data collection should, in fairness, be considered in the context that, at the time, the deaths attributed to anthrax were not definitively linked to terrorism.

As should be expected, corporate spokspersons admitted that they were largely unprepared for such a threat. Few had crisis management plans in place to deal specifically with the threat of terrorism. Most showed a strong preference to turn to state and local, rather than federal, authorities for information, and a preference for the telephone.

Often, researchers include study limitations (and perhaps strengths) in this section. We stated earlier that every method had its strengths and weaknesses. You made trade-offs when making each of your decisions. Now is the time to discuss those trade-offs and their implications to the research. Tell us: If you knew then what you know now, if you had to do it over again, what you would do differently. Perhaps you might want to suggest the next step in future research in this area; what specifically would you suggest. This section also acts as your concluding section, and every good Communication scholar knows that we use our Conclusion to remind our audience what you've just told them. Please note that it is inappropriate to introduce new data, new information, new results, or new references to literature in the Discussion and Conclusion section (Pyrczak & Bruce, 1992).

Evaluating and Critiquing Quantitative Research ▼

When you are reading a journal article, proofreading your own research paper, or perhaps helping a fellow student by critiquing his or her research, what should you be looking for? What are the criteria for evaluating good quantitative research?

Not surprisingly, how you evaluate and critique a research study depends on the type of research it is. For all research, however, there are some general items you want to examine.

First, you want to take a look at the validity and reliability threats we discussed throughout this textbook and compare the design of the research against those threats. For example, was the sampling procedure subject to selection bias? Was the observation subject to the Hawthorne Effect? Does the sample adequately represent the population?

You want to take a look at the sample size and determine if the study has sufficient statistical power to address the Hs and RQs. What's the quality of the instruments used? Did the researcher report validity and reliability statistics or have a good rationale for using these measurements?

Overall, you want to answer the following questions in a critique of quantitative research:

    a. What was the reason for conducting this study?

    b. What did the researcher intend to accomplish?

    c. How were the participants selected and assigned? Which, if any, were lost and how did this affect validity and reliability?

    d. Were the measurement instruments valid and reliable?

    e. What was the study procedure? What did participants do? How were they measured? With what and by whom? Were testing conditions uniform? Were factors other than the independent variable operating?

    f. How were the data analyzed? Was the analysis appropriate and accurate?

    g. What were the major conclusions? Were they justified? Can the results be generalized? (Girden, 2001, p. 8)

When critiquing survey research, the two most important things you should look at are the validity and reliability of the questionnaire and measurements used, and the sample design. Because a survey especially is a methodology intended to generalize to a population, this last criteria is especially important. Here's a composite list of what Girden (2001) calls "caution factors when evaluating research" (p. 67):

Sampling Factors:

    1. The sample frame

    2. The criterion of exclusion

    3. The response return rate (is it less than 70%)?

    4. If the sample size is appropriately large for desired statistical power

    5. The method used to contact nonresponders

    6. The likelihood that characteristics of nonresponders introduced bias

Procedural Factors:

    7. If participants were randomly assigned to groups or otherwise ensured group equivalence

    8. If testing or observation was conducted throughout representative days, times, locations, etc.

Measurement Factors:

    9. The nature of the questionnaire or measurement instrument (is it relevant to the purpose of the study?)

    10. The reliability and validity of the questionnaire or measurement instrument

Data Collection Factors:

    11. The number and characteristics of interviewers, observers, or data collectors

12. The training and supervision of interviewers

13. If interviewers or data gatherers do not affect participant performance; if appropriate, if test administrator was naïve with respect to study purpose

14. The uniformity of the interview setting or testing conditions

Analytical Factors:

15. If the analysis appropriately controls for extraneous variables

16. If appropriate statistical procedures were computed, appropriate to the variables and RQs or Hs

17. If statistical analysis was appropriately accurately performed and interpreted

(pp. 67, 96, 100, 219, 240)

We would like to add one additional area for evaluation criteria: ethics. It's important to determine if the study followed acceptable ethical procedures. Was the study conducted under the supervision of an institutional IRB? Were appropriate informed consent procedures followed? Were vulnerable populations properly protected?

So What?

In this chapter, we've pulled the book thus far together for you. We've shown you what to do with your data once it's collected, how to write it up once it's analyzed, and how to evaluate it once it's been written. We've shown you how researchers in the positivist paradigm—those who believe life can be measured and who want to do so—conduct research. We've shown you how quantitative researchers incorporate their ontology, epistemology, and axiology into research practice and how this carries through in the questions they ask, hypotheses they test, methods they design, data they collect, and statistics they use to analyze the results. It also carries into how they write their results and make their claims. In our next section, we'll show you how the other half lives—how qualitative researchers see their own research world.

Glossary

Central tendency
Also called summary statistics. It is a measure that represents the "typical" number in an array (distribution) of data. Depending on the type of data you are working with, this can be the mode, median, or mean.

Confidence level
Refers to the probability that I'm "close to correct" when I infer population characteristics based on my sample. How close I am to correct is the margin of error.

Correlation
The statistical test designed to test for linear relationships between variables when you have interval or ratio variable. When one variable occurs, the other variable tends to be present as well.

Correlation coefficient
Indicated by the Greek letter r (pronounced "rho"). It is a number that represents the extent that variables are related or go together and the magnitude of their

relationships. Correlation cannot identify causation. Just because two variables are related or vary together, we cannot determine whether one causes the other. Range from +1.0 to –1.0. +1.0 indicates a positive relationship. –1.0 indicates a negative relationship. 0 indicates no relationship between the variables in question.

Inferential statistics

The type of statistic used when gathering information about a population based of the sample. The type of statistics used with significance testing.

Leptokurtic distribution

A distribution of scores that has stronger consistency around the mean than in a normal distribution. This type of distribution has a high peak, representative of the fact that there are a large number of scores in the center of the distribution. Leptokurtic graphs also have a small range, showing that there is a relatively small difference or variance between scores.

Mean

A measure of central tendency; the arithmetic average, computed adding the scores together and dividing by the total number of score.

Measures of dispersion

Measures that represent the distribution of scores in a data array. Dispersion can be thought of as statistics that represent differences in our data, whether it's the overall distance between the high and low scores (range), an average of how far the scores are from our mean (variance), or the standard deviation or square root of that variance.

Median

A measure of central tendency that represents the exact center point of our data set when it's put in numerical order. Median is the appropriate measure of central tendency for ordinal data. For example, a data set consisting of scores of 1, 3, 5, 9, 17 would have a median of 5, since it is the center point of our array. Median can help control for outliers in our data sets as in the above example. Even though 17 is an extreme value, 5 is still our median. If there is an even number of participants the two middle numbers will be "tied" and will be averaged together to get the median. The median is also sometimes used for higher levels of data than ordinal because it controls for outliers.

Mesokurtic distribution

Having a normal bell shaped curve; a normal distribution of scores. This type of distribution has a moderate peak, representative of a normal number of scores in the middle of the distribution. A mesokurtic distribution also has a normal range with gradually sloping curves. When a mesokurtic distribution is perfectly centered, and not skewed in either direction, it is said to be *normal*.

Mode

The appropriate measure of central tendency for nominal data. The mode refers to the most frequently occurring value in our distribution. For example, a sample of communication studies students at UNC Charlotte might reveal that there are more female students than male students. Since the value "female" occurs more often in our data set, this value would be the mode.

Multiple regression

Represented by the symbol R, this predicts the dependent variable's value from two or more independent variables. Used when testing curvilinear effects that can't be tested with linear correlation methods, and for testing the effects of extraneous variables.

Negative correlation

Occurs when one variable increases, while the other variable decreases, thus, indicating two variables that vary in opposite directions.

Negatively skewed

More scores are on the right side of the graph—or higher than the mean.

Platykurtic distribution

Indicates a flat distribution of scores (farther away from the mean than in a normal distribution). This type of distribution has a low peak, representing the fact that a relatively small number of scores are in the middle of the distribution. Platykurtic graphs also have a wide range, which represents a large amount of variance in scores.

Population parameters

Population characteristics based on the sample characteristics.

Positive correlation

Occurs when both variables vary in the same direction.

Positively skewed

More scores tend toward the left side of the graph, or lower than the mean.

Range

A measure of dispersion that refers to the difference between the highest and lowest values in a data set. Calculated by subtracting the lowest score from the highest score. A data set with values between 1 and 29 would have a range of 28.

Regression

For interval or ratio, data, the procedure that looks at the pattern in a data distribution to make predictions about future patterns. This procedure finds the "line" that best fits your data distribution. This is also known as prediction. It is another way to look at relationships between interval or ratio variables. The term refers to a *line of best fit* and is based on an algebraic equation (regression equation) that takes into account the regression line, the slope (the angle of the line), and intercept (the point at which the line intersects the y-axis).

Significance testing

Testing to determine the probability of there being a "true" difference between scores of a data set. Involves testing a null hypothesis in order to prove it, and therefore disprove the difference.

Skewness

Either positive (lower than mean) or negative (higher than mean), is the uneven, sloping, or unsymmetrical graph of scores. Refers to the condition that occurs when more scores tend to be higher than the mean (negative skewness), or lower than the mean (positive skewness).

Standard deviation

One of the most commonly reported summary statistics for interval and ratio data is the square root of the variance. A measure of dispersion that represents the typical amount an entry deviates from the mean. Mathematically, it's the variance (the square of the average distance of scores from the mean) translated back into the original unit of measure by calculating the square root.

Statistical significance

The probability of there being a "true" difference between scores of a data set, as opposed to a perceived difference that may occur, but might in reality be simple "overlapping" of margins of error.

Stepwise selection

A method of inserting independent variables into an equation for multiple regression. Each independent variable is subjected to a significance test, starting with the smallest p value, and then proceeding to the next smallest and so on, until there are no more variables with statistically significant probabilities. Also called stepwise regression.

Variability

Contrasted with central tendency, variability refers to the differences in our data, how wide the range is, and how far a given value might be from the measure of central tendency. Variability is another word for dispersion.

Variance

A specific measure of dispersion that represents the average of how far our data is from our mean. Mathematically it is calculated by squaring the average distance of scores from the mean. It could also be referred to as the average of the sum of the squares, because it's computed by squaring the deviation scores.

References

Babbie, E., Halley, F., & Zaino, J. (2003). *Adventures in social research: Data analysis using SPSS 11.0/11.5 for Windows*, 5th edition. Thousand Oaks, CA: Pine Forge Press.

Babbie, E., Halley, F., & Zaino, J. (2007). *Adventures in social research: Data analysis using SPSS 14.0 and 15.0 for Windows*, 6th edition. Thousand Oaks, CA: Pine Forge Press.

Boster, F. J., Shaw, A. S., Hughes, M., Kotowski, M. R., Strom, R. E., & Deatrick, L. M. (2009). Dump-and-Chase: The effectiveness of persistence as a sequential request compliance gaining strategy. *Communication Studies, 60*(3), 219–234.

Botta, R. A., & Dumlao, R. (2002). How do conflict and communication patterns between fathers and daughters contribute to or offset eating disorders? *Health Communication, 14*(2), 199–219.

Girden, E. R. (2001). *Evaluating research articles: From start to finish*. Thousand Oaks, CA: Sage.

Gordon, J., & Berhow, S. (2009). University websites and dialogic features for building relationships with potential students. *Public Relations Review, 35*(2), 150–152.

Gravetter, F. J., & Wallnau, L. B. (1986). *Statistics for the behavioral sciences: A first course for students of psychology and education*. St. Paul, MN: West Publishing.

Ivory, J. D., & Kalyanaraman, S. (2009). Video games make people violent—Well, maybe not that game: Effects of content and person abstraction on perceptions of violent video games' effects and support of censorship. *Communication Reports, 22*(1), 1–12.

Pyrczak, F., & Bruce, R. R. (1992). *Writing empirical research reports: A basic guide for students of the social and behavioral science*. Los Angeles: Pyrczak.

Reinard, J. C. (2006). *Communication research statistics*. Thousand Oaks, CA: Sage.

Rodgers, J. L., & Nicewander, W. H. (1988). Thirteen ways to look at the correlation coefficient. *The American Statistician, 42*, 59–66.

Salmon, C. T., Park, H. S., & Wrigley, B. J. (2003). Optimistic bias and perceptions of bioterrorism in Michigan corporate spokesperson. *Journal of Health Communication, 8*, 130–144.

Williams, F. (1968). *Reasoning with statistics: Simplified examples in communications research*. New York: Holt, Rinehart and Winston.

RESEARCH UNDER THE QUALITATIVE PARADIGM

Part **4**

QUALITATIVE APPROACHES TO COMMUNICATION STUDIES RESEARCH

14

CHAPTER OUTLINE

1. Qualitative Approaches to Research
   a. Attributes and Appropriateness
      i. Research Questions and Study Objectives
      ii. Qualitative Writing
      iii. Relationship to Participants and Cultures
   b. Characteristics of Qualitative Researchers
   c. Theoretical Approaches to Qualitative Inquiry
2. Methods and Approaches to Qualitative Research
   a. Ethnography
      i. Autoethnography
      ii. Chicago School of Ethnography
      iii. Ethnomethodology
      iv. Ethnography of Communication
      v. Critical Ethnography
   b. Narrative Research and Narrative Ethnography

   c. Phenomenology
   d. Grounded Theory
   e. Case Study
   f. Conversation Analysis (CA)
   g. Discourse Analysis
   h. Qualitative Textual Analysis
      i. Content Analysis
      ii. Rhetorical Criticism
         A. Argumentation analysis
         B. Neo-Aristotelian criticism
         C. Burkean criticism
         D. Narrative criticism
         E. Metaphoric criticism
         F. Fantasy theme analysis
         G. Feminist and ideological criticism
         H. Semiotic analysis
   i. Performance Studies
   j. Feminist Studies
3. So What?

KEY TERMS

Autoethnography	Conversation analysis	Ethnography
Bracketing	Critical ethnography	Ethnography of communication
Case study	Dialogic	Ethnomethodology
Chicago School of Ethnography	Discourse analysis	Evocative
Content analysis	Emergent design	Fieldwork

Grounded theory

Inductive reasoning

Informants

In vivo

Multivocal

Narrative ethnography

Narrative research

Naturalistic

Performance studies

Phenomenology

Reflexivity

Rhetorical criticism

Social constructionism

Theoretical sampling

Theoretical saturation

CHAPTER OBJECTIVES

1. To understand under what conditions, research questions, and study objectives qualitative research is appropriate
2. To understand the different approaches to qualitative research and when each is appropriate
3. To understand the characteristics of the main methods of qualitative research used in communication studies

▼ Qualitative Approaches to Research

Attributes and Appropriateness

Research Questions and Study Objectives. Generally speaking, qualitative research is an appropriate methodology for communication studies researchers to use to describe or understand communication and interaction patterns, possibly within and between texts, dyads, groups, cultures, and contexts; to understand the influence of society, relationships, environment, or interactions on behavior; to closely examine interactive events in their natural settings; and to examine **reflexivity**—how your own thoughts, feelings, and behaviors interact with your research site and your research itself (Bochner & Ellis, 1992; Gill & Maynard, 1995). Qualitative research lets us understand, describe, and get close to the people or contexts we're studying. It lets us understand how people see the world. Qualitative research answers questions such as: What is going on here? How do *they* do it? What does it mean to them? How do they interpret what it means to others? How can we describe and interpret how they act, what they tell us they know, and how they justify their actions? The *data* for qualitative research consists of words: transcripts, quotes, field notes, and texts.

Qualitative research is what's called interpretive, as opposed to the objective approach of quantitative research (Creswell, 2007). While, in quantitative research, something is either statistically significant or it's not, or the null hypothesis is either accepted or rejected, qualitative research is much more subject to inference, impressions, and a more inductive form of reasoning. **Inductive reasoning** discovers patterns, inferences, and conclusions from studying and observing certain phenomena.

reflexivity
How one's own thoughts, feelings, and behaviors interact with his or her research site and his or her research itself.

inductive reasoning
Reasoning that discovers patterns, inferences, and conclusions from studying and observing certain phenomena.

Qualitative research is appropriate to use when something needs to be explored (when not much is known about a topic) or when we need a complex, in-depth, detailed understanding about something, especially within its environment or context. We also use qualitative research to investigate a complex or sensitive issue that cannot be reduced to a simple, objective, quantitative study (Creswell, 2007).

Many qualitative communication researchers study patterns, symbols, norms, rules, and assumptions in a culture to understand how people create meaning and how these meanings influence what people do and why they do it. In what ways do qualitative researchers study the things they study? They ask people, watch people, observe, participate, interview, review documents, and gather life histories, among other things. Qualitative research is **naturalistic**—it's often conducted *in the field* (qualitative researchers conduct *field work*)—where participants live, work, and play. Qualitative research is often conducted **in vivo**—in a natural setting; qualitative researchers observe interactions, talk to people, or participate in events as they are happening. Qualitative research typically uses an **emergent design**, revising the study (including sampling, data collection, data protocols, coding, and analysis) as the study emerges and progresses (Creswell, 2007).

Qualitative Writing.   Qualitative research in communication studies often has an emphasis on the writing process, and the writing is often viewed as a method of analysis itself (Richardson, 2003), as the writing process gives the researcher an opportunity to focus analytically on the meaning and significance of the data. Qualitative approaches in our field are often known for using engaging, intimate, vulnerable forms of writing that are **evocative** (they evoke emotions and engagement on the part of the reader), reflexive, multivocal, and **dialogic** (they engage the reader in conversation with the research), often using first person, narrative, literary, and dramatic language (Creswell, 2007; Ellis & Bochner, 2000; Reed-Danahay, 2001; Tedlock, 2000).

Qualitative writing is **multivocal**, in that it frequently includes multiple voices—it might be written from different points of view (including the researcher and multiple stakeholders or participants). Qualitative research is characterized by its attempt to understand the multiple realities represented by many different participants and stakeholders (Creswell, 2007). These multiple realities are incorporated into a qualitative research study by including joint narratives, quotes from different participants, and member checks—giving participants (or people who are representative of your participants) a copy of the tentative findings and integrating their feedback into your analysis.

Qualitative writing is reflexive in that the qualitative researcher might write him- or herself into the analysis. Reflexivity refers to the acknowledgment of the influence of the researcher and the researcher's frame of reference on the research participants and the research itself. Reflexive writing finds where the researcher intersects with the research and discusses and analyzes that intersection (Macbeth, 2001). Qualitative researchers are especially sensitive to the privileges of their academic voice over other voices (especially those of

naturalistic
Research that is conducted in the field or where participants live, work, and play.

in vivo
Research that takes place in a natural setting.

emergent design
A study design in which methods (including sampling, data collection, data protocols, coding, and analysis) are revised as the study emerges and progresses.

evocative
A form of writing used in qualitative research to evoke emotions and engagement on the part of readers.

dialogic
A form of writing used in qualitative research to engage readers in conversation with the research.

multivocal
A form of writing that frequently includes multiple voices; it might be written from different points of view (including researchers and multiple stakeholders or participants).

their study participants) and are reflexive in their writings about this privilege (Macbeth, 2001). Qualitative researchers are also reflexive in that they are often transparent in writing about the story behind the research—the data collection story, for example, which gives the reader an opportunity to evaluate and critique the process and interpret the results in light of this back-story (Macbeth, 2001).

Qualitative findings are often written as provisional texts, and qualitative research, because it is often preliminary and exploratory, is considered unfinished and ongoing (reality changes as you're describing it). Qualitative writing is characterized by a flexibility of form, and qualitative research reports in our field can range from the traditional to the artistic (poetic ethnography, for example). The goal in writing qualitative research is often to be accessible, to change or impact the reader, to get a response from the reader, or to open a conversation with the reader.

Relationship to Participants and Cultures. Rather than seeking the objectivity and detachment quantitative researchers try for, qualitative researchers often purposely engage in relationship with their participants, infusing their methods with empathy, "sympathetic introspection derived from personal encounters" (Patton, 2002a, p. 49), and "put[ting] oneself in the other person's shoes, from trying to discern how others think, act, and feel" (p. 49). The goal in qualitative research is often to be useful (to society, to study participants), connected, and personal. Qualitative researchers acknowledge that research is biased and infused with their own values and assumptions, and, rather than trying to remain objective, take those biases into account during the research process.

Characteristics of Qualitative Researchers

Qualitative researchers tend to be people who have inquiring minds. They like ambiguity and complexity; to ask questions; to interact or be with people; to analyze immediate experience; and, perhaps, to question authority. In qualitative research, the data collection instrument is the researcher—you. You aren't using scales, measurements, or instruments through which to filter the information— you're filtering the data through yourself—your mind, your impressions, your intuitive sense.

✳ Theoretical Approaches to Qualitative Inquiry

✳ **social constructionism**
A perspective suggesting that communication is the vehicle through which reality is understood, constituted, and represented, and it is through communication that beliefs and meanings are constructed and negotiated.

Much qualitative research in the field of communication studies approaches inquiry from a social constructionist perspective. **Social constructionism** suggests that communication is the vehicle through which reality is understood, constituted, and represented, and it is through communication that beliefs and meanings are constructed and negotiated. Identity is constructed through interaction with each other (Foster & Bochner, 2008). The social constructionist's approach to communication inquiry involves the following guiding principles:

︶1. Language is fundamental to the construction of social situations.

︶2. Multiple social realities exist, and research should work to capture and report the multiple truths.

⌒ 3. Meaning is produced through relational communication.

⌒ 4. Context, situations, and circumstances are significant to meaning.

⌒ 5. Researchers affect the subjects of study, and study subjects affect researchers as well.

⌒ 6. A goal of research should be moral, ethical, critical, and political change.

⌒ 7. Researcher subjectivity is acknowledged. *Values & biasyzes are important*

⌒ 8. The aim of research is authenticity, credibility, and trustworthiness.

⌒ 9. Research seeks to understand and foster dialogue (Foster & Bochner, 2008; Patton, 2002b).

Other communication studies qualitative research operates from an artistic and evocative framework (Patton, 2002b), which seeks creativity, aesthetic quality, and interpretive vitality. Research from this perspective has the goal of connecting with the audience, being provocative, and feeling authentic. This type of research is often literary, creative, poetic, artistic, and performative.

Still other qualitative research in communication studies takes a critical change perspective. The critical approach to research always has as its goal to identify power and control strategies in a society or culture. Critical research typically takes as its mission social critique—the study of marginalized, oppressed, disenfranchised, or disadvantaged populations with the aim to promote social justice among these populations. Critical researchers do this by questioning the social implications and moral issues of action and by seeking shared understanding of the social action (Patton, 2002b).

. . . .

Methods and Approaches to Qualitative Research   ▼

There are quite a number of methods and approaches to qualitative research used by communication researchers, and there are a myriad of categorizations of these approaches. For the purposes of understanding the approaches used in our field, we'll start by listing the key methods or approaches researchers in our field use, discussing where the research focus is for each, and move on to describing and explaining each method. In this chapter and Chapter 15, we'll give you more information about conducting each type of qualitative research project.

Qualitative methods in communication studies can be divided by what each method or approach focuses on studying. Some methods focus on understanding stories. Others focus on studying contexts; lives; cultures; written discourse; oral discourse or conversations; lived experiences; views, values, beliefs, feelings, assumptions, and ideologies of people; or patterns of behavior, beliefs, and language (Creswell, 2007). While these methods each approach the research problem differently, their boundaries are not firm, and in much actual research these methods overlap.

The following table, derived from Creswell (2007, pp. 78–79) and others as cited, summarizes each qualitative approach as it is conducted in communication studies:

Method	Focus On Describing/ Understanding Communication as It Relates to:	Characteristics
Ethnography	A culture or cultural group.	Uses observations, interviews, focus groups, artifact analysis, introspection to study group or culture. Analysis could be thematic, narrative, descriptive.
Narrative Research	Individuals' stories, the role of personal narratives in interactions and relationships (Foster & Bochner, 2008).	Primarily uses personal, in-depth interviews or introspection to study individual stories. Analysis can be thematic or narrative.
Phenomenology	Meaning within lived experience.	Can study individuals or groups, through interviews, document or artifact analysis, introspection or focus groups. Analysis is usually thematic or descriptive, focusing on meanings of phenomena.
Grounded Theory	Behavior within social situations and multiple realities.	Studies individuals or groups primarily through interviews, focus groups, observations, or introspection. Analysis involves selective coding and theoretic discussion.
Case Study	Illustrative case.	Studies individual cases (people, events, or groups) through interviews, focus groups, observations, document or artifact analysis, or introspection. Analysis is typically descriptive.
Conversation Analysis	Interpersonal social action in sequences of utterances and interaction as agents of action and activity (Wooffitt, 2005).	Study of verbal interaction between individuals in terms of what was said and the way it was said, and the activities performed by these utterances. Analysis consists of elements of transcriptions with details, such as turn-taking, delivery, and other verbal and nonverbal details, and resulting sense-making related to those utterances.
Discourse Analysis	Creation of reality in (usually) oral discourse and interactions (Foster & Bochner, 2008).	Studies discourse in spoken (or written) linguistic events, from interviews, focus groups, observations. Analysis links context, discourse, and resulting meaning or reality (Wooffitt, 2005).

Textual Analysis	Creation of meaning in (usually) written texts and artifacts.	Interpret characteristics (content, structure, and function) of a message, derived from written text or artifact or other social communicative form. Analysis investigates construction of meaning, power, or persuasion resulting from the message, related to societal influences and message outcomes.
Performance Studies	Both formal and informal performances of self, identity, and meaning.	Studies performances (formal—theatrical, and information—performance of self) through observation and participation, and reenacts them, recreating and interpreting them through the performance.
Feminist Research	Power and gender in a culture.	How conceptions of gender are produced and maintained in texts. This is a critical methodology, and analysis focuses on how language, discourse, and culture constructs power and control.

Ethnography

Ethnography, simply put, is the study of a culture. Communication ethnography is the study of communication in a culture. Ethnography is characterized by immersion in a culture—called **fieldwork**—in order to fully understand beliefs and practices in context. This immersion usually occurs through observations, various types of participation, and formal interviewing and informal conversations. Ethnography frequently makes use of key participants, called **informants**, who can act as co-researchers and help the researcher explain and make sense of the culture (Atkinson, Coffey, Delamont, Lofland, & Lofland, 2007). Within the method called *ethnography* are many subareas, which we will now explain in more detail. You may notice as you look through these descriptions that the areas sound as if they might overlap. In fact, they do, but researchers usually begin their research at one of the traditions.

Autoethnography. Ellis and Bochner (2000) are known for the development of **autoethnography** in communication studies. Autoethnography is a type of ethnography in which the culture you're studying is a culture of which you're an integral part. It's to ethnography what autobiography is to biography. Ellis and Bochner describe five forms of autoethnography:

1. Reflexive ethnographies that provide researchers an opportunity to critically view the experiences of a particular cultural community.

2. Native ethnographies in which ethnographers reflect on their own membership in a historically marginalized or mysterious culture.

3. Complete-member-researcher/ethnographies where a member of a culture reports on that culture for outside interpretation.

ethnography
The study of culture.

fieldwork
Data collection in a naturalistic environment.

informants
Key participants who can act as coresearchers and help the researcher explain and make sense of a culture.

autoethnography
A type of ethnography in which the culture being studied is a culture of which the researcher is an integral part.

4. Literary autoethnographies in which writer/researchers describe their culture to those unfamiliar with the culture.

5. Personal narratives that are critical autobiographical stories of experiences. They provide the audience an opportunity to access and interpret those experiences to make sense of society.

Carolyn Ellis is known for writing narrative autoethnographies, studies which use narratives about her own life to make critical statements about the larger culture in which she is a part. In a piece called "Katrina and the Cat: Responding to Life's Expendables" (Ellis, 2007), she used a personal story of rescuing an injured cat to relate to the situation of poor people in New Orleans, Louisiana, in the aftermath of the hurricane Katrina. The story leads to the questions of whether she adequately cared for the cat and whether we as a society adequately care for people who need our help.

Chicago School of Ethnography.   The **Chicago School of Ethnography** was developed by sociologists at the University of Chicago between 1917 and 1942. The Chicago School of Ethnography focused on reflexive interactional communication to understand how people use communication for sense-making (Deegan, 2007). This perspective on ethnography was grounded in the theory of social interactionism, a communication theory that studies interrelationships between relational participants by understanding that meaning resides not in the individuals, but in their negotiated everyday interactions, and by understanding the interrelationships between individuals, the larger community, and their social experience (Reusch & Bateson, 1951; Blumer, 1969; Goffman, 1959, 1967; Laing, 1961; Mead, 1934). The Chicago School of Ethnography studied urban settings and marginalized people. Their studies were characterized by informal conversational language depicting everyday life. Their studies included research on hobos and gangs, juvenile delinquency, small town life, race relations, and mental disorders (Deegan, 2007). Although this form of ethnography was founded by sociologists, their emphasis on interaction and meaning forms the basis of our interpersonal communication field today.

In the Chicago School tradition, Smith (2008), for example, conducted a long-term ethnography of professional wrestling, looking at the ways wrestlers use interactions in the ring and the gym to give meaning to their physical suffering and pain. He analyzed the ways wrestlers use their bodies in the context of pain and what their interactions say about the meaning they bring to their pain. Another example of an ethnography is Desantis's exploration of the health and wellness rationalizations some cigar smokers make (Desantis, 2003)

Ethnomethodology.   Developed by Harold Garfinkel in 1967, **ethnomethodology** focuses on understanding the lived experience and lived practices from the point of view of those within the experience (Pollner & Emerson, 2007). Rather than using formal data collection techniques, researchers following this approach use forms of participant observation to attend to what interactional participants think is important or *accountable* (able to be noticed and accounted for). Ethnomethodology studies interactions in everyday life and attempts to understand ordinary unnoticed interactions. Ethnomethodologists suggest that

Chicago School of Ethnography
Grounded in the theory of social interactionism, this communication tradition studies interrelationships between relational participants by understanding that meaning resides not in the individuals, but in their negotiated everyday interactions, and by understanding the interrelationships between individuals, the larger community, and their social experience.

ethnomethodology
This approach focuses on understanding the lived experience and lived practices from the point of view of those within an experience.

researchers "make the familiar strange," or seek to see meaning in the ordinary. They also stress reflexivity, which they refer to as the meaning constructed in an interaction while the action is taking place (Pollner & Emerson, 2007). Conversation analysis, the study of everyday talk (discussed later in this chapter) is associated with ethnomethodology (Ten Have, 2007). For a recent example of ethnomethodology, we can look at the research of Frers (2009), who looked at how patients' medical files are used as one part of doctor-patient interactions to organize medical discussions, control access to information, establish boundaries, distribute medical access, and create meaning.

Ethnography of Communication.   This method was developed in the 1960s by John Gumperz and Dell Hymes to study speech events in the context of community (Keating, 2007). Their research focused on the meaning resulting from shared beliefs, values, and social interaction in a culture. They looked at actual speech exchanges and their social meaning—actual language use in context. **Ethnography of communication** is characterized by its focus on communication competence, or the social rules, norms, skills, and structures that a communicator needs to be able to follow in order to communicate appropriately in a specific speech community. This method is also characterized by its use of speech acts, speech events, speech situations, and speech communities and units of analysis. Unlike other types of ethnography that focuses on everyday speech, ethnography of communication focuses on routine or ritualized forms of communication in a society (e.g., ceremonial events). This type of ethnography has been used to study classroom interactions between teachers and students, language usage in various cultures and countries, and politeness and formality (Keating, 2007). Phillips (2009) followed the tradition of ethnography of communication as she studied the African American gang practice of writing while dancing. She discussed how gang members use this writing with their feet as a form of language expression to perform racial politics. Some other interesting applications of ethnography of communication include studying the use of music in the workplace (Korczynski, 2011) and the experience of Mexican American fathers and mothers who had gone through the death of their child (Russell-Kibble, 2011).

> **ethnography of communication**
> *The study of speech events and their meaning in a culture.*

Critical Ethnography.   **Critical ethnography**, as with all critical methodologies, is the study of power and control. Critical ethnography is the practice of ethnography for the purpose of critique of cultural power differentials (Foley & Valenzuela, 2007). Critical ethnographers, as with all other ethnographers, view positivist objectivity as a myth, and acknowledge their own biased viewpoints and backgrounds inherent in their research. Critical ethnography is often an action-oriented method in which participants see the possibility of their participation resulting in changes to social problems. Today's critical ethnographers utilize introspection, memories, dreams, and autobiography as ways of knowing and seeing power and control in society. Critical ethnography is characterized by conversational, informal interviewing; collaborating with participants; reader-friendly writing; and offering participants the opportunity to edit or give feedback on transcriptions and findings (Foley & Valenzuela, 2007). Winkle-Wagner (2008) conducted a critical ethnography to study the

> **critical ethnography**
> *The study of how power and control in a culture is constructed through communication.*

way black undergraduate college women negotiated identity as they navigated issues of feminism, race, and gender. She used ethnographic methods to look at how these women constructed strength, assertiveness, and empowerment at a predominantly white college.

Narrative Research and Narrative Ethnography

Narrative inquiry is a field in progress. There are actually two different types of narrative research: *analysis of narratives* (the study and analysis of the stories people tell), and *narrative analysis* (using narratives to write your findings) (Creswell, Hanson, Clark, & Morales, 2007). Some studies do both—using narratives to tell the story of peoples' stories. **Narrative research** is appropriate to investigate research questions that deal with the life experiences of individuals or when the use of stories facilitates understanding of the issue under study (Creswell et al., 2007).

narrative research
Research that investigates research questions dealing with the life experiences of individuals or when the use of stories facilitates understanding of an issue under study.

In analysis *of* narratives, researchers study oral or written narratives received during an interview, fieldwork, or everyday conversation. Narrative may occur as a story told by a study participant—perhaps a short story about an event, a story told as a life history, or an autobiographical story (Chase, 2000). Oral history is used to describe the meanings attributed to certain historical events by those who experienced those events (McMahan & Rogers, 1994; Thompson, 2000). This type of narrative research stems from sociologists from the Chicago School and later from anthropologists. Both disciplines were able to study social institutions and cultures from the stories shared by others. Personal narratives provide insight into historical events and social movements. For example, the civil rights movement sparked interest in slave narratives. The second wave of the women's movement also produced interest in women's life stories and experiences, particularly as the silenced group.

Narrative researchers often take on an *authoritative* voice; that is, they interpret the narration. Sometimes it is necessary for researchers who publish oral histories or life histories to employ a muted *supportive* voice. For example, a researcher may preface a personal narrative with brief commentary about the context of a situation or experience. Finally, the researcher's *interactive* voice surfaces when there is an interaction between the researcher's and the narrator's voices (Bamberg, 1997). Narrative analysis is often a specialized form of ethnography.

narrative ethnography
A form of ethnography that uses a narrative voice to help readers understand a culture.

Narrative ethnography, or narrative autoethnography, uses the narrative voice to help the reader understand a culture. Narrative ethnography is typically written in the first person, in an evocative, active voice. One key characteristic of this type of research is the restorying of the participants' stories into a chronological narrative with plots, time, place, and scene (Creswell, Hanson, Clark, & Morales, 2007).

Whether conducting analysis of narratives or narrative analysis, there are five analytic lenses through which researchers examine narrative work (Chase, 2000):

1. Narratives are treated as a unique discourse. Narrative research is an organization and understanding of past experiences.

2. Narratives are viewed as verbal action. The narrator is shaping reality with his or her words.

3. Stories are "both enabled and constrained by a range of social resources and circumstances" (p. 657). This lens is used to determine similarities and differences between narratives.

4. Narratives are viewed as "socially situated interactive performances" (p. 657). A narrative requires a narrator and listener.

5. Narrative researchers frequently consider themselves to be narrators as they interpret the subject matter they have studied. Often, first person is used to relay a story or experience.

Narrative research typically uses in-depth interviews and document or artifact analysis for data collection (Creswell et al., 2007).

Using analysis of narratives, Davis (2008a), in "Final Stories: The Ultimate Sensemaking Frame," analyzed stories told by her mother prior to her death, and Montalbano-Phelps (2003) conducted an analysis of narratives of domestic violence survivors, identifying several major themes within those narratives. Using narrative ethnography in "A Family Jigsaw Puzzle: Secrets and Gaps," Davis (2009) used a narrative approach to tell a story of secrets within her family of origin.

Phenomenology

Phenomenology—developed by Edmund Husserl and Martin Heidegger—is the study of experience, in order to understand—in great depth—the nature, essence, and meaning of that experience. The goal of phenomenology is to understand an experience, uncontaminated by other theories or assumptions. One of the key aspects of phenomenological inquiry is to undertake a systematic identification of the researchers' preconceived ideas and thoughts, in order to be able to focus on understanding the experience with an open, blank mind (called **bracketing**). As Starks and Trinidad (2007) explain it, "phenomenology contributes to deeper understanding of lived experiences by exposing taken-for-granted assumptions about [our] ways of knowing" (p. 1373).

Phenomenologists frequently gather data through in-depth retrospective interviews or focus groups in which participants are encouraged to relive, explain, and describe experiences in great detail. Phenomenologists seek to understand embodied experience, to understand a phenomenon as completely as if they had experienced it themselves (Starks & Trinidad, 2007). Sometimes phenomenologists use their own personal experiences for analysis, and these accounts are similar to autoethnographic accounts. Researchers conducting phenomenology might also use observation methods in which they observe people participating in the phenomenon under study, as well as document or artifact analysis (Creswell et al., 2007; Starks & Trinidad, 2007).

Phenomenological analysis consists of thick descriptions of the phenomena that are then categorized into units or themes to describe the *essence* of the experience (Creswell et al., 2007; Starks & Trinidad, 2007).

✳ phenomenology
The study of experience, in order to understand, in great depth, the nature, essence, and meaning of that experience.

• bracketing
Undertaking a systematic identification of a researcher's preconceived ideas and thoughts, in order to be able to focus on understanding an experience with an open, blank mind.

Merrill and Grassley (2008) studied the experiences of overweight female patients to understand their encounters with health-care services and providers from their points of view. They used what's called a "hermeneutic phenomenological approach," which refers to the interpretation of lived experience. They used face-to-face interviews with eight women, and analyzed the data using a framework commonly used by phenomenologists, Van Maanen's lifeworlds of lived space, lived body, lived time, and lived relations.

Grounded Theory

grounded theory
A systematic approach to understanding and analyzing participants' experiences.

The process of **grounded theory** was originally developed by Barny Glaser and Anselm Strauss (Glaser & Strauss, 1967; Strauss & Corbin, 1990), but most communication studies researchers that use grounded theory use a constructivist approach to grounded theory developed by Kathy Charmaz (2000), so we will discuss Charmaz's version here. The goal of grounded theory, says Charmaz, is to learn "what our research participants' lives are like. We study how they explain their statements and actions, and ask what analytic sense we can make of them" (pp. 2–3). Grounded theory seeks to understand interaction within social practices and the resulting meaning (Starks & Trinidad, 2007). Grounded theory is appropriate for research questions that focus on experiences over time within a social context (Creswell et al., 2007).

theoretical saturation
The collection and analysis of data until no new categories of theories are identified.

There are two main ideas incorporated into grounded theory: We are developing theories that are grounded in the data and that surface through the **theoretical saturation** of categories (we collect and analyze the data until no new categories of theories are identified); and our design is *emergent*—we analyze, collect data, reanalyze, interpret, and change our design as we go along. The process of grounded theory allows for surprises, fresh ideas, and exploration (Charmaz, 2006). The theories derived in grounded theory are explanations of social processes—grounded theory answers the question of "How does the social process of 'X' happen in the context of this environment?" (Starks & Trinidad, 2007). Unlike phenomenology, whose focus of analysis is within the specific phenomenon, the focus of a grounded theory analysis is to develop a social model or theory (Creswell et al., 2007).

theoretical sampling
Choosing a sample based on the people, events, groups, and so on, who can shed light on a theory being investigated.

Researchers conducting grounded theory typically use observation and in-depth interviews in which participants describe their experiences (Starks & Trinidad, 2007). Grounded theory involves a systematic process of synthesizing data throughout the course of a study (Charmaz, 2006). Grounded theory typically uses a **theoretical sampling** method—you choose your sample based on the people, events, groups, and so on, who can shed light on the theory you are investigating. As you collect your data, your theory may change and, as a result, your sampling design may change also. In the next chapter, we'll talk more about the steps involved in coding data under a grounded theory methodology; but for now, you should know that in grounded theory, coding begins when you collect your first piece of data. As you code and collect your data, you start to define and categorize the data. You interact with the data and pose questions while coding and collecting. Your emerging interpretations shape your data collection (who you talk to, what you attend to, what you ask them) as well as your data coding. This starts the chain of theory development, which also emerges as you work with your data.

For example, Becker, Ellevold, and Stamp (2008) used a grounded theory framework to analyze self-report interview and observation data about defensive communication among romantic couples. They developed a theory of defensive communication that they illustrated through narrative.

Case Study

The key thinkers in case study research are Robert Stake and Robert Yin. A **case study** is an in-depth study of a particular case (or multiple cases). A case is defined as a *bounded unit*, and could be a person, a group, an organization, a culture, or a community. Case study research is appropriate for research questions that focus on an in-depth understanding of a specific issue or example (Creswell et al., 2007). A case study is similar to ethnography in that it uses an immersion method to fully understand the case. As with ethnography, case studies typically involve multiple data sources such as observation, in-depth interviews, and perhaps, artifact analysis. With a case study, the objective is to fully understand that case or to use that case to understand an issue or a theory. Sometimes a researcher will use multiple cases to compare cases, but often a case study will have a sample size of one—one case. The rigor in this method comes from the immersion in the case—the amount of time spent in the field and the ability of the researcher to fully and completely describe, understand, and explain the case. Analysis of a case study typically focuses on description and understanding, although categorization of concepts or themes might be done as well (Creswell et al., 2007). For example, Huang Chua (2009) used an analysis of two case sites to compare restrictions on speech in virtual communities and the contradiction between these restrictions and collective identity.

case study
An in-depth study of a particular case (or multiple cases).

Conversation Analysis (CA)

Conversation analysis was developed by Harvey Sacks and Emanuel Schegloff and was influenced by the work on interaction of Erving Goffman and Harold Garfinkel's ethnomethodology (Ten Have, 2007). CA is an investigation of social interaction between humans, most especially of everyday, ordinary conversation, called in CA "talk-in-interaction" (p. 4). Conversation analysts record natural interactions and then listen for context and structure. The goal of CA is to explain *how* people talk with each other.

Conversation analysis researchers look at characteristics of talk, such as pacing, turn-taking, delivery, words, sounds, silences or spaces, overlapped speech and sounds, volume, and other verbal and nonverbal details. CA is especially known for its unique form of transcription that provides detail on turn-by-turn conversation sequences and structure. For example, brackets in transcripts indicate where conversational turns overlap with each other. Numbers in parentheses indicate elapsed time (pauses) between utterances. Underscoring indicates stress in pitch. A period indicates a fall in tone. Arrows indicate a raising or lowering of pitch. Colons indicate prolonging of a sound. Equal signs indicate no gap between lines. A degree sign means that the utterance is relatively quiet. A question mark indicates a rise in tone, and so on. Reading—and writing—CA transcripts is an art and a skill.

conversation analysis
An investigation of social interaction between humans, most especially of everyday, ordinary conversation.

Ten Have (2007, p. 96) gives the following excerpt of a CA transcript:

1. Maude: I says well it's funny; Missi:z uh: ↑Schmidt ih you'd think she'd help<.hhh
2. Well (.) Missiz Schmidt was the one she: (0.2) assumed respo:nsibility for the three
3. specials.
4. (0.6)
5. Bea: Oh↓*::. °°M-hm, °°=

In conversation analysis (CA), there are three assumptions of conversational organization:

1. Talk is action—language conveys a message.
2. Action is structurally organized—single acts are organized into sequences.
3. Talk creates and sustains intersubjective reality—conversation creates meaning. (Perakyla, 2005).

Good and Beach (2005) used CA to analyze gift giving in children's birthday parties. They looked at gift opening activities as interactional and embodied actions. Characteristic of CA, they specifically identified "an extended summons–answer sequence involving initiation of a gift-opening, enthusiastic response cries, positive assessments of the gifts, the offering and prompting of thanks, and related actions" (p. 565). They noted that the rituals constitute a "complex social system where adults model and facilitate the construction and integration of past, present, and future relationships" (p. 565).

Discourse Analysis

discourse analysis
The study of spoken or written discourse— studies speech acts—from the content of the discourse, to its delivery (paralanguage, speech, grammar), to its context, and the meaning deriving from each of these, to understand how people use language to construct ideas, meanings, and identities.

Discourse analysis—the study of spoken or written discourse—studies speech acts—from the content of the discourse, to its delivery (paralanguage, speech, grammar), to its context, and the meaning deriving from each of these, to understand how people use language to construct ideas, meanings, and identities (Starks & Trinidad, 2007). This type of analysis might focus on relational roles in the interaction; language use, exchange, or persuasion strategies; conversational turns; interactional and relational history of the participants; and nonverbal strategies. Discourse analysis takes a wide view of the context of the interaction. While both CA and discourse analysis focus on the specific utterances (or discourse) and the meaning resulting from it, they differ in terms of their primary focus. As you saw in the last section, CA focuses primarily on how people talk, while discourse analysis focuses on how that talk constructs meaning.

Data collection in discourse analysis involves ways of finding discourse— recorded transcripts of conversations, interviews, or focus groups are ideal, as are transcripts from Internet messaging or chat groups and perhaps discursive texts such as letters, e-mail, or journal accounts. Field notes of discourse are also sometimes used, albeit they are less than ideal. Observation of discourse and the resulting transcripts might be supplemented by in-depth interviews in which the study participants discuss meaning related to the discourse. Discourse is analyzed through a *close look* at the communication, especially at its significance, activities, identities, relationships, politics, connections, sign systems, and knowledge, to understand how language constructs social realities (Starks & Trinidad, 2007). Final analyses typically use descriptions of the language and discourse and a discussion of the ways that this language constructs meaning (Starks & Trinidad, 2007).

Critical discourse analysis is the study of how different texts, or discourses, create power and inequality in society (de Fina, Schiffrin, & Bamberg, 2006). Historical discourse analysis studies discourse in its historical context (Perakyla, 2005).

In an example of discourse analysis, Elliott Mishler (2007) looked at the way time is constructed through language of sexual abuse survivors in a way that allowed them to restory their past and construct new identities for themselves.

Qualitative Textual Analysis

The purpose of textual analysis is to interpret the characteristics of a message. Textual analysis typically takes a social constructionist point of view in looking at the meanings formed by the messages in a text. Textual analysis answers questions such as: "How were they able to persuade?" or "How is this concept constructed through the text?" Texts can include transcripts of speeches; written conversations (letters, email, Internet messaging, chat groups); journals, diaries, or blogs; personal records (medical records or employment records); newspapers or magazines; audio or videotapes (personal or commercial) or films; books; pictures, architecture, or paintings; Web sites; organizational materials (employee manuals or PR releases); and advertising materials.

A textual analysis may look at the way that words or phrases are used to construct an idea, or it may look at general topics or ideas that are constructed in the text, or it may compare the two. Researchers using textual analysis may describe the content, structure, or functions of a message. They may evaluate the message on its strengths or weaknesses (e.g., how well did a speech communicate an idea), or they may study how the communication in a message is related to societal influences or historical context. There are two main types of textual analysis: content analysis and rhetorical criticism.

Content Analysis. Chapter 12 talked about quantitative content analysis, in which researchers count and measure characteristics within a message. **Content analysis** can also be used as a qualitative method. Qualitative content analysis describes elements in a message, often mass media messages (television or film, advertisements, news stories). This method is different from other types of textual analysis or coding in that, in content analysis, code categories are determined *before* you begin collecting data. Your research question sets up your categories—perhaps you want to see ways that women are depicted in a popular television show, for example, so you might have a coding scheme that consists of four codes: villain, victim, survivor, and rescuer. Content analysis coding schemes can be somewhat more complex than this, but content analysis uses a

content analysis
When used as a qualitative method, used to describe elements in a message.

finite number of categories. While content analysis describes the content of a text, or what message a text conveys, rhetorical criticism focuses on the structure of a text, or how the text conveys that message.

Chen (2008) used a qualitative content analysis to analyze a Chinese TV drama, *The Gobi Mother*, a highly popular television show in China. She identified several themes that helped explain the success of the show: fate and faith; favor and face; foes, friends, and family; home, happiness, and harmony despite harsh circumstances. She concluded the main character's use of a sincere, simplistic, and down-to-earth communication style as resistance to prestige, power, and position was a key to the show's success.

rhetorical criticism

The study of the ways that written or spoken language (such as speeches, books, images, performances, texts, and films), in their historical and cultural context, work—to persuade, instruct, inform, entertain, arouse, engage, and convince.

Rhetorical Criticism. **Rhetorical criticism** is the study of the ways that written or spoken language (e.g., speeches, books, images, performances, texts, and films), in their historical and cultural context, work—to persuade, instruct, inform, entertain, arouse, engage, and convince. In short, rhetorical criticism seeks to understand how symbols act on people. The practice of rhetorical criticism goes back to the rhetoric and oratory of Plato, Aristotle, Gorgias, Cicero, and Socrates, in fifth century BCE, and, as such, this method is the foundation of our field of speech communication. A researcher using rhetorical criticism might compare the purpose of a message with the outcome of that message. You might look at the message in light of its historical or societal context, or you might take a critical look at how power is constructed in the message.

There are many types of rhetorical criticism, and many of these methods reflect certain philosophies in the history of our field. We're going to discuss some of the main ones in our field: argumentation analysis, Neo-Aristotelian criticism, Burkean (dramatistic) criticism, metaphoric criticism, narrative criticism, fantasy theme analysis, feminist criticism, ideological criticism, and semiotics. Which type of rhetorical criticism you use really depends on what you think is going on in the text and whose rhetorical philosophy you choose to follow. To begin a rhetorical criticism, you need to read the text and ask yourself: What message is the writer or speaker attempting to convey with the text, and what strategies is the author or speaker using for his or her appeal to that message?

ARGUMENTATION ANALYSIS. If you want to analyze how well the argument is made in the text, you might use an *argumentation analysis*. Toulmin (Bizzell & Herzberg, 1990, p. 1105) called this *practical reasoning* and suggested that what we know is derived by assumptions, beliefs, and persuasion. An argumentation analysis answers two types of questions: analytical and substantial. Analytical questions are concerned with: "Am I arguing *rightly*?" In other words, analytical questions look at errors of structure in a speech or text, such as formal inconsistencies. Substantial questions are concerned with: "Are these the *right* (or relevant) arguments to use when dealing with this kind of problem, in this situation?" (Toulmin, 1990). Toulmin argued that an argument persuades by its force or delivery, more so than by its structure. Toulmin said that truth is socially derived in discourse. Argumentation analysis often uses each of the elements in Toulmin's Model of Argument for its analysis:

1. Claim (assertion, conclusion)
2. Data (grounds, evidence)
3. Warrant (justification)
4. Backing (additional evidence)
5. Modal qualifier (strength of movement from data to claim)
6. Rebuttal (instances where warrant will not justify claim)

Weger and Aakhus (2003) used argumentation analysis to look at how electronic media (chat room interactions) facilitates public discourse and participation. They looked at the utility, or use, of the arguments and procedures in the chat rooms. They specifically looked at the elements in the chat rooms that support, and hinder, critical discussion.

NEO-ARISTOTELIAN CRITICISM.   Another way to analyze a textual argument is to use *Neo-Aristotelian criticism*. Neo-Aristotelian criticism analyzes the persuasive ability of a text by Aristotle's five criteria: type of persuasive argument, organizational structure, style, nonverbal, and speaker memory or control of the speech. When you think of Neo-Aristotelian criticism, think of your public speaking class. When your instructor gave you feedback on your speeches, he or she was likely using a form of Neo-Aristotelian criticism.

Recall that Aristotle said that persuasion was built on one of three types of arguments: appeals to ethos (reputation of the speaker), appeals to pathos (emotions), or appeals to logos (logic). A Neo-Aristotelian criticism might discuss which appeal the text's argument was based on, how the structure and delivery of the argument supported that appeal, where the text was effective, and where it was ineffective.

Aristotle discussed the importance of logos and ethos in *Rhetoric*: "Whether our argument concerns public affairs or some other subject, we must know some, if not all, of the facts about the subject on which we are to speak and argue" (Aristotle, 1990, p. 184). He also said, "There are three things which inspire confidence in the orator's own character—the three, namely, that induce us to believe a thing apart from any proof of it: good sense, good moral character, and goodwill. . . . The way to make ourselves thought to be sensible and morally good must be gathered from the analysis of goodness already given: the way to establish your own goodness is the same as the way to establish that of others" (p. 161). Cicero in *Of Oratory* cited the importance of pathos: "We require a man of sharpness, ingenious by nature and experience alike, who with keen scent will track down the thoughts, feelings, beliefs, and hopes of his fellow-citizens and of any men whom on any ideas he would fain win over by his work" (Cicero, 1990, p. 224).

McGee (1998) used Aristotle's concept of ethos (speaker's reputation) in the gubernatorial campaign of self-avowed racist David Duke to examine Duke's use of a religious conversion to construct a new ethos for himself in the campaign.

BURKEAN CRITICISM.   *Dramatistic criticism* is based on the work of Kenneth Burke, who looked at all language as made up of dramatic elements. Burke said that we are "symbol using animals" (Burke, 1990a), and suggested that it is crucial that we understand how our cultural symbols construct our ideas of reality; how our symbolic actions construct attitudes, beliefs, motivations, ideologies, cohesion, and divisions. Burke was concerned with analyzing language and how language is a model of our reality. Burke's pentad, the five characteristics on which he analyzed a message, include the act (the specific message), the purpose of the message, the agent or person communicating the message, the agency or medium of the message, and the scene or context of the message. A Burkean analysis might look at the ways these five elements work together, which elements are more emphasized than others, and whether the interaction of these elements is effective in constructing the message or persuasive argument (Burke, 1990b).

DePalma, Ringer, and Webber (2008) used Burke's dramatistic pentad to look at Sharon Crowley's book advocating negotiation, dialogue, and dissent as a means of facilitating public discourse (called "Toward a Civil Discourse"), and Barack Obama's "Pentecost 2006 Keynote Address." They suggested that both author's attempts (the act) to provide ways to bridge liberals and conservatives (the purpose) instead eliminated the possibility for dialogue.

NARRATIVE CRITICISM. If you think that the argument is written as a narrative or story, you might decide to do a *narrative criticism*. Narrative criticism looks at the stories being told in a text, and analyzes them by narrative elements—setting, characters, events, time, relationships, audience, and theme. Wolfe (2008) examined Dr. Seuss's *The Lorax* using narrative criticism to suggest the plot, imagery, and color served as propaganda for the political activism environmental movement.

METAPHORIC CRITICISM. If you think the text's persuasion comes from the use of metaphors in the language, a *metaphoric criticism* would look at the use of metaphors to construct a specific meaning. Davis (2007), for example, studied the use of metaphor to construct the concepts of life and death in the case of the legal and political arguments for and against the removal of life support from Terri Schiavo in Florida in 2005.

FANTASY THEME ANALYSIS. If you think the text is using language in ways that construct mythic themes of good and evil, for example, a *fantasy theme analysis* looks at how a text uses mythic stories, such as war, villains, and heroes. Zagacki and Grano (2005) conducted a fantasy theme analysis of radio talk shows in Baton Rouge, Louisiana, and their communication about the Louisiana State University's "Fighting Tigers" college football team. Looking through the lens of the fantasy of sport, they found that the talk shows promoted fantasies about college athletics that solidified regional identity, pride, and masculinity.

FEMINIST AND IDEOLOGICAL CRITICISM. Perhaps you want to study how the text constructs power and control in society. *Feminist criticism* looks at how power related to gender is constructed in a text. Twentieth-century feminist rhetorician Kristeva looked at the ways that gendered social conditions are embodied in language (1990). She noted that language is open to interpretation and multiple meanings and advocated the use of language to change society by emphasizing language's power to build community. *Ideological criticism* is also an approach that looks at the use of cultural texts and artifacts to construct power. Ideological criticism analyzes text to identify ways they construct a cultural ideology over competing ideologies. Researchers using this method might look at terms such as *freedom* to identify how they construct dominant meaning in a society and then how this meaning affects behaviors and beliefs. This type of analysis exposes the hegemony—hidden power in a society—by exposing the dominant discourses that reify cultural beliefs and ideas.

In an example of feminist criticism, Walsh, Fürsich, and Jefferson (2008) examined two U.S. situation comedies—*The King of Queens* and *According to Jim*—in which "smart, witty, and attractive women . . . are married to inept, overweight, and immature men" (p. 123). They discussed the ways the shows reaffirm male dominance and trivialize sexism through their use of plot, characters, setting, structure, and humor.

SEMIOTIC ANALYSIS.   *Semiotics*, based on the work of philosophers and linguists de Saussure and Peirce is the study of symbol systems and the ways that reality is constructed through the symbolic process of communication (Leeds-Hurwitz, 1993). Semiotics is based on three principles: Language is a symbolic system that represents reality (the extensional world); via the use of language, we assign meaning to our extensional world; and this meaning is influenced by our cultural experiences. Meaning resides in social relations. Semiotic analysis looks at *signs* (smallest elements of meaning in interaction), *symbols* (a type of sign that has specific cultural meaning), and *codes* (sets of related signs and rules for their use), and the relationship between signs and codes, and codes and cultures. An example of a social code is clothing; a bride's white dress would be a sign within the code of clothing. An example of a symbol is the Christmas tree. Semiotic analysis looks at how social codes and symbols create meaning in a culture (Leeds-Hurwitz, 1993).

Page (2006) conducted a semiotic analysis to examine advertisements created for Kohler's "As I See It" ad campaign, which Page claimed "has delivered romanticized and fantasized portraits of high-end kitchen and bath fixtures" (p. 90). She specifically looked at the way the symbols, metaphors, and allusions to myth unintentionally create a relationship between females and products, commodities, self-alienation, sexual activity, and desire.

Performance Studies

In **performance studies**, researchers represent cultural experiences by observing and reenacting culturally situated communicative acts to reflect an interpretation of cultural practice through human expression. The communicative act performed can either be a cultural text or an ethnographic account, which is why performance studies are sometimes known as *performance ethnography* because they represent a culture through performance. Performance ethnography creates an appreciation for representation of others by enabling the actor to fully embody the others' experience. This embodiment of cultural practice also results in a critical observation of knowledge (Alexander, 2005). In other words, when I perform your actions as if I were you, I can more fully understand your experience and your situation. In addition, when you see my performance, you

performance studies
Researchers represent cultural experiences by observing and reenacting culturally situated communicative acts to reflect an interpretation of cultural practice through human expression.

can more fully understand yourself and others. In the performance, the audience is allowed to see others related to how they see themselves. For this reason, performance studies combine theory and praxis (practice or normal behavior) as they perform theory and make it alive to the audience (Jones, 2000).

Performance ethnography is considered a standpoint epistemology because it is a particular moment of knowing that allows participants and the audience to understand themselves and others through and as the other. In conducting performance studies, researchers must try to separate their own feelings from the situation under observation. It is important to balance your everyday experiences with your commentary on the subjects. As a performance studies researcher, you would practice reflexivity. You would clearly define yourself in relation to the people being portrayed, your research intentions, and your prior knowledge. Since it is impossible to separate life stories from those cultural, social, and political contexts that influence experiences,; and since cultural, social, and political contexts impact the performance itself (actors, setting, audience perspectives) (Jones, 2000), performance studies reflect culture and experience.

Performance studies are also a critical method because they shed light on cultural hegemony by identifying dominant characters who regulate norms in situational and environmental membership. Alexander (2005) notes that as a moral discourse, performance studies fill the gaps between the known and the unknown, as well as the self and others. Performance studies contribute to the understanding of social life as a whole, by examining the intent of social behavior, and considering the moral and theoretical assertions inherent in the action. Jones (2000) highlights the value of performance in social activism (i.e., women's movement, civil rights, AIDS activism, etc.). Such performance asks the audience to critically examine the issue at hand.

Madison (1998) suggests that performance matters because it is action in the world, and voice is intrinsically tied to experience. Performance studies creates a space to critically examine social systems; motivates performers with rhetorical currency to make social changes; urges audience members, as a collective unit, to make changes; and teaches audience members to recognize social disparities and work to liberate the oppressed.

A variation on performance studies or performance ethnography is performative writing, writing that is written in a manner that is meant to be read aloud or performed. Liamputtong and Rumbold (2008) call this type of research *presentational knowing*, referring to expressive forms of performative arts-based research methods, and in their book on arts-based research methods, Davis and Ellis (2008) discuss their use of introspective fiction, including fictionalized narrative accounts, poetry, and reflections, to bring their research to life. Other researchers use other forms of performative research methods: drawings to explore the complexity of human experience (Guillemin & Westall, 2008); dance (*ethnodance*) to uncover and explore knowledge and meaning (Cancienne & Bagley, 2008); the study of music to understand the construction of meaning (Aldridge, 2008) and use of music to provide insights into social understandings (Daykin, 2008). Pelias's (2002) study of his relationship with his son is written as a play script, and Pelias calls this method a "strategy of writing that lets the heart be present" (Ellis et al., 2008, p. 257). Jones's (1999) performative ethnography using Billie Holiday's blues lyrics to illustrate her reasoning can be considered performative writing, and Davis's (2008b) work "A Funeral Liturgy," about funeral rituals, is written as a liturgy meant to be read aloud, responsively.

Feminist Studies

Feminist communication scholars look at how conceptions of gender are constructed through discourse, language, communication (verbal and non-verbal), messages, or texts. Much feminist scholarship commences from both a Foucauldian and postmodern feminist sense of power and resistance, sex and gender, agency, and passivity. Foucault's unique contribution was to question how discourses and associated practices came to be accepted as true or legitimate, and how these *normalized* discourses become objects for thought, to reimagine power as a productive force and to question the normalizing, long established, and societal practices associated with bias and the development of an ethic of the self (Miller, 2008; Motion & Leitch, 2007). Foucault's work was especially important in understanding power as it is experienced and conveyed in everyday practices and discourses, and a Foucauldian perspective examines the *biopolitics* that use the body as a field for power, control, and discipline (Deveaux, 1994).

Generally, Foucauldian feminist scholarship (see Trethewey, 1999, for example) explores women's gendered embodiment of self within social, personal, and professional identities. Other feminist scholars, for example, see women's issues, such as anorexia, as a function of gendered discourse and power (see Moulding, 2006; Whitehead & Kurz, 2008). Feminist scholars use many methods to study these issues, including ethnography, autoethnography, and phenomenology. Trethewey, for example, used in-depth interviews to look at the ways women "discipline their bodies" as they adorn, carry, and size their bodies in socially acceptable ways. Davis and Sharpe (2008) used autoethnography to explore the struggle to resist the hegemonic pressures on women to use their bodies as physical capital through following diet and exercise strategies.

So What?

As stated earlier in this chapter, these descriptions and categorizations are not mutually exclusive. In communication studies, it would be common for a study to be thought of as a feminist narrative ethnography, for example. It is also common for an ethnographic study to use grounded theory as a coding and analysis method, or for an ethnography to be reported as a case study. A textual analysis might very well take a critical focus, and phenomenological research might be written as a narrative. You might conduct a phenomenological ethnography in which you use ethnographic methods to understand lived experience. What is important is that the method(s) or approach(es) used be appropriate to the RQ or study objectives and that the researcher employ accepted procedures to carry out the study.

Good qualitative research is rigorous. This means that good qualitative research is reflexive. Good qualitative researchers engage in empathy, respect, and rapport toward their research participants and care about the research practices they use. They are accountable for their actions and are aware of the ethics of their practices. Good qualitative researchers remember that all knowledge is partial. They are open to the unexpected and unanticipated, and are also open about their research procedures, findings, and their claims, boundaries, and limits. Good qualitative researchers are fully engaged in the research process (Davies & Dodd, 2002). And, as Lincoln and Cannella (2004) claim, qualitative research is rigorous in that "it makes its premises, biases, predilections, and assumptions clear up front" (p. 181). We would argue, it also works appropriately within the limits and opportunities those premises, biases, predilections, and assumptions represent. It is also rigorous in that it explores and documents lived experience (Lincoln & Cannella, 2004); immerses itself in the culture, text, or discourse under study; points out societal oppression and control; and gives voice to marginalized people (Lincoln & Cannella, 2004).

Now that we have described the main types of qualitative research used in the field of communication studies, we will move to Chapter 15 in which we discuss how to conduct them. Chapter 15 will discuss the specific procedures for collecting qualitative data, and Chapter 16 will discuss the methods of coding, analyzing, and writing qualitative research. Chapter 16 will also discuss criteria for critique of qualitative research.

Glossary

Autoethnography
A type of ethnography in which the culture being studied is a culture of which the researcher is an integral part.

Bracketing
Undertaking a systematic identification of a researcher's preconceived ideas and thoughts, in order to be able to focus on understanding an experience with an open, blank mind.

Case study
An in-depth study of a particular case (or multiple cases).

Chicago School of Ethnography
Grounded in the theory of social interactionism, this communication tradition studies interrelationships between relational participants by understanding that meaning resides not in the individuals, but in their negotiated everyday interactions, and by understanding the interrelationships between individuals, the larger community, and their social experience.

Content analysis
When used as a qualitative method, used to describe elements in a message.

Conversation analysis
An investigation of social interaction between humans, most especially of everyday, ordinary conversation.

Critical ethnography
The study of how power and control in a culture is constructed through comunication.

Dialogic
A form of writing used in qualitative research to engage readers in conversation with the research.

Discourse analysis
The study of spoken or written discourse—studies speech acts—from the content of the discourse, to its delivery (paralanguage, speech, grammar), to its context, and the meaning deriving from each of these, to understand how people use language to construct ideas, meanings, and identities.

Emergent design
A study design in which methods (including sampling, data collection, data protocols, coding, and analysis) are revised as the study emerges and progresses.

Ethnography
The study of culture.

Ethnography of communication
The study of speech events and their meaning in a culture.

Ethnomethodology
This approach focuses on understanding the lived experience and lived practices from the point of view of those within an experience.

Evocative

A form of writing used in qualitative research to evoke emotions and engagement on the part of readers.

Fieldwork

Data collection in a naturalistic environment.

Grounded theory

A systematic approach to understanding and analyzing participants' lives.

Inductive reasoning

Reasoning that discovers patterns, inferences, and conclusions from studying and observing certain phenomena.

Informants

Key participants who can act as co-researchers and help the researcher explain and make sense of a culture.

In vivo

Research that takes place in a natural setting.

Multivocal

A form of writing that frequently includes multiple voices; it might be written from different points of view (including researchers and multiple stakeholders or participants).

Narrative ethnography

A specialized form of ethnography that uses a narrative voice to help readers understand a culture.

Narrative research

Research that investigates research questions dealing with the life experiences of individuals, or when the use of stories facilitates understanding of an issue under study.

Naturalistic

Research that is conducted *in the field* or where participants live, work, and play.

Performance studies

Researchers represent cultural experiences by observing and reenacting culturally situated communicative acts to reflect an interpretation of cultural practice through human expression.

Phenomenology

The study of experience, in order to understand, in great depth, the nature, essence, and meaning of that experience.

Reflexivity

How one's own thoughts, feelings, and behaviors interact with his or her research site and his or her research itself.

Rhetorical criticism

The study of the ways that written or spoken language (such as speeches, books, images, performances, texts, and films), in their historical and cultural context, work—to persuade, instruct, inform, entertain, arouse, engage, and convince.

Social constructionism

A perspective suggesting that communication is the vehicle through which reality is understood, constituted, and represented, and it is through communication that beliefs and meanings are constructed and negotiated.

Theoretical sampling

Choosing a sample based on the people, events, groups, and so on, who can shed light on a theory being investigated.

Theoretical saturation

The collection and analysis of data until no new categories of theories are identified.

References

Aldridge, D. (2008). Therapeutic narrative analysis: A methodological proposal for the interpretation of musical traces. In P. Liamputtong & J. Rumbold (Eds.), *Knowing differently: Arts-based and collaborative research methods* (pp. 205–228). New York: Nova Science.

Alexander, B. K. (2005). Performance ethnography: The reenacting and inciting of culture. In N. K. Denzin & Y. S. Lincoln (Eds.), *The Sage handbook of qualitative research* (pp. 411–441). Thousand Oaks, CA: Sage.

Aristotle. (1990). Rhetoric. In P. Bizzell & B. Herzberg (Eds.), *The rhetorical tradition: Readings from classical times to the present* (pp. 151–194). Boston: Bedford St. Martin's Press.

Atkinson, P., Coffey, A., Delamont, S., Lofland, J., & Lofland, L. (2007). *Handbook of ethnography.* Thousand Oaks, CA: Sage.Bamberg, M. (1997). Positioning between structure and performance. *Journal of Narrative and Life History,* 7, 335–342.

Bateson 1951 missing reference here

Becker, J. A. H., Ellevold, B., & Stamp, G. H. (2008). The creation of defensiveness in social interaction II: A model of defensive communication among romantic couples. *Communication Monographs,* 75(1), 86–110.

Bizzell, P., & Herzberg, B. (Eds.). (1990). *The rhetorical tradition: Readings from classical times to the present.* Boston: Bedford St. Martin's Press.

Blumer, H. (1969). *Symbolic interactionism: Perspective and method.* Berkeley: University of California Press.

Bochner, A., & Ellis. C. (1992). Personal narrative as a social approach to interpersonal communication. *Communication Theory, 2,* 65–72.

Burke, K. (1990a). Language as symbolic action. In P. Bizzell & B. Herzberg (Eds.), *The rhetorical tradition: Readings from classical times to the present* (pp. 1034–1041). Boston: Bedford St. Martin's Press.

Burke, K. (1990b). A grammar of motives. In P. Bizzell & B. Herzberg (Eds.), *The rhetorical tradition: Readings from classical times to the present* (pp. 992–1018). Boston: Bedford St. Martin's Press.

Cancienne, M. B., & Bagley, C. (2008). Dance as method: The process and product of movement in educational research. In P. Liamputtong & J. Rumbold (Eds.), *Knowing differently: Arts-based and collaborative research methods* (pp. 169–186). New York: Nova Science.

Charmaz, K. (2000). Grounded theory: Objectivist and constructivist methods. In N. Denzin & Y. S. Lincoln (Eds.), *Handbook of Qualitative Research* (pp. 509–535). Thousand Oaks, CA: Sage.

Charmaz, K. (2006). *Constructing grounded theory: A practical guide through qualitative analysis.* Thousand Oaks, CA: Sage.

Chase, S. (2000). Narrative inquiry: Multiple lenses, approaches, voices. In N. K. Denzin & Y. S. Lincoln (Eds.), *The Sage Handbook of Qualitative Research* (pp. 651–679). Thousand Oaks, CA: Sage.

Chen, Y. (2008). Fate, faith, family: Communication and harmony in Chinese TV drama The Gobi Mother. *China Media Research, 4*(4), 50–58.

Cicero, M. T. (1990). Of oratory. In P. Bizzell & B. Herzberg (Eds.), *The rhetorical tradition: Readings from classical times to the present* (pp. 200–250). Boston: Bedford St. Martin's Press.

Creswell, J. W. (2007). *Qualitative inquiry and research design: Choosing among five approaches.* Thousand Oaks, CA: Sage.

Creswell, J. W., Hanson, W. E., Clark, V. L. P., & Morales, A. (2007). Qualitative research designs: Selection and implementation. *The Counseling Psychologist, 35*(2), 236–264.

Davies, D., & Dodd, J. (2002). Qualitative research and the question of rigor. *Qualitative Health Research, 12*(2), 279–289.

Davis, C. S. (2007). The social construction of life, death, and disability in the Terri Schiavo Case. In J. L. Werth & T. Lillie (Eds.), *End of life issues and persons with disabilities* (pp. 167–182). Austin, TX: Pro-ED.

Davis, C. S. (2008a). Final stories: The ultimate sensemaking frame. *Storytelling, Self, and Society, 4,* 1–19.

Davis, C. S. (2008b). A funeral liturgy: Death rituals as symbolic communication. *Journal of Loss and Trauma, 13*(5), 406–421.

Davis, C. S. (2009). A family jigsaw puzzle: Secrets and gaps. *The International Review of Qualitative Research, 1*(4), 433–452.

Davis, C. S., & Ellis, C. (2008). Autoethnographic introspection in ethnographic fiction: A method of inquiry. In P. Liamputtong & J. Rumbold (Eds.), *Knowing differently: Arts-based and collaborative research methods* (pp. 99–118). New York: Nova Science.

Davis, C. S., & Sharpe, D. (2008). *From couch to 5K: Exercise and the body politic.* Unpublished manuscript. Charlotte, NC: The University of North Carolina at Charlotte.

Daykin, N. (2008). Knowing through music: Implications for research. In P. Liamputtong & J. Rumbold (Eds.), *Knowing differently: Arts-based and collaborative research methods* (pp. 229–244). New York: Nova Science.0 0

Deegan, M. J. (2007). The Chicago School of Ethnography. In P. Atkinson, A. Coffey, S. Delamont, J. Lofland, & L. Lofland (Eds.), *Handbook of Ethnography* (pp. 11–25). Thousand Oaks, CA: Sage.

De Fina, A., Schiffrin, D., & Bamberg, M. (2006). *Discourse and identity.* New York: Cambridge University Press.

DePalma, M., Ringer, J., & Webber, J. (2008). (Re)Charting the (dis)courses of faith and politics, or rhetoric and democracy in the Burkean barnyard. *RSQ: Rhetoric Society Quarterly, 38*(3), 311–334.

Desantis, A. D. (2003). A couple of white guys sitting around talking: The collective rationalization of cigar smokers. *Journal of Contemporary Ethnography, 32*(4), 432–466.

Deveaux, M. (1994). Feminism and empowerment: A critical reading of Foucault. *Feminist Studies, 20,* 223–248.

Ellis, C. (2007). Katrina and the cat: Responding to society's expendables. *Cultural Studies/Critical Methodologies, 7*(2), 188–201.

Ellis, C., & Bochner, A. (2000). Autoethnography, personal narrative, reflexivity: Researcher as subject. In N. Denzin & Y. Lincoln (Eds.), *The handbook of qualitative research* (2nd ed., pp. 733–768). Thousand Oaks, CA: Sage.

Ellis, C., Bochner, A., Denzin, N., Lincoln, Y., Morse, J., Pelias, R., & Richardson, L. (2008). Talking and thinking about qualitative research. *Qualitative Inquiry, 14*(2), 254–284.

Foley, D., & Valenzuela, A. (2000). Critical ethnography: The politics of collaboration. In N. K. Denzin & Y. S. Lincoln (Eds.), *The Sage handbook of qualitative research* (pp. 217–234). Thousand Oaks, CA: Sage.

Foster, E., & Bochner, A. (2008). Social constructionist perspectives in communication research. In J. A. Holstein & J. F. Gubrium (Eds.), *Handbook of Constructionist Research* (pp. 85–106). New York: Guilford.

Frers, L., (2009). Space, materiality, and the contingency of action: A sequential analysis of the patient's file in doctor-patient interactions. *Discourse Studies, 11*(3) 285–303.

Gill, V. T., & Maynard, D. W. (1995). On labeling in actual interaction: Delivering and receiving diagnoses of developmental disabilities. *Social Problems, 42*(1) 11–37.

Glaser, B. G., & Strauss, A. L. (1967). *The discovery of grounded theory: Strategies for qualitative research.* Chicago: Aldine Publishing Company.

Good, J. S., & Beach, W. A. (2005). Opening up gift-openings: Birthday parties as situated activity systems. *Text 25*(5), 565–593.

Goffman, E., (1959). *The presentation of self in everyday life.* Garden City, NY: Doubleday.

Goffman, E., (1967). *Interaction ritual: Essays on face-to-face behavior.* Garden City, NY: Doubleday.

Guillemin, M., & Westall, C. (2008). Gaining insight into women's knowing of postnatal depression using drawings. In P. Liamputtong & J. Rumbold (Eds.), *Knowing differently: Arts-based and collaborative research methods* (pp. 121–140). New York: Nova Science.

Huang Chua, C. E. (2009). Why do virtual communities regulate speech? *Communication Monograph, 6*(2), 234–261.

Jones, S. H. (1999). Torch. *Qualitative Inquiry, 5,* 235–250.

Jones, S. H. (2000). Autoethnography: Making the personal political. In N. K. Denzin & Y. S. Lincoln (Eds.), *The Sage handbook of qualitative research* (pp. 763–791). Thousand Oaks, CA: Sage.

Keating, E. (2007). The ethnography of communication. In P. Atkinson, A. Coffey, S. Delamont, J. Lofland, & L. Lofland (Eds.), *Handbook of ethnography* (pp. 285–301). Thousand Oaks, CA: Sage.

Korczynski, M. (2011). Stayin' Alive on the factory floor: An ethnography of the dialects of music use in the routinized workplace. *Poetics, 39,* 87–106.

Kristeva, J. (1990). Women's time. In P. Bizzell & B. Herzberg (Eds.), *The rhetorical tradition: Readings from classical times to the present* (pp. 1251–1266). Boston: Bedford St. Martin's Press.

Laing, R. D. (1961). *Self and others.* London: Tavistock.

Leeds-Hurwitz, W. (1993). *Semiotics and communication: Signs, codes, cultures.* Hillsdale, NJ: Lawrence Erlbaum.

Liamputtong, P., & Rumbold, J. (2008). *Knowing differently: Arts-based and collaborative research methods.* New York: Nova Science.

Lincoln, Y. S., & Cannella, G. S. (2004). Qualitative research, power, and the radical right. *Qualitative Inquiry, 10,* 175–201.

Macbeth, D. (2001). "Reflexivity" in qualitative research: Two readings, and a third. *Qualitative Inquiry, 7*(1), 35–68.

Madison, D. S. (1998). Performance, personal narratives, and the politics of possibility. In S. J. Dailey (Ed.), *The future of performance studies: Visions and revisions* (pp. 276–286). Annandale, VA: National Communications Association.

McGee, B. R. (1998). Witnessing and Ethos: The evangelical conversion of David Duke. *Western Journal of Communication, 62*(3) 217–243.

McMahan, E., & Rogers, K. L. (1994). *Interactive oral history interviewing.* Hillsdale, NJ: Lawrence Erlbaum.

Mead, G. H. (1934). *Mind, self, and society.* Chicago: University of Chicago Press.

Merrill, E., & Grassley, J. (2008). Women's stories of their experiences as overweight patients. *Journal of Advanced Nursing, 64*(2), 139–146.

Miller, L. (2008). Foucauldian constructionism. In J. A. Holstein & J. F. Gubrium (Eds.), *Handbook of constructionist research* (pp. 251–274). New York: Guilford.

Mishler, E. G. (2007). Narrative and identity: The double arrow of time. In A. de Fina, D. Schiffrin, & M. Bamberg (Eds.), *Discourse and identity.* New York: Cambridge University Press.

Montalbano-Phelps, L. L. (2003). Discourse of survival: Building families free of unhealthy relationships. *Journal of Family Communication, 3*(3), 149–177.

Motion, J., & Leitch, S. (2007). A tool box for public relations: The oeuvre of Michel Foucault. *Public Relations Review, 33*(3), 263–268.

Moulding, N. (2006). Disciplining the feminine: The reproduction of gender contradictions in the mental health care of women with eating disorders. *Social Science & Medicine, 62*(4), 793–804.

Page, J. (2006). Myth and photography in advertising: A semiotic analysis. *Visual Communication Quarterly, 13*(2), 90–109.

Patton, M. Q. (2002a). *Qualitative research and evaluation methods.* Thousand Oaks, CA: Sage.

Patton, M. Q. (2002b). Two decades of developments in qualitative inquiry: A personal, experiential perspective. *Qualitative Social Work, 1*(3), 261–283.

Pelias, R. J. (2002). For father and son: An ethnodrama with no catharsis. In C. Ellis & A. P. Bochner (Eds.), *Ethnographically speaking: Autoethnography, literature, and aesthetics* (pp. 35–43). Walnut Creek, CA: Alta Mira.

Perakyla, A. (2005). Analyzing talk and text. In N. K. Denzin & Y. S. Lincoln (Eds.), *The Sage handbook of qualitative research* (pp. 869–886). Thousand Oaks, CA: Sage.

Phillips, S. A. (2009). Crip walk, villain dance, Pueblo stroll: The embodiment of writing in African American gang dance. *Anthropological Quarterly, 82*(1), 69–98.

Pollner, M., & Emerson, R. M. (2007). Ethnomethodology and Ethnography. In P. Atkinson, A. Coffey, S. Delamont, J. Lofland, & L. Lofland (Eds.), *Handbook of ethnography* (pp. 118–135). Thousand Oaks, CA: Sage.

Reed-Danahay, D. (2001). Autobiography, intimacy, and ethnography. In P. Atkinson, A. Coffey, S. Delamont, L. Lofland, & J. Lofland (Eds.), *Handbook of ethnography* (pp. 407–425). London: Sage.

Richardson, L. (2003). Writing: A method of inquiry. In N. K. Denzin & Y. S. Lincoln (Eds.), *Collecting and interpreting qualitative materials* (pp. 499–541). Thousand Oaks, CA: Sage.

Ruesch, J., & Bateson, G. (1951). *Communication: The social matrix of psychiatry.* New York: Norton.

Russell-Kibble, A. (2011). *Mexican American parents' perceptions of cultural influences on grieving the death of their child.* (Unpublished doctoral dissertation). University of Arizona, Tucson, Arizona.

Smith, R. T. (2008). Pain in the act: The meaning of pain among professional wrestlers. *Journal of Qualitative Sociology, 31,* 129–148.

Starks, H., & Trinidad, S. B. (2007). Choose your method: A comparison of phenomenology, discourse analysis, and grounded theory. *Qualitative Health Research, 17*(10), 1372–1380.

Strauss, A., & Corbin, J. (1990). *Basics of qualitative research: Grounded theory procedures and techniques.* London: Sage.

Tedlock, B. (2000). Ethnography and ethnographic representation. In N. K. Denzin & Y. S. Lincoln (Eds.), *Handbook of qualitative research* (pp. 455–486). Thousand Oaks, CA: Sage.

Ten Have, P. (2007). *Doing conversation analysis: A practical guide.* Los Angeles, CA: Sage.

Thompson. P. (2000). *The voice of the past: Oral history.* Oxford, UK: Oxford University Press.

Toulmin, S. (1990). The uses of argument. In P. Bizzell & B. Herzberg (Eds.), *The rhetorical tradition: Readings from classical times to the present* (pp. 1105–1122). Boston: Bedford St. Martin's Press.

Trethewey, A. (1999). Disciplined bodies: Women's embodied identities at work. *Organization Studies, 20*(3), 423–450.

Walsh, K., Fürsich, E., & Jefferson, B. (2008). Beauty and the patriarchal beast: Gender role portrayals in sitcoms featuring mismatched couples. *Journal of Popular Film & Television, 36*(3), 123–132.

Weger, H., Jr., & Aakhus, M. (2003, Summer). Arguing in Internet chat rooms: Argumentative adaptations to chat room design and some consequences for public deliberation at a distance. *Argumentation & Advocacy, 40*(1), 23–38.

Whitehead, K., & Kurz, T. (2008). Saints, sinners and standards of femininity: Discursive constructions of anorexia nervosa and obesity in women's magazines. *Journal of Gender Studies, 17*(4), 345–358.

Winkle-Wagner, R. (2008). Not feminist but strong: Black women's reflections of race and gender in college. *The Negro Educational Review, 59*(3–4), 181–195.

Wolfe, D. (2008). The ecological Jeremiad, the American myth, and the vivid force of color in Dr. Seuss's *The Lorax. Environmental Communication, 2*(1), 3–24.

Zagacki, K., & Grano, D. (2005). Radio sports talk and the fantasies of sport. *Critical Studies in Media Communication, 22*(1), 45–63.

COLLECTING QUALITATIVE DATA

15

CHAPTER OUTLINE

KEY TERMS

Account analysis, critical incident, episode analysis, and protocol analysis interviews

Active-member researchers

Advice questions

Aided account

Artifacts-as-texts

Behavior or experience questions

Co-constructed interview

Complete-member researchers

Complete observer

Contrast question

Creative interviewing

Descriptive observation

Descriptive questions

Devil's advocate question

Epiphany interviews

Feeling question

Field notes

Field sites

Fieldwork

Focus groups

Focused observation

Gatekeepers

Hypothetical interaction

In-depth interviews

Interactive focus groups

Knowledge question

Life history interviews

Life story interview

Motive questions	Participant observation	Scratch notes
Native-language questions	Peripheral-member researchers	Selective observation
Naturalistic observation	Personal narrative interview	Sensitizing concepts
Observations	Polyphonic interviewing	Sensory questions
Observer-as-participant	Posing emergent ideas	Structural questions
Once-upon-a-time question	Posing the ideal	Time-line questions
Opinion or value question	Quotation questions	Topical interview
Oral history interviews	Raw data	

CHAPTER OBJECTIVES

1. To learn how to design a methodology (sample design, selecting a field site, data collection) for the main approaches and methods of qualitative research
2. To learn how to collect data for the main approaches and methods of qualitative research
3. To learn how to take field notes in qualitative research
4. To learn how to transcribe qualitative recordings
5. To learn how to apply the main qualitative concepts to specific methods and approaches

▼ # Design Considerations for Qualitative Methods

As we stated in the last chapter, conducting qualitative research frequently involves an *inductive, emergent* process of study design, data collection, preliminary analysis, redesigning, recollecting, reanalyzing, and so on.

Sampling

In qualitative research, as we stated in Chapter 8 on sampling, sample size depends on the scope and objectives of the study (Starks & Trinidad, 2007). We also stated that most qualitative methods rely on *purposive sampling* methods, looking for participants who have experienced the phenomena or issue under study (Starks & Trinidad, 2007). Depending on the study objectives, qualitative research projects might also use other sampling methods such as *theoretical construct sampling, maximum variation sampling, typical instance sampling*, or *extreme instance sampling*. Potential participants may be identified through *snowball* or *network sampling*.

Phenomenological research typically has small samples, because phenomenologists are not looking to sample from a wide range of experiences—they want detailed information about a very specific experience. Phenomenological research typically uses sample sizes from one to ten participants (Starks & Trinidad, 2007); people who have experienced the phenomena under study. For that reason, phenomenological research typically uses purposive sampling or theoretical construct sampling.

In grounded theory, you're done when you're done—when you've collected enough data to understand and explain the full complexity of the culture you're studying; when you have detailed descriptions of the ways that participants view the world; when you fully understand underlying issues, changes over time, and multiple viewpoints; when you can develop analytic categories; and when you understand differences and nuances in your data (Charmaz, 2006). Grounded theory is more interested with immersion in a culture than in sample size. In a grounded theory study, achieving understanding and rapport with our participants is more important than the number of participants we talk to. Having said that, however, grounded theory often has larger sample sizes than other qualitative methods because it uses theoretical sampling, involving participants with different experiences to compare and explore different aspects. In grounded theory, the sample size is complete when the study reaches *theoretical saturation*—when no more theories or constructs emerge by the data. Grounded theory research typically uses samples ranging from ten to sixty participants (Starks & Trinidad, 2007).

There are as many sampling strategies in ethnographic research as there are types of ethnographic research. An ethnography that takes a grounded theory stance might utilize theoretical sampling such as in grounded theory, or an ethnography that has a phenomenological approach might sample purposively for phenomenological understanding. Other ethnographies might want people who represent different types of experiences, so they might use typical instance, maximum variation, or extreme instance sampling. Many ethnographies are methodologically case studies and might only study one culture or field site, but even with small samples or single site samples, all ethnographers typically conduct long periods of fieldwork (up to twelve months of observations—or more) and multiple interviews of many participants in that one site.

Conversation analysis (CA) and discourse analysis also might have a very small sample size, depending on the study objectives. Sometimes a single conversational event might be sufficient, other times, more discourses might be required to compare across people or settings (Starks & Trinidad, 2007). Sometimes in CA, sampling is thought of as collecting a specimen, and you would want one or more specimens that are representative of the category you are studying (Ten Have, 2007). In their study on public discourse surrounding the Young Women's Christian Association of America decision to reverse its mandate of single-sex membership, Harter, Kirby, and Gerbensky-Kerber (2010) drew upon nearly six years of public discourse as their sampling. Both CA and discourse analysis of studies would be likely to use purposive sampling and might, depending on the research question or study objectives, use maximum variation or typical instance sampling.

Sampling is not really a concept used in case studies, at least not in the traditional sense. While we said in Chapter 14 that a case is a **bounded unit**, determining what the exact bounds of your case are may not be as easy as you might think. A case certainly can consist of one individual (if that person exemplifies a phenomenon or issue you want to study), but a case may also be an organization, a program, an event or activity, a time, or a process. Sometimes, your *case* may be the same as a *research site* (see the next section), especially if you are studying organizations or groups. Before you decide on your sampling strategy, you need

bounded unit
A case.

to make sure you're clear on the bounds of your case—what qualifies as being *in* the case, and what is *out*? Case studies use purposive sampling strategies, cases chosen specifically for their characteristics related to the issues you are studying. While you may likely be studying one case, in order to fully understand that case, you might do many observations over time, conduct multiple interviews with many different people, and look at quite a few records. As with ethnography and phenomenology, the hallmark of case study data collection is to immerse yourself in the case until you have reached saturation—until no new insights, understandings, or descriptions occur (Baxter & Jack, 2008).

It's also possible to do a multiple case study, when you want to compare one organization or program with another, for example, or when you want to replicate a case to understand the situation under study even more fully or understand the situation from different nuances or angles. Again, sampling or sample size is not really the relevant question to ask here. Instead, you want to determine what it is you are trying to compare or replicate. If, for example, you want to understand how Medicaid versus non-Medicaid health-care providers communicate with patients, you might want to use as one case a health-care clinic that takes Medicaid, and as a second case, one that does not (Yin, 2009).

Sampling in textual analysis, including content analysis and the different types of rhetorical analysis, depends completely on your research question or study objectives. If, for example, you want to know how doctors are depicted in the television show *House*, you might actually randomly sample ten episodes from the 2008 season and analyze them. If you want to understand how Martin Luther King Jr. constructed hope in his famous "I Have a Dream" speech, you would be studying the population—that one speech.

Perhaps your rhetorical analysis is less specific than that; let's say you want to understand how gender is constructed through women's clothing styles. You would have to first *operationalize* your variables—which women, which styles, and then determine how to identify those texts. You might operationalize your variable as women on your college campus, and their everyday style of dressing. Then, you might use typical instance sampling, which might consist of going to the food court in the student activity center and taking field notes on the clothing you see.

When your textbook author Christine Davis (2007) wanted to analyze the use of language to construct the concepts of life and death in the Terri Schiavo legal case, I decided to go to newspaper accounts that described how both sides of the debates talked about the situation. Rather than going to all newspaper accounts, I used the newspaper that was local to the situation, the *St. Petersburg Times*, because I thought it would have the most thorough coverage of the debate. Within that parameter, I analyzed the population (all) of newspapers throughout the duration of the court case. Thus, I analyzed the population of articles within a purposive sample of newspapers.

Selecting and Accessing a Field Site

field sites
Groups, organizations, or cultures in which research is conducted.

Some types of qualitative research—ethnographic research, phenomenological research, grounded theory research, case studies, and CA and discourse analysis, most frequently, sample within **field sites**—within groups, organizations, or cultures. The type of field site you choose will depend, again, on your research question or study objectives. Christine Davis, for example, has conducted ethnographic research at a hospice organization (Davis, 2010) and within a children's mental health system of care (Davis, 2006, 2008). If you wish to study communication within an organization, you might select one specific organization to study based on the same factors on which you'd base your sample selection—your initial theoretical construct, the amount of variability you want at your site, if you want an organization that is typical, or if you want an organization that is atypical.

Once you've determined what type of site you wish to study, you need to gain access to the site. Most ethnographers, for example, gain access to the site through *informants*. Sometimes it's as simple as knowing someone at the site—the higher the rank, the better. Other times, you need to make an appointment with management (if it's an organization) or a respected group member or leader, then sell yourself and the project. You'll need to get past the organizational **gatekeepers**, and you may not always know who they are until after you think you have approval to conduct the research. Ironically, Christine Davis, while writing this book chapter, was attempting to collect data within a field site—a local children's mental health system of care. She thought she had permission from the people in charge of giving her referrals to potential study participants, but after she began trying to collect data, the research was blocked by a gatekeeper higher up in the site she had not known to contact. As of this writing, she is attempting to gain access to another alternative site. In naturalistic research, you have to be flexible and prepared for changes and setbacks.

gatekeepers
Management (if it's an organization) or a respected group member or leader who grants approval to conduct research in a given field site.

Frequently, rather than being given *carte blanche* approval, access is negotiated. For example, I might want to observe child and family team meetings, and to do that, I might ask to be given names of all caregivers of children to obtain their permission to attend. The gatekeeper might tell me that I can only attend meetings of children with one kind of disorder, but not another (because of concerns about risk or their different funding requirements for different diagnoses). Perhaps the site might want to give me access, but only if I provide them with copies of my videotapes of the meetings for their training purposes; however, that would go against IRB guidelines for anonymity. Instead, I might offer to give them deidentified typed transcripts and also offer to conduct training for them based on the study findings. As in any negotiation, it's important to think about what's in it for the site—how the risks (and perceived risks) can outweigh the benefits. At the very least, you might be inconveniencing people at the site, and in health-related sites gatekeepers might be concerned that your presence will affect provision of care. You need to address these concerns up front.

Once you have access to a site and before you start formal data collection, it's a good idea to familiarize yourself with the environment. Do some informal *hanging out*. If it's an organization, take a tour. If it's a town, study a map. Ask the gatekeepers or informants to brief you on what to expect and how to act. Actually, that's one of the key roles of the informants—they are people who are in the culture or site you wish to study who are willing to act as a guide and translator of cultural practices and jargon or language (Fontana & Frey, 2003).

You may have to gain access only once, such as accessing a health-care organization. Or you may have to gain access each time you talk to new participants, such as talking to people in a public place such as a shopping mall, or attending a series of health-care team meetings for which you have to get access for each meeting separately. In his study on cigar smokers' rationalization of smoking behaviors, Desantis (2003) spent time in the same cigar shop over a matter of years, for a total of six hundred hours of fieldwork.

You have to decide how to present yourself—as a student, a professor, or one of the participants. This is an important consideration, and one that will shadow you throughout the study. You may want the respect (and cooperation) of the professionals or managers at your site, but you also need the rapport and trust of the employees, patients, or members at the site, as well. It's a fine line. Desantis (2003) was first a cigar shop regular prior to engaging in both participant observation and interviewing. This allowed him a type of privileged access to be both friend and researcher to the others he studied.

To get good information, you need to be in the field (involved with the site) long enough to gain the trust of the study participants. This will occur over time as they become familiar with you. You also have to establish rapport with study participants in order to get good trustworthy information. How you access the site affects both of those factors.

Ethical Issues

Chapter 5 has already talked about the ethical issues to be considered in data collection, but we'd just like to remind you of a few of them now. In most qualitative research, you must obtain informed consent from study participants before conducting data collection. This is easy enough when conducting in-depth interviews. However, it becomes problematic when doing observations or when taking field notes in public places. The general rule is that if a person is identifiable to anyone (including you), you must obtain informed consent from him or her. If you are observing a group, every person in the group must give consent in order for you to observe them. What if you are observing in a large site such as an organization? There's no way you can get every organization member to give consent. That may not be practical, but you must get consent from the people you will be doing any identified interaction with. That doesn't mean that you need consent if you're just going to say "hello" when passing someone in the hallway, but you do need consent if you plan to have a long conversation with a person, and especially if you plan to write about a person specifically (identified or not) in your findings.

How you identify participants in your report is also an important ethical decision. Sometimes you will be reporting their comments anonymously or they will be identified by role (i.e., mother, or provider). Other times, you might give them pseudonyms. Other times, they might give you permission to use their real names. Make sure each person in the study is clear up front how his or her name will be used. Also make sure everyone understands fully if you will be using actual quotes, narratives, stories, or other information that may identify him or her. Sometimes, the ethical thing to do is to let those involved read the report before it's finalized so they can flag any passages they think might blow their cover.

Data Collection

Observations

Qualitative researchers use **observations** to gain insight into the obligations, constraints, motivations, and emotions that participants experience as they complete everyday actions. Observations help us understand the complex, lived experience of human beings. Qualitative researchers conducting studies such as ethnography, case study, phenomenology, and others often use observational techniques in natural settings, which is why it is sometimes called **naturalistic observation**. Observation in natural settings is also frequently referred to as **fieldwork** (Angrosino & de Pérez, 2003). Often, observation is referred to as **participant observation** because you are participating in the life of others. But, remember, you are still observing as a naïve outsider who doesn't understand exactly what's going on and needs to ask, explore, and try on the experience. In addition, you will never truly be able to understand the experience from a first person point of view (Rock, 2007). You might observe one time, or you might observe multiple times over a long period of time, likely months, maybe years.

Types of Observers. Observation can be formal or informal. You can, for example, simply hang out. Or you can become more involved—become a volunteer, join a group, move in. Some ethnographers take on the role of **complete observer**, in which they have little to no interaction with the people being observed. This is done rarely, however, partly due to the incompatibility of informed consent procedures with lack of interaction with participants, and partly because researchers recognize that there really is no such thing as no interaction or true objectivity. Researchers need to be aware that the very act of observing a setting will in fact influence and change behaviors of the people being observed. Many researchers instead do **observer-as-participant**, in which the researcher interacts casually with participants, but still remains primarily an observer and does not become a member of the group being studied.

Other researchers take on the role of **peripheral-member researchers**, researchers who have some level of involvement with a group without core group involvement. **Active-member researchers** become involved with central activities of the group but do not fully commit themselves to the group. **Complete-member researchers** study settings in which they are already members or with which they are already affiliated (Angrosino & de Pérez, 2003).

Types of Observations. There are several ways to observe. In **descriptive observation**, usually done when you are first in the field, you observe everything, no matter how small. You take nothing for granted. In **focused observation**, conducted after you've been in the field for a while, you ignore things that are irrelevant, and you define irrelevant based on your initial analyses, interviews, grounded theory open coding, and so on. In **selective observation**, as your

observations
A way to gain insight into the obligations, constraints, motivations, and emotions that participants experience as they complete everyday actions.

naturalistic observation
The use of observational techniques in natural settings.

fieldwork
Conducting observations in natural settings.

participant observation
When a researcher is participating in the life of others, but is still observing as a naïve outsider who doesn't understand exactly what's going on and needs to ask, explore, and try on the experience.

complete observer
Researchers that have little to no interaction with the people being observed.

observer-as-participant
Researcher interacts casually with participants, but still remains primarily an observer, and does not become a member of the group being studied.

peripheral-member researchers
Researchers who have some level of involvement with a group without core group involvement.

active-member researchers
Researchers that become involved with central activities of the group but do not fully commit themselves to the group.

complete-member researchers
Researchers who study settings in which they are already members or with which they are already affiliated.

descriptive observation
Everything is observed, no matter how small, and is usually done when a researcher is first in a field.

focused observation
Things that are irrelevant are ignored and not observed; usually done when a researcher has been in a field for a while.

selective observation
Researchers concentrate on certain activities based on additional analyses, interviews, coding, and so on, as their time in a field is winding down.

field notes
A record of what was meaningful during an observation.

scratch notes
Rough notes that are embellished upon shortly after an observation.

time in the field is winding down, you concentrate on certain activities, again based on additional analyses, interviews, coding, and so forth (Angrosino & de Pérez, 2003).

What specifically do you observe? People—who is involved and who is not involved; the setting, the context, or the scene; and your impressions. Of course, remember that you're communication researchers, so you're observing communication—communication acts or interactions; how, when, and where they communicate; and what their communication means.

How Do You Remember What You're Observing? You take **field notes.** Field notes are taken in all sorts of ways: notebook, sketch pad, tape recorder, video recorder, laptop, even napkins, or, when necessary, the palm of your hand. Field notes are a record of what was meaningful. They include mental observation, note taking during or after the observation, recording during or after, and journals or diaries highlighting your impressions as you interact in the field. Write it down, record it, remember it—the only rule is to do what you need to do so that you can vividly recall it later. You'll usually write rough notes, often called **scratch notes,** then embellish those notes soon after for more *detailed field notes.*

Here's an example of field notes your author Christine Davis took for research on hospice in which I observed hospice team meetings and interactions with patients (Davis, 2010). I was an observer-as-participant. I took brief notes in a notebook during most of the hospice team meetings I attended, and I dictated more detailed field notes into a small tape recorder after the meeting was over. Notice how the field notes represent a sort of stream-of-consciousness notation of my descriptive observation. I noted everything, since at this point I didn't know what my point of my analysis was going to be.

field notes following shadowing nurse C. with A. Ironically as I'm driving here the song "Spirit in the Sky" is playing and that makes me think of A. as I think of her corner table with all the religious icons, her candles, she's always got at least one candle burning, some of the candles are in virgin mary decorated vases or glasses. She's got a statue of virgin mary that's got neon lights that blink surrounding her. That's always kind of in the background of the room, a lot of beadwork and candles around. She's rearranged her bed this time, I haven't seen her in awhile. She recently finished a chemotherapy treatment and is just blown up. Evidently that's partly due to the chemotherapy and partly due to the fact that her cancer has spread; she's got a huge mass, that's involving the bladder and the kidneys and the nurse verified later that it's also spread to her spine and she also has a compression fracture in her spine. The dr told her that since the cancer was in the bladder, that's causing a lot of her swelling. Her abdomen is huge. Very tender to the touch. She and the nurse talked about her pain. She described her pain as being centered in the abdomen and hips and was a sharp stabling pain that's going on and on that's aggravated by movement or activity. When she took her pain medication and lay down and relaxed that seemed to help. She also later talked about a pain that was shooting up her back from her hips and abdomen and later she talked about another pain in her abdomen that was a tearing pain and the nurse verified that was probably due to the mass pressing against all sorts of organs. She's having a great deal of nausea, vomiting, after her last chemo she just stayed in bed for 3 days, she was all worn out. When the nurse met with her, she sat down on the side of her bed, held her hand the entire time, actually had her hand on her arm the entire time, after a lot of questions about the pain, asked her to rate her pain on a scale of 1 to 5, asked her about nausea symptoms, questions about how often she urinated and how often she moved her bowels, to see what, she explained later, to see what organs were being affected, symptoms from the cancer and from the chemo I think also. She talked her about do you want to continue the chemo because of the side effects, and the pt said yes, they agreed that the side effects went on for 3 days but was helping a lot of the symptoms, was shrinking the primary tumor in the cervix and so that's alleviating symptoms. A. said that her leg which had been all swollen, was that went down with them chemo, so she's willing to take 3 days of misery for another 3 weeks of feeling better before her next bout with chemo. She also said the dr said that with the cancer in the bladder that was also contributing to the blood clots and that would continue as well, and she's been in the hospital recently to have a screen put in for blood clots. The dr nurse practitioner evidently went out week before last to straighten out her medication so she seems to be doing better. She was so sick after the chemo that she was not well enough to say she was out of her pain medication so she's been taking it max. so the nurse sat on her bed, asked her a lot of medical questions, asked her a lot of questions about if she's taking care of her kids, are her daughters helping out at all, is she standing up for herself. A. did say that she was in bed for 3 days, she sent the kids out of the room and didn't do anything and the daughters seemed to at least leave her alone. It's not clear if they understand how sick she is but they at least seem to at least be leaving her alone. Also, she said when her boyfriend's over there, they don't leave the kids with her, they look in the room, see the boyfriend there, and leave her alone. So she seems to be doing some things to stand up for herself. The nurse talked about, if she wanted to go into the hospice home after her next bout with chemo, just to get some relief, and have somebody to take care of her. A. didn't respond, didn't look to me like she was pleased with the idea; it looked to me like she was not pleased with the idea, but she didn't respond one way or the other. they are seeing her twice a week now,

What Observers Observe.   Observation as a data collection method is used in many of the qualitative methodologies, with a slightly different focus for each.

In phenomenology, researchers observe participants in their natural environment to find information about their lived experience and resulting meaning (Starks & Trinidad, 2007). Grbich (2007) calls phenomenological observation "bathing in the experience as it occurs" (p. 88).

In grounded theory, researchers observe social processes in their natural environments, which help them see the affect of the environment on behavior and meaning (Starks & Trinidad, 2007). Since, in grounded theory, you shape and reshape your data collection and refine your study design as you try out tentative concepts, theories, and analysis throughout your study, you might return to the field to observe different things, explore additional questions or experiences, or otherwise move along your ideas as they emerge (Charmaz, 2006). Field notes in grounded theory might include descriptions of both individual and collective behaviors, much detail including stories and observations, processes you consider to be significant, things that participants tell you they consider to be interesting or problematic, participants' language use, scenes and contexts, and analytical thoughts and ideas. Observations in a grounded theory project focus on processes—what is related to what else, what are the practices in the site, how are people organized, and what are the social networks. In grounded theory, you will be looking for data that lets you compare across time, across categories, and between concepts. In grounded theory research, think of fieldwork as an opportunity to "dig into the scene" (p. 23).

In discourse analysis, researchers would observe speech-in-action (Starks & Trinidad, 2007) and would likely also record the actual discourse used, giving a well-rounded picture of discourse and meaning. CA does not use observation per se, especially with field notes, but instead CA uses recordings of natural interactions (Ten Have, 2007).

In-Depth Interviews

in-depth interviews
Opportunities for participants to describe their worlds, in concert and negotiation with researchers. Such interviewing involves co-constructing a narrative with a participant—to understand his or her history and version of the story and the ways that he or she makes sense of his or her actions in the context of his or her cultural narratives.

The same qualitative approaches that use observations (ethnography, grounded theory, phenomenology, case study, action research, discourse analysis), as well as conversation analysis, also frequently use **in-depth interviews** as a method for collecting data. In qualitative research, think of the interview as an opportunity for the co-construction, exchange, and negotiation of ideas, information, and meaning. Qualitative interviews resemble conversations between equals who systematically explore topics of mutual interest. Interviews are opportunities for participants to describe their worlds, in concert and negotiation with researchers. Such interviewing involves co-constructing a narrative with a participant—to understand his or her history and version of the story and the ways that he or she makes sense of his or her actions in the context of their cultural narratives. The goal of qualitative interviewing is to establish rapport with participants and to understand and learn from participants. When interviewing, qualitative researchers seek to understand participants' perspectives on an experience, because remember, in qualitative research, we want to retrieve experiences, gain insight, obtain information, obtain descriptions, foster trust, understand sensitive relationships, or create discourse to analyze (Fontana & Frey, 2003; Fontana & Prokos, 2007; Madison, 2005; Roulston, deMarrais, & Lewis, 2003; Silverman, 2003).

Interviews can help us understand a phenomenon: They can help us identify it, discover it, and explain it; we can listen to participants' thoughts, ideas, feelings, and behaviors about it. Interviews can let us understand participants' natural attitudes, life experiences, preferences, intentions, and behaviors, and in doing so, we can better understand their language, knowledge, and experience (Fontana & Prokos, 2007).

Here's an excerpt from an interview with a hospice chaplain in a study concerning the experience of hospice (Davis, 2010). Notice how it sounds like a natural conversation.

> *I take a bite of cake as Father Logan and I chat. "So, would you say hospice is a spiritual organization?" I ask.*

> *He pauses for a minute and then responds thoughtfully. "I do not agree with this dichotomy between the spiritual and the secular. As I understand life, and from a biblical perspective, all of life is spiritual. Sitting here talking to you is an act of spirituality. Taking care of a patient physically, medically, is an act of spirituality because the body is as much of a person as the soul. You can't really take care of one part separate from the other. They are intertwined."*

I nod. "You know, it seems to me somehow, by addressing the physical, hospice actually takes care of the spiritual." He licks a bit of icing off his fork, then leans forward, gesturing with his fork as he talks. "That gets back to hospice's philosophy of health care, which is holistic. I think the patients appreciate us because they feel loved and valued. Somebody cares."

"One of the things I notice is how you all touch the patients. I see a lot of hugging and touching."

"Yeah," he agrees. "One of the first things I noticed when I started with hospice is all the touching that goes on, among the hospice worker, the patient, and the caregiver. Touching people on the shoulder, rubbing their back."

"Do you do a lot of touching yourself?"

"When I go to visit a patient, I might touch them on the back. If they're bad off, I'll make sure I rub their hand or their arms. Because touch communicates love and care."

I think of my dad when he was sick and how much touching meant to both of us. I nod.

He continues. "There are thousands of nerves in the skin. Touching speaks volumes to the patient and the caregiver. By the family seeing you touch the patient in some way, their burden is eased as well." (pp. 35–36).

Phenomenology and grounded theory would use interviews to obtain the participants' stories or accounts of the experience as retrospective account. Both types of researchers would probe and clarify throughout the interview to obtain details (Starks & Trinidad, 2007). Phenomenological interviewing would include nonstructured interviews that you can follow up on to understand the participant's experience. You would return to each participant multiple times to make sure you fully understand (Grbich, 2007).

Grounded theorists begin their research with **sensitizing concepts**—initial ideas, concepts, interests to pursue and sensitize you to ask certain kinds of questions and look for certain kinds of information. These sensitizing concepts give you a starting point for data collection but they are only a starting point in grounded theory—you let the data help you develop your thoughts, theories, and ideas and you follow those as you refine your study. Therefore, interview guides in grounded theory are open ended and emergent, subject to change as the study—or the interview—progresses (Charmaz, 2006).

sensitizing concepts
Initial ideas, concepts, or interests to pursue and sensitize people to ask certain kinds of questions and look for certain kinds of information.

Grounded theory interview questions center around the central question of grounded theory, "What's happening here?" Grounded theory interviewing will be formed by what you've observed in the field, as you ask participants questions about meanings, processes, and control related to actions and behaviors you've seen. A grounded theory interview will consist of a few good open ended questions that let your participant do most of the talking, yielding an in-depth exploration of the participant's experience. Questions such as: "Tell me about," "How," "What," and "When" are useful in helping participants give rich responses. Grounded theory interviewing investigates taken-for-granted aspects of life to understand participants' meanings, intentions, and actions.

In grounded theory, data collection, coding, and analysis are simultaneous. As the issues become clearer and more specific, researchers can hone in on participants' issues, interests, and concerns with more specificity. The interviewer is an active participant in the process. Grounded theory uses multiple interviews to delve deeper into salient topics.

Discourse analysts would conduct in-depth interviews to elicit participants' language, and perhaps to clarify the participants' intended meaning for their discourse (Starks & Trinidad, 2007). CA does not usually use interviews as a source of data, since CA considers interviews to be too subject to researcher's manipulation or construction, and CA seeks to analyze more pure forms of natural conversation (Ten Have, 2007).

Types of Interviews.

Life story interview
Participant discusses the significant streams of his or her life.

Oral history interviews
Participant discusses his or her stories about a significant historical moment in his/her life.

Personal narrative interview
Participant discusses an event or experience.

Topical interview
Participant discusses a specific topic, program, issue, or process.

Polyphonic interviewing
Captures and retains individual voices of the participants.

Epiphany interviews
Participant discusses certain turning points in his or her life.

critical incident, episode analysis, account analysis, and protocol analysis interviews
Participant discusses and reconstructs a specific experience in a specific context.

co-constructed interview
A collaboration in which the researcher and participant are full partners in the interview.

Types of Interviews. Interviewing can be structured, semi-structured, or unstructured. Most qualitative interviews in communication studies are fairly unstructured and open ended. In unstructured interviews, you discuss with participants their (and perhaps your) inner thoughts and feelings. You modify the interview as you go along. You would think of this type of interview as a guided conversation. Your goal is to be dialogic and interactive, understanding each other at a deep level of meaning (Fontana & Frey, 2003).

A **life story interview** documents all the significant streams of a person's life, to provide understanding of the larger cultural or historical frames. This can take a linear narrative form (what happened next), or can be more performative (tell me a story, or role play this situation). Full life history interviews are rare, but often aspects of a life might be examined in an interview. Life story interviews often look at turning points or disjunctures in a person's life as a way of studying identity, conflicts, and so on. **Oral history interviews** capture people's stories about their lives. Oral history is a person's recounting of a significant historical moment in their life, and would ask the participant to "give me your experiences of this historical time or event." A variation, life history interviews, takes place over several days in multiple sessions as people go about their everyday lives and give oral reports about their lives. A **personal narrative interview** is a person's recounting—telling a story about—an event, experience, or point of view. A **topical interview** consists of a person's discussion of a topic, program, issue, or process. In **polyphonic interviewing**, the voices of the participants are recorded with minimal influence from the researcher and are reported separately (from each other) as individual voices, multiple perspectives, and differences between each are highlighted rather than glossed over. **Epiphany interviews** are interviews in which people tell about certain moments in their lives that are turning points; participants' transformational, existential moments in their lives. They provide rich, meaningful data.

Critical incident, episode analysis, account analysis, and protocol analysis interviews all ask participants to tell about a specific experience in a specific context, for example, "Tell me about a good day at work or school." In this type of interview, participants might reconstruct a scene, complete with dialogue/ role playing, and the interviewer might ask questions such as "What did you mean when you said that?" or "What were you thinking when that happened?"

Some qualitative researchers use what's called a **co-constructed interview**, an interview that is a collaboration between researcher and participant—the researcher and participant are full partners in the interview. The conversation between them is as important as the response given by the participant. **Creative interviewing** is adaptive to situations. These types of interviews may consist of multiple sessions over many days. They may be more intimate and dialogic, or may include shared stories between researchers and participants (Fontana & Frey, 2003; Madison, 2005).

Types of Questions. There is an almost unlimited list of types of questions you can ask in qualitative research. The purpose in giving you this list isn't as much to make you memorize lists, but to tweak your curiosity and generate ideas for your interview processes. Remember, too, that while the questions you ask are important, your questions will evolve and improve as you spend more time in the field.

Here are some of the types of qualitative interview questions mentioned in the literature:

- → **Advice questions:** Asking participants to give advice to a person in a similar situation, yielding information on beliefs or understandings.
- → **Aided account:** Use of video, picture, or graphics to ask questions about specific experiences.
- → **Behavior or experience questions:** Asking for more information about an action or behavior.
- → **Contrast question:** Asking for unlike comparisons in order to understand something by understanding what it is not. For example, "What's the difference between 'a' and 'b'?"
- → **Descriptive questions:** Asking participants to recount (in detail) or recreate a phenomenon or experience, like a verbal tour of the phenomenon.
- → **Devil's advocate question:** Why should 'a' happen or not happen?
- → **Feeling question:** Ask participant to discuss how they feel or are emotionally affected by a phenomenon.
- → **Hypothetical interaction:** What would you do if 'x' did 'y'?
- → **Knowledge question:** Asking a participant for specific factual information about a topic and how one attains this type of information.
- → **Motive questions:** What were you trying to accomplish, why do you think he or she said that?
- → **Native-language questions:** What do the terms mean, who uses them, when, in what context, and so on.
- → **Once-upon-a-time question:** Asking participants to narrate an experience related to a phenomenon.
- → **Opinion or value question:** Asks a person to discuss a belief or judgment they have about an issue.
- → **Posing emergent ideas:** It's sounding like "this" is going on, how does that resonate with your own experience?
- → **Posing the ideal:** Describe the ideal—organization, situation, state of affairs, goals, and so on.
- → **Quotation questions:** Giving participants a direct quotation from another interview or observation and asking for their feelings or opinions about it.

creative interviewing
Adaptive interviewing that may consist of multiple sessions over many days, more intimate and dialogic sessions, or shared stories between researchers and participants.

→ **Sensory question:** Attempting to understand how a participant experiences a phenomenon from a sensory point of view (what do they see, hear, feel, taste, smell).

→ **Structural questions:** Questions that require explanation and explore contextual information (how does something work? how do you—the participant—structure knowledge?). For example, "What are all the different ways to do this?" or "What are all the stages/ranges?"

→ **Time-line questions:** What happened next? (Fontana & Frey, 2003; Madison, 2005).

While the questions you ask are important, your attitude and stance during the interview is equally important. When going into an interview, you should have excitement, naïveté, active and sympathetic listening, awareness of status differences, patient probing and clarifying, and also an inquiring mind—the strong desire to find out and understand the answers to the questions you are asking (Fontana & Frey, 2003; Madison, 2005).

Here are some general interviewing tips:

- Start with ice breaker questions.
- Move on to more general questions.
- Depending on study objectives and RQs, you may share your opinions with participants, or you may not.
- Remember that the goal is to create shared meaning; you want to observe nonverbals that are also communicating meaning in the interview.
- Keep the interview questions natural and conversational.
- Avoid irrelevant questions and topics.
- Listen for slang, jargon, and so forth—ask participants to explain terms to you to help you understand them; avoid using slang yourself unless you know the participant understands it.
- It's okay to be broad in your questions, but make sure both you and the participant are clear what you are asking about.
- Ask one thing at a time.
- Don't embarrass your participant.
- Keep the questions in a flow.
- Order or group the questions in a logical sequence.

Good interviewing requires good listening skills. I'm sure you remember these skills from your Introduction to Communication class, but let's review them anyway. Good listening involves listening for both content and feelings. You exhibit good listening skills through appropriate eye contact and body language and through, frankly, intent listening. It's important to listen carefully enough that you know when you have received a complete response and when you have not. When you have not, or when the person's response raises additional questions (which it often will), you should probe and clarify. Often, in in-depth interviewing, probing, and clarifying yields the most meaningful information of the entire interview.

When do you probe and clarify? When the person says something that can have more than one meaning (e.g., nice, perfect, boring, attractive, exciting, convenient, lovely, unusual, different), you should ask him or her to define the term by asking, "What does *nice* mean to you?" or "What do you mean by *nice*?" When the person gives you a generalization ("Everybody likes ice cream,"), you might ask, "What do *you* like about it?" When she is vague ("Sometimes I think about it"), you would ask her to be more specific ("Tell me about a specific time you thought about it"). When he contradicts something he said earlier, you might say, "I'm confused. Maybe I misunderstood, but didn't you say earlier _____ ?" When she needs to elaborate, you can ask, "Tell me more about that." You might need her to say more, and you can give her a silent probe with a questioning look (raised eyebrows, frown, head tilt), hand gestures (roll hands for "tell me more"), or a head nod. If he seems to need encouragement to continue talking, you can say, "I see!" or "Uh huh," or you can ask, "And then?" or "What happened next?" To get additional facts or a more accurate understanding, you can ask, "Can you clarify that for me?", "Could you describe that once more? I'm not sure I understand.", "What do you mean by that?", "Help me understand.", "I'm unclear how you came to that conclusion. Can you tell me more?", or "I've lost you. Can we go back to _____ ?"

To show you understand, or to help his label his feelings/experiences, you can probe or clarify for feelings by saying, "You feel that _____ ", "At that point you were feeling _____ ", "You were [angry] at that moment . . .", "I can hear the [sadness] when you tell that story . . .", "I can sense the [frustration] you must have felt," or "If I understand correctly, you're feeling _____ ".

To check your meaning and interpretation and to show you are listening and understanding, you can say, "As I understand it, you _____ ", "Am I right in saying that this is the way you see this situation?", "If I were to say that, would I be on target?", "Would it be accurate to say you thought _____ ?", or "If I understand how you see this situation, it's _____ ?"

To help her define a situation, explore aspects, or examine attitudes, you can ask, "What led you to make that particular decision?", "How would you describe the problem as you see it now?", "How would you assess the situation at this point in time?", "What values might have prompted you to take that action?", or "What is the key issue for you right now?"

Probe and Clarify:

1. When the person says something that can have more than one meaning
2. When the person gives you a generalization
3. When the person contradicts something he or she said earlier
4. When the person needs to elaborate
5. If the person needs encouragement to continue talking
6. To show you understand
7. To help the person label his or her feelings/experiences
8. To check your meaning and interpretation
9. To show you are listening
10. To help the person define a situation, explore aspects, or examine attitudes

Challenges. Just because we said that qualitative interviewing resembles a conversation, please do not think that if you can converse, you can automatically interview. Interviewing is more difficult than it looks. One reason is that despite your best intentions and preparation, you never know ahead of time exactly what will happen in an interview. Our questions and our participants' responses are always more ambiguous than we think they will be. You have to be flexible and prepared for anything (Fontana & Frey, 2003; Roulston et al., 2003).

Roulston and colleagues (2003) interviewed student interviewers and gathered information on the challenges they faced in their first interviews. They had lots of challenges. They encountered unexpected participant behaviors such as participants who were late to the interview. The room was noisy, and the environment was distracting to both the researcher and the participant. Participants were uncomfortable with the note taking or tape recording of the interview. The interviewers didn't receive the responses they expected to receive. They had difficulty being flexible in terms of going where the participants' answers took them. They didn't know how much to talk, or they talked too much or not enough. They had difficulty being mentally present throughout the interview and able to attend to what the participant was saying. They had difficulty keeping the conversation related to the research topic. They were uncertain about what they were really asking or really wanting to find out from the interview. They had problems asking questions that were clear and concise. They had difficulty dealing with emotionality of the participants. They had trouble asking difficult questions. They couldn't create rapport in the interview. Finally, they felt overwhelmed by everything they had to do at once during the interview. What went well among the student interviewers was turning the interview into a conversation in which participants were relaxed and open.

Interviewing Challenges:

1. Participants late to the interview
2. Distracting, noisy environment
3. Discomfort with note taking or tape recording
4. Unexpected responses
5. Being flexible
6. Talking too much or not enough
7. Being mentally present throughout the interview
8. Keeping the conversation related to the research topic
9. Determining what they really wanted from the interview
10. Asking clear and concise questions
11. Dealing with participant emotionality
12. Asking difficult questions
13. Creating rapport in the interview
14. Being in control of everything they had to do at one time in the interview

There are other potential errors you need to guard against as well. Make sure you give the participant enough time to give you a complete answer. Don't interrupt participants before they've given you a complete response. Learn to live with silence while your participant is thinking and pondering your question. Remember to ask only one question at a time. Make sure your questions are clear. Guard against half-listening and missing an opportunity to probe appropriately. Be careful not to "feed" answers to participants or put words in their mouth. And, definitely, don't talk down to participants.

Focus Groups

Focus groups are in-depth group discussions on a specific situation or topic of interest, made up of five to twelve participants and a moderator (or two co-moderators). They provide participants a forum to discuss differing perspectives. Developed in the 1950s by sociologist Robert Merton and psychologist Paul Lazerfeld, the first focus groups were used for media testing. They have been used primarily in the marketing field for decades, but they have been more recently (re)discovered by social scientists. Each field has its own take on facilitating and analyzing focus groups, and one of the first decisions to make is whether you plan to focus on the individual or the group as your unit of analysis. In social science research, especially in communication studies, the objective of focus groups is to better understand group dynamics, and in these contexts, focus groups are used primarily for exploratory or phenomenological (understand *lived experience*) research. You might use focus groups with ethnographic, phenomenological, and grounded theory research, as well as for action research, case study research, discourse analysis, or content analysis.

focus groups
In-depth group discussions on a specific situation or topic of interest, made up of five to twelve participants and a moderator (or two co-moderators).

Focus groups are group interviews in which the interviewer is called a *facilitator*. The facilitator leads a small group of people, usually somewhere between five to seven individuals, in a relatively open discussion about a specific product or program.

Here's an excerpt from a focus group with a children's mental health-care team, as they metacommunicate about their team communication (Davis, 2013, forthcoming):

We start with the collage exercise.

"This is a collage that represents this team," I explain. "Your impressions of the team. I brought new magazines this time," I say, referring to the fact that they did the same exercise in the previous focus group.

"Did you say nude magazines?" Mr. Camelini asks incredulously.

"This is getting interesting!" says Margie, the Center for Children and Families' therapist who is helping videotape the meeting.

After some joking, the group settles down quickly to the task, looking through magazines, cutting, and gluing. Alan, Nancy, and Peggy help clear off lunch debris. Alan stands to reach magazines. Jane, Mr. Stewart, Mr. Camelini, Peggy, and Nancy sit comfortably as they look through magazines. Alan puts his magazine down and holds out his hand. Without a word being exchanged, from across the table, Peggy hands him scissors. There is some chatter about the magazine pictures.

Peggy asks, "Did we do this wrong last time so we have to do it again?"

"No!" I protest. "I thought it was so interesting, I wanted to do it again!"

Jane shows Peggy a picture.

Alan and Mr. Stewart compare pictures. Alan asks him, "You want me to put that in? Where do you want to put it?"

"We're trying to get in Kevin's mind!" Mr. Stewart responds.

"That's a good one!" Alan comments.

Jane studies a page. "45 Top Descriptions of Kids. All You Need to Know," she reads out loud.

"We should cut it out and paste it in your office," Peggy offers.

Mr. Camelini stands up and picks up a glue stick.

"This is more fun than taking pictures," Alan comments, referring to his videographer role in the last focus group.

I notice that Jane and Peggy are chatting. Mr. Camelini is working on his own, slightly away from the table.

The intercom blares, "The fire alarm will be going off. Please disregard it." Nobody seems to pay the message any attention. The fire alarm never does go off.

. . .

I watch as a poster begins to form. In the top center a headline says "Lifetime." There is a picture of a broken teacup with a band aid mending the break. In the center is a Lexus. I see a tossed salad. A picture of a room, neat as a pin, with hardwood floors and perfectly lined up files. A cartoon of a woman comforting a young boy, with a young girl crying in the background. "Hope" reads one headline. "Walls" in another. A mirror. A satellite. A young boy waiting for a ball to come down from the air. A picture of two boys in a classroom, raising their hands, with a headline "Education," and a sub-head "Concern. Worldwide." Another headline, "Oh, I wish. . . ." Small girls playing soccer, great effort showing on their faces. Finally, a headline that reads: "Deeper Into the Mind-Bending Universe Than You've Ever Been: A Guide in Plain English." That would make a good title for my book, I think to myself.

"Okay," I say. "Explain to me what we've created. What are we saying about our team here?"

"In the center I put the Lexus," Mr. Camelini answers first. "When we first met, we didn't know each other and we were pulling in different directions, but now we're a fine-tuned machine, moving along," he explains.

"Ooh," I respond. "You guys are a Lexus now. Cool. What else is here?"

"I put a salad," says Nancy, "'cause I think of this as healthy for ourselves and for the family."

Jane and Mr. Stewart are flipping through magazines. Alan and Mr. Camelini watch them. Peggy gets up to get a soft drink.

Nancy leans forward and points to the poster. "This is a person doing his own thing and going his own way, and this is a group of people all working together to get to the goal." She looks at Alan and watches his reaction. He studies the board for a minute.

"*Soccer players. Great,*" *I comment.*

"*Get to the goal. That's neat,*" *says Alan.*

"*Literally, get to the goal,*" *I respond.*

"*Since we're close to the last day of school,*" *Alan says,* "*I found this headline of concern about education. This other picture would represent a radar, that we're still trying to listen very carefully and figure out what's going on. This other picture represents a goal that the family has, their house.*"

Mrs. Stewart comes back in the room and gets a drink. She looks over the poster and dabs glue under the corners of one of the pictures.

"*What's the coffee cup?*" *I ask.*

"*It's broken. The band-aids are there to help,*" *says Peggy.*

"*Anything else up there we haven't talked about?*" *I ask.*

"*Oh, I wish,*" *says Jane, with feeling.*

"*Oh I wish,*" *I repeat, momentarily confused, then I see the phrase on the poster.* "*Right.*"

"*They wish for a lot of things,*" *says Jane.*

"*There's the most important right there,*" *adds Mrs. Stewart, pointing to the* "*Lifeline*" *headline.*

"*You can wish, you can hope,*" *Jane adds.*

. . .

"*That's great. What's the cartoon?*" *I wonder.*

"*That reminded me of when Kevin was in here with us today,*" *Nancy answers.* "*We all have a different perspective of him. This person on the team is going one way, another person is going another way, but we can all bring our perspective. Kevin can bring his and help us to understand some of the things he's thinking about. The team has a common goal from different perspectives.*" *I notice that everyone is leaning forward, listening to her intently.*

I glance at my watch and move quickly to my next question. "*What's it like being a member of this team?*"

"*Complicated is the best word I can come up with,*" *Mrs. Stewart responds. She is still standing, leaning against the back of her chair.*

"*In what way?*" *I ask.*

"*Well,*" *she answers, looking around the table at everyone,* "*we're all trying to figure out what's driving Kevin, what his ultimate motives are, and so far we're coming up empty. It's hard to come up with the answers if you don't know the question.*"

Mr. Stewart leans back in his chair and puts his hands behind his head. "*Yeah!*" *he responds.*

Mrs. Stewart continues, "*That's basically what it is. What's making Kevin do this, and then how do we solve it? It's like trying to put the cart before the horse,*" *she explains in a serious tone, as if she's teaching a classroom of children.*

"*What was the question?*" *Peggy asks, as everyone laughs.*

"What's it like being a member of this team?" I answer, then smile. "But you could answer any question you feel like answering."

"I got off from thinking about what she was saying," Peggy says. "One of the things that I get from the team is that so often, when I'm working with families, I feel like I'm by myself."

The door opens and the woman from the front office comes in and whispers something to Mrs. Stewart, who says 'okay,' then sits down in her chair.

Peggy continues, "Then I'm running around trying to connect everybody, and having everyone at the table really helps do that. We're all communicating at the same time and we all see what happens at the same time. For me, being part of the team really makes me feel less alone in what I'm trying to do."

The door opens again, then closes.

"I would mirror that. I agree," says Alan.

Mr. Stewart responds. "We agree. 'Cause a lot of times we feel like we're alone, trying to deal with this. But with the group, we don't feel so alone."

. . .

"I feel some frustration," says Mr. Camelini, seemingly ignoring the diversion at the other side of the table. "On one hand, it's great to have parents here, but like Mrs. Stewart said, I'm not sure how much progress we've made. When I'm in these meetings, I'm always torn; I want to be in the classroom."

"It's taking time away from your class," I acknowledge.

"Yes."

"We very much appreciate your. . ." Alan starts to say.

"Spending a lot more time with one student than I am with the others," Mr. Camelini interrupts.

Mrs. Stewart sits forward. "Like I said, Kevin's complicated. Finding out why he does what he does would make dealing with him so much easier, but we wind up with more questions than we have answers." Her hands are expressive and everyone is listening attentively to her. "One minute we think we know why Kevin does some of what he does, and then the next minute that whole idea is shot out of the water because he's done something worse than what he had done before. That's what makes this whole situation complicated for everyone. . . ."

Peggy interrupts. "I do think it's frustrating because sometimes when we're trying to figure out why, we can get stuck there. One of the good things about a team is that if we do get stuck, there's always someone that can pull us out a little bit. We may never know why, but there's people, yourself included," she looks at Mrs. Stewart, "who know what works and doesn't work. So in that way I think a team approach is good. Sometimes it's frustrating because team involvement slows down the pace. So we have to have everybody on board from the beginning."

Alan nods. "It's one of those balance things. Sometimes, if you were just working on your own, it would be so much faster, 'cause it's just you doing it with the family, where with a team it does take longer to get everybody on board."

Peggy continues. "But who's to say that with the team approach we don't get where we're going, maybe a little slower, but maybe a little more lasting than you would with individuals?"

When the door opens again, Jane looks up and leaves the room. When Jane returns a moment later, she walks over to Mr. Camelini, shows him a paper, and steps back out of the room.

Mrs. Stewart jumps in. "They say too many cooks spoil the broth, but in this instance, I think the number of cooks actually makes the broth better, because they're each putting in a separate ingredient and not the same thing. No two people are going to put in the same idea, or look at something the same way."

"This is a good team," Alan says.

I ask my next question. "If you guys were making a movie of this team, what would the movie be like? Where would it take place?"

"I think the location we're at right now would be perfect," Mrs. Stewart answers. "The whole school environment."

"Documentary," Alan comments.

"Who would be there?" I ask.

"People like us," Mrs. Stewart says.

"Except Mr. Stewart would be called Julius Caesar," Alan interjects.

"Not hardly. I'm no Cleopatra!" Mrs. Stewart says.

"Demi Moore would play me," I say as everyone laughs. "What would be happening?"

"Exactly what is happening now," Mrs. Stewart answers. "Discussing what's the best way to help Kevin. Find out what's eating him, and what we can do to put a halt to it."

Nancy agrees. "I really like that idea. I was thinking the same thing. I think it would be real interesting if we were making a movie, to have this be part of it. Then, we'd follow Kevin through his whole day, starting at home, coming to school, going to class, riding the bus back home; brief little segments of each one, and then us as a team coming together with Kevin and talking about it." Everyone is nodding.

"Movies have to have a plot," I say. "What would the plot be?"

Peggy answers first. "The first thing that came to my mind was The Bad News Bears."

There's a knock on the door again, but no one comes in.

"That sounds like Kevin sometimes!" Mrs. Stewart says, laughing.

Peggy continues. "They're just a mess, with the whole sports theme, and the story is about the team and where they came from and where they went."

"The second one, Breaking Training," *Mrs. Stewart adds.*

"I haven't seen that one." Nancy says.

"They play baseball," Peggy explains. "Somebody winds up having to put a group of kids who can't do much of anything together to play ball, and they have nothing. They don't have uniforms. I don't remember who was in charge of them."

"*Who* was *in charge of them?*" *Mrs. Stewart says thoughtfully.*

"*I want to say Rodney Dangerfield. No?*" *Peggy thinks.*

"*No, that was another soccer movie,*" *Alan says.* "*It wasn't Walter Matthau, was it?*" *he asks.*

"*I think it was. Yeah, it was Walter Matthau,*" *Mrs. Stewart confirms.*

Peggy continues. "*But anyway, through the course of the movie, they are a really good little ball playing team and they learn a lot about each other.*"

I ask, "*Movies have to have dialogue. What would people be saying?*"

Alan answers, "*They wouldn't be saying just stuff about Kevin. 'Cause I don't think this is just all about Kevin. It's about your whole family,*" *he says to the Stewarts.*

Jane comes back into the room and returns to her seat at the table.

"*It's about the entire family and the group itself,*" *Mrs. Stewart says.*

"*How they interact with us,*" *Mr. Stewart adds.*

"*I'm not even sure that Kevin would be the star,*" *Alan thinks.*

"*Who's the star?*" *I ask.*

Mrs. Stewart answers, "*Actually, I think the entire team.*"

"*An ensemble,*" *Alan says.* "*Just like* Friends.*"

"*But the entire team would be the actual stars of the movie,*" *Mrs. Stewart says.*

Peggy speaks up. "*I was thinking of the show* 24. *Every hour you see is an hour in the day, and there's 24 hours and there's 24 shows. It's a drama. I think it's in a hospital.*"

"*He's a spy,*" *Alan remembers.*

"*A spy. Even though we're not that exciting, I see it focusing on different parts of us, like Mr. Camelini in the classroom, you two at home, and individual therapy,*" *Peggy says.*

Mrs. Stewart interjects. "*I can give a good example too. Like* CSI. *They got two different cases going on at once, but they go back and forth between what one group is doing to solve this, to what this second group is doing, and sometimes the two overlap. They become one case instead of two separate ones. Basically, that's exactly what's going on here. We have the team at school, then we have us at home, and when we come together at school, the two overlap into one. So it's a two-part thing.* CSI *actually fits the bill best because they have two cases going on at the same time.*"

"*What would people be looking like, body language and facial expressions?*" *I ask.*

"*A variety,*" *Peggy answers.* "*I don't think we could pin that down. Even when one person's talking, everybody's reacting differently. Sometimes I'm listening, sometimes I'm not. I might look like I'm listening, I might not be.*" *Everyone laughs.*

Mrs. Stewart says softly, "*That's perfect. We have laughter. We all have concerns about Kevin, but in different ways.*"

Advantages to Focus Groups.   There are many advantages to focus groups. Foremost is that you can see group interaction in action. Focus groups can be a forum to provide a voice to marginalized groups. In some ways, focus groups are more naturalistic than some other data collection methods, in that they tap into the usual *modes of communication* and *everyday social practices* that constitute people's social lives—they mirror social interchange in a relatively naturalistic way. For communication scholars, focus groups are studied in the context of interactions with others—human experience is constructed within specific social contexts—so you can watch the process of collective sense-making through interactions of participants. Also, with focus groups, the relationship between the researcher and the participants is less hierarchical—the balance of power shifts from the researcher to the participants in a focus group. Of course, focus groups are inherently biased due to the interactional nature of method.

Uses for Focus Groups.   In academic research, focus groups can be used for application or evaluation of theories, or to study applied contexts of theories. They are used for exploratory tasks such as creating messages, collecting information, identifying beliefs, discovering attitudes, explaining processes, generating thoughts, feelings, and behaviors. They are also used for experiential (or phenomenological) tasks, such as observing natural attitudes, life experiences, preferences, intentions, behaviors; understanding language, knowledge, and experience. With focus groups, you can gain insights into attitudes, beliefs, motives, behaviors of participants, explore how people act, behave, think—you can observe their behavior in process, hear reactions to ideas, and see things from a different (the participants') perspective. In marketing and communication research (particularly media research), focus groups are especially useful to let you discover factors that may motivate purchase, product use, brand loyalty, or product trial; understand how people use a product or service, or how they perceive a communication act; understand the attitudes and values associated with product use, purchase, brand loyalty, and so on; understand how groups interact or communicate as a group, understand how people influence each other through language and conversation; and get ideas for language, visuals, and imagery to use in communication efforts.

Also salient for communication research, focus groups are specifically useful to listen to people talk in a group, to listen for group-generated language, to listen to people bouncing ideas off of each other, and to listen to how people influence each other.

Focus Group Characteristics.   Groups may consist of people who have little in common, or people who have a lot in common (or who know each other), but homogeneous is not necessarily better—it may be advantageous to watch people disagree with each other or have to explain themselves.

Focus groups traditionally use in-depth techniques, such as nondirective interviewing, loosely structured questions, projective techniques, indirect approaches to asking questions, nonverbal questioning, such as visualization or role playing, to focus on getting interactive discussion.

The focus group itself generally has four main stages:

1. 8–10 minutes: Introduction
2. 10 minutes: Rapport-building
3. 60 minutes: In-depth investigation
4. 8–10 minutes: Closure

Focus Group Moderating or Facilitating. The moderator is the instrument of research in focus groups—the importance of the moderating role cannot be overemphasized.

Qualities of a good moderator include:

- Expresses warmth and empathy
- Appears kind, yet firm
- Is actively involved
- Pays close attention
- Is a good listener
- Pursues understanding of meaning and intents
- Demonstrates unconditional positive regard
- Links trains of thoughts and divergent comments
- Demonstrates incomplete understanding (sophisticated naïveté)
- Expresses interest in new ideas

A good moderator encourages all group members, demonstrates flexibility, demonstrates sensitivity and respect, demonstrates a research orientation (a questioning mind), is a quick starter and initiator, demonstrates quick thinking, has stamina (facilitating focus groups is tiring!), displays an appropriate sense of humor, and shows a genuine interest in what participants have to say.

As in in-depth interviews, focus group moderators need to use unconditional positive regard as you show respect for an opinion without appearing to reinforce it. You should also, as appropriate, exhibit listening skills, probe for clarity, practice flexibility by following up on unexpected issues, practice sensitivity to emotional level of discussion, encourage the expression of different opinions, respond to nonverbals as well as verbals, and be attentive to both process and content.

interactive focus groups
A variation on traditional focus groups, in which the researcher(s) participate with team members in figuring out and interpreting their interactions and behavior.

Interactive Focus Groups. **Interactive focus groups** are a variation on traditional focus groups, in which the researcher(s) participate with team members in figuring out and interpreting their interactions and behavior. Unlike researchers using traditional focus group methods, interactive facilitators strive to create a type of polyphonic interviewing, in which multiple perspectives (including theirs) are sought and discussed (Fontana & Frey, 2003). In traditional focus groups, participants are strangers to each other and thus have little consequences past the group session for their conversation (Myers, 1998). In contrast, these focus groups consist of participants already in an existing *bona fide* group, and the purpose is to observe how their prior group culture interacts in this environment. Also, unlike traditional focus groups, which are highly constrained and organized, in interactive focus groups, the discussion is as unstructured as possible, allowing for multiple perspectives. While interactive focus groups have a *ringleader*, all participants are coresearchers, yielding a group process somewhere between that of a leaderless group and a group with all leaders. At different times, different participants may take the lead. At other times, the discussion seems more chaotic and unfocused.

Interactive focus groups are often held in multiple focus group sessions, which let us build upon previous sessions and encourage reflection, empathy, and trust between sessions. One of the main advantages and purposes of these focus groups are their ability to provide insights into complex behaviors and motivations by observing the group interaction effect in action.

There are specific ethical concerns to be taken into consideration when designing a study using an interactive focus group methodology. The first is the confidentiality of the information discussed. While group members can be asked to maintain both confidentiality and anonymity, participants cannot control this, nor guarantee it. Participants in interactive focus groups are especially vulnerable to group coercion or pressure to disclose information participants may not have intended to disclose. Creating a safe environment in which participants can share painful and emotional experiences is a challenge that must be met in any focus group, but especially in interactive focus groups because of the tendency for deeper disclosure in these sessions.

Texts and Artifacts

In ethnography, phenomenology, case study, and grounded theory, analysis of texts and other artifacts supports the interviewing and observation. Rhetorical scholars and content analysis researchers study texts, as well as **artifacts-as-texts**. Researchers have been known to study clothing and personal adornment (hair, makeup, jewelry); architecture, buildings and grounds, decorating; garbage bags; personal memorabilia; documents (corporate, personal); memos; logs, diaries and journals; records (health records, driver's licenses, building contracts, bank statements, other legal or formal records); visual media (photographs, video); evidence of cultural rituals (wedding programs, marriage certificates) and behavior (shopping); cultural symbols (regalia, tombs, art); and community and social artifacts (roads, transportation) (Charmaz, 2006; Hodder, 2003). Denzin (2008) offers a critical examination of the painting "The Grand Canyon of the Yellowstone"; he explores historical documents surrounding this piece. In her piece on torch songs—songs about unrequited love—Jones (1999) explored her own experience with and about questions surrounding torch songs.

There are many good reasons for analyzing text, documents, and artifacts—called *material culture* by Hodder (2003): Access is easy, cost to access is low, information may differ from other data collected (allowing you to triangulate or crystallize your data), they allow you to understand the perspectives of others and to pay attention to your own understandings of and experiences with those same texts; and because texts endure and give historical insight and social context (Charmaz, 2006; Grbich, 2007; Hodder, 2003). Because text is written, it is an artifact that is capable of transmission, manipulation, and alteration, being used in different ways through time, and can thus acquire new and different meanings over time. Texts and artifacts are "material traces of behavior" that are left behind and give a different insight than interviews or personal communication. What people say is often very different than what people do, and texts and artifacts were constructed to *do* something. "They can be understood only as what they are— . . . produced under certain material conditions . . . embedded within social and ideological systems . . . designed specifically to be communicative and representational" (Hodder, 2003, pp. 157, 160).

artifacts-as-texts
Sources of information that supplement interview and observational data, such as photographs, clothing, buildings, pottery, tools, and so on.

▼

Data Transcription

raw data

Data that consists of interview and focus group transcripts, detailed field notes from observations and interviews, texts themselves, and any field notes taken from reading and examining texts and artifacts.

Raw data in qualitative research consists of your interview and focus group transcripts, detailed field notes from observations and interviews, texts themselves, and any field notes you take from reading and examining texts and artifacts. Just as your data in quantitative research must be reliable and valid, so must your qualitative data.

The most important, yet challenging, task in preparing your data is doing proper transcription of interviews and focus groups. When transcribing, it is important to keep all words and punctuation as close as possible to the actual speech. As you're typing, you need to type the text as close to the participants' natural speaking voices as possible. The text should be a verbatim account; do not edit or reduce text. Many researchers suggest including mispronunciations, slang, grammatical errors, nonverbal sounds (laughs, sighs), and background noises in your transcripts. If you also have a videotape of your interview, focus group, or observation, it's easiest to transcribe the dialogue from the audiotape, then fill in nonverbal communication (eye contact, body language, facial expressions, description of the environment, silence or pauses) from the video. Or, these can be noted in field notes while you are there. If so, you may want to merge the two (transcript of dialogue with notes on visual nonverbal), because it may assist your analysis to have both of these things on the same file.

When you're transcribing, keep participants' identities anonymous. When you come to a person's name or other identifying piece of information in a tape, type a _____ , or substitute his or her role in the study (e.g., parent or teacher). So, for example, if a participant in a focus group uses the name of a teacher, saying: "Mrs. Smith praised my child," you would type, "Teacher praised my child," or " _____ praised my child."

Challenges. There are numerous challenges to transcription. Transcription is tedious and boring. It is an intensive, tough, lonely, and tiring task. You've got to approach it with an inquiring mindset—keep up your excitement about delving deeply into your data. The primary challenge is in understanding what people are saying. People talk in incomplete sentences and they overlap speech (talk over each other). In addition, you might be dealing with poor tape quality and distracting or disturbing background noises. Also, it's not always clear when punctuation is necessary, and sometimes (oral) punctuation makes a big difference in the meaning of a sentence. Even misunderstanding or dropping words can change the meaning of a message (McLellan, MacQueen, & Neidig, 2003; Roulston et al., 2003).

Conversation Analysis (CA). We discussed in Chapter 14 the unique characteristics of transcription in Conversation Analysis (CA). In CA, it is especially important to transcribe both what is said and how it is said. When transcribing and analyzing conversations in CA, it's also important to remember CA's reminder that the transcription is not the data, the transcription is just a way to capture the actual data—the conversation. In CA, tapes are transcribed as "actual words as spoken" and "sounds as uttered" (Ten Have, 2007, p. 98). CA transcription accounts for identification of participants (by first name, initial, random letter, or role); words as spoken; sounds as uttered (e.g., hmm, tch, eh); spaces and silences; overlapped speech and sounds; and pacing, stretches, stresses, and volume. Ten Have suggests transcribing in rounds: Start with a transcription of the words, go back through and add the sounds, go back through and add spaces and silences, and so on. Chapter 14 lists many of the transcription conventions used in CA. In a study on joint laughter in workplace meetings, Kangasharju and Nikko (2009) found through conversational analysis that shared laughter can be used by leaders to create a positive work environment, as well as help remediate issues and reduce tension associated with those issues.

So What?

In Chapter 14, we discussed many of the different types of qualitative research. In this chapter, we discussed the different ways you can collect your qualitative data. As you can see, many of these types and ways overlap, and many different ways of data collection can be used for many different types of qualitative research. Often, distinctions between approaches to qualitative research are a result of which approach researchers were trained on in graduate school. In other cases, distinctions are small and are based on slight differences in researchers' ontology, epistemology, or axiology. Sometimes, approach and data collection decisions are based on sensitizing concepts researchers enter the field with, or based on their research question or prior knowledge, and other times, these decisions are based on an initial examination of the data. Regardless of the approach and type of qualitative research being used, all qualitative research should be conducted using careful, rigorous, systematic, and ethical practices. In Chapter 16, we will show you what to do with the mountains of data you collected from this chapter.

Glossary

Active-member researchers
Researchers that become involved with central activities of the group but do not fully commit themselves to the group.

Advice questions
Asking participants to give advice to a person in a similar situation, yielding information on beliefs or understandings.

Aided account
Use of video, picture, or graphics to ask questions about specific experiences.

Artifacts-as-texts
Sources of information that supplement interview and observational data, such as photographs, clothing, buildings, pottery, tools, and so on.

Behavior or experience questions
Asking for more information about an action or behavior.

Bounded unit
A case.

Co-constructed interview

An interview that is a collaboration between researcher and participant—the researcher and participant are full partners in the interview.

Complete-member researchers

Researchers who study settings in which they are already members or with which they are already affiliated.

Complete observer

Researchers that have little to no interaction with the people being observed.

Contrast question

Asking for unlike comparisons in order to understand something by understanding what it is not.

Creative interviewing

Interviews that may consist of multiple sessions over many days. They may be more intimate and dialogic, or they may include shared stories between researchers and participants.

Descriptive observation

Everything is observed, no matter how small and is usually done when a researcher is first in a field.

Descriptive questions

Asking participants to recount (in detail) or recreate a phenomenon or experience, like a verbal tour of the phenomenon.

Devil's advocate question

A type of interview question in which the participant is asked to argue for or against a position.

Epiphany interviews

Interviews in which people tell about certain moments in their lives that are turning points; participants' transformational, existential moments in their lives.

Feeling question

Asking participants to discuss how they feel or how they are emotionally affected by a phenomenon.

Field notes

A record of what was meaningful during an observation.

Field sites

Groups, organizations, or cultures in which research is conducted.

Fieldwork

Conducting observations in natural settings.

Focus groups

In-depth group discussions on a specific situation or topic of interest, made up of five to twelve participants and a moderator (or two co-moderators).

Focused observation

Things that are irrelevant are ignored and not observed, and is usually done when a researcher has been in a field for a while.

Gatekeepers

Management (if it's an organization) or a respected group member or leader who grants approval to conduct research in a given field site.

Hypothetical interaction

A type of interview question in which the participant is asked what he/she would do in a hypothetical situation.

In-depth interviews

Opportunities for participants to describe their worlds, in concert and negotiation with researchers. Such interviewing involves co-constructing a narrative with a participant—to understand his or her history and version of the story and the ways that he or she makes sense of his or her actions in the context of his or her cultural narratives.

Interactive focus groups

A variation on traditional focus groups, in which the researcher(s) participate with team members in figuring out and interpreting their interactions and behavior.

Knowledge question

Asking a participant for specific factual information about a topic and how one attains this type of information.

Life story interview

An interview that documents all the significant streams of a person's life, to provide understanding of the larger cultural or historical frames.

Motive questions

A type of interview question in which the participant is asked about their motive when they were doing or saying something.

Native-language questions

Asking participants what terms mean, who uses them, when they use them, what context they are used in, and so on.

Naturalistic observation

The use of observational techniques in natural settings.

Observations

A way to gain insight into the obligations, constraints, motivations, and emotions that participants experience as they complete everyday actions.

Observer-as-participant

Researcher interacts casually with participants, but still remains primarily an observer, and does not become a member of the group being studied.

Once-upon-a-time question

Asking participants to narrate an experience related to a phenomenon.

Opinion or value question
Asks a person to discuss a belief or judgment they have about an issue.

Oral history interviews
Interviews that capture people's stories about their lives.

Participant observation
When a researcher is participating in the life of others, but is still observing as a naïve outsider who doesn't understand exactly what's going on and needs to ask, explore, and try on the experience.

Peripheral-member researchers
Researchers who have some level of involvement with a group without core group involvement.

Personal narrative interview
A person's recounting—telling a story about—an event, experience, or point of view.

Polyphonic interviewing
An interview in which the voices of participants are recorded with minimal influence from researchers and are reported separately (from each other) as individual voices, multiple perspectives, and differences between each are highlighted rather than glossed over.

Posing emergent ideas
A type of interview question in which the interviewer asks the participant about ideas that are emerging to the researcher at that point in the research.

Posing the ideal
Asks a person to describe the ideal—organization, situation, state of affairs, goals, and so on.

Quotation questions
Giving participants a direct quotation from another interview or observation and asking for their feelings or opinions about it.

Raw data
Data that consists of interview and focus group transcripts, detailed field notes from observations and interviews, texts themselves, and any field notes taken from reading and examining texts and artifacts.

Scratch notes
Rough notes that are embellished upon shortly after an observation.

Selective observation
Researchers concentrate on certain activities based on additional analyses, interviews, coding, and so on, as their time in a field is winding down.

Sensitizing concepts
Initial ideas, concepts, or interests to pursue and sensitize people to ask certain kinds of questions and look for certain kinds of information.

Sensory questions
Attempting to understand how a participant experiences a phenomenon from a sensory point of view (what does he or she see, hear, feel, taste, smell).

Structural questions
Questions that require explanation and explore contextual information.

Time-line questions
Questions that ask what happened in a time series.

Topical interview
A person's discussion of a topic, program, issue, or process.

References

Angrosino, M. V., & de Pérez, K. A. M. (2003). Rethinking observation: From method to context. In N. K. Denzin & Y. S. Lincoln (Eds.), *Collecting and interpreting qualitative materials* (pp. 107–154). Thousand Oaks, CA: Sage.

Baxter, P., & Jack, S. (2008). Qualitative case study methodology: Study design and implementation for novice researchers. *The Qualitative Report, 13*(4), 544–559.

Charmaz, K. (2006). *Constructing grounded theory: A practical guide through qualitative analysis.* Thousand Oaks, CA: Sage.

Creswell, J. W., & Miller, D. L. (2000). Determining validity in qualitative inquiry. *Theory into Practice, 39*(3), 124–130.

Davis, C. S. (2007). The social construction of life, death, and disability in the Terri Schiavo Case. In J. L. Werth & T. Lillie (Eds.), *End of life issues and persons with disabilities* (pp. 167–182). Austin, TX: Pro-ED.

Davis, C. S. (2008). Competing narratives: How peer leaders use narrative to facilitate change in community mental health groups. *Small Group Research: An International Journal of Theory, Investigation, and Application, 39*(6), 706–727.

Davis, C. S. (2010). *Death: The beginning of a relationship.* Hampton Press.

Davis, C. S. (2013, forthcoming). *Constructing hope: Inside team care in children's mental health.* Walnut Creek, CA: Left Coast Press.

Denizin, N. K. (2008). Drawn to Yellowstone. *Qualitative Research, 8,* 451-472.

Desantis, A. D. (2003). A couple of white guys sitting around talking: The collective rationalization of cigar smokers. *Journal of Contemporary Ethnography, 32,* 432-466.

Fontana, A., & Frey, J. H. (2003). The interview: From structured questions to negotiated text. In N. K. Denzin & Y. S. Lincoln (Eds.), *Collecting and interpreting qualitative materials* (pp. 61–106). Thousand Oaks, CA: Sage.

Fontana, A., & Prokos, A. H. (2007). *The interview: From formal to postmodern.* Walnut Creek, CA: Left Coast Press.

Grbich, C. (2007). *Qualitative data analysis: An introduction.* Los Angeles, CA: Sage.

Harter, L., Kirby, E., & Gerbensky-Kerber, A. (2010). Enacting and disrupting the single-sex mandate of the YWCA: A poststructural feminist analysis of separatism as an organizing strategy. *Women & Language, 33,* 9-28.

Hodder, I. (2003). The interpretation of documents and material culture. In N. K. Denzin & Y. S. Lincoln (Eds.), *Collecting and interpreting qualitative materials* (pp. 155–175). Thousand Oaks, CA: Sage.

Jones, S. H. (1999). Torch. *Qualitative Inquiry, 5,* 280–304.

Kangasharju, H., & Nikko, T. (2009). Emotions in organizations joint laughter in workplace meetings. *Journal of Business Communication, 46,* 100–119.

Madison, D. S. (2005). *Critical ethnography: Methods, ethics, and performance.* Thousand Oaks, CA: Sage.

McLellan, E., MacQueen, K. M., & Neidig, J. L. (2003). Beyond the qualitative interview: Data preparation and transcription. *Field Methods, 15*(1), 63–84.

Myers, G. (1998). Displaying opinions: Topics and disagreement in focus groups. *Language in Society, 27,* 85–111.

Rock, P. (2007). Symbolic interactionism and ethnography. In P. Atkinson, A. Coffey, S. Delamont, J. Lofland, & L. Lofland (Eds.), *Handbook of ethnography* (pp. 26–38). Los Angeles, CA: Sage.

Roulston, K., deMarrais, K., & Lewis, J. B. (2003). Learning to interview in the social sciences. *Qualitative Inquiry, 9*(4), 643–668.

Silverman, D. (2003). Analyzing talk and text. In N. K. Denzin & Y. S. Lincoln (Eds.), *Collecting and interpreting qualitative materials* (pp. 340–362). Thousand Oaks, CA: Sage.

Starks, H., & Trinidad, S. B. (2007). Choose your method: A comparison of phenomenology, discourse analysis, and grounded theory. *Qualitative Health Research, 17*(10), 1372–1380.

Ten Have, P. (2007). *Doing conversation analysis: A practical guide.* Los Angeles, CA: Sage.

Yin, R. K. (2009). *Case study research: Design and methods.* Thousand Oaks, CA: Sage.

WRITING, ANALYZING, AND CRITIQUING QUALITATIVE RESEARCH

16

CHAPTER OUTLINE

1. Coding Qualitative Data
   a. Coding Process
   b. Methods of Categorizing
      i. Thematic Analysis
      ii. Analysis by Sensitizing Concepts
         A. Frame Analysis
         B. Social Network Analysis
         C. Event Analysis
         D. Schema Analysis
         E. Interpretive Thematic Analysis
   c. Coding in Grounded Theory Research
   d. Coding in Phenomenological Research
   e. Coding in Conversation Analysis (CA)
   f. Coding in Discourse Analysis
   g. Coding in Textual and Artifact Analysis and Rhetorical Criticism
   h. Coding in Content Analysis

   i. Coding in Narrative and Performative Research
2. Analyzing Qualitative Data
3. Writing Qualitative Findings
   a. Summary or Traditional Method of Writing
   b. Dramatic or Scenic Method of Writing
   c. Writing Phenomenological Findings
   d. Writing Grounded Theory Findings
   e. Writing CA Findings
   f. Writing Discourse Analysis Findings
   g. Writing Performance Texts
   h. Writing Narrative Texts
4. Evaluating and Critiquing Qualitative Research
5. So What?

KEY TERMS

Axial coding	Ethnodrama	Negative case analysis
Card pile sort	Event analysis	Schema analysis
Code book/code list	Frame analysis	Sensitizing concept
Creative analytical practices	Inter-coder reliability	Social network analysis
Data coding	Interpretive thematic analysis	Summary method of writing
Dramatic or scenic method of writing	Metacodes	Thematic analysis

CHAPTER OBJECTIVES

1. To learn how to code, analyze, and write qualitative research under the main approaches and methods
2. To understand how to appropriately and accurately code and analyze qualitative data
3. To understand how to interpret qualitative results
4. To understand how to write quantitative research reports
5. To learn how to approach and critique qualitative research

Coding Qualitative Data

data coding
The categorization of data to make it manageable.

In quantitative research, you reduce your data into something manageable through the use of summary and descriptive statistics: mean, median, and mode; and standard deviation, variance, and range. In qualitative research, you reduce your data into something manageable through the use of **data coding**, or categorizing the data.

Coding Process

There are several different, specific types of coding, some with very specific methods of coding and some with more general approaches to coding. Regardless of the type, coding generally consists of a multistep process that involves, first, reading through the data (transcript, recording, field notes, texts, etc.) and jotting down notations on what you think the data are saying. In this stage, it's important to be familiar with your data and with what it is saying. In fact, you are ready to analyze when you can answer this question: "What are you finding out?" Hopefully, you've been thinking about your findings as you move through your data collection, and you've hopefully been jotting down thoughts, ideas, and notes in your field notes, but this is the stage to start pulling it together in your mind and on paper. Here's an example of analytical notations in the field notes from the hospice research Christine Davis conducted (2010):

> They then talked about new admissions again talking about the people as people, kind of almost gossiping about them in a good sense. Talking about their situations, kind of by the RN's talking about the physical, went into talking about what they called readmits, some of this was interrupted by when the dr came in and he also did a little bit of chatting and gossiping and kind of friendly conversation about the pts, not only having the symptoms but also the pts as people and personalities and relationships and talking in those terms. Later on, in an interesting contrast, the female nurse practitioner came in about the first ½ of her section was pretty cut and dried, almost staccato voice, boom boom boom. And I noticed that when the RN's responded to her, they were speaking very clinically, very symptom oriented, it was a very interesting contrast. The doctor actually took what the nurses said and took their recommendations and seemed to defer to them. the nurse practitioner actually argued with them on 1 or 2 cases. And really seemed to be barking orders as opposed to working collaboratively. It was an interesting contrast between the dr and the np.

This first step is followed by a step in which you review your notations and begin to build a **code list or code book**, which is an organized listing of your categories and codes and the rules for documenting and applying them. Your code book should include a detailed description of each code, inclusion and exclusion criteria, examples of text for each code, and examples of text that would *not* fall in each code. Code books are developed and refined as the study progresses. As you move through your coding process, you might turn some themes into subthemes, you might delete other themes, and you might refine or combine other categories (Ryan & Bernard, 2003).

code book/code list
An organized listing of categories and codes and the rules for documenting and applying them.

Here's part of the code book for the hospice research project conducted by Christine Davis (2010).

1. Introductions
   a. My introduction to team
   b. Patient's introduction to terminal illness
2. Deepening
   a. Getting used to team
   b. Patient getting used to illness
3. Coming to terms
   a. Becoming part of the team
   b. Patient's coming to terms with illness
4. Endings
   a. Leaving the team
   b. Leaving Patients
5. How does Hospice construct humanness
   a. Dignity
   b. Free will
   c. Individual responsibility
   d. NOT perfect
   e. Respect and Acknowledge feelings

Finally, the last step in coding is to connect actual data (lines of discourse, quotes, words, portions of narrative or text) to each code. In this step, you will somehow mark or tag your text according to which category it belongs in (Ryan & Bernard, 2003). Some people do this by hand, highlighting text and writing next to it a number corresponding to the category. Many researchers use coding software—HyperRESEARCH, NVivo, and Atlas/ti are three major ones used—to perform this step. A word of caution: Statistical software like SPSS does compute your statistics for you. However, coding software does not code your data for you. The software just gives you a way to record your codes that provides an easily sorted output so that analyzing them is much easier than sifting through your coded data by hand.

Another approach to data sorting is to use a **card pile sort**. You would go through your field notes and interview transcripts and write all the answers to the research question you find in the data. Write each answer on a separate index card, then put them in piles according to semantic groupings (which ones seem to have similar meanings). You would sort and resort the piles, merging and subdividing the piles until no further subdivision is possible. You might first

card pile sort
Using index cards drawn from field notes to create semantic groupings.

sort by variations, layers, or dimensions. You might then classify each of these into subgroups or types. The list of piles becomes your code list or code book (Grbich, 2007).

Methods of Categorizing

Thematic Analysis.   Regardless of whether you use written notation or sort piles, you need a method of categorizing. The most common coding method is a **thematic analysis**, a method of categorizing your data into thematic categories. How you select your categories depends on your research question (RQ), study objectives, and method or approach to your research. You may have come into your research with a **sensitizing concept**. Perhaps you knew you wanted to study the use of certain types of language (gendered language, for example). Your coding categories would then reflect the different categories of gendered language. Perhaps you wanted to understand a lived experience; in this case, you might code more openly, letting the data itself suggest themes and categories. Perhaps you had a series of RQs; for each RQ, you would use a sorting technique to find all the possible responses found in the data to that question. You might sort the data by responses related to a particular issue (Grbich, 2007).

Analysis by Sensitizing Concepts.   There are many categorization schemes based on sensitizing concepts derived from your RQ, study approach, or your data.

FRAME ANALYSIS.   **Frame analysis** consists of sorting your data by the interpretive frames within which we construct meaning and understanding. For example, I might see the world through multiple frames such as parent, professor, and writer. Or I might make sense of an illness situation through the frames of physical sensations or pain, cost or financial parameters, lifestyle or ability to maintain daily activities, and so on (Grbich, 2007).

SOCIAL NETWORK ANALYSIS. **Social network analysis** consists of sorting by the relationships involved in a group. For example, in a health-care team meeting, you might observe relationships between the case manager and the caregiver, between the case manager and the health-care provider, or between the caregiver and the health-care provider (Grbich, 2007). Your code list might then consist of:

- Case manager-caregiver relationship
- Case manager-health-care provider relationship
- Caregiver-health-care provider relationship

EVENT ANALYSIS.   In **event analysis**, you might sort by the perspectives of a specific event represented in the interview accounts (person one's perspective, person two's perspective, and so on). You might also use codes that represent structural aspects of the event (time, space, location, context, culture, etc., depending on what emerges from your data) (Grbich, 2007).

---

thematic analysis
A method of categorizing data into thematic categories.

sensitizing concept
The issue you are attempting to address or answer in your research, based on your RQ, study approach, or data itself.

frame analysis
The sorting of data by the interpretive frames within which meaning and understanding is constructed.

social network analysis
Consists of sorting by the relationships involved in a group.

event analysis
The sorting of data by the perspectives represented in interview accounts.

SCHEMA ANALYSIS.   **Schema analysis** consists of close reading of texts or discourse, in which you look for clues in the discourse that tell you what people might be thinking or believing that would cause them to say what they are saying. You would want to pay specific attention to their patterns of speech, key words and phrases, use of metaphors, and repetition of ideas. You might be looking for participants' personal semantic networks—repetitive ideas associated with people's assumptions or meanings. You would also need to look at what is not said—these reflect assumptions people make about what "everyone knows" (Grbich, 2007).

INTERPRETIVE THEMATIC ANALYSIS.   In **interpretive thematic analysis**, you code with your analysis in mind. As you read through your data, themes begin to emerge. You begin clustering categories, grouping for similarities, always keeping in mind your analysis, presentation, readership, and audience. As you build these categories, you would examine the emerging topics within each category. You would compare and contrast each topic with the other topics in a cluster, looking for overlapping topics, distinctions, topics that should be moved to a different cluster, and topics that should be eliminated. You adjust your topics and clusters as you identify linkages and themes. These themes then guide your analysis (Madison, 2005).

Coding in Grounded Theory Research

Grounded theory is a specific approach to data coding and analysis. In Chapters 14 and 15, we talked about philosophical underpinnings of grounded theory, and how data are collected in grounded theory research. Grounded theory's method of coding is the foundation of the approach, and coding in grounded theory follows a very specific, rigorous process. In fact, grounded theory's coding process is one of the most systematic and rigorous coding processes in qualitative research.

Grounded theory coding takes into account the relationships between the data and the categories. In grounded theory, codes and categories are mutable (changeable) until late in the project, but coding in grounded theory research actually begins as soon as you begin collecting your data.

As you collect your data, you would do open coding—initial coding of data and jotting down emerging themes, thoughts, ideas, or concepts. This process will continue throughout your data collection and will create sensitizing concepts that will inform your data collection efforts.

When you have completed data collection, you finalize your open coding to do what's called **axial coding**: creating codes that connect categories (called **metacodes**). As you refine your axial codes or metacodes, you go through a process of **negative case analysis**—constantly comparing existing codes with new data, adding new codes (or revising existing codes) until all cases of data are accounted for in the coding scheme. You're done creating categories when you reach *theoretical saturation*, when no new themes or meanings are derived.

schema analysis
Consists of close reading of texts or discourse, in which researchers look for clues in the discourse that tell us what people might be thinking or believing that would cause them to say what they are saying.

interpretive thematic analysis
Coding and categorizing data for themes and topics according to your analysis plan.

axial coding/ metacoding
Codes that connect categories.

negative case analysis
The process of constantly comparing existing codes with new data and adding new codes (or revising existing codes) until all cases of data are accounted for in the coding scheme.

Coding in Phenomenological Research

Coding in phenomenological research uses a systematic procedure that categorizes specific statements into "clusters of meaning" that represent the phenomena. In phenomenological analysis, as you are collecting the data, you begin to form ideas about patterns, relationships, and connections. You use written descriptions to uncover the essence of the phenomenon through different layers of interpretation. You identify key themes that occurred as you yourself interacted with your participants, or with your data itself (Grbich, 2007; Starks & Trinidad, 2007).

Phenomenological coding and analysis uses a multistep process:

1. Identify categories of meaning related to the RQ and construct a code list of these themes.
2. Isolate natural meaning units (phrases with a single meaning) and add these to the code list.
3. Select themes that are central to the experiences of participants and write a descriptive comment about each theme.
4. Write a narrative about the participants' experiences with the phenomenon and relate it to the interpretive themes you selected.
5. Collect these narratives and themes and combine them into related field of interconnections.
6. Rank the themes in terms of frequency and intensity.
7. Group themes into subthemes and metathemes.
8. Identify additional or overriding themes that explain the phenomena.
9. Write a narrative about the phenomenon, including your own personal experience with the phenomenon, description of the phenomenon from the literature, and your interpretive themes from your research.
10. Distill the narrative into one final description to form your conclusion.

In phenomenology, the final narrative may use more poetic or other creative forms of writing to distill the experience.

Coding in Conversation Analysis (CA)

CA does not use categorization as data reduction, per se. Rather, coding and analysis in CA identifies *devices* used by conversational participants and discusses and describes those devices. CA coding consists of identifying speech characteristics such as: types of statements (assertions, declarations, directives, commissives, or expressives); turn taking, gaps, and pauses between speakers; and structural and verbal and nonverbal patterns. CA coding and analysis consists of detailed transcriptions of conversations (using CA notations as described in Chapter 14) and a sense-making process within an episode of talk, using your intuitive sense to interpret what certain types of speech characteristics mean (Grbich, 2007).

Rather than forming categories, CA utilizes an inductive process in which you work back and forth between your transcript and your analysis. This involves a three-step process in which you (1) identify sequences of related talk, (2) examine how the speakers take on certain roles or identities through their talk, and (3) look for outcomes of the talk and work backward to trace the way that outcome was produced (Silverman, 2003).

Coding in Discourse Analysis

Coding in discourse analysis involves identifying meaning, themes, and roles constructed through language and finding examples of the ways that language constructs that reality. This typically involves categorizing the discourse into themes, statements, arguments, challenges, or ideas, and connecting these categories to their historical, social, economic, and/or political context. You would especially look for places the discourse has disunity and discontinuity and try to identify where the limits of the discourse are (Grbich, 2007; Starks & Trinidad, 2007).

Coding in Textual and Artifact Analysis and Rhetorical Criticism

Texts and artifacts are specifically communicative and symbolic, and coding in textual analysis consists of examining what the texts and artifacts communicate and symbolize. You might be looking for semiotic codes—systems of meaning in a culture (e.g., in our culture, ties represent formal attire). You might examine where power and control are communicated, for example, how a space is designed to symbolize power, prestige, value, and domination. When interpreting material culture, you would ask questions about how beliefs, ideas, and intentions impact the use and meaning of the artifact. Look at the artifact within its context—what are its boundaries? What is similar to it? What is different from it? What are the rules of representation? What are the social and material implications of practices? What is the representational symbolism, as well as the practical meaning? (Hodder, 2003).

In textual analysis (and analysis of artifacts-as-texts), you might use one of several coding methods to actually categorize your data: grounded theory or schema analysis, for example. You might look for metaphors, repetitions of words, or shifts in content. As with other types of coding, you would typically let the categories or themes emerge from the data, but you can also find your themes from literature, use that list as a starting point, and add more themes as you go through your data. Sources of themes can include literature reviews, professional definitions, local commonsense constructs, researchers' values, and your own prior experience (Ryan & Bernard, 2003).

Remember that with a textual analysis, you're answering questions such as:

1. What are people saying about "x"?
2. How did he or she say "x"?
3. How were they able to persuade "x"?
4. How is "x" concept constructed through the text?

Also remember that the purpose of a textual analysis is to describe the content of the text and make claims about what the text *does* and how it does it. Therefore, your codes for a textual analysis will be based on categories that answer your question(s).

In rhetorical criticism, how you categorize your data depends on which type of rhetorical criticism you plan to conduct, so that's probably a good place to begin. As we discussed in Chapter 14, the type of rhetorical analysis you do might depend on what you *see* in your data. So, if you read your text and notice that the use of metaphors is especially strong, you might decide to do a metaphoric analysis. If you think that a speech uses dramatistic elements to persuade, you might decide to do a dramatistic analysis. You might be struck by the use of mythic stories and proceed toward a fantasy theme analysis. Therefore, you have to read through your text, perhaps making notations to yourself on what you're noticing, before you can determine which sensitizing concept on which you will categorize your data. If you're conducting a NeoAristotelian criticism, for example, you'll want to code specifically looking for ways the speaker/writer used invention, arrangement, style, delivery, and memory to persuade. You might also have to code for what the speaker is trying to persuade you to do. In a narrative criticism, you might examine and code the text for places where the speaker/writer is using setting, characters, events, and so forth to persuade or communicate. And, in a Burkean analysis, you might be coding for act, purpose, agent, agency, and scene, looking specifically for places and example of where each of these elements contributes to the message and how they do so.

Here's an example. When your author Christine Davis (2007) was analyzing the newspaper articles of the Terri Schiavo account, I first read through the articles, jotting down ideas in the margins of the pages as I read. I was really struck with the use of metaphoric language, and at the same time, I was struck with how each side seemed to play a duel with language to depict ideas of *life* and *death*. When I began coding the data, I made coding notations again in the margin of the pages, coding each article as "life" or "death." I also began open coding to come up with categories of metaphors. I first jotted down words depicting the metaphors used, for each article. Similarly to grounded theory coding, I next took those open codes and compared them, combined them, and refined them to come up with a finite list of metaphors and metaphoric categories. I last went back and recoded each article, assigning it to one or more of the metaphoric categories. Finally, I went through each article again and made notes to myself about how much each of the metaphors seemed to contribute to the overall *life* and *death* arguments.

Coding in Content Analysis

A key characteristic of coding in content analysis is that your codes are developed ahead of time. Rather than emerging from the data, they instead reflect your literature review, theory, and RQ. For example, if you think that children's television perpetuates stereotyped gender roles, you might code the characters in television shows by a predetermined typology of such roles (e.g., mother, housewife, businessperson). Qualitative content analysis might categorize the texts by content, context, linkages, possible interpretations, purpose, or meaning.

In a research project studying social support in children's mental health treatment team meetings, Christine Davis created the following content analysis code list to determine what types of social support are observed in meetings. The list of types of social support was derived from literature research on the topic, and it was developed when I designed the study, before I ever looked at the data.

1. Instrumental: Helping or doing things for him or her
2. Emotional: Emotional support
3. Informational: Providing information
4. Tangible: Material aid or giving him or her things or money
5. Positive social interaction: Companionship
6. Affectionate: Love and affection
7. Esteem: Raising his or her self-esteem
8. Network: Connecting the person to others
9. Listening: Nonjudgmental listening support
10. Emotional challenge: Challenging recipient to evaluate his or her attitudes, values, feeling
11. Reality confirmation support: A person similar to the recipient thus confirms the recipient's view of the world
12. Task appreciation support: Acknowledging the recipient's efforts and expressing appreciation for work
13. Task challenge support: Challenging way of thinking about task or activity to stretch, motivate, or lead recipient

In content analysis, **inter-coder reliability** is an important concept, and usually two coders code the data then compare the percentage of agreement between coders. Inter-coder reliability of 70 percent to 80 percent is usually considered to be acceptable (Grbich, 2007).

inter-coder reliability
The level of agreement between two or more coders.

Coding in Narrative and Performative Research

Some forms of qualitative research, especially narrative ethnography or performance ethnography, seek to represent the data through narrative, description, or other arts-based forms. Sometimes these narratives, poems, or works of art are based on themes derived from coding the data as we've described above; other times, the narratives are organized chronologically or for otherwise aesthetic reasons, and no formal coding scheme is used.

• •

Analyzing Qualitative Data   ▼

Once you've coded your data, it's time to do your *data analysis*—the process of labeling your raw data and finding patterns, themes, concepts, and propositions. This stage bridges the gap between your data, your codes, and your written report. Of course, as a good researcher you will be mentally and informally analyzing the data as you move throughout your study, but when you're finished coding, and before you start writing, it's a good idea to take a step back and do some analytical thinking and note taking on your research. This step consists of memo writing in which analytical interpretation lends a structure to the process. As with every other step in your research, this step will reflect your research questions or study objectives. In this stage, you are attempting to answer your RQs, using your data and the coding of your data to do so. So, you're looking at your themes, and asking yourself what they mean (in terms of answering your RQs and objectives), as you build your conclusions and inferences. You're looking for first order explanations (what you think is going on), as well as second order explanations (what your research participants think is going on). You're looking for patterns within and between categories, comparing your emerging findings with existing theories to see where your data might agree with, expand upon, or change theory. You are seeking to understand meaning as it is created from within the data. You will build ideas and theories inductively as you move from coding to analysis. As you continue to immerse yourself in the data, you will tune into ideas that inform what meanings you make of your data. Your final step will be to refine, communicate, support, explain, and substantiate your ideas, as you write them in your report (Charmaz, 2000).

As you build ideas and refine them, you might discuss them with your informants. This might take place as formal "member checks" (interviews or focus groups with study participants or people who are similar to study participants to get their feedback on your findings), or they might be more informal conversations. Here's an example of a conversation I (Christine Davis) had with two key informants in my children's mental health research (Davis, 2013, forthcoming). You might note that one of the key conclusions I came up with in this project was that the team used communication to construct hope for themselves and the family. Can you see how that idea was beginning to develop?

Two weeks later, I have a chance to discuss my ideas about the research with Nancy and Alan. We're at Jason's Deli again. I eat here at least once a week. I munch on salad as we talk.

"One of the things that I'm trying to do with this research," I explain, "is to not be the expert, imposing my opinion on the rest of the team. I want this to be a partnership between me and the team. One of the things I'm discovering is how hard it is not to play the expert role. I wonder if it's hard for you and all the other professionals on the team, to have the family be a real true partner on the team."

Nancy answers first. "The more frequently the team meets, the better it is to have them be viewed as a full partner. It's much better that there is a team, because otherwise they're asking me for things. This way, I can say wait for the team to decide instead of being the gatekeeper. I also think the team realizes their partnership more when they meet regularly."

Alan nods. "We've talked about this before. You have a situation of power, no matter what. If you're just talking about us being case managers, I don't even think about it anymore, being the professional versus the family, because we just do what we need to do to get things better."

"But isn't the power differential still there, even if you don't think about it?" I protest.

"To complicate matters," Nancy adds, "the financial assistance fund puts them in a subservient role since they have to ask for it, and it's the state's money. We have to make decisions that are not just about adhering to the family's choice. A good example is the situation with the gas. I can't as an administrator just hand them the money because

she wanted to go specifically to another, more expensive, company 'cause she was mad at the first company. By statutes, I had to say no, and that was a power decision. But I don't know that power necessarily needs to be looked at as something that is either inherently positive or negative. It's how you use it."

"How about the other professionals on the team?"

"That depends. As far as the regular team members, I don't know that I've been aware of any abuse of power or anything like that. The school psychologist definitely came over as the big expert, talking about a lot of negative things," Alan says.

"He didn't really understand our team," Nancy adds. "He was just invited that day as a guest."

"I don't think it was his fault," Alan responds, "but he came over powerfully and very negatively. I don't think it was his intention to do that, but at the same time I don't think he saw that family with the level of respect that the team members that know them do."

I nod. "I felt that he de-humanized them. Would you agree with that?" Alan smiles. "I think that's what I just said."

"I've been noticing how the family, especially Kevin, seems to be doing better, and I wonder why you think that is," I ask.

Nancy sits forward. "I've thought a lot about this. We've given them more structure. The family financially isn't able to go a lot of places, and with the behavioral rewards, they now they have something to look forward to every week. On Monday, they're already looking forward to what they're going to do on Saturday, and so they have a hope of things getting better."

Writing Qualitative Findings ▼

When writing the report of your findings, continue to keep your study objectives and RQs in mind. It's a good idea to write by an outline, and we'll give you a sample outline in a minute. You'll likely include both description and analysis, perhaps using verbatim quotes to support your claim(s). Your claim will consist of the theme or thread that forms the *backbone* of your findings. Quotes serve as evidence for your claim. Many researchers include recommendations where appropriate—for future research, for organizations, and so on.

It's easy to get carried away when writing up qualitative research. Since your evidence can be quite wordy and long, if you try to include all good pieces of evidence, your paper could easily reach 50 to 100 pages! For journal articles, you want to end up with a paper that is 25 to 35 pages long, not counting the title page, appendix, and references. Therefore, you'll need to balance providing evidence for your claims with only including the most persuasive evidence. For example, if you're organizing your paper thematically, with quotes to support each theme, include enough quotes to support but not too many—usually two to three good quotes for each theme should suffice.

Summary or Traditional Method of Writing

summary method of writing
A method of writing in which researchers give readers summaries of what happened and what was discovered during research.

Caulley (2008) lists two basic ways to write qualitative research reports. One is the more traditional method. Caulley calls this the **summary method of writing**, in which you give the reader summaries of what happened and what you discovered in your research. Textual and rhetorical analyses are usually written in this style, and ethnographic findings sometimes use this style, as well.

In this style of writing, you will make sure you specifically address your RQ or study objectives and include rich illustrative examples that support each of your findings—give enough detail to help the reader understand the coding process and support your themes with quotes or excerpts. You will demonstrate how the themes relate to each other and provide adequate amounts of evidence to support your claims. Finally, you will present the results in an understandable, well-organized manner (Ponterotto & Grieger, 2007). Traditionally written qualitative research reports typically follow an outline that looks like this:

A. Title page (1 page)
B. Abstract (1 page, 100–200 words)
C. Introduction (may include literature review or literature review may be a separate section) (6–7 pages)
D. Research questions or study objectives (1 paragraph)
E. Methods (6–7 pages)
F. Results (6–7 pages)
G. Discussion (5–6 pages)
H. Limitations and suggestions for future research (1/2 page)
I. References (3 pages)

Review Chapter 4 for more information on how to write a title page, abstract, and literature review. Your final paper picks up where that chapter left off.

The Introduction should introduce us to your topic, describe the nature of the situation, and provide an overview of the selected topic. Use this as an opportunity to justify your research and your selection of the topic, and preview what good reading the paper will do. Show us how your research furthers scholarly understanding of communication or responds to a need in society. Describe the prevalence of the problem you're solving, and the implications for individuals, families, organizations, and/or society at large. Focus your research by indicating why others should be interested in the selected topic. Convince the audience that the topic is worthy of study. Include a literature review that justifies your topic, introduces relevant theory, summarizes previous research done in the area, and leads us to your specific research and your argument and claim.

The conclusion of your introduction should be that *this* certain type of research is needed on *this* specific topic. That should lead us right into your research questions or study objectives.

In your Methods section, you will describe in detail what methodology you used. You may need to cite research to justify why you chose the method you chose; at the very least it should be clear how your method specifically addresses your research questions or study objectives. You'll need to define and describe your population and sample. Tell us what your sampling design is. Who did you talk to? How many people did you talk to? When/where/how? How did you select your sample? How, where, what, and when did you observe? How did you enhance credibility, crystallization, and ethics? What are your variable(s) and how did you define them conceptually and operationally? What information did you gather? What sensitizing concepts did you use? How did you code and analyze the results?

Sometimes, the Results and Discussion sections are merged together. Usually, the Results section explains and describes the themes, with supporting quotes or snippets from your transcripts or field notes serving as evidence for each one. You would use the Discussion section, then, to give your *big picture* analytical opinion on what this all means, how it answers your RQs, and how it is important to your community or to society. This is where you would show us that your study has social validity—the social value or importance of the topic to society (Ponterotto & Grieger, 2007).

In the final section, you would let us know what limitations you see for your research. Maybe you would do things differently if you had to do it over— perhaps you weren't able to sample as broadly as you would have liked, or perhaps, in retrospect, you would have liked to have spent more time in the field. Then, suggest future research for us—what future research might your study point to? This is your chance to justify your next research project.

The following sample gives you an excerpt from a more traditionally written qualitative paper. It illustrates how specific quotes are used to support each of the suggested themes (Cohen, 2009, pp. 402-403).

Findings

Women in the focus groups told numerous stories about the last time they thought about cancer. The women also expressed the problematic integration of their loved ones' cancer and breast cancer experiences with their personal beliefs about cancer (and orientation to cancer communication). As this analysis will explore in detail, these women had no trouble recounting their cancer experiences; their discussion evidenced recurring problems shared by African American women integrating conflicting and uncertain beliefs about cancer and breast cancer.

Theme 1: Pervasive Worry about Cancer and its Prevalence among African American Women

Women expressed the belief that when they think about cancer, they think about the number of people they know who have died from cancer among family and loved ones and their pervasive worry. Such pervasive worry required acknowledgement and the negotiation of the relational and situational meaning of cancer. And women often

From "Naming and Claiming Cancer Among African-American Woman" by E. L. Cohen, *Journal of Applied Communication Research, 37(4)*. Copyright © 2009. Reprinted by permission of Taylor & Francis Ltd, www.informaworld.com.

recounted the number of people in their lives afflicted with cancer. For example, one participant reported:

> My grandmother, she died, she had both breasts removed before she died. And moles on her face, she had those removed, too, she had cancer. But every day, I think about cancer. I work with people every day that's got cancer. I work with a lady, where I work, she's got cancer. She's had all the radiation . . . I work with her every day. And my friend, one of my best friends, she has cancer now, and she's not doing so well . . . it's a constant thing. (4a: 479–484. Note: Parenthetical notations include focus group number, participant identification letter and line numbers from the transcript.)

Women were comfortable acknowledging the many times they thought about cancer, particularly as a diagnosis accompanying the news of their loved ones' death:

> . . . I think about it a lot. I have had relatives who have had it. And then I have a constant reminder that something always happens, like somebody that you know died, like a couple months ago a young lady died that I didn't even know . . . she was a school friend . . . she had breast cancer and she died. (1d: 370–374)

Discussion also revealed knowing cancer as a cause of illness within a family depends on a person's family history. Several discussions across groups reflected the sentiment that many women did not grow up going to the doctor frequently, and often did not have a cancer diagnosis or received one when it was "almost too late." One participant acknowledged "Cancer is really prevalent on both sides of my family and both of my grandfathers have passed away before they even got the chance to acknowledge it" (2e: 574–576).

Participants documented a lay understanding of cancer consistent with the belief that cancer is something that is lurking but available to be discovered. As one participant opined:

> Yeah. That's what is so urgent about cancer. You may not even know you have it and all of a sudden, you go to the doctor and they say, "You've had this for years," or whatever. It's like it lays dormant in your body, so it's really important for that information to be out there. And it's almost impossible not to have cancer in the back of all of our minds because many times you're conscious of your body and you look in the mirror at yourself, you know that you can be a potential cancer risk. It can happen. (4b: 531–537)

They also spoke of the difficulty reconciling their probabilistic orientation not to "acknowledge" the urgency of cancer and the fear of death is "constant," with their distrust of doctors as well as their need for information and cancer detection. This difficulty reflected a felt ambivalence and uncertainty about cancer clearly expressed by these women.

Theme 2: Ambivalence and Pervasive Forms of Uncertainty

Women's stories touched on the ambivalence about hearing methods to prevent cancer and expressed a variety of pervasive uncertainties associated with a disease diagnosis. Ontological uncertainties can be understood from an individual's

---

dramatic or scenic method of writing
A creative, nonfiction method of writing that is often written as a series of scenes connected by a series of narrative summaries.

Dramatic or Scenic Method of Writing

The second way to write your qualitative findings is the **dramatic or scenic method of writing**, what Caulley (2008) calls *creative nonfiction* writing. Ethnographic researchers in communication studies frequently use this style of writing for their findings.

In this style of writing, you would actually show a scene of what happened rather than describe it or tell about it. This is more compelling reading. Usually written in present tense, this style of writing is more action-oriented. It's often written as a series of scenes connected by a series of narrative summaries. Depending on the research and on your style of writing, sometimes there will be more narrative summaries than scenes, and other times there will be more scenes than narrative summaries. Davis (2010, pp. 75-76), for example, wrote her hospice ethnography as a narrative.

* * *

During Barbara's next visit to Marian, they discuss her pain medication.

"You know, Marian, if you're too sick to take your medications, you need to call us. We can send somebody out to help," Barbara fusses gently.

"I know, honey, but I was too sick to call," Marian defends herself weakly. "I was too sick to take my pain medication; it hurt so bad!"

"What dosage are you taking now?" Barbara asks as she checked Marian's pulse.

"I'm on the maximum dosage now."

Barbara sits on the edge of Marian's bed as she asks her about her pain. "Where is your pain now, on a scale of 1 to 10?"

"It's about a five, but when the pain medication kicks in, it's a zero. It's just I was too sick to take my pain medication," Marian offers.

"Do you want to go to the Hospice Home to get your pain relief under control?" Barbara offers. "That will give you somebody around the clock to help take care of you."

75

76   *Chapter Nine*

Marian doesn't respond, but she doesn't seem pleased with the idea.

"I'm coming out twice a week to see you now, okay?" When Marian nods, Barbara continues her instructions. "If you stabilize, we might drop it back to once a week, but I want to keep an eye on you. Especially on your pain. Since it was so out of control the other day."

"Once I got back on my pain mediation properly, the pain is more under control now," Marian responds.

Barbara pauses at the door before leaving. "Call us if it happens again," she instructs firmly.

When you write up qualitative research findings using a dramatic or scenic method, you want to use realistic details; concrete nouns with concrete adjectives that appeal to the senses (sight, sound, smell, taste, touch); words that imply emotion; conversations to convey emotion and to pull the reader into the story; and active verbs (he pushed her down) rather than passive verbs (she was pushed down). Include thick description about details, contexts, emotions, relationships, feelings, history, voices, actions, and meanings. Adequately describe the research participants so your reader can actually see them. Use reflexive writing—include yourself and your biases, frames of reference, and personal connections to the topic in the writing. How can you write such detail? By capturing it in your field notes. Write detailed notes about the environment and context. You never know what details you might want to use later. Write detailed notes about dialogue, or—even better—tape record the dialogue so you can use it later. Open and close the writing with a narrative; the first narrative to set the stage and the second to conclude it (Caulley, 2008; Ponterotto & Grieger, 2007). The sample below, also from the hospice ethnography, gives you an example of rich, detailed narrative writing (Davis, 2010, p. 2).

2 *Chapter One*

her husband, John, died 15 years earlier. She doesn't like being in the hospital, not one bit. It brings back too many unhappy memories. Since John's death, she has tried to remain optimistic and upbeat, especially in front of her daughter, Katherine. But today she has a bad feeling. They're doing a biopsy to check out some pain she has been having. "Just a routine precaution," the doctor said. But she has a bad feeling. A really bad feeling.

"Hey, honey, what do you say we get out of here and you take me over to the mall?" Marian asks the aide who's wheeling her out of her hospital room down the hall toward the operating room.

He laughs loudly and repeats her question. "Take you to the mall!" He laughs again as he continues pushing her. She can feel her pulse quickening, her breaths becoming shallower. The blanket covering her is soft, and she feels its weight as she shivers underneath it. Cold, she feels cold, down to her bones. The cold comes from deep within her and mingles with her fear as it spreads from her toes to her stomach to her throat. They're moving quickly, and Marian looks up at the ceiling tiles as they float by. White square after white square. Row after row of tiles in a white checkerboard pattern. White checkerboard merges into the tops of white walls. People walking by are a blur of flesh-colored faces above white jackets. White. White everywhere.

"Here you are," the aide says, as he parks the stretcher in what looks like a small empty cubicle. "This is a holding room. You're going to wait here until they're ready for you." He pauses at the edge of her sight. "Good luck."

She looks around. More white tiles, more white walls on each side of her. A gray curtain, pulled back, on the wall in front of her feet. Beyond, she can see what looks like a nurse's station. The nurses' desk area is light gray, the lights are dim, and the room is empty. It looks brand new, clean, with no evidence of a person anywhere. No papers, no clutter, no coffee cups. She is in here alone, and it feels like a ghost town.

Marian takes a deep breath and closes her eyes.

Writing Phenomenological Findings

A phenomenological analysis will typically include a rich detailed narrative that clearly communicates the experience under study. As Starks and Trinidad (2007) explain, "By the end of the story the reader should feel that she has vicariously experienced the phenomenon under study and should be able to envision herself . . . coming to similar conclusions about what it meant" (p. 1376). Phenomenological studies are often reported as narratives, perhaps as blended accounts from different participants' points of view, often written to allow the reader to experience the phenomenon (Starks & Trinidad, 2007). Following is an excerpt from a phenomenological paper (Beabout, Carr-Chellman, Alkandari, Almeida, Gursoy, Ma, Modak, & Pastore, 2008, pp. 218– 219) about the perceptions of New Orleans educators on the process of rebuilding the school system after Hurricane Katrina. You can see this paper was written as a more traditional paper, organized around themes with quotes for supporting evidence.

From "The Perceptions of New Orleans Educators on the Process of Rebuilding the New Orleans School System after Katrina" by Brian Beabout et al, *Journal of Education for Students Placed at Risk, Vol. 13, No. 2, January 4, 2008,* reprinted by permission of Taylor & Francis Group, www.informaworld.com ∎

Findings

Our findings indicate that a wide range of factors have influenced educators' perspectives on this unique process of drastic school change. Among others, comments addressed topis ranging from district communication and leadership, the need for accountability, the lingering challenges of the pre-Katrina system, and concerns about working conditions. This variety is consistent with our view of schools as complex social systems. Viewed through the lens of chaos theory, three dominant themes emerge: the current culture of uncertainty in New Orleans, a mix of hope and cynicism for the future, and the lack of revolutionary change. A detailed analysis of these three themes and their relation to chaos theory follows.

Current Culture of Uncertainty

In 2005 and early 2006, the uncertainties of living in post-Katrina New Orleans have included disrupted mail, spotty communication, unreliable utility services, disrupted social networks, skyrocketing housing costs, and increased violent crime. These factors have lent a mood of indeterminacy to life in New Orleans, a feeling that has deeply affected educators living there. This uncertainty, felt by educators tasked with reform, can be described on several different levels: the citywide level, the school system level, and the school site level.

The Road Home: Citywide Uncertainty

Predicting student enrollment is a task central to the planning of any school district (Hartman, 1999). The extreme uncertainty surrounding the return of New Orleans' population has remained a topic of intense interest in the rebuilding process (Hill & Hannaway, 2006; Ritea, 2007; Troeh, 2006; Warner, 2005). With returning children a key determinant for how much funding is available for hiring teachers and opening school buildings, the future of the school system rests on the decisions of thousands of New Orleans families displaced by the storm across the state, the region, and the nation. As educators discussed their experiences with change, the impossibility of estimating how and when the population would return figured large in their comments:

Again, the whole problem and the most confusing thing is that nobody really knows what the whole system and the whole city will be like in the next 12 months . . . . We have a staff meeting and we talk about doubling or tripling enrollment. How many students can our school handle? How many faculty would we have to hire? What would it look like? What classes would we offer? You know, I can't honestly imagine everything because all of the variables make me imagine chaos (Charter School Teacher).

Writing Grounded Theory Findings

Grounded theory research is often organized thematically, with each concept or theme supported by snippets of quotes from interviews or field notes. The theories themselves might be explained in a diagram or in a written explanation (Starks & Trinidad, 2007). The following is an example of a grounded theory paper. Note how the paper is organized by theme, with each theme supported in this case, both by literature and by supporting quotes (Becker, Ellevold, & Stamp, 2008, p. 96).

Relational Concerns. The final contextual condition influencing the process of defensive communication is relational concerns, which comprises romantic partners' underlying anxiety about the relationship. The two main relational concerns pertain to uncertainty and identity. Participants in dating relationships expressed concerns about relational uncertainty that often colored the process of defensive communication. For example, Christy and Derek, a dating couple, experienced defensiveness when Derek joked about her dating someone else.

> D: Um, we went [to the restaurant] and we go out to eat a lot, but it had been a week or two weeks since we were even there. And then umm, we sat in this one booth and we sat in this booth once before but it was like maybe a month ago. We sit down and she was like we sat in the same seat. So she got a little nickname from me and I chuckled and I was like you must be getting me confused with one of your other ones because we didn't even come here yesterday let alone sitting in this booth.

> I: How do you feel you were approaching the situation when talking with her?

> D: Umm, in a light joking manner because we I mean, we were just hanging out at that time. I mean I knew how she felt about me and vice versa but that is as deep as it went. I mean if she was with someone else, there was nothing I could say or do about that. So it was mostly in a joking manner.

> I: Did you suspect that maybe she had been there with someone else?

> D: Yeah. She is smart, okay? And I can understand that there is some knuckle head who can't remember this or that, who we were sitting at a table and we got the same table that we were sitting in yesterday. I mean I don't think that I had even her the day before you know, and that is what makes me think that maybe it was. (5:I:B:147–172)

> Uncertainty often resulted from jealousy about the partner's fidelity or interest in another person, threats of relationship termination, lack of relational maintenance, or unclear

Writing CA Findings

CA writing typically does not include much in the way of theoretical or literature discussions, and tends, instead, to provide detailed discussion of the transcripts and the meaning resulting from the communication patterns. A CA report usually involves use of extensive transcripts as data evidence (Grbich, 2007). The following gives a great example of a CA analysis as it uses the unique CA notation in the text (Good & Beach, 2005, p. 573).

The first extract to be analyzed comes from Kristine's seventh birthday party and represents a prototypical gift-opening sequence, as described in Figure 2. Kristine is sitting in a chair by the side of the pool, with a stack of wrapped gifts to her right. Her grandma is behind her and Mom is to Kris's left, holding a pad of paper and writing down what each gift is and whom it is from. Immediately in front of Kristine is a group of girls sitting in the pool, watching Kristine open the gifts. Although they are in the pool, they still create their own little intense focus cluster to watch the opening and see the gifts. Dad is seen walking back and forth through the scene, cleaning up wrapping papers and helping to entertain the guests. It is clear, then, that the gift-opening system involves more than just the birthday girl and the gifts she is opening.

    Extract (1) begins at the moment Kris picks up a gift. This excerpt occurs five and one-half minutes into the gift-opening portion of the party and displays Kris opening a gift from Judy, a friend who has been going back and forth between the pool and Jacuzzi, about 30 feet away:

(1) *SDCL: Birthday Party: Age 7*
     ((Grma = Grandma; Wen = Wendy))
 1 Kris: [((Selects and holds gift))
 2 Kris: [Who's this one fro[m?
 3 Kim: [JUDY!

Writing Discourse Analysis Findings

A discourse analysis will typically be written as a discussion of the outcomes of language, supported by evidence from the participants' narratives to explain how language was used to construct meaning (Starks & Trinidad, 2007). It might be written thematically or topically, or in a narrative format. The sample below gives an example of a critical discourse analysis by De Melo Resende (2009, p. 373), on the discourse in a Brazilian apartment building meeting about homeless people in the vicinity.

Although the phrase 'homeless people' appears in the text only once, it is clear that this is the theme of the circular. Further, although the reference to 'homeless people' is a general reference, in the first paragraph ('as causas que levam os moradores de rua a permanecerem mais tempo em um só lugar'/'the causes that led the homeless people to remain longer in one place'), the rest of the text makes it clear that the focus is on this one specific group. However, this specification is not done explicitly, rather, it is taken as understood. The group in street circumstances is referred to through pronominalization ('eles', 'deles'/'they', 'them'). This pronominal representation of the group implies a dichotomic division 'we' versus 'them' (especially in '*their* remaining near to *our* building' ['a permanência *deles* perto do *nosso* prédio'], my italics). This indicates the group's social exclusion and the negating of the problem: the real problem is not their street circumstances but 'their remaining near our building'.

An evaluation of the group is made through the structuring of assumptions. See the excerpt highlighted in example (2), original bold:

(2) . . . as causas que levam os moradores de rua a permanecerem mais tempo em um só lugar **é a facilidade de obterem as coisas básicas necessárias como: comida, roupas, calçados e dinheiro, sendo este último transformado nas drogas que utilizam.**

Gostaria também de colocá-los a par, uma informação, passada na reunião, de que existem duas ou três pessoas recentemente libertadas da penitenciária e que estão ainda na condicional, entre eles.

. . what leads homeless people to remain longer in one **place is the fact that it is too easy to obtain basic goods such as food, clothing, shoes and money, the**

The following is an example of a discourse analysis of narratives told by women in interviews about their sister (Tannen, 2008, p.217).

I encountered a similar use of dialogue in another woman's account of a problematic sister—in this case, the speaker's own. This conversation, too, was with a woman I was meeting for the first time. She began by rolling her eyes when she answered in the affirmative my question about whether she had a sister. She then established the big-N Narrative that would drive everything else she told me: She and her sister did not have a good relationship because of her sister's selfishness and self-centeredness. In particular, the sister did not fulfill family responsibilities but relied on her (older) sister, the speaker, to do everything. To support this evaluation of her sister, the speaker told me a small-n narrative: when their father was nearing the end of his life and the family was gathered by his bedside, her sister decided to leave. "You'll be there," she said. "You can tell me what's happening."

In this instance, too, the coherence principle of the big-N Narrative driving the speaker's discourse was a sister's callousness, selfishness, and failure to fulfill responsibilities as a family member. The specific event recounted—the sister's departure at the time of their father's death—was a small-n narrative that supported the big-N Narrative or theme: my sister and I are not close because she is irresponsible and selfish. As in the previous example, the big-N Narrative is motivated by the Master Narrative that sisters are expected to be close. In this example, as in the one immediately preceding, the key involvement strategy was constructed dialogue, which was effective because it capped and helped create a scene that dramatized the speaker's point. The word "dramatize" is not only metaphoric; it captures the sense in which framing discourse as someone's speech is not passive "reporting" of words uttered by another but rather

Writing Performance Texts

Performative and artistic styles of writing allow for creative opportunities to communicate your study results. More and more, ethnographies in communication studies are written as performative texts. It's important to remember, however, that your findings drive your writing, not the other way around. For example, you might want to use a poetic method of writing the results because you feel that represents a more evocative style of communicating that reminds you of your research participants or scene. You might use ethnodrama to communicate the dramatic nature of the phenomenon you studied. In her research on funeral communication, Davis (2008) wrote her findings as a liturgy to communicate the ritualistic elements found in her research. This style of writing lets you use the style itself as a statement of resistance—as a way of using the text itself to suggest different ways of being, reflecting, and seeing the world, and as a way to possibly create change in society. A good performance text offers a way for the audience to relive the experience through the eyes of the writer or performer. Poetry and other creative forms of writing and presenting engage the listener's body to let the reader feel the world you're studying. Ethnographic drama can allow conflicting voices to be heard, can give voice to people or things who don't normally have voice, and can recreate emotionally laden experiences. Done well, this type of research contributes to our understanding of your research and of our world, has aesthetic merit, is reflexive, has emotional and intellectual impact, and expresses and embodies a lived experience (Denzin, 2003; Richardson, 2003).

Performative writing and creating—what Richardson (2003) calls **creative analytical practices**—turns your text into an evocative artistic representation. You can perform your research as radical street or public performances, such as rallies, puppet shows, marches, vigils, choruses, clown shows, or ritual performances. You can do a co-performance in which you bring the audience into the text and invite them to share the experience with you. You can advocate for a specific cause by creating an exhibition out of something that has happened; asking people to confront something that they normally don't think about or interact with; showing an idealized version of reality, or depicting traditional, culturally shared beliefs or values. Texts might be written as poetry, synthesizing the most important and salient meaning, symbolism, and interpretation into poetic lines, using poetic rhythms to convey speech, incorporating pauses, repetitions, narrative strategies, and rhythms in the speech into your poem. Texts might be turned into art, recreating the essence of the experience into an art form—painting, sculpture, music (Denzin, 2003; Richardson, 2003).

Ethnodrama is the presentation of data in staged performance, with a plot, characters, dialogue, and stage movements. Scripts are derived from your field notes, interview transcripts, document analysis which you put together in a "narrative collage" (Grbich, 2007, p. 65). Frequently, following an ethnodrama performance, open discussions between audience and performers can occur to facilitate dialogue and understanding (Grbich, 2007).

creative analytical practices
A form of performative writing and creating that turns text into an evocative artistic representation.

ethnodrama
The presentation of data in staged performance, with a plot, characters, dialogue, and stage movements.

The following two samples give you examples of performative writing (Davis, Delynko, Cook, 2010; Holman Jones, 2011, p. 328).

Glory days.
Sharing, showing,
    weaving a pattern of dreams and hope,
      rebirth and resurrection.
        Understanding. And
          connection.
Not all survived.
    Some problems intruded.
      Some dreams eluded.
Some voices stayed voiceless.
    and some's status are erased
We offer insight into
    lives we cannot relate to.
      To say,
        these are not others.
          They are not
them.
    They are us.
We offer stories to show
    men without homes are still
      men.
Men ill,
    can try again.

Literature and Theoretical Basis

Stigma

Undesirable difference[1]
Undesirable
    Other[2]
Outgroups.
Out,
    groups!
Out,
    other![3]
Out of sight,
    out of mind.
      Out of their mind,
        out of our mind.
    Discounted deviant.
      Social death.
      Disconfirmed.
      Socially liminal.
      Socially ambivalent.[4]
Dedicated to preserving the social order through providing
an example of unacceptability for the rest of society[5]

Homelessness

According to the National Alliance to End Homelessness, in
January 2005, there were 10,765 homeless people in North
Carolina, 2,196 in Mecklenburg County.

Two-thousand, one hundred ninety-
    six
      nameless, faceless, homeless deviant others.[6]
Careful!
    They may be dangerous!
      Disruptive!
        Unasthetic![7]
Remember:
    God helps those
      who help themselves!
        Homeless aren't.
          Homeless don't.[8]
They:
    Are lazy.
    Won't work
    Can't relate.
      Can't
      relate.[9]
They are
    Runaways
      From abused homes
        With trust issues,
          Support issues,
            Deviant peers
        Isolation,
          Depression.[10]
            Drug abuse: Cause? Effect? Both.
              Social environment. Poverty.[11] Disability.[12]
They are
    Alone.[13]
They have
    Each other.
      Well, some of them do
some of the time.
    Closeness.
    Aloneness.

Poverty

Income:
    The cost of participating in our social system[14]

Standpoints

Social memberships.
    Views of the world.
      Perspectives of others
        about others.
Folk history
    of oppressed group.
Oppositional voice
    from the standpoint
      of the opposition.

From "Lost and Found" by
Stacy Holman Jones, *Text and
Performance Quarterly, Vol,
31, No. 4.* Copyright © 2011.
Reprinted by permission of
Taylor & Francis Ltd, www.
informaworld.com.

328   *S. Holman Jones*

"Grandma, I want to you to know how your love made me." Her eyes open again, now pale blue water. You watch each other, waiting.

> Pulse, push, breathe. Pulse push
> breathe. Pulse, push breathe. Her eyelids
> fall, closing embrace.

Door

Your husband looks at you and his silent questions pierce your skin. You breathe in sharply and push out the words, "I need to tell you something." He clenches his jaw. He nods. You lose your nerve. "Let me take a shower and then we'll talk." He turns and leaves the bedroom.

You undress and step into the scalding water. You stand there, breathing and willing yourself to stop, to put your arms out and break the fall, to be still. You let the water flow over you until it runs cold. You dry yourself, get dressed, and meet him on the sidewalk.

You walk several blocks without speaking. He looks at you, willing you to meet his gaze. He waits. You let the momentum of your movement still your pulse and quiet the fear rising in your throat. You say that you have fallen for her.

He drops to his knees on the sidewalk. He says, "Jesus." He stays down and you say you are sorry again and again. You wait. He puts his palms on the ground and pushes up, then begins walking away. You follow. He is angry, hurt, incredulous. He asks you what this means. You say you don't know. He asks you if you still love him. You say you don't know. He asks you if you want to stay in the relationship. You say you don't know. He asks you if this means you're a lesbian. You say you don't know.[25]

You wait. He stares hard at you, then lowers his head. "I don't know *you*. I don't even recognize you." You hear something—a faint clicking sound—and turn your head. It could have been anything—a leaf falling, a twig snapping.

> One door slamming
> shut and another opening
> suddenly makes sense.[26]

You see your chance, your choice. You say, "Yes."

Hold

> He insists: *you* call
> the social worker and say,
> "the adoption's off."

You agree, trying to diffuse his anger and sadness and ignore your own. But each time you pick up the phone to call, the recriminating sound of the dial tone taunts you. You push the receiver back into its cradle. With each failed call, your husband

Writing Narrative Texts

As you've seen from examples above, many communication researchers use a narrative writing approach which blends narratives from the participants' points of view with narratives from their own point of view (as researcher). Researchers using the narrative approach might also include autoethnographic narratives on their own personal reflections on issues raised in the course of doing the research. Narrative writing often includes sections of grounded theory or thematic analysis with supporting literature. Good writing of this style is an evocative narrative, reminiscent of a novel, with characters, plot, action, and movement that uses plot and character development to illustrate themes.

▼ Evaluating and Critiquing Qualitative Research

When evaluating your own qualitative research or when critiquing qualitative research you read in journals, the following list of criteria is a good guide.

Ethical criteria: Did the researcher prevent harm, discomfort, distress to study participants? Did the benefits outweigh risks or cost to participants? Were the study participants coerced or unduly influenced? Were vulnerable subjects used, and if so, were proper safeguards in place? Were any participants deceived? Were appropriate consent procedures implemented? Was the privacy of participants safeguarded or appropriately disclosed? Was the research approved and monitored by an IRB?

RQ criteria: Did the researcher appropriately define the scope of the problem? Does the research have significance for society/academia? Was the research problem formally, clearly, and concisely stated?

Design/methodology criteria: Was the design the most appropriate for the RQ? Is the study externally valid? What were the major limitations of the design? Were the limitations acknowledged by the researcher and taken into account in interpreting the results?

Sampling criteria: Was the target population identified and described? Were eligibility criteria specified? Were the sampling selection procedures appropriate and clearly described? How adequate was the sampling plan in yielding a representative sample? Were there factors that affected the representativeness of the sample? Were possible sample biases identified and accounted for in the study? Was the sample size sufficient?

Data collection criteria: Did the RQ lend itself to the type of data collection? Did the data collection adequately cover the complexities of the problem under study? Who collected the data? Were data collectors qualified? How were they trained? How was the data gathered? Was it potentially distorted?

Analysis criteria: Was the coding sufficient, correct, and appropriate? Was an appropriate amount of quotes, supporting evidence reported? Was the information appropriately summarized and clear? Were the findings adequately supported? Were the findings appropriately tied to theory and concepts (if applicable)?

Writing criteria: Was the report written in a clear, concise manner? Was it well organized? If it was a narrative, was the writing action-oriented and evocative? Did the writing include thick description? Was the writing sufficiently reflexive? Did the writing reflect the findings, tone, and concepts you wanted to convey?

So What?

This chapter showed you how to pull together your data, organize it, analyze it, and write it. As you have seen, there are many approaches to take when conducting qualitative research. Decisions you make early on regarding sampling, data collection, sensitizing concepts, and coding procedures, will affect how you write your findings as well as the credibility of your findings. As you're analyzing and writing your quantitative research, keep in mind the goal of all types of qualitative research—to describe communication (in all forms) and to understand how that communication constructs or creates ideas, reality, and outcomes.

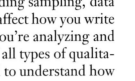

We hope throughout this book you've been inspired to conduct research for yourself. We trust you've learned how to be a critical consumer of all types of research, as well as learned how to appreciate all types of research for the strengths and limitations they bring to the researcher's toolkit. Thanks for sticking with us. Where are you on the stages of learning? Think about how much more you know now than you did in the beginning of the semester. Congratulations! You've made it through Communication Research Methods!

Glossary

Axial coding/metacoding
Codes that connect categories.

Card pile sort
Using index cards drawn from field notes to create semantic groupings.

Code book/code list
An organized listing of categories and codes and the rules for documenting and applying them.

Creative analytical practices
A form of performative writing and creating that turns text into an evocative artistic representation.

Data coding
The categorization of data to make it manageable.

Dramatic or scenic method of writing
A creative, nonfiction method of writing that is often written as a series of scenes connected by a series of narrative summaries.

Ethnodrama
The presentation of data in staged performance, with a plot, characters, dialogue, and stage movements.

Event analysis
The sorting of data by the perspectives represented in interview accounts.

Inter-coder reliability
The level of agreement between two or more coders.

Interpretive thematic analysis
Coding and categorizing data for themes and topics according to your analysis plan.

Negative case analysis
The process of constantly comparing existing codes with new data and adding new codes (or revising existing codes) until all cases of data are accounted for in the coding scheme.

Schema analysis
Consists of close reading of texts or discourse, in which researchers look for clues in the discourse that tell us what people might be thinking or believing that would cause them to say what they are saying.

Sensitizing concept
The issue you are attempting to address or answer in your research, based on your RQ, study approach, or data itself.

Social network analysis
Consists of sorting by the relationships involved in a group.

Summary method of writing
A method of writing in which researchers give readers summaries of what happened and what was discovered during research.

Thematic analysis
A method of categorizing data into thematic categories.

References

Beabout, B., Carr-Chellman, A., Alkandari, K., Almeida, L., Gursoy, H., Ma, Z., Modak, R., & Pastore, R. (2008). The perceptions of New Orleans educators on the process of rebuilding the New Orleans School System after Katrina. *Journal of Education for Students Placed at Risk, 13*(2), 217–237.

Becker, J. A. H., Ellevold, B., & Stamp, G. H. (2008). The creation of defensiveness in social interaction II; A model of defensive communication among romantic couples. *Communication Monographs, 75* (1), 86–110.

Caulley, D. N. (2008). Making qualitative research reports less boring: The techniques of writing creative nonfiction. *Qualitative Inquiry, 14*(3), 424–449.

Charmaz, K. (2000). Grounded theory: objectivist and constructivist methods. In N. K. Denzin & Y. S. Lincoln (Eds.), *Handbook of qualitative research* (pp. 509–535). Thousand Oaks, CA: Sage.

Cohen, E. L. (2009). Naming and claiming cancer among African American women: An application of Problematic Integration Theory. *Journal of Applied Communication Research, 37*(4), 397–417.

Davis, C. S. (2007). The social construction of life, death, and disability in the Terri Schiavo case. In J. L. Werth and T. Lillie (Eds.), *End of Life Issues and Persons with Disabilities* (pp. 167–182).

Davis, C. S. (2008). A funeral liturgy: Death rituals as symbolic communication, *Journal of Loss and Trauma, 13*(15), 406–421.

Davis, C.S., Delynko, K.M., & Cook, J. (2010). Oral history of McCreesh Place, apartment building for (formerly) homeless men: Advancing the warp and balancing the weave. *Cultural Studies-Critical Methodologies, 10*(5).

Davis, C. S. (2010). *Death: The beginning of a relationship.* Cresskill, NJ: Hampton Press.

De Melo Resende, V. (2009). "It's not a matter of inhumanity": A critical discourse analysis of an apartment building circular on "homeless people." *Discourse and Society, 20,* 363–379.

Denzin, N. K. (2003). The practices and politics of interpretation. In N. K. Denzin & Y. S. Lincoln (Eds.), *Collecting and interpreting qualitative materials* (pp. 458–498). Thousand Oaks, CA: Sage.

Good, J. S., & Beach, W. A. (2005). Opening up gift-openings: Birthday parties as situated activity systems. *Text, 25*(5), 565–593.

Grbich, C. (2007). *Qualitative data analysis: An introduction.* Thousand Oaks, CA: Sage.

Hodder, I. (2003). The interpretation of documents and material culture. In N. K. Denzin & Y. S. Lincoln (Eds.), *Collecting and interpreting qualitative materials* (pp. 155–175). Thousand Oaks, CA: Sage.

Madison, D. S. (2005). *Critical ethnography: Methods, ethics, and performance.* Thousand Oaks, CA: Sage.

Ponterotto, J. G., & Grieger, I. (2007). Effectively communicating qualitative research. *Counseling Psychologist, 35*(3), 404–430.

Richardson, L. (2003). Writing: A method of inquiry. In N. K. Denzin & Y. S. Lincoln (Eds.), *Collecting and interpreting qualitative materials* (pp. 499–541). Thousand Oaks, CA: Sage.

Ryan, G. W., & Bernard, H. R. (2003). Data management and analysis methods. In N. K. Denzin & Y. S. Lincoln (Eds.), *Collecting and interpreting qualitative materials* (pp. 259–309). Thousand Oaks, CA: Sage.

Silverman, D. (2003). Analyzing talk and text. In N. K. Denzin & Y. S. Lincoln (Eds.), *Collecting and interpreting qualitative materials* (pp. 340–362). Thousand Oaks, CA: Sage.

Starks, H., & Trinidad, S. B. (2007). Choose your method: A comparison of phenomenology, discourse analysis, and grounded theory. *Qualitative Health Research, 17*(10), 1372–1380.

Tannen, D. (2008). "We've never been close, we're very different": Three narrative types in sister discourse. *Narrative Inquiry, 19*(2), 206–229.Fig. 7

APPENDICES

Appendix A

Writing Research Proposals

1. *Introduction:* Introduce us to your topic and tell us why you are interested in studying it. You may introduce us to any theoretical or conceptual framework you plan to use for your research project. State upfront the specific aims of this project. You can explain them in detail later in the proposal, but give us a preview of what we're about to read.

2. *Rationale:* Justify your selection of the topic. Convince the audience that the topic is worthy of study, that it is interesting and significant.

3. *Literature Review:* Use your literature to further develop your idea to further convince us that research on the topic is necessary, and your proposed way of conducting the research is the best way to do it. Make sure your literature review is comprehensive and, again, points to your project as the next missing piece of information. Use the literature to explain your theoretical or conceptual framework.

4. *Research Questions, Study Objectives, or Hypotheses:* What, specifically, will this study be focusing on?

5. *Methodology:* Your method should be justified by your Research Questions; be very specific in terms of what you will be doing. We want to be sure the methods used are appropriate for your research questions, and that what you propose to do is feasible and doable.
   a. *Method:* Which method or approach will you use (be specific)?
   b. *Population:* How have you operationalized your population?
   c. *Sample:* What is your sampling design and how does it represent the population?
   d. *Information to be Collected or Instruments to be Used:* Justify the selection of the instruments and discuss their validity, or explain how you chose the information to be gathered.
   e. *Validity, Reliability, Credibility, Crystallization:* How will you ensure study quality?
   f. *Ethics:* How will you ensure ethical treatment of your study participants?
   g. *Variables:* What are your main variables and how have you conceptualized and operationalized them?

6. *Analysis Plans:* How do you plan to analyze the data? What statistical tests will you use to test your hypotheses? What coding and analytical method will you use?

(Morse, 2003; Sandelowski, 2003)

7. *Limitations and Suggestions for Future Research:* What will this study not allow you to do? What future research will this study lead to?

8. *Time/Duration of Project:* Include a timeline outlining each step of your proposed research.

9. *Appendix*
   a. Copy of instrument or study protocol
   b. Consent form
   c. IRB application

References

Morse, J. (2003). A review committee's guide for evaluating qualitative proposals. *Qualitative Health Research, 13*(6), 833–851.

Sandelowski, B. (2003). Writing a qualitative proposal. *Qualitative Health Research, 13*(6), 781–820.

Appendix B

[CAREGIVER CONSENT]

Dept. of Communication Studies
9201 University City Blvd.
Charlotte, NC 28223

Informed Consent for
Children's Mental Health Child and Family Team
Meeting Communication Study

Project Title and Purpose:

You are invited to participate in a research study titled "Children's Mental Health Child and Family Team Meeting Communication Study." This is a study to look at communication in child and family team meetings between your providers and your family. I want to use this information to help providers better communicate with families.

Investigator(s):

This study is being conducted by Christine Davis in the Department of Communication Studies at the University of North Carolina (UNC)–Charlotte.

Description of Participation:

As part of this research study, I would like to attend your upcoming child and family team meeting. I'd like your permission to observe and videotape the meeting and ask you and the other people attending the meeting to fill out a short questionnaire at the end.

Length of Participation:

The only time you will spend on this study is time you will already be spending in attending the meetings plus the extra 15 minutes to fill out the questionnaire at the end. If you decide to participate, this will be one of 25 meetings observed, and you will be one of 25 caregivers participating.

Risks and Benefits of Participation:

There are no known risks to participate in this study. However, there may be risks that are currently unforeseeable. There are no direct benefits to you, but the benefits of participating in this study are helping improve communication between providers and caregivers and families. In addition, I will give you $25.00 as appreciation for your participation, and if your child attends, I will give him or her $5.00.

Volunteer Statement:

You are a volunteer. The decision to participate in this study is completely up to you. If you decide to be in the study, you may stop at any time. You will not be treated any differently if you decide not to participate or if you stop after you have started. The information you provide will not affect the services your child and family are getting now or in the future. Taking part in the study is completely up to you, and even if you decide during the meeting that you no longer want to participate, you can just let me know. The meeting will be held and you will receive services whether or not you choose to participate in this research.

Anonymity:

The data collected, including the videotape and the questionnaire, will not contain any identifying information or any link back to you or your participation in this study. The following steps will be taken to ensure this anonymity: your name will not be written down anywhere but the consent form. The consent form will be kept separate from the videotape and the questionnaire. Names will not be used when transcribing the videotape.

Fair Treatment and Respect:

UNC–Charlotte wants to make sure that you are treated in a fair and respectful manner. Contact the University's Research Compliance Office at 704-687-9999 if you have any concerns about how you are treated as a study participant. If you have any questions about the project, please contact Dr. Christine Davis, Department of Communication Studies, UNC–Charlotte, 9999 Colvard, 9201 University City Blvd., Charlotte, NC 28223, 704-687-9999, xxx@uncc.eduw

Participant Consent:

I have read the information in this consent form. I have had the chance to ask questions about this study, and those questions have been answered to my satisfaction. I am at least 18 years of age or an emancipated minor*, and I agree to participate in this research project. I understand that I will receive a copy of this form after it has been signed by me and the principal investigator.

_____   _____   _____
Participant Name (PLEASE PRINT)   Participant Signature   DATE

_____   _____
Investigator Signature   DATE

*Emancipated Minor (as defined by NC General Statute 7B-101.14) is a person who has not yet reached his or her 18th birthday and meets at least one of the following criteria: (1) has legally terminated custodial rights of his or her parents and been declared emancipated by a court; (2) is married, or (3) is serving in the armed forces of the United States.

Appendix C

How Your Objective, Research Question, and/or Hypothesis Relates to Your Methodology

If your objective, research question, and/or hypothesis is:	Then your chosen method should be:
To test causation	Experimental design (Chapter 12)
To assess (measure) beliefs, attitudes, opinions; to collect (measure) retrospective information about behavior, meaning	Survey (Chapter 10)
To analyze (in a measureable way) the content of messages such as media messages; to measure how information is exchanged through text or media messages	Quantitative content analysis (Chapter 11)
To analyze (in a measurable way) the content of interpersonal messages; to measure how information is exchanged interpersonally	Interaction analysis (Chapter 11)
To understand, describe, explain communication in a culture or cultural group	Ethnography (Chapter 14)
To understand, describe, explain communication in a culture in which the researcher is an integral part	Autoethnography (Chapter 14)
To understand, describe, explain meaning within lived experience	Phenomenology (Chapter 14)
To describe and understand group discourse/conversation in action	Focus groups (Chapter 15)
To describe and understand creation of reality in (usually) oral discourse and interactions	Discourse analysis (Chapter 14)
To describe and understand interpersonal social action in sequences of utterances and interaction as agents of action and activity	Conversation analysis (Chapter 14)
To analyze (in a descriptive way) the content of messages such as media messages	Qualitative content analysis (Chapter 14)
Describing or understanding communication in individuals' stories, and the role of personal narratives in interactions and relationships	Narrative research (Chapter 14)
Describing or understand communication as it relates to behavior within social situations and multiple realities	Grounded theory (Chapter 14)
Describing or understanding communication as it relates to illustrative case(s)	Case study (Chapter 14)
Describing/understanding communication as it relates to creation of meaning in (usually) written texts and artifacts	Textual analysis (Chapter 14)
Describing/understanding communication as it relates to both formal and informal performances of self, identity, and meaning	Performance studies (Chapter 14)
Describing/understanding communication as it relates to power and gender in a culture	Feminist research/Critical-cultural studies research (Chapter 14)

(Continued)

If your objective, research question, and/or hypothesis is:	Then your chosen method should be:
To understand how symbols act on people—the ways that written or spoken language (such as speeches, books, images, performances, texts, and films), in their historical and cultural context, work—to persuade, instruct, inform, entertain, arouse, engage, and convince	Rhetorical criticism (Chapter 14)
To understand how well the argument is made in a text	Argumentation analysis (Chapter 14)
To study the persuasive ability of a text by Aristotle's five criteria	Neo-Aristotelian criticism (Chapter 14)
To study how our symbolic actions construct our ideas of reality, based on Burke's Pantad	Dramatistic criticism; Burkean criticism (Chapter 14)
To understand the stories being told in a text, based on narrative elements	Narrative criticism (Chapter 14)
To study the use of metaphors in a text to construct a specific meaning	Metaphoric criticism (Chapter 14)
To look at how a text uses mythic stories and themes	Fantasy theme analysis (Chapter 14)
To understand how cultural texts and artifacts (dominant discourses) construct power in a society	Ideological criticism (Chapter 14)
To understand how reality is constructed through the use of symbol systems (signs, symbols, codes)	Semiotic analysis (Chapter 14)

Appendix D

STATISTICS DECISION CHART

What type of data do you have?	What do you want to do?		
	Summarize Data	**Test for Differences between Groups**	**Test for Relationships between Variables**
Nominal	Look at measures of central tendency: 　Mode Display data visually: 　Frequency Table 　Pie chart 　Bar chart	Analyze the distribution of the independent or dependent variable: 　Chi Square Compare 2 or more independent or dependent categories: 　2-variable Chi Square	Cramer's V
Ordinal	Look at measures of central tendency: 　Median Display data visually: 　Frequency table 　Bar chart	Analyze the differences between 2 groups: 　Mann-Whitney U Test Analyze the differences between 3 or more groups: 　Kruskall-Wallis Test Examine the differences between related scores: 　Wilcoxin Sign Test	Spearman's Rho
Interval/Ratio (Scale)	Standardize your data 　Z-Scores Determine measures of central tendency: 　Median 　Mean Determine measures of dispersion: 　Range 　Variance 　Standard deviation Display data visually: 　Bar chart 　Line graph	Estimate data: 　Estimate confidence levels and margin of error Examine differences between 2 unrelated groups: 　Independent samples t-test Examine differences between 2 related groups: 　Paired t-test Compare 3 or more groups on their distribution on one variable: 　One-way analysis of variance (ANOVA) followed by a TUKEY ad-hoc test Compare 3 or more groups and their differences over time: 　Repeated measures ANOVA followed by a TUKEY ad-hoc test	Test for a statistically significant relationship between variables: 　2 variables: 　Pearson-Product Moment Correlation 　3 or more variables: 　Correlation Matrix Predict outcomes: 　Regression analysis

INDEX

R